METTERNICH

METTERNICH

ALAN PALMER

WEIDENFELD AND NICOLSON
5 Winsley Street London W1

137410

ISBN 0 297 99448 4

Printed in England by C. Tinling and Co. Ltd,
London and Prescot

6

M5618P

CONTENTS

ILLUSTRATIONS

Between pages 70 *and* 71

Metternich as a young diplomat (*Ullstein Bilderdienst*)
The coronation of Emperor Francis, 1792 (*Archiv Gerstenberg, Frankfurt*)
Princess Eleonore (*Ullstein Bilderdienst*)
Metternich's audience with Napoleon, Dresden 1813 (*Staatsbibliothek, Berlin*)
Napoleon at the battle of Wagram (*Mansell Collection*)
Viscount Castlereagh (*Mansell Collection*)

Between pages 134 *and* 135

Emperor Francis of Austria (*by gracious permission of Her Majesty The Queen*)
Letter from Metternich to Hardenberg, September 1813 (*Archiv Gerstenberg, Frankfurt*)
Tsar Alexander I, Emperor Francis and King Frederick William III of Prussia after the battle of Leipzig (*Archiv Gerstenberg*)
Frederick William III of Prussia (*Staatsbibliothek, Berlin*)
Emperor Francis returns to Vienna, June 1814 (*Osterrische Nationalbibliothek, Vienna*)
Victory banquet at the Guildhall (*Guildhall Library*)

Between pages 198 *and* 199

The Congress of Vienna (*Archiv Gerstenberg, Frankfurt*)
A ball at Princess Metternich's, late 1814 (*Staatsbibliothek, Berlin*)
Dorothea Lieven (*Tate Gallery*)
Metternich's daughter Clementine, by Sir Thomas Lawrence (*Mansell Collection*)
Princess Melanie
Emperor Ferdinand (*Osterrische Nationalbibliothek, Vienna*)
Metternich's summer residence (*Historische Museen der Stadt Wien*)

Between pages 262 *and* 263

Rioting at the western entrance to Vienna, March 1848 (*Archiv Gerstenberg, Frankfurt*)

PREFACE

Clement von Metternich held continuous office at the head of Europe's affairs for a longer period of time than any other statesman in modern history: he became foreign minister of the Austrian Empire in the autumn of 1809 and he did not resign until the spring of 1848. For thirty-three of these thirty-nine years his statecraft and philosophy of government determined the political pattern of the continent. The 'Age of Metternich', though often impatiently dismissed by historians as a mere interlude, lasted for twice as long as the 'Age of Napoleon' which preceded it and for half as long again as the 'Age of Bismarck' which followed it in the closing decades of the century. Moreover Metternich's actual participation in public events covered an even wider span: in 1790 he performed official duties during the coronation of Leopold II as Holy Roman Emperor of the German Reich; and in 1859 his advice on questions of war and peace was still being sought by Leopold's great-grandson, Francis Joseph. On his first visit to London, in 1794, he was entertained by the Prince of Wales, the future George IV; and on his penultimate visit to the Rhineland, sixty-three years later, he was able to offer his choicest wines to another Prince of Wales, the future Edward VII. Metternich's mother had known Maria Theresa at the height of Habsburg splendour: his youngest daughter was to outlast the Habsburg Monarchy itself.

Yet, whether playing a leading part in Europe's drama or walking-on before its colourful backcloth, the Metternichs rarely won a good notice from the critics. The haughty superiority of father and son was mocked in the French press as early as 1798, and cartoonists half a century later were no kinder to the fallen Chancellor and his third wife as they sped across the continent to exile in England. More, however, was at fault than character. The incredible vanity of the Metternichs might merit an occasional lampoon but not the endless pages of hatred and contempt with which European radicals assailed their name over four decades. Such sustained vituperation was a direct consequence of Clement Metternich's policy rather than of his failings in personality. As early as 1820 he was regarded as the pillar of an international order which perpetuated autocracy and denied sovereignty to peoples striving for recognition; and for thirty years the so-called 'Metternich System' was associated with repression of civil liberty and with negative government.

A generation easily thrilled by the collective emotion of Romantic revolt could never look on Metternich's conservative classicism with sympathy or understanding. He seemed urbanely doctrinaire in a world of stifled enthusiasm, and few people warmed to his philosophy.

Metternich's unpopularity is hardly surprising. He set himself against the prevailing mood of his age and of the half-century which followed his death. While accepting the existence of territorial States and striving for guarantees of their stability, he could never acknowledge the claims of a Nation. He rejected the idea that community of language, sentiment or race provided a basis for political unity; and he insisted that representative government was a weak and unsatisfactory method of administration which restricted the initiative of those in power while permitting unwarranted authority to a popular demagogue. Though he respected the traditional rights of ancient institutions, such as the British Parliament or the Hungarian Diet, he was convinced that constitutional forms were neither for export nor for emulation. Nationalism and Liberalism remained equally abhorrent doctrines to him, the product of that French Revolution against which he saw himself in conflict throughout his life. In their place he evolved a cumbersome set of political principles, pompously propounded over the years in earnest memoranda heavy with profundity. He offered a threefold creed: a belief in an essential community of interest which bound together the European States; a belief in the need for vigilance against political excess; and a belief in the virtues of a balanced order, both between governments and between classes within society. These ideas were based upon a haphazard search for immutable laws of political behaviour and none of them were in the least original, for they seem to owe something to Voltaire's 'Great Republic' and even more to Aristotle; but they provided Metternich with a code of respectable obscurity in which he might envelop what was basically a day-to-day and hand-to-mouth policy.

Yet Metternich was not primarily a theorist nor even a constructive statesman. Though he prided himself on a logical scientific approach to political problems, his gifts were those of an artist. He practised the skills of diplomacy with greater fluency than any contemporary except Talleyrand, from whom he had learnt many of the refinements of the game. But he possessed the opportunity, denied to Talleyrand, of shaping the very character of statecraft in an era of external peace. Metternich's achievements are essentially transitory, victories of intrigue rather than of creative conviction, triumphs of expediency more than of principle; but the distinctive features of diplomacy during the Hundred Years Peace were perfected by the Austrian Chancellor and passed into general usage at a time when Europe's fate was determined by its chancelleries to a greater extent than ever before or since. The assumption that Great Powers together form a European Concert and share a responsibility for the international order; the acceptance of negotiation as a protracted undertaking rather than as a swiftly concluded episode; the primacy of confidential exchanges over public dispute; the persuasiveness hidden behind an elaborate comedy of manners – all these aspects of what Sir Harold Nicolson has called the old diplomacy were formed while Metternich was master of its conventions, and many reflect the qualities of his own personality. To understand the idiom of his Europe, it becomes essential to understand the man.

He puzzled observers in his own age and baffled their immediate successors: how could such a lightweight sit so heavily on the world? Nineteenth-century German historians, academic lenses tinted with patriotic colours, viewed the Rhinelander who had passed into Austrian service with scant sympathy. The great Prussian scholar, Heinrich von Treitschke, writing in the 1880s, virtuously lamented his 'spiritual narrowness' and his 'thorough understanding of all the meanest motives in human nature' while complaining that his 'empty mind' remained unresponsive to 'the dynamic forces of History'. Treitschke's prejudices were perpetuated by other historians in his own country and by writers in Britain and the United States, where academic fashion at the end of the century was heavily Germanic in form. Thus a Metternich legend seeped into the general textbooks of two continents, with the Austrian Chancellor appearing as some Mephistophelian compound of trickery and harassment; and even today this distorted picture has not entirely been expunged from their pages. On the other hand, after the First World War, several historical commentators began to laud Metternich's foresight in checking the growth of nationalist fervour, some even claiming to find among his potpourri of political maxims a conservative philosophy of general validity. He was, it now appeared, an early champion of federalism and a good European, eager to offer a weary continent relief from the threat of war; and it seemed almost as if his shade was looking benevolently down on the green tables of Geneva and Locarno. This impression was at least as convincing as the older one but it was not so popular with English readers, who have long expected continental statesmen to exude a whiff of brimstone rather than an odour of sanctity.

Metternich was by no means indifferent to what future generations would think of him, though he had every confidence in their verdict. 'My name is linked with so many great events that it will accompany them to posterity', he declared in a private letter written when his life still had forty years to run; and he added, 'A century hence, authors will judge me very differently'. There is no doubt he had every intention of assisting them to think rightly about him. He drafted three autobiographical fragments and gave instructions to his son, Richard, that these reminiscences should be published twenty years after his death, together with selections from his archives. The Collected Papers duly appeared in the early 1880s and the documents they included have proved a rich mine of information, even though they were pruned and edited. Unfortunately the autobiographical sections were less successful. They showed traits hardly endearing to his readers: a gift of invention; a tact of omission; and a claim of infallibility. 'He dazzles himself with his brightness in the mirror which he holds perpetually before his eyes', wrote Albert Sorel, master-craftsman among the French historians of diplomacy. The *Memoirs* did not improve Metternich's reputation as much as he had assumed or his son anticipated.

But the reminiscences, though for the most part limited to his early years, have their value. They confirm a characteristic which his acquaintances had often noted and placed on record: he always regarded the years of Napoleonic upheaval as the prime of his public life; and what followed was for him a protracted epilogue, though it dragged on for a third of a century. Others might assess his policy as custodian of autocracy and high priest of the status quo: he was concerned to show himself as the diplomat who had outwitted Napoleon. In retrospect life became for Metternich a cavalcade of set-pieces through which he moved gracefully in command of every scene. But memory lingered rarely in Vienna: he saw himself time and time again at the Tuileries or St Cloud, sharpening phrases he had almost used, recounting compliments the Emperor failed to offer; or he re-captured in his mind that final meeting at Dresden, when the marriage-broker turned antagonist and Romance sank to reality. There followed a climax at Leipzig (where they made him a Prince), a long journey through the winter snows of France to victory celebrations, and a congress in Austria's capital city.

All these episodes filled Metternich's table talk. Anthony Trollope's mother, visiting the Chancellor in 1836, caught him dwelling on that last encounter with the Emperor of the French; and in his years of exile after 1848 his conversation, which some thought tedious, sparkled when he recalled the First Empire. Countess Lieven, listening to Metternich for the first time in 1818, was delighted by his tales of the fallen Emperor; and we find them still talking of him when they meet thirty years later. It is as if Napoleon, even in death, overshadowed the Chancellor of Europe.

And here is the most curious paradox of Metternich's career. For, vainest of statesmen though he was, he never sensed such distinction in the epoch to which historians appropriated his name as in the reflected glory of Napoleon's Empire. The key to this seeming incongruity of character lies in Metternich's place of birth and the challenge of his early years.

ROCOCO

A Rhineland family

Until the present century the towns of the middle Rhine and Moselle valleys remained living symbols of a unique society. Outwardly as German as the neatly walled vineyards around them or the rich groined vaulting of their Gothic churches, they retained from a mediaeval past the intensive uncertainties of a frontier region. Compact and tidy, with pepper-pot roofs high and pointed and four or five rows of shutters set close together, their houses thrust upwards like the earliest rural settlements rather than sprawl along the riverbank in the ill-discipline of the modern city. Belfries and Romanesque towers clustered protectively over the lower slopes of the hills; and above them the slitted lanterns of a fortress stood sentinel. At times they seem to have been not so much communities of burghers and traders as extensions of castles and monasteries, bound in by ramparts and gates. They were everywhere concerned with security, disturbingly aware of an indefinite future.

Nor is this surprising. These valleys are the historic crossroads of the West, with the confluence of the Rhine and Moselle equidistant from Versailles and Potsdam, from the Channel coast and the lateral wall of the Alps. Founded originally as camps or posting stations by the Romans, their towns long marked the border between Latin civilization and the barbarian tribes, a division perpetuated through the duchies of the early Middle Ages to the rivalries of the Reformation and never wholly eradicated by later empires. Little worlds of their own, proud of ancient liberties and steeped in local patriotism, Mainz, Coblenz, Trier and Frankfurt gained unity only from the rivers which linked them together, binding them also to the greater cities of Cologne and Strasbourg. Paradoxically they became at the same time bastions of particularism and monuments to a culture which was European in spirit and not specifically the heritage of any one people. It was in the archetype of these small Rhenish towns, Coblenz, that Clement Metternich was born on Wednesday, 15 May 1773. The traditions of the Rhineland, limited in vision but non-national in character, shaped the pattern of his life; perhaps they even dominated it.

His full name, Clement Wenceslas Lothar von Metternich-Winneburg-Beilstein, is in itself a sonorous commentary on his antecedents and their social aspirations.[1] He was christened Clement Wenceslas in honour of his spiritual lord and temporal sovereign, the Elector of Trier; and Lothar was added to this discreetly chosen combination to commemorate an ancestor who had himself ruled in Trier on the eve of the Thirty Years War. The Metternich family origins, although fashionably obscured by legendary romance, were impeccably aristocratic, with claims reaching back over eight centuries to the Empire of Henry the Fowler and possibly to the Carolingian nobility. But the Metternich titles reflected an eminence which was narrowly parochial. Beilstein, for example, was a ruined keep dominating the right bank of the Moselle almost halfway between Coblenz and Trier: it had belonged to the Metternichs since Lothar's day. And Winneburg was an even older castle some ten miles north-west of Beilstein: they had held the place for centuries. They had, moreover, given the family name to a village which sprang up on their original Rhenish lands two-and-a-half miles to the west of Coblenz and on the crest of the first heights met by travellers along the old road to Trier. Their dignities were almost a geographical gazetteer of the lower Moselle valley; and these steeply sloping vineyards and rich orchards were their true heartland.

They were not, however, the sole territorial possessions of the family. Heinrich Metternich, head of a regiment at the Battle of the White Mountain in 1620, had won himself an estate in the wider dominions of the Empire, Königswart in Bohemia, a full three hundred miles east of Coblenz beyond the forests of Thuringia and the Erzegebirge Mountains. Yet although Königswart had been family property for a century and a quarter before Metternich's birth, it was still looked upon as alien land; and his kinsmen were no more tempted to settle in its wild pine-covered hills than the great landowners of the English ascendancy to live in Ireland. In this attitude there was, perhaps, a lack of foresight. Other aristocratic dynasties – some of them, indeed, Czech rather than German in origin – prospered as territorial magnates in Bohemia appreciably enriching the chronicles and coffers of the Empire. But the distinction that surrounded such names as Kaunitz, Schwarzenberg, and Czernin had as yet eluded the Metternichs. Their existence was graciously acknowledged by the Imperial court in Vienna but they always cut a very small figure beside these proud families from Bohemia and their peers in Hungary. No one east of the Rhineland took the Counts Metternich very seriously, despite the sixteen quarterings on their heraldic arms.

For most of the eighteenth century it had not mattered very much. The Habsburg rulers in Vienna were still titular Holy Roman Emperors,

the formally elected masters of all the German lands. But in the Rhineland the Emperor's suzerainty was solely honorific: he had no power to
intervene in the internal affairs of the small states; and he could only
induce them to undertake common action in war or diplomacy with the
backing of the Imperial Diet, an institution so corrupt and dilatory that
it was no more than an archaic curiosity. The princes whose words were
law along the middle Rhine were the rulers of Mainz and Trier, both
of them high dignitaries in the Catholic hierarchy and among the nine
Electors responsible for preserving the empty myth of a common
German Reich. The Archiepiscopal Elector of Mainz (who was also
Primate of Germany until 1801) ruled an area as large as the English
counties of Devon and Dorset; and the Archiepiscopal Elector of Trier –
which, significantly, was in those days more often known by its French
name, Trèves – was prince of a region almost as large as the English
county of Norfolk and including, besides the city of Trier, most of the
Moselle valley and Coblenz itself. For many generations the fortunes of
the Metternichs had been closely linked to the polity of these ecclesiastical princes, and their patronage had been considerable.

Metternich's father, Francis George Charles, was sustained by an
agreeably comfortable revenue from his estates and greater social ambition than his immediate ancestors. In many ways he was typical of the
eighteenth-century aristocracy in a petty state except that he had even
less common sense than most of his fellow nobles and much more money
to fritter away. His portrait looks too true to be flattering: a well-cared-
for face but drink-worn and fattening, with pouched eyes and loosely
boorish lips, as heavily German as the Hanoverian Georges. The testimony of contemporaries is no kinder to his reputation: 'a boring babbler
and chronic liar,' wrote Count Frederick Stadion to the Emperor Joseph
II in 1785; and six years later, when he was the Imperial plenipotentiary
in Brussels, the Archduchess Marie Christine begged her brother (the
Emperor Leopold) not to send letters to her by the official courier since
there was no certainty when the Count would get round to opening the
despatch boxes from Vienna.[2] Others found him arrogant, pedantic,
inclined to fuss over petty ceremonial, and obstinate. In retrospect his
serene bumbling seems the most endearing trait in his character.

Yet these strictures were passed on the Count in middle age; and as
a young man no doubt he showed more attractive qualities, for he was
able to make himself known in Vienna and marry a woman of beauty
and intellect with ready access to the Empress Maria Theresa. He was
born in March 1746 and inherited the family sinecure of Chamberlain
to the Elector of Mainz, but he began his career in diplomacy as the
representative in Vienna in 1768 of his own prince-bishop, the Elector
of Trier (that same Clement Wenceslas after whom he was to name his
eldest son). It was an interesting moment in the history of the Habsburg

lands. Maria Theresa was forty-eight and in the twenty-ninth year of her reign. Prostrated with grief at the death of her husband in August 1765, she had insisted on sharing formal sovereignty with her son, Joseph II, and withdrew from government. But when Joseph sought to sweep the dead wood out of the Imperial administration, Maria Theresa found the spectacle of a revolution from above a remarkable restorative for melancholia. Tactfully she began to exercise once more that patient political sense which had already marked her out as the wisest of the Habsburgs. When Count Metternich arrived in Vienna he astutely avoided committing himself to either the 'Empress' or 'Emperor' faction, preferring the group associated with Kaunitz, the elder statesman who managed Austrian foreign policy from 1753 to 1792. It was with the backing of Kaunitz and the support of Maria Theresa that he negotiated a marriage with Maria Beatrice von Kagenegg, a young girl of personality whose sharp wit and impulsiveness had attracted the warm-hearted sympathy of the Empress. The Kagenegg lands were in the Breisgau which, until 1806, was a Habsburg enclave in southwestern Germany and the wedding was celebrated in Freiburg early in January 1771, just four weeks after Beatrice's fifteenth birthday. Soon afterwards she returned with the Count to Coblenz, for he had been appointed a Councillor of State to the Elector of Trier, with responsibility for foreign affairs.

Childhood in Coblenz (1773–84)

The Metternichs took up residence in the family house in the Münz Platz, a massive barrack built in 1674, its austere walls relieved only by a double line of dormer windows. It was there that their four children were born. The eldest was a girl, baptized Pauline.* Clement followed in May 1773 and a second son, Joseph, eighteen months later. A third son, born in 1777, died in infancy. Most of the childhood of both the surviving boys and Pauline was spent at Coblenz, for in the year of Clement's birth the Count had carried out his personal diplomatic revolution, entered the Habsburg service and immediately became Minister of the Imperial court to the Elector of Trier, a curious reversal of rôles and one which seems to have owed much to Beatrice's thrust and ambition. The Count was also accredited to the two other ecclesiastical Electors in the Rhineland, the Archbishops of Cologne and Mainz and in 1777 his responsibilities were extended to all Westphalia. After

* There is a minor mystery over the precise date of Pauline's birth. In the Austrian *Biographisches Lexikon* it is given as 29 November 1772. This date is accepted by such authorities as Srbik and Corti. But it seems to me biologically improbable that she was born only twenty-four weeks before Clement; and her birthday is more likely to have been 29 November 1771, nearly eleven months after her parents' marriage. Dr Helmut Mathy gives this date in his *Franz Georg von Metternich*, p. 29.

Maria Theresa's death in 1780 he continued to hold the post for the first six years of Joseph II's reign. The duties were not over-taxing, but the prestige was locally considerable.

Metternich himself says little about Coblenz in his *Memoirs*: there is only a confused picture of badly paved streets, of gimcrack signboards hanging like banners from the shop fronts, and of neatly trimmed shrubs planted in disciplined line before the Elector's palace.[3] Nor do other impressions seem more exciting. That engagingly eccentric traveller, Baron Riesbeck, anatomizing Germany in the early 1780s, found Coblenz 'a very pretty, though somewhat dead town, which contains about twelve thousand inhabitants'.[4] Although Riesbeck's comments are often startlingly subjective – 'Cologne is the ugliest town in all Germany,' he says – his terse dismissal of Metternich's birthplace is apt enough. The political and social changes of eighteenth-century Germany passed by Coblenz. Nothing of moment happened there between the retreat of a French army in 1688 and the advance of a French army in 1794. In Brandenburg a new city and a parvenu dynasty had emerged to challenge the traditional hegemony of Habsburg Vienna; but the shadow of Prussia did not as yet impinge on the middle Rhine. In Weimar an intellectual awakening, which coincided with Metternich's early years, proclaimed the spiritual unity of the German people; but Weimar was a hundred and seventy miles from Coblenz and a world away. In Hanover, at Göttingen, a Renaissance re-born brought humanism back to universities inhibited by Lutherans and Jesuits; but there were no academic institutions in Coblenz to be stimulated by Herr Gesner's neo-classicism. It should not, however, be thought that Coblenz was ignorant of the Renaissance. A new palace beside the Moselle was completed for the Elector in 1784 and its Ionic portico owed something to Raphael while a 'Last Supper' in the chapel owed a great deal more to Leonardo. Faithful imitation was a passable substitute for genius, and far safer than originality: it may well have been the first lesson Metternich learnt from his environment.

Fortunately he owed most of his early education to his mother. Still in her twenties, she possessed a quick intellect able to soften the obscurantist overtones of an ecclesiastical principality with a healthy cynicism. The family accepted Christian beliefs without troubling the mind over theological exactitude; they scrupulously observed the punctilio of Catholicism as the bedrock of order. The children received religious instruction from the Abbé Bertrand, a member of the Piarist order, a congregation founded in counter-reformation Rome for the education of the poor and never so intellectually zealous as the Jesuits. There was even a cautiously Voltairian deism about the atmosphere of the Metternich household and the Count himself secretly swore the oaths of Freemasonry in a rare moment of free thought.

French influences were strong. Coblenz was a city within the general
orbit of French ideas: for although Strasbourg is nearly two hundred
miles farther up the winding Rhine, the river formed so natural a route
of communication that the distance seemed far less; and there were
parts of French Lorraine which were comparatively accessible along the
Moselle valley. Moreover Countess Beatrice was sympathetic to French
culture. The marriage of the Dauphin to Maria Theresa's daughter in
the spring of 1770 had made an impression on a precocious girl who was
only a few months younger than Marie Antoinette. She prided herself
on the elegance of her French literary style and saw to it that Clement
could write French prose with grace at an early age. He was, indeed,
for many years happier at expressing himself in French than German;
and the correspondence between son and mother remained in French
for as long as she lived. He assiduously kept abreast of French literature
and read the French press and periodicals even in his retirement, and
yet he was never able to understand France or respect the French
nation. It was not the least of his defects.

Metternich's father did not take any great interest in his son's formal
education, apart from a few growls at the backwardness of his German
and much pompous advice in the general style of Polonius.[5] But
the Count did expect Clement to accompany him on some official
journeys, although never to Vienna. Thus at the age of six he was taken
to Strasbourg, where medical research had popularized a preventive
safeguard against cowpox which involved taking the disease in a mild
form. The boy was subjected to this primitive method of inoculation (as
George III of England had been, in London, before him) and suffered
no ill effects. Other expeditions were less eventful. To attend a predominantly ecclesiastical gathering in Cologne at the age of seven was
no doubt extremely boring; and it is hard to see why a lad of thirteen
should have been introduced to the prince-bishoprics of Hildesheim and
Paderborn unless to convince him by contrast that his native city was a
haven of gaiety and progress. On the other hand, he remembered
vividly in later years a visit to Königswart in midsummer, 1786. It was
the first time that he had entered the Habsburg lands and the journey
was prompted by a decision of his father to pull down the old castle at
Königswart and build a residence of dignity; but all this excitement
was cut short by news of the death of Frederick the Great of Prussia and
the hurried return of the Count to his diplomatic duties.[6]

Contact with the French Revolution

By then Clement already had a private tutor, or at least one shared with
Pauline and Joseph. John Frederick Simon was introduced into the
Metternich household by the Countess Beatrice in the autumn of 1784

to supplement – and perhaps even to offset – the teachings of the Abbé
Bertrand. Simon's subsequent career makes his appointment seem, in
retrospect, remarkable; for, less than eight years after taking up his
duties in Coblenz, he was a fanatical Jacobin in Paris 'appealing to
vulgar passions', as his one-time pupil wrote later in his *Memoirs* with
bland distaste. But in 1784 Simon had much to commend him, especially
to a mother who delighted in sense and good taste and who believed
that both virtues sprang more naturally from a French mind than one
trained in Germany. Simon, in fact, bridged both cultures. Born in
Strasbourg in 1751, he came from an Alsatian middle-class family,
Lutheran in origin. For two years he had taught in the famous experi-
mental school at Dessau in Anhalt recently established by the educational theorist Johann Basedow. There he married the niece of
Joachim Campe, a scholar whom Countess Beatrice knew and respected.
Simon admired Basedow's principles, his stress on teaching modern
languages by a direct method, his cavalier disregard of formal classical
studies and, above all, his insistence on a rigorous training of the body
as well as the mind. But Basedow had the administrative vagueness of a
dedicated crank, and Simon left Dessau to set up a girls' school at
Strasbourg and, when that failed, a tutorial establishment at Neuwied,
only eight miles down the Rhine from Coblenz. Ill fortune followed him
there, too, for his wife died soon after her return to Germany. It was at
this moment that Countess Beatrice invited him to take charge of the
education of her three children. There was probably no one in Coblenz
better fitted for the task; but the appointment is an interesting commentary on the breadth of her intellectual sympathies, for she knew
well enough that Simon was no conventional pedagogue.[7]

'The doctrines of this Jacobin ... inspired in me a revulsion which
age and experience have only increased,'[8] wrote Metternich in his
fragmentary autobiography in 1844, the rounded sententiousness tripping heavily from the pen. But it was not always so. For five years the
three children enjoyed their tutor's company, for he was a patient
teacher, generous in mind. As late as the spring of 1789 Pauline, a dull
but earnest girl, was corresponding at length with him over the possibility of rationalizing the early chapters of 'Genesis', a task well within
the compass of his essentially Voltairian philosophy.[9] He was, moreover,
sufficiently a disciple of Basedow to insist on physical education; and
Clement retained into middle age the slim poise of an athlete's frame,
tall and elegant. He was already a competent horseman and, under
Simon's instruction, he became a powerful swimmer. The indignation
with which Metternich saw his tutor turn Jacobin was genuine enough,
but it did not run so deeply as the autobiographical record would
suggest at first glance. Elsewhere, in a passage written in 1820, Metternich describes Simon as 'the kindest soul in the world', one who

'embraced the universe with his love and philanthropy'; and, at the height of his power in 1829, he was prepared to receive Simon in Vienna, listen to his projects for a new encyclopaedia and find in him a septuagenarian optimist, as much Pangloss as Voltaire.[10]

In the summer of 1788 there was, however, still no sign of Simon's pending apostasy, and it seemed good sense to send Clement and Joseph to the university in his home city, Strasbourg. Their names were duly enrolled on the specially exalted register, *Matricula Serenissimorum et Illustrissimorum*, under the date 12 November 1788.[11] They were accompanied by both Simon and the Abbé Bertrand, and accommodated at first in the lavishly Baroque residence of Prince Maximilian of Zweibrücken, a member of the House of Wittelsbach who was at that time commander of the Royal Regiment of Alsace but who became, in 1805, the first King of Bavaria. Even when they moved into less exquisite lodgings Prince Max continued to act as guardian. His wife, a princess of Hesse-Darmstadt, was a friend of the Countess Beatrice and was admired and respected both in France and the German states. Gossip, finding little at fault with the Princess, turned eagerly to her husband and was not disappointed; for Prince Max, at thirty, showed a desire for feminine society which was full-blooded rather than refined. While his prowess in such matters won him admiration from the soldiery, it lessened his virtues as a champion of youthful morals. Clement, however, found him an agreeable patron who 'fulfilled his charge in a most cordial manner'.[12]

At the age of fifteen such privileged treatment was not inclined to lessen Clement's self-conceit nor to endear the Metternich brothers to those fellow students who lacked sixteen quarterings in their social equipage. Simon did all he could for the young man. He induced him, for example, not to wear the short top-knotted wigs (*toupets*) affected by the nobility: they were, he argued, not merely effeminate but time consuming since they required powdering and pomading. Clement was 'happy, handsome and lovable', wrote Simon to Count Metternich a few days before the formal matriculation ceremony. Perhaps so: but there were others who, in later years, maintained that they had found him a refined liar and a braggart. There may well be justice, too, in these recollections for, though Clement had inherited his mother's brains and good looks, he was also his father's son.[13]

Strasbourg was one of the best universities in Europe in these last years of the old order. It was far more cosmopolitan in composition than Oxford and Cambridge or the German universities. The largest single group came, indeed, from Alsace and Lorraine, almost all of them to study law; but a quarter of the whole body of students came from the other provinces of France and a similar proportion from Germany and the Habsburg lands. There was a score of Russians (mostly aristocrats,

but many from simpler homes and supported by generous grants from
the Academy of St Petersburg) and some English and Swiss. Metternich
certainly made acquaintances among the nobility from most states but
it is unlikely that he ever tasted the full blended society which the
university could, in theory, offer. The gulf between gentlemen and
commonalty was as broad as at Oxford and Cambridge, where the
eighteenth-century aristocrats wore golden tassels on their academic
caps. At Strasbourg there were opportunities for riding, fencing and
dancing, a theatre for which a student took out a subscription (and with
good reason, for the talents of the Strasbourg *Comédie* were far above
those of the French provinces), and numerous salons, some intellectually
stimulating and others purely convivial.[14] Clement Metternich participated fully in this social life, even to the extent of taking lessons in
playing the violin, a skill for which he showed aptitude and sensitivity;
but he also attended lectures and tutorial sessions so that he appears to
have spent more hours in formal study than his English contemporaries.
A letter to his father in the week he matriculated outlines a day divided
into three sections: a morning at lectures or with his tutors; an hour of
science followed by an hour of music in the afternoon, and at four
o'clock attendance, with his brother Joseph, at a course of historical
lectures. Sundays and Thursdays were left free and so, it would seem,
were the evenings. Undergraduates rarely keep the good resolutions of
their university honeymoon days and it is likely that Metternich's zest
for learning soon flagged; but there is no doubt that he sat at the feet of
the distinguished Professor Koch who lectured on German law, on the
virtues of the Peace of Westphalia, and, with coincidental topicality, on
the comparative history of revolutions. Koch, a Montesquieu with an
Alsatian accent, had evolved his own ponderously tabular method of
instruction: it was a style which weighed down Metternich's written
analyses for half a century or more.[15]

His mother continued to send her favourite child good advice by
letter. One Wednesday in the following summer she wrote: 'In Germany
you must admire German music and in France French music; and it is
like that with most things' (*enfin il en va de tout ainsi*).[16] As a primer of
dissimulation the precept was sound enough; but it was a little difficult
just then for a sixteen-year-old student to know how far tact should
stretch approval. For that Wednesday an assembly at Versailles began
to speak of a French constitution; on the following Tuesday the Bastille
was stormed; and by the next Friday (17 July) King Louis XVI, brother-
in-law to the Emperor, had ridden to the Hotel de Ville in Paris and
donned the red, white and blue cockade of revolution. Events were
rapidly outpacing Professor Koch's lectures.

At Strasbourg, isolated from the rest of France by the Vosges, the
gathering storm had as yet produced no more than a ground swell of

discontent. On Saturday, 18 July, the town senate met as usual and discussed a demarcation dispute between rival guilds over shipping on the Rhine. The first rumours of what had happened in the capital reached the city that evening, excitement mounted on Sunday and overspilled on Monday when printed accounts confirmed the news from Paris. That afternoon Arthur Young, English agronomist and itinerant reporter extraordinary, arrived in Strasbourg to find 'a detachment of horse with their trumpets on one side, a party of infantry with their drums on the other, and a great mob halloing'.[17] It was, however, on the whole a cheerful crowd, not so much threatening authority as revelling in revolution. Yet, as Metternich was to find on another occasion, the mood of a mob is fickle. At noon on Tuesday a mass of idle onlookers in the market square, stirred by wild tales of imminent repression, swung unexpectedly into anarchy: armed with crowbars and axes they rushed the town hall (*Stadthaus*). Fascinated, Arthur Young noted in his journal the minutiae of the riot. Metternich too observed what was happening, but as his flow of reminiscence rarely touched an event in which he did not participate, he says little of this first impression of revolution. 'Surrounded by a number of dull spectators who called themselves the people, I had been present at the plundering of the Stadthaus in Strasbourg, perpetrated by a drunken mob,' he wrote many years later.[18] Although a more dramatic event than his disdainful prose suggests, it was not in itself an historical turning point, and the day ended in near bathos. For that evening Metternich's patron and protector, Prince Maximilian, ordered cavalry from the Royal Regiment of Alsace to clear the streets. There was no bloodshed: the crowd dispersed exhausted, amiable and comfortably cheered with pillaged wine. Two days later a young man found with coins stolen from the town hall was publicly hanged. Order was thus seen to be restored; and as the poor wretch came from Mainz, Alsatian patriotism was not affronted.

The news from Strasbourg horrified Countess Beatrice, downstream in Coblenz, where such civic giddy-mindedness was as yet unthinkable. On 28 July she wrote to her son urging him to leave 'that accursed city of Strasbourg' and take refuge with her brother at Freiburg, sixty miles away in the Breisgau.[19] But her panic was premature. Spasmodic disturbances continued for some time in Strasbourg, like tremors after an earthquake. There was even a minor mutiny among troops of the garrison. Yet there was never any direct threat to the aristocracy; and Metternich was able to complete another year at the university.

By strictly academic standards it cannot have been of much value to him; for there was little formal teaching. His own ex-tutor, Simon, plunged wildly into revolutionary politics, translating the 'Declaration of the Rights of Man' into German, assuming the editorship of a patriotic weekly and, by January 1790, dominating the local Jacobin club, 'the Society of the Friends of the Constitution'. Other university teachers and instructors were swept along in the liberal effervescence, some of them scientists and several of them ecclesiastics. Professor Koch, too staid a lawyer to sympathize with revolutionaries, had nevertheless to leave Strasbourg for Paris early in the New Year so as to defend the traditional liberties of the university against those in the capital who saw social justice only in uniformity. It was all sadly different from those early weeks of lectures and reading and music; and yet, in their way, the fifteen months which followed the sacking of the *Stadthaus* were the most formative period of Metternich's education. Revolution became for him the supreme bogey; but it was to be another fifty-eight years before he saw it again as a raw force of disintegration in the streets.

The Coronation of Leopold II (1790)

There followed a contrast so striking as to be hardly less memorable. In September 1790 he left Strasbourg to attend the coronation of Leopold II as Holy Roman Emperor at Frankfurt on 9 October (for Joseph II had died in the previous February). It took place in a blaze of archaic pageantry, so that it was almost as if a fumbling institution, which at heart did not believe in itself, was seeking to exorcize the egalitarian devilry of the French by the ritual and ceremonial of centuries. Count Metternich inevitably held a position of some importance at Frankfurt. He was a representative of the Bohemian aristocracy who was also familiar with the Rhenish ecclesiastical Electorates, and he was determined – or Beatrice was for him – that he would outshine the great magnates flocking in from the distant provinces of the Empire; and he succeeded. Ninety-eight coaches brought the Metternichs to town. 'His retinue was the most brilliant at the Austrian court', wrote a French aristocratic observer wistfully. The Count was reported to have spent ten thousand florins (about £1,500) on personal liveries for the ceremony, and even then to have struck a bargain and obtained them second-hand.[20]

Leopold II was too experienced and intelligent to be impressed by such blatant ostentation: but not so his heir, the Archduke Francis. Having been bullied into inferiority for ten years by his uncle Joseph II, the twenty-two-year-old Archduke was inclined to think highly of any dignitary who treated him with deference. Count Metternich seemed a fine fellow: he presented his eldest son to the Archduke; and Clement thus met for the first time the future sovereign who was to create him Prince and Chancellor.

No one, indeed, at Frankfurt that autumn could have failed to notice the Metternichs. For by now Countess Beatrice was thrusting forward not only her glittering noodle of a husband but Clement, who had been appointed to the high-sounding dignity of Ceremonial Marshal to the Catholic Bench of the College of the Counts of Westphalia. The post was largely honorific but it opened to him all the doors that mattered. He enjoyed the occasion and, failing to sense its basic artificiality, turned it into a minor personal triumph. Moving at ease among the illustrious names of the Empire, he seemed a handsome piece of human Rococo. As yet he had not completed his formal education, but at seventeen he had arrived. Only time would show if there were more to him than a porcelain butterfly.

WORLD IN FERMENT

Metternich at Mainz University

Although Clement Metternich had made a felicitous entry on the diplomatic stage at Frankfurt, he was still too young to be a regular performer; and for both father and son the coronation festivities proved ultimately no more than a lively intermezzo. The Count grovelled before his new sovereign and was rewarded with responsibilities for which he was ill suited; for on 30 December 1790 he was appointed Minister Plenipotentiary to the States General of the Austrian Netherlands, and departed for Brussels. Clement, wishing to continue his study of law and diplomacy, had by then already taken up residence at Mainz. The Rhenish city lacked the academic prestige of his former university but the tocsin of revolt was sounding with such menacing urgency in Strasbourg that no aristocrat could serve out an apprenticeship in state-craft there. Mainz, on the other hand, had considerable advantages for Metternich: the Electorate was part of his homeland, a little world in which he cut a fine figure; its university was well equipped for the scientific studies in which he delighted to dabble; and, though there were radical freaks among its lecturers, the sound conservative teachings of Nicholas Vogt were an antidote to dangerously subtle analyses or flights of philosophical fancy. Thus while Count Metternich was seeking in 1791 to play off against each other the rival Belgian patriot factions, Clement Metternich was learning from Professor Vogt the comforting doctrine that good government depends for survival upon a balance between extremes.[1] There was, in fact, little to choose between the applied politics of the father and the aphorisms diligently recorded by his son. The concept of a stable equilibrium appealed equally to both Metternichs, for it assumed a condition of repose natural to their temperaments.

Metternich remained at the University of Mainz until the summer of 1792 although he spent the vacations with his father in Brussels learning the technique of administration by working in the Chancery. Life in both Brussels and Mainz was overshadowed by the dramatic events across the French frontier. Even before the storming of the Bastille there

had been a determined effort by the Belgians to throw off Habsburg
rule, and insurgent unrest forced the Austrian garrisons to withdraw
from the larger cities in November 1789 and fall back on the Meuse.
Two months later a United States of Belgium was proclaimed in
Brussels and it was not until the last weeks of 1790 that the Austrian
Army restored order in its Netherland possessions. By the following
July, when Count Metternich arrived as the Emperor's political representative, there was a deceptive calm throughout Hainault and
Brabant. For the next two years the Belgian democrats continued to
look to Paris for liberation and their pleas did not go unheeded. An
abler and less indolent administrator might have rallied the Emperor's
Belgian subjects around the Catholic hierarchy against the godless mob
of revolution, but not Count Metternich. After a few months of comprehensive tolerance he seemed to lose interest in his task. Perhaps at heart
he had come to accept Austria's exclusion from the southern Netherlands as inevitable. Perhaps he failed to diagnose the nature of the
revolutionary contagion, for both he and the Countess Beatrice listened
too readily to the venomous belittling of the Parisian governments by
the *émigrés* (who had begun to settle in Brussels in the first winter of the
new order). Whatever the reason, he failed to build up any national
front to resist the revolutionary armies, and at the end of 1792 they
flooded almost unchecked across the Flanders plain. Later, Clement
Metternich was to maintain that during his father's tenure of office in
Brussels he had gained experience of value in his own career; but it
was hardly an administration to emulate.[2]

The impact of the Revolution upon Mainz was different. Johannes
von Müller, the Swiss scholar who was both secretary to the Archiepiscopal Elector of Mainz and a historian of distinction, had greeted
news of the fate of the Bastille with an enthusiasm similar to that of
Wordsworth or Herder: it was for him the happiest event since the fall
of the Roman Empire. But during the very period that Metternich was
at the university Müller's views hardened and within three years he was
speaking out against 'the monster tyranny of the French madmen'.
Although there were some imperturbably incorrigible Jacobins, of
whom the most notorious was George Forster, the University librarian,*
the majority of academics in Mainz followed Müller into disillusionment
and revulsion. Nor is this surprising. Like Brussels and Turin, the
Rhineland cities had sprung to life as centres of French *émigré* activity.
The most determined counter-revolutionary groups were in Coblenz,
but it was in the tiny court of the Elector of Mainz that the first wave

---

* George Forster (1754–92) was a distinguished naturalist, who had sailed around the
world with Captain Cook. Another of the so-called Jacobins in Mainz was a Professor
Mathais Metternich (1758–1825), who edited a news-sheet, *Der Bürgerfreund*. He was pre-
sumably a distant relative of the future Austrian Chancellor. On Mainz in 1792–93, see
Agatha Ramm, *Germany 1789–1919* (pp. 28–31).

of exiles sought to perpetuate the fading enchantments of Versailles and the Trianon. The Elector, himself a natural hedonist despite his ecclesiastical responsibilities, allowed full play to their frivolity. No one at his court accepted as final the passing of the age of privilege and elegance, least of all young Metternich. Its cultured sensualism flattered his affectations.

For, even at Mainz, Metternich's physical features and personality showed almost all the characteristics of later life. Tall, with blond curly hair, blue eyes and a high forehead, he was readily accepted into society. His manners were exquisite and he possessed a conversational agreeability which brought to gossip the lustre of good talk. As his career progressed he was to acquire a stiff and condescending graciousness of expression and it became all too easy for eyebrows which in youth showed naïve surprise to be raised in cynical disapprobation. Perhaps as a student he enjoyed a sense of fun which was held in restraint in his years of authority, for a tale is told of a night in Brussels when, having dined well, Clement amused himself by hacking off the noses of statues in a trim eighteenth-century park.[3] But such gestures of revolt were rare indeed. For the most part he remained an urbane observer of the ancient régime in liquidation, inwardly aware of its isolation and unreality but delighted by its sumptuous idleness. Elsewhere contemporaries were greeting a Romantic dawn: Metternich preferred the soft afterglow of tradition and order.

Yet despite his discreetly elaborate behaviour he was sufficiently a product of his day to thrive on the storm and stress of emotional attachment. He had met a goddess briefly in Brussels in the previous year: now she was in Mainz. 'I made the acquaintance at this time,' he wrote a quarter of a century later, 'of a young woman of my age, a delightful creature full of charm, good sense and wit. She belonged to one of the distinguished families of France. I loved her as only a young man could and she loved me with all the simplicity of her heart.' Her name was Marie-Constance de Caumont la Force and she was the nineteen-year-old daughter of the Comte de Lamoignon, former Keeper of the Seals at Louis xvi's court. She was also, inconveniently perhaps, the wife of a French aristocrat a few months her senior. Her portrait shows a tall and full-bosomed girl with gently sloping shoulders, an oval face with eyes set far apart, a broad forehead and delicately seductive lips. She possessed an ethereal beauty that warmed Mainz with admiration, as others besides Metternich have testified. The fact that for four years she had been not unhappily married and that, despite Metternich's avowals of her natural innocence, she manifestly enjoyed flirtations with the cavaliers around her made Marie-Constance unobtainably desirable. Clement and his friend, the future Marquis de Bouillé, would frequently walk beside her house above the Rhine assuring each other

with almost terrifying intensity that their hearts were over-flowing with
love for Madame de Caumont. It was a situation worthy of at least an
operatic aria, more fittingly a duet. Clement himself clearly regarded
the attachment as the first of his *grands amours*. On his admission it
continued for three years – that is, until his own marriage – and he
tried unsuccessfully to pick up the threads of the romance as soon as he
arrived in Paris as ambassador in 1806; but Marie-Constance chose to
remain with her husband and children on the family estate in Normandy
(where she died in 1823). They continued to exchange warm-hearted
letters for more than thirty years. Yet, for all Metternich's persistence,
the affair may have been no more than an adolescent infatuation. 'When
we were with each other,' he later explained, 'we gave such assurances
of our love that, as the future stretched so far before our eyes, we postponed the sequel to so much passion until a more convenient moment.'
Marie-Constance was an intelligent girl; and she had enjoyed herself
at Mainz.[4]

A second coronation; a military expedition; and a mission to London (1792–4)

Metternich's days of study and festivity in Mainz were interrupted at
the beginning of March 1792 by the sudden death of the Emperor
Leopold and the accession of his twenty-four-year-old son, Francis. It
was a bad moment for a change of sovereigns, for the Girondist Government in Paris had, throughout the winter, been pressing for a crusading
war to liberate the peoples of Europe and there were hotheads in
Vienna and among the *émigrés* in the Rhineland who were eager for the
opportunity to accept the Girondist challenge. Leopold's counsel might
still have kept the peace – he had clamped down on the *émigrés* in
Coblenz shortly before he died – but the inexperienced Francis carried
little weight and, within seven weeks of his accession, the French had
declared war on Austria.[5] It was to be more than twenty-three years
before genuine peace returned to Europe.

Neither Austria nor her Prussian ally was mobilized or prepared for
war. Fortunately it did not seem to matter: the two French columns
which crossed the frontier of the Austrian Netherlands and advanced on
Tournai and Mons disintegrated at the first signs of battle. The German
states had no intention of beginning a campaign so early in the summer.
They would wait until the harvest was gathered in. By then the French
people might have risen against their incompetent government. Meanwhile there was certainly time to crown the new Emperor at Frankfurt.
He was the fifty-fourth Emperor since Charlemagne and the twentieth
Habsburg to be thus honoured.

It was only twenty-one months since the last coronation: the stage
properties were at hand; and the actors knew their rôles.[6] Once again

the electors, princes and magnates descended on the Imperial city, golden coaches brightly burnished in the midsummer sun. Once again fastidious outsiders, jealous of Frankfurt's traditions, complained of the overcrowded inns, of the unimaginative food, of the endless commotion in the cobbled streets. Once again Metternich, a veteran at the age of twenty, was Marshal to the Catholic Bench of the College of the Counts of Westphalia. And once again the ceremony was followed by a banquet and a ball, formally opened on this occasion by Clement Metternich, in pale green satin and a lace cravat, partnered by Princess Louise of Mecklenburg (who was to marry into the Hohenzollern family in the following year and become the best-loved, and most mourned, Queen of Prussia). Small wonder that to Metternich the 'pageant and cere-monies' seemed 'of a more imposing character' than in 1790; and they were followed by protracted celebrations in Mainz, where the Elector was eager to show the young Emperor the splendours of his court. But, even more than at the previous coronation, men were conscious of the revolutionary shadows in the West, seeing them not so much a menace, as an affront to the divinity of monarchy. It was, perhaps, an accident that the climax of the festivities was reached on 14 July, the third anniversary of the fall of the Bastille. The coincidental timing, if such it was, produced strange contrasts. In Frankfurt the Emperor Francis, robed in the traditional dalmatic, received the insignia which had been in Habsburg hands for half a millennium. In Paris, almost at the same hour, his aunt watched with tearful alarm as her royal husband moved through a throng of hostile citizens to an improvised altar in the Champ de la Fédération. For on the very day that the Emperor Francis made his first appearance as a crowned sovereign, King Louis XVI made his last. Within ten weeks France was to be a republic; and, though this seemed far less likely, within a decade and a half the Holy Roman Empire itself would be a thing of the past.

With the coming of the war Metternich's days of formal study were ended. From Mainz he travelled back to Coblenz where the Duke of Brunswick had set up his headquarters for the invasion of France.[7] The Prussians were encamped in the village of Metternich itself and there were, in all, some seventy-two thousand Allied troops in the immediate vicinity of Coblenz, confident that they would cut through the French Army like a butter-knife and reach Paris before the leaves of autumn fell. They left Coblenz on 30 July but moved so slowly that it was not until 19 August that they crossed the frontier. The weather then broke and in place of the cloudless sun of the Frankfurt festivities there was an endless downpour of rain which bogged down Brunswick's army as it moved into the Argonne. Yet it had its victories: Longwy fell on 23 August and Verdun on 2 September. Metternich, like everyone else, eagerly awaited news of the final breakthrough to Paris. He was by then

in Brussels, conscious that the destruction of French resistance by
Brunswick's men would relieve his father of his greatest concern, a
campaign to liberate Belgium. But the reports that reached Brussels
from the Argonne were unbelievably bad. Brunswick's advance ended
in the cannon fire of Valmy on 20 September. The Prussians were said
to be conducting secret negotiations with Dumouriez, the French
commander, and another enemy force under Custine had begun to press
forward from Alsace on Speyer and Worms. It was small comfort to
know that reinforcements were moving slowly across the Empire from
the Austrian lands and Hungary.

Worse was to come. By the middle of October Brunswick's troops
were back across the frontier and Custine advancing almost unimpeded
up the Rhine valley. On 21 October he occupied Mainz and a few days
later Frankfurt, the coronation city, fell to the army of the new Republic.
Only Coblenz, which was ringed by fortified hills, continued to defy the
invaders and even there the Metternich estates were ravaged by the
contending armies. Meanwhile Dumouriez was poised for the anticipated invasion of Belgium. On 6 November he defeated the Austrians
at Jemappes, a small town on one of the few hills near Mons. There
were no more natural barriers before Brussels. Hurriedly the Austrian
administration evacuated the city, the Metternichs fleeing north-
eastwards to Roermond on the Meuse and eventually reaching the
comparative safety of Coblenz. It had been a humiliating experience;
and it is interesting that when Metternich came to write his *Memoirs* he
chose to ignore these weeks entirely in the narrative of his early life.

There followed, not the disaster which Count Metternich by now
anticipated, but a period of intrigue and tragi-comedy. The French
over-reached themselves, speedily alienating the population of both
Belgium and the Rhineland by a policy of annexation and exploitation
while risking a protracted struggle by declaring war on Holland and
Britain. At the same time a new Austrian army, under Coburg, concentrated west of the Meuse and in March 1793 began a counter-
offensive. Dumouriez was defeated at Neerwinden, east of Louvain,
and by the early spring the Metternichs were back in Brussels seeking
once more to reconcile the Belgians to Austrian rule. By now, to
Clement Metternich's satisfaction, the French republican government
was openly split into hostile factions. With confusion at home there was
a lively prospect of treason at the front. On 2 April the French Minister
of War and three commissioners from the Convention arrived at
Tournai to arrest Dumouriez. But even this operation was bungled.
They were themselves arrested by Dumouriez, handed over to the
Austrians and interrogated by Clement Metternich, who had been sent
by his father on a special mission to the Austrian commander.[8] Three
days later Dumouriez too came over to the Austrians. He seemed a

worthwhile prize, for he was not only the victor of Valmy and Jemappes, but the man who had been Foreign Minister when war was declared on Austria. With evident elation young Metternich saw him set out under escort from Brussels down the long road which was to take him to Regensburg and Vienna and ultimately, after nineteen years of exile in England, to a grave beside the Thames at Henley. For Metternich his defection confirmed the worthlessness of republican rule and its transient hold on the loyalties of men of good breeding. Already the former Marquis de Lafayette had deserted to the Prussians (and was, for his pains, languishing in Spandau jail) and, at the very moment of Dumouriez's flight, Citoyen Talleyrand was on his way across the Atlantic having decided that the banks of the Delaware offered more peace than the Seine and less commitment to a cause than the Rhine or the Scheldt. But as yet Talleyrand was of small importance compared to Lafayette and Dumouriez; and it is probable that Clement Metternich had not even heard of him.

But the war continued, despite Dumouriez's treason. So far Metternich had not seen any military action. He was to have his opportunity in the following month. Coburg's army, more than half of it Austrian, moved sedately forward through Flanders and at last reached the barrier fortress of Valenciennes, on the French frontier. Established practice dictated that such citadels should be besieged: Coburg always obeyed the precepts of the textbooks; and for two months Valenciennes was entrenched, undersapped and blockaded. When it fell, on 28 July, military punctilio was duly observed and regimental bands played ceremonially as swords were handed over and flags honoured. The siege was a classical example of an old-style military exercise, as formal as a minuet and as decorous as a parade. Among the observers of these operations was Clement Metternich, who was able to dine elegantly at the headquarters of one or other of the Allied staffs and live in reasonable comfort. Years later he wrote, 'I . . . therefore had the chance to observe war closely . . . In the course of my lengthy public career, I have often had cause to congratulate myself on the experience I thus gained.'[9] The fact that, in that long life, there was never again a military enterprise so antiquated as Coburg's cumbersome campaign seems to have escaped his attention. Within a few months Carnot had begun the revolution in warfare which Bonaparte completed and Clausewitz analysed. Metternich's amateur dabbling in siege operations was worthless; and yet he continued to believe that, in those two months of a glorious summer, he had received a practical education in the science of arms. A boundless capacity for self-delusion lay high among his attributes.

Yet Coburg's army was an inter-Allied force, and it is probable that the connections Metternich made in the British camp at this time were of more value to him than the perfunctory knowledge he acquired of warfare. The joint British-Hessian-Hanoverian expeditionary force was commanded by Frederick, Duke of York, the second son of King George III; and it may well have been through his patronage that when, in the early spring of 1794, Metternich was despatched to London on a special mission he was received at court and admitted to society with a generous hospitality rarely shown towards a young diplomat of little standing. Officially he had been sent across the Channel by his father to assist Count Desandrouin, the Treasurer-General of the Austrian Netherlands, to negotiate a British loan; but he had never before visited a capital city and his private contacts were of more significance than the occasional moments he spent in public business.[10] He met Pitt and Burke, dined with Fox and Grey and Sheridan (although he appears not to have enjoyed their company), listened to debates in the Lords and the Commons, and sat for some hours in Westminster Hall as the trial of Warren Hastings dragged interminably into its sixth year of melodramatic abuse. He was flattered by the thirty-one-year-old Prince of Wales (whom he describes, a little unexpectedly, as 'one of the most handsome men I ever saw') and treated with kindness by the King.[11]

Since his life was spent mainly in the Rhineland and Central Europe it is hardly surprising that the most lasting impressions he retained of England were of her unique character as a naval power. Early in May 1794 he watched, from a hill above Cowes, as the Channel Fleet formed up to escort a convoy of merchantmen to the East Indies and another convoy to the West Indies. 'I consider this the most beautiful sight I have ever seen' he wrote forty years later, adding for good measure, 'the most beautiful that human eyes have ever beheld.'[12] He also subsequently claimed to have been with Admiral Howe in his flagship on 30 May when news came that the French Fleet was at sea and to have begged Howe to allow him to stay aboard for the naval battle which all felt to be at hand, a request Howe allegedly refused. But unfortunately this tale of how he narrowly missed 'the glorious First of June' off Ushant bears all the stamp of a raconteur's licence; for on 30 May Howe was not in Portsmouth but fogbound down-Channel some three hundred miles to the west, having been patrolling the Biscay sea-lanes for all the last fortnight in May. It is, of course, possible that Metternich asked to be allowed to observe a naval action at a meeting with Howe two weeks, rather than two days, before the battle; but it is equally possible that the incident took place only in his retrospective imagination. His wish to see a naval bombardment was fulfilled a few weeks later when the vessel on which he was a passenger from Harwich to the Netherlands was blown off course and caught in crossfire between the forts of Dunkirk and a British flotilla, commanded by a Captain

Sidney Smith, whom he was to meet many years later at the Congress of Vienna. It was not the type of action for which he had hoped.[13]

Flight to Austria; and marriage to Eleonore von Kaunitz (1795)

He left Harwich in September 1794 as the Emperor's Minister Plenipotentiary to the United Netherlands at the Hague. News of this appointment reached him while he was in London and may, indeed, explain why he had received such courteous attention. It was an impressive designation for a young man of twenty-one but he arrived in Holland only a few days before the vanguard of French invaders and was forced to spend an undignified month pursuing the government to which he was accredited from one Dutch city to another until he eventually found it, an exiled and powerless rump, on the Lower Rhine.[14] For during his sojourn in England the military balance was drastically changed on the continent. Coburg's defensive position in Flanders was swept aside by the inspired revolutionary armies of Carnot, and when Coburg broke off the battle of Fleurus on 26 June 1794 he handed the Low Countries to France for twenty years. Nine days later there was a desperate conference between Coburg and the Duke of York outside a village called Waterloo, where the Duke believed there was a ridge on which Brussels could be defended. But Coburg would have none of it. Brussels was abandoned once more and Count Metternich fled to Dusseldorf, where on 19 July his Emperor coldly told him that he had dissolved the administration of the Austrian Netherlands. The British fell back through Ostend, Neuport and Antwerp to stand at last along the dreary banks of the Waal while the Austrians trailed away to the east, amid bitter recriminations from an ally who felt betrayed. It was, indeed, a sorry passage of arms, reflecting little credit on the enterprise of the military commanders or their willingness to wage a protracted campaign.

That autumn the French advanced in the Rhineland. Cologne and Bonn fell swiftly to the revolutionary army and on 23 October the tricolour flag was hoisted over Coblenz. 'All intelligent Frenchmen know that Coblenz is really in France,' Robespierre had declared shortly before the war began;[15] and, though he was no longer alive to direct policy, it seemed in those early months of military administration that Coblenz might indeed be incorporated in the Republic. Every one of the Metternich estates was confiscated, seventy-five square miles of land from which the Count had drawn an income of over £25,000 a year. The family fortune and its political influence had fallen rapidly to a low ebb, for the Emperor Francis had himself been in Belgium that spring and was so unimpressed by the Count's method of government that he did not hesitate to blame him for the maladministration which underlay the military reversals. The Count received scant sympathy when he arrived in Vienna that October.

The Emperor was particularly incensed at two aspects of the Count's policy: his leniency towards the political demands of the people of Brabant; and his attempt to arm the peasantry against the invader, a measure which the Habsburg government maintained had played straight into the hands of the revolutionaries. The Count had no political allies at court: foreign affairs were controlled by Baron Thugut as 'Minister of State for the Chancellery' (*Haus-Hof-und Staatskanzlei*); while the Emperor's own opinions were still carefully implanted by his former tutor, Count Colloredo; and neither had any liking for such a palpably ambitious family as the Metternichs, father, mother and son. For Clement, too, was eclipsed by the shadows falling on his father.[16] He had supported the Count's activities in the Austrian Netherlands with laudably filial respect and had published a pamphlet, with ill-disguised anonymity, defending his father's policy and maintaining that the only way to fight a revolution was to raise a people's army pledged to defend their homes against anarchy and plunder.[17] It was a fine piece of writing but ill-timed; and it could, perhaps, be argued by his enemies that had Clement not dallied so long in London his services as envoy at the Hague might have achieved greater cohesion among the Allies. Although his later assertion to an American visitor that he had contemplated emigrating to the United States need not be taken seriously, his career certainly appeared to have ended before it had begun. In the middle of November 1794 he joined his parents in Vienna; it was not the happiest of introductions to his sovereign's capital city.

He spent the rest of the winter with his attention divided between the delights of Viennese society (where he was treated with considerable reserve) and management of the one remaining family estate, Königswart in Bohemia, 160 miles north-west of Vienna. Neither of the Metternichs was employed in the Emperor's service for more than two years after the flight from the Netherlands, but by the beginning of 1795 Francis had sufficiently relented to authorize payment of a pension to the Count as compensation for his lost properties in the Rhineland. It was, however, the Countess Beatrice who thrust the family back up the social ladder, even enabling it to reach a higher level of acceptance than at Frankfurt and Mainz. For this remarkable woman had by no means lost the intelligence and forcefulness with which, in her youth, she had won her way into the court of Maria Theresa. She retained one connection of inestimable value, her friendship with the Kaunitz family. The old Chancellor, who had been her patron a quarter of a century ago, had died early in 1794 but his son had married a companion of her childhood, Princess von Oettingen-Spielburg, to whom a daughter had been born in October 1775. At nineteen Eleonore von Kaunitz, grand-daughter of Austria's greatest statesman of the century, was a highly eligible bride for any suitor. There was talk of a marriage alliance with the Palffys or with the Colloredos, then at the peak of social influence. But within six weeks of reaching Vienna, Beatrice set about negotiating the union of Eleonore and Clement with all the single-mindedness which Eleonore's grandfather had shown when he achieved the 'Diplomatic Revolution' of 1756–7; and Count Metternich and his son dutifully followed Beatrice's lead.[18]

It must be admitted she soon had a firm ally in Eleonore herself. Still a romantic at heart, she was flattered by Metternich's good looks, poise and – if the testimony of her aunt may be believed – by the fact that he was alternately 'modest and enterprising'. Clement had no illusions about the marriage. Eleonore was small and plain, with so few features on her face that she presented an insoluble problem to the portrait painters; for try though they did to depict her as a wistful doe, she invariably appears on canvas as a frightened mouse. But as Metternich's own inclinations were always towards a lioness or an eagle, it made little difference. He respected Eleonore, and his letters both before and after the wedding show that he felt genuine affection for her; but there is little doubt that the greatest attraction was her dowry and that her only fascination for him was membership of the Kaunitz family.

Her father viewed Countess Beatrice's intrigues with distaste and Eleonore's infatuation with gloomy resignation. He regarded Metternich as a shallow creature who was far too polished in his manner towards women, languidly flippant and careless hearted. His daughter insisted that he was an earnest scholar with sound religious principles; her world was as yet a small one. Even before her father gave his consent to the betrothal, she was carrying cuttings of Clement's hair in a locket round her neck. Metternich spent most of July 1795 on the Kaunitz estate in Moravia and when in August he moved on to Prague and Königswart she was delighted by the letters which reached her day after day. But her father's hostility was not lessened by closer acquaintance with the family; and Count Metternich's assertion that his son was as much a prodigy as the younger Pitt somehow failed to impress him. Eventually Prince Kaunitz imposed two conditions: Eleonore should continue to reside with her family as he considered she was too young to set up a separate establishment; and his future son-in-law was not to serve as a diplomat so long as he was alive. It is significant that although both of these stipulations cut across Beatrice's plans for her son, Metternich was prepared to accept them rather than lose the opportunity of converting himself from a dispossessed Rhinelander to an Austrian aristocrat of the highest standing.

They were married on 27 September 1795, a fortnight before Eleonore's twentieth birthday, on the country estate which Chancellor

Kaunitz had created at Austerlitz on the central Moravian plateau, fourteen miles east of Brno.[19] Ten years later its name resounded across Europe as the sabres of the Grand Army scattered Russians and Austrians on the heights west of the village, but in 1795 it remained isolated and barely known among its orchards and vineyards, the mock Renaissance chateau hidden by an avenue of chestnuts stretching for a mile towards the hills. On that Sunday the whole countryside around Austerlitz was in festive mood for, with that curious patriarchal egalitarianism of the central European nobility, six peasant couples had been invited to share the nuptial blessing bestowed on Eleonore and Clement. In the evening there were gifts for the villagers, wild dancing to gipsy violins, and new wine to be tasted; and on the next day the Metternichs joined Prince Kaunitz in a pheasant shoot. It was a splendid triumph for Countess Beatrice, and there is no reason to suppose that Eleonore was unhappy.

The Metternichs in Viennese Society and at the Congress of Rastatt (1798–9)

The couple wintered in the Kaunitz town residence in Vienna, some ninety miles from Austerlitz. Although Thugut still treated the Metternichs with inhospitable frigidity, they were elsewhere well received and Clement was once again able to delight the salons with his elegance, courtesy and good taste. In later years he maintained that he used these early months in Vienna to continue his studies, oblivious of the Revolution ravaging the continent: 'I diligently attended lectures on Geology, Chemistry and Physics', he wrote. 'Then, too, as afterwards, I followed with attention the progress of medical science'.[20] He certainly amused himself with science much as another great statesman, Lord Salisbury, was to do at the end of the century. But this self-portrait of a young aristocrat happily fiddling with test-tubes while Europe burns is not entirely convincing. There is no doubt that at times the family chafed at its exclusion from political affairs and it is probable that Clement was trying, cautiously, to build up a faction in the salons of the capital, although 'interests' and 'connections' in the Habsburg autocracy were both more exclusive and more amorphous than in the eighteenth-century parliaments of Britain.

Before the end of the year the Metternichs suffered a social misfortune. One of Clement's earliest patrons was the Princess Liechtenstein (who had known his mother since childhood and who was an aunt of Eleonore). The Liechtensteins were among the greatest feudal magnates of the Empire and indeed of Europe. Their estates in Bohemia and Moravia covered nearly five hundred square miles and they had, as well, other lands in Silesia and Lower Austria; and the backing of this princely dynasty, together with the Kaunitz connection, could carry

Metternich to the pinnacle of influence if the Emperor determined to dispense with Thugut and his policy. On 8 December Eleonore and Clement held their first grand reception and ceremonial dinner. As the illustrious names of Habsburg society echoed through the antechamber so bad news travelled with them. That morning the young Prince Karl of Liechtenstein, Eleonore's cousin and Clement's boon companion on the eve of their wedding, had been gravely wounded in a duel with a man of little account fought over a woman of no reputation. On Christmas Eve he died. Illogically the superstitious minds of Vienna held the tragedy to be a sinister omen for the Metternichs; and, although Princess Liechtenstein survived for another sixteen years, she was too broken in spirit to advance the cause of the young couple whose entry into society was so associated with her son's folly and death.[21]

Eleonore had, of course, other connections of social value. The Kaunitz family were close friends of the Prince de Ligne, who had once exchanged intellectual pleasantries with Voltaire and Rousseau and 'enlightened' the great despots of Berlin and St Petersburg. Although in his sixties, he still strove – not without success – to preserve his reputation as the finest conversationalist of his age and Clement was welcome in such company as a ready listener, astute enough to feed a wearying wit with apt responses. There were, too, the Kinsky and Clary dynasties, who had intermarried with the Kaunitz family (and with almost everybody else who mattered as well); and the Metternichs were received by the Schwarzenbergs and the Lobkowitzs and the Esterhazys. It was gratifying to sparkle in such brilliance, and their marriage was a happy one. In the middle of January a daughter was born to them and named Marie, and Clement remained for many months a proud and jubilant father.

Yet his public career had still not advanced since the disastrous autumn of 1794: it was closed to him by the veto of his father-in-law and the stubborn hostility of Thugut. But in September 1797 one obstacle at least was removed; for Prince Kaunitz suddenly fell ill and died. The other barrier, too, seemed by now less inflexible. The character of the war against France had changed dramatically with the victories of General Bonaparte in the plains of Lombardy. After a year of independent command the twenty-seven-year-old Corsican had carried his army into Carinthia in the spring of 1797 and the Austrians concluded an armistice when his troops were only a hundred miles from Vienna itself.[22] Six months later this provisional armistice of Leoben was succeeded by the formal Treaty of Campo Formio. Its terms were hard, for they were dictated by Bonaparte himself. The Austrians were forced to recognize the annexation of Belgium to the Republic, the transformation of northern Italy into a French dependency, and the extension of France's eastern frontier to the Rhine.

There was indignation in Vienna against a Foreign Minister who accepted such conditions. Thugut was shaken, but he did not fall for he was a man of courage and determination. He made it clear to Emperor Francis that for him Campo-Formio was no more than a sealed truce and that he intended to open negotiations for a new coalition to resume the war against France; but he was forced to make gestures to his domestic enemies. At Campo-Formio it had been agreed that there would be a congress to determine compensation for the German princes dispossessed of the left bank of the Rhine. It was to Austria's interest for the Congress to be prolonged until Thugut reached agreement with Britain and Russia. Who better qualified to safeguard the Emperor's interests at such a gathering than that master of circumvention and delay, Count Francis George Metternich? He accepted the post of Imperial Plenipotentiary to the Congress and insisted on taking his eldest son to Rastatt as secretary.[23] When, after six weeks of preliminary exchanges, the formal Congress opened on 19 January 1798, Clement Metternich was duly appointed a representative for the Westphalian Counts. The Habsburg delegation was completed by Count Ludwig von Lehrbach, as spokesman for the Austrian lands, and Count Ludwig Cobenzl, plenipotentiary for the Kingdoms of Hungary and Bohemia: both Lehrbach and Cobenzl seem to have regarded the Metternichs with almost as much suspicion as they did the delegates of the French Republic.

The Rastatt Congress was a futile exercise in diplomacy, and perhaps it was always meant to be. To the French the small Imperial city between the Rhine and the Black Forest should, by rights, have been the cemetery in which the Holy Roman Empire would be interred after dissection. But as the proceedings at Rastatt dragged on through the spring and summer of 1798 into a second winter, it became clear that there was no one in Paris who could take responsibility for signing the Empire's death certificate. It had been assumed when the delegates travelled to Rastatt that this task would be undertaken by General Bonaparte: he had made a brief visit to the city before the Congress officially opened but he left on the very day the Metternichs arrived, without meeting them. Clement's letters to his wife show the extent to which everything at the Congress seemed to depend on Napoleon's movements. On Sunday, 17 December, he was expected 'next Tuesday'; and when Tuesday passed with no Bonaparte, Clement wrote: 'We expect him tomorrow'. There followed three letters in the next fortnight announcing the imminence of his arrival. By 6 January there is an assurance that 'our affairs will move more swiftly when Bonaparte has arrived', and a week later a firm statement, 'There is no doubt that he will return'. By 27 March he was writing, 'the non-arrival of Bonaparte is now certain': by 8 May, 'the return of Bonaparte is certain'; and by

15 May, 'Bonaparte has left Paris for Toulon although a courier has been sent' telling him the Austrians 'await him at Rastatt'.[24] He never came. By the end of July he was in Cairo; but the Congress still looked for an authoritative lead from the French. It finally dispersed in March 1799; by then, Bonaparte was outside Acre.

Metternich found Rastatt a bore. At first it had seemed an intriguing observation post from which to scrutinize and assess the strange phenomenon across the Rhine in France. He disliked and despised most of what he saw: the formal dress of the French delegates, so vulgar that a gentleman 'would hesitate to wear it in the early morning'; the liberty of thought which forced Alsatian peasants to cross the Rhine to find churches where they might keep the solemnities of Holy Week; the pyramid of almond-cakes decorated with tricolour flags which 'quite took away the appetite' when he dined with the principal French representative; the revolutionary cockades which the *Comédie Française* fastened to the costumes of Molière's characters so as to identify them with the new order. 'Good God!', he wrote to Eleonore a week after his arrival, 'how changed is this nation. Neatness and elegance beyond compare has given way to the deepest slovenliness and in place of perfect amiability there is now sinister truculence.'[25]

The conversation of the French was at times obsessive. 'All they dream of in France ... is an invasion of England,' he complained to Eleonore. One man proposed 'going over in a balloon'; another 'pretended to have invented a type of boat which would pass unseen beneath the waters'; and yet another, 'the most fanatical of all, would have guns manufactured which would have a range of fifty miles and destroy England from batteries in France.'[26] He was sure, he said, that Eleonore would dismiss these ideas 'as the plans of madmen', but no doubt their recounting would amuse the salons of Vienna. Clearly the scientist in Metternich was not impressed.

It was interesting to see Frankfurt and Strasbourg once more but he was soon complaining that at Rastatt 'all days are alike'. 'There is nothing so wearisome under the dome of heaven as a ball at Rastatt,' he wrote early in 1798. He described to Eleonore how he was visiting the theatre, playing 'games of chance' in the evening, and – in a rare note of enthusiasm – how he had conducted an orchestra at a subscription concert and played in a quartet 'with a talented young violinist and two amateurs'. French lampoons suggested that Metternich's pursuits were rather less innocent; and there was a persistent tale – which improved in the telling – that one evening father and son encountered each other in the same private room of a notoriously open house. On 25 September 1798, a scurrilous French newspaper, *Le Publiciste*, gave him the doubtful honour of a pen-portrait: 'Some day', it declared, no doubt with esoteric humour, 'he may well follow in his father's footsteps ... He

should not however mistake haughtiness for dignity, and since he himself consorts with low company he should refrain from treating certain
better men disdainfully.'²⁷ The ponderous rebuke may have been
deserved; but the happiness with which he went on leave to his family
in Vienna and later welcomed Eleonore's decision to take up residence
in Rastatt rings too genuinely through his letters to be feigned. And yet
one wonders why she chose to leave the delights of Viennese society for
the unending dreariness of a congress that refused to come to the boil.

By the spring of 1799 Austria was again at war with France and they
were back in Vienna. His family was growing. A son, Francis, was born
in February 1798 and his wife was expecting their third child. It was
born in June and baptized Clement; but within a few days he died, and
in the following November Francis, too, contracted a lung infection
from which he never recovered. During these months of tragedy
Metternich remained a private citizen, disinclined after the frustrations
of Rastatt to continue in the diplomatic service. Once more he drifted
through the salons, resumed his scientific studies, and consoled himself
with music. Occasionally he carried out court functions for Emperor
Francis, who chided him for his apparent indolence and urged him to
hold himself in readiness for further orders. But the old century slipped
away with no word from the Imperial palace. Thugut was still in charge
of foreign affairs although, as the Second Coalition fell from triumph to
disaster, he earned himself an unpopular reputation as a warmonger.

In June 1800 Bonaparte, now First Consul of the Republic, defeated
the Austrians at Marengo; and in the first week of December General
Moreau snatched victory from the Archduke John at Hohenlinden. By
the middle of the month the French had reached the great Benedictine
abbey of Melk, high above the Danube and only fifty-five miles due
west of the capital. For a second time Emperor Francis sought peace
from the French, and an armistice was concluded at Steyr on Christmas
Day. This time there was no saving Thugut. 'All sections of the people
are unanimously of the opinion that Your Excellency is holding up the
conclusions of peace, and will always hold it up,' wrote the Emperor in
a note of dismissal to Thugut on the first day of 1801.²⁸ His responsibilities for foreign affairs were handed over to Ludwig Cobenzl,
although both Colloredo and Francis himself took an active part in the
formulation of policy for the next five years. Peace was concluded at
Lunéville, early in February 1801: the Treaty confirmed the territorial
losses of Campo-Formio, adding to them a further weakening of
Habsburg influence in Italy. The Empire was exhausted and in desperate need of peaceful convalescence.

Clement Metternich did not think highly of the Colloredo–Cobenzl
partnership. It was fashionable to deride Colloredo as an unimaginative
and foppish courtier and, although his relations with Cobenzl had

become more friendly during their dreary sojourn in Rastatt, there remained a certain cold reserve. Cobenzl's father had, however, once been a supporter of Count Metternich; his wife had been, since childhood, a friend of Eleonore; and Metternich's own inclination was at this time rather more towards Cobenzl's policy of appeasement than an endless conflict with France. Both men believed, at heart, that eventually Consul Bonaparte would tame the aggressive instincts of 'the barbarians' west of the Rhine. It was likely that Metternich would have returned to diplomatic service soon after Cobenzl's appointment; but he was indirectly approached by the Emperor even before Cobenzl had returned from St Petersburg, where he was serving as Austrian ambassador. The Emperor offered him the choice of three posts: he might go as Minister to the Imperial Diet at Regensburg; or to the Danish Kingdom of Copenhagen; or the Saxon Kingdom in Dresden.[29] Metternich maintains, not altogether convincingly, that he was reluctant to give up his private life for affairs of state and that he was induced to consider the offer only after a personal appeal by the Emperor to his sense of duty. But, whatever the precise circumstances of the offer, he chose wisely. At Regensburg he would have had to sit by the disintegrating corpse of the Holy Roman Empire, and life would have become a perpetual Rastatt. Had he travelled to Copenhagen, he would have been on the outer fringe of affairs; but Dresden's central position had for many decades given the city greater importance than the strength of the Saxon Kingdom warranted. He accepted the Dresden post at the end of January 1801; his appointment was confirmed on 5 February, three days after the conclusion of the Peace of Lunéville. There was no sense of urgency. He stayed for part of the summer in Vienna, moved to Königswart in the autumn and, once he was certain that all was well with the family estate, he journeyed to Dresden, which was less distant from Königswart than was Vienna. He arrived there at last on 4 November.[30]

DRESDEN AND BERLIN

At the Court of Saxony (1801–3)

The acceptance of the Dresden appointment was a significant turning point in Metternich's career. At the age of twenty-seven, he was beginning almost half a century of service to 'Austria', a concept which, although not achieving Imperial dignity until 1804, was already tacitly recognized as the only effective means by which the Habsburg realm might contribute to the European state system in the post-revolutionary era. Outwardly, of course, the Dresden post made no difference to Metternich's personal loyalties; he remained the servant of the ruler in Vienna. Henceforth, however, he saw the problems of the continent less as a dispossessed Rhinelander and far more as a Central European. Although at times mourning sentimentally the passing of a familiar order, he tended to leave the fate of the former ecclesiastical principalities in the west to others. As he wrote later, he had no wish 'to witness the obsequies of the noble German Empire'; and remembrance of things past is certainly no way of advancement.

Before setting out for Dresden, Metternich spent several weeks in Vienna and there received what nowadays would be regarded as an extensive briefing on the German problem. From Count Ferdinand Trauttmansdorff, the head of the diplomatic service, he received the general advice to regard every Prussian initiative with suspicion and hostility while urging respect for the deliberations of the Imperial Diet at Regensburg; and he also offered the helpful suggestion, tendered with the cynicism of a veteran bureaucrat, that he should send frequent despatches whose worth would be assessed by their length rather than by any succinct analysis. His principal instructor in these matters was, however, Baron Karl Daiser von Sylbach, a State Counsellor who at the age of forty-six had an experience of German affairs going back to the days of Kaunitz. It is difficult to estimate the extent of Daiser's influence on Metternich; but it is probable that a memorandum which Metternich prepared shortly before his departure for Saxony was as much a pupil's tribute to an able tutor as a work of original thought and composition.[1]

This document was written in the form of 'Instructions' and Metternich evidently hoped that he would be authorized to use its proposals as a basis for his conduct and policy in Dresden. In this he was to be disappointed for its recommendations showed greater independence and authority than could be tolerated in a fledgling envoy to a comparatively minor court. It remains, nevertheless, an interesting historical curiosity, not least because in later years Metternich was to use so many of its ideas as a framework for his principles of action.

The 'Instructions' are primarily an analysis of political events from 1790 to 1801. There is, in this document, far less condemnation of the Revolution as a source of disintegration than in Metternich's earlier writings and a more statesmanlike appraisal of the rivalries between the Great Powers, notably Prussia and Russia. France had attained primacy on the continent not only through her military victories but because of the failure of the other nations to maintain a proper balance in Europe. Greed for Polish lands had distracted the Russians and Prussians: the partition of Poland, which was 'contrary to all principles of sound policy', was evidence of a 'blind desire for aggrandizement' in both St Petersburg and Berlin. Britain, too, though hostile to French ambitions, had neglected Europe for the sake of maritime conquests. The coalition of 1798 had left the Austrians to face the French and they had, in consequence, suffered more from the re-shaping of the map of Europe than any other power. But Metternich was by no means pessimistic over the situation in 1801. He argued that the loss of the Austrian Netherlands was an indirect advantage to the dynasty, for they had been an expensive luxury, so remote as to be scarcely defensible. Similarly although the changes in Italy robbed the Habsburgs of a traditional sphere of influence, they created new opportunities on the Adriatic where the Austrians had become heirs to the commercial oligarchs of Venice. But he insisted that Austria's central position on the continent made it essential for her to think, not so much of territorial compensation, as of 'laying the foundations of a European political system'. Saxony and the other German states ought therefore to look for leadership to Vienna rather than to Paris, Berlin or St Petersburg; for only Vienna could establish the equilibrium which Europe needed for her convalescence.

It was not long before Metternich realized that these fine sentiments were wasted on the Court of Saxony. Frederick Augustus III, Elector of Saxony since 1763, was a naïvely honest dilettante in his early fifties, much addicted to the cultivation of ornamental gardens and the memory of Camillo Marcolini, the beloved favourite of his youth.[2] As yet the French Revolution had made little impact upon his politics and even less on his way of life. 'To judge from this court alone,' Metternich wrote, 'one might have believed the world was standing still.'[3] Etiquette,

costume, manners and customs were fifty years out of date: the whole
atmosphere of Dresden was too formalized and leisurely even for
Metternich. He had believed that his post would serve as a sounding-
board for the intrigues of the Russians and Prussians but the trivia of
court ceremonial effectively muffled any vibrations from St Petersburg
or Berlin. For months nothing happened and there was little enough to
include in those lengthy despatches which Trauttmansdorff had pressed
him to send. His British colleague, Sir Hugh Elliott, informed Metternich that he personally had a simple solution: if his government asked
for news, he invented it and subsequently sent another courier with a
further despatch denying its authenticity. There was a considerable air
of make-believe about this tiny baroque court: it was so full of charm
that there was no room for serious politics and every suggestion from
Metternich for closer links with Austria was received with blandly conciliatory indifference. Frederick-Augustus had no wish to offend the
French or the Russians or the Prussians or anybody else for that matter;
there was still so much work to be done in the rose-gardens.

Metternich unquestionably enjoyed the light-hearted frivolity of
Dresden. The city had long delighted in its reputation for amorous
escapades and he was soon able to provide the gossips with the scandal
that titillated their lives. Katharina Bagration was the eighteen-year-
old wife of one of Russia's most distinguished and popular generals,
temporarily out of favour at St Petersburg. Before her marriage in 1800
she had been the Countess Skavoronski and was of Latvian origin. Her
features were pale, their alabaster quality emphasized by her dark hair;
she was small in figure and her face had the angelic sweetness of a
porcelain nymph from neighbouring Meissen. She became Metternich's
mistress soon after his arrival at Dresden and, in the late summer of
1802, she gave birth to a daughter who was baptized Clementine and
acknowledged as Metternich's child even by his wife, Eleonore.*⁴ Nor
was Katharina his only liaison in Dresden. It was there that he met
Wilhelmine, daughter of the last Duke of Courland, and at that time
married to the *émigré* Prince de Rohan Guemenee who was serving with
the Austrian Army. When Metternich first knew Wilhelmine she was
only twenty but her exotic temperament had already made her
notorious, 'a volcano belching forth ice' wrote the Countess of Boigne,
who had no reason to love her.⁵ As the Duchess of Sagan she was to
pursue Metternich, and many other public figures, for almost four
decades, at times tantalizingly elusive and occasionally driving her admirers into hostility by a mocking arrogance. She was a far more

---

* Clementine Bagration was brought up as an Austrian by the Metternichs and accommodated, with a nurse, at Baden, near Vienna. She married an Austrian General, Count
Otto Blome, in 1828 but died in childbirth a year later. She is the only known illegitimate
offspring of Metternich.

predatory animal than Katharina Bagration, although less ravishing and – at least in the later years – less outrageous. Metternich was infatuated with both these women at Dresden and, it would appear, with others; but he continued to show a sincere affection towards Eleonore. Society was puzzled by the abundance of his attachments and by the sensible charity of his wife. When, in January 1803, Eleonore gave birth to their fourth child, Victor, there were some who maintained that she had found consolation with a lover and that Metternich was not the boy's father; but there seems no ground for the calumny. Dresden was permissively free in its love-making although inclined, from time to time, to castigate itself with waves of censorious prurience.

It would, however, be a mistake to assume that Metternich spent all his leisure hours in Dresden – and there were many of them – in amatory dallying. In July 1802 he made the acquaintance of that implacable foe of Napoleon, Friedrich Gentz, a man who for thirty years was to serve him as confidant, mentor and critic.[6] Gentz had been born into a middle-class family in Prussian Silesia in 1764. He had studied philosophy under Kant at Königsberg and at the age of thirty won renown in Berlin as the author of good polemical journalism denouncing the French Revolution. He became a Prussian civil servant but continued to write extensively, especially in the *Historisches Journal* which he founded in 1799. His analyses were so good that they were even circulated in translation in London, where they attracted the attention of Pitt. It seemed as if Gentz would become the supreme political commentator of his age. He became, instead, the most bribed official in Europe; for Gentz had a weakness for gambling, good food and actresses, and was in these early years nearly always in debt. When Metternich met him for the first time he was about to transfer service from Prussia to Austria although it was known that, until Pitt's fall in February 1801, he had existed on generous subsidies from London. No one trusted him but everyone sought to tap his knowledge and benefit from his political acumen. His character was full of contradictions: a vain flatterer whose writings sparkle with astringent criticism; a grasping spendthrift who would fritter away his takings on the favourite of the moment; a lonely sensualist whose intellectual ruthlessness was countered by sentimentality over flowers and children. His friendship with Metternich, although developing more slowly than he chose to admit, was of major significance for Europe; for it was the pragmatism of his mind that translated Metternich's nebulous concept of European order into political terms. Without Gentz, Metternich would have made scarcely more impact on Europe than his ridiculous father. The £150 sterling which he lent Gentz in Dresden at their second meeting was, in time, repaid with ample interest.

Metternich established other contacts of importance at Dresden,

though none were to have such momentous consequences as his meeting
with Gentz. He renewed acquaintance with the Marquis de Moustier,
whom he had known at Strasbourg and who was now one of Talleyrand's most trusted envoys. He met, for the first time, Count Karl
Nesselrode, a young Baltic German who was already high in the esteem
of Tsar Alexander I and who became the Tsar's personal agent in Paris
and, in due course, his Foreign Minister. And despite his efforts to
frustrate French policy he became friends with Count Alexandre de la
Rochefoucauld who, as a member of one of the noblest French families,
had been sent by Napoleon to flatter and cajole the etiquette-ridden
Frederick Augustus into collaboration. This was a task which de la
Rochefoucauld found extremely tedious. Lacking Eliott's irresponsible
inventiveness, he was forced to fill his despatches to Paris with meteoro-
logical observations; and his chief delight seems to have been a sparring
match with Metternich over precedence in matters of protocol, a contest almost invariably won by the French. But Metternich's elegance
and personal charm always made him acceptable to his professional
enemies and he had too many cultural tastes in common with de la
Rochefoucauld to allow policy to dictate private conduct.[7]

Within a few months of his arrival in Dresden, Metternich had
realized that he was becalmed in an agreeable backwater. This was not
entirely a consequence of the military weakness of Saxony or of its
ruler's indecision. Metternich's term of residence in Dresden coincided
with a period of relative tranquillity. The continent was in an almost
Hobbesian condition of neither war nor peace. The Russians and the
French had signed a convention providing for co-operation in settling
Europe's affairs early in October 1801, and at the same time the
negotiations began between Britain and France which led in March
1802 to the conclusion of the Treaty of Amiens. A fourteen-month truce
settled on Europe; and momentarily there seemed hope of a genuine
peace.

If, however, the generals were inactive in 1802, the diplomats were
not.[8] The new order in Germany, vaguely foreshadowed in the treaties
of Campo-Formio and Lunéville, had still to be worked out in detail.
Throughout the year an Imperial deputation chosen by the Diet at
Regensburg thrashed out the shape of the new Germany, reporting their
deliberations to both French and Russian mediators. By the end of
February 1803 they had completed their work, and Austria was shocked
and humiliated by an Imperial Recess (*Reichsdeputationshauptschluss*)
which destroyed the municipal and ecclesiastical structure of the old
Germany without offering Austria anything by way of compensation
(except a minor adjustment of frontiers in the South Tyrol). Nothing
brought home more clearly the reality of the defeats of 1797 and 1800
than the character of the Recess. Bavaria, Württemberg, Baden and

Prussia all received territory at the expense of the old petty principalities and Imperial cities in order to offset the aggrandizement of France on the left bank of the Rhine. The form of the Electoral College was changed and the composition of the Imperial Diet. In both institutions Protestants were at last in a majority and if ever a new Emperor were elected it seemed improbable that he would be a Habsburg or, indeed, a Catholic. Metternich was instructed to emphasize to Frederick Augustus that Saxony was the only one of the old electoral states which had received no territorial adjustment and that, in consequence, it was essential for Saxony and Austria to work together as revisionist members of the Diet. But Frederick Augustus, although as usual agreeing with Metternich, preferred to appease Prussia and France.

The Imperial Recess had two indirect consequences for Metternich. His father, deprived for all time of his lands on the Rhine, was awarded a new estate at Ochsenhausen, near Ulm, with the rank of Prince and a scat in the Imperial Diet. And the need to improve the diplomatic representation of Austria at St Petersburg led to a major re-shuffling of posts in which Clement Metternich was assigned the important embassy at Berlin. There were mild protests from those who had little sympathy for the family in Vienna. Colloredo defended the appointment in a confidential note to Thugut: 'Count Metternich is young but by no means maladroit. We shall see how he shapes up to Berlin. In Dresden they are well pleased with him, though not so much with Madame.'⁹ It was a patronizing and unchivalrous end-of-term report, but Colloredo rarely extended generosity outside the narrow ranks of the feudal aristocracy and, as a clericalist of limited understanding, he had no liking for the Kaunitz connection.

Metternich was informed of his appointment to Berlin early in February 1803 and, indeed, had a meeting that month with Count Philip Stadion, whom he was replacing at the Prussian court. But once again there seemed no urgency in Metternich's professional itinerary.¹⁰ Stadion duly went to St Petersburg while Berlin was left in the care of a *chargé d'affaires*. Metternich stayed on in Dresden until the end of May, spent some of the summer with his father at Ochsenhausen and the remainder in Vienna, returned to Dresden in the early autumn and only crossed into Prussia in the fourth week of November 1803. It is hardly surprising that Gentz, travelling from Vienna to London and back in his efforts to stir up resistance to the French, complained in his diary that his new and generous friend showed 'a marked inclination for indolence'.¹¹ These were months of portent for all Germany. The Anglo-French conflict was renewed on 16 May and Bonaparte poured troops into Hanover. The French speedily exhausted its resources but continued to hold it thereafter as a territorial bait whose offer of cession might tempt the Prussians into co-operation and alliance. There was certainly a need for Austria to be represented by a spokesman of authority in Berlin; but it must be admitted that, for the moment, he could tender nothing more substantial than fair words and ponderous advice. Austria counted for little under the amiable and ineffective partnership of Colloredo and Cobenzl.

Wooing Prussia (1803–5)

Life in Berlin was duller for Metternich than in Dresden. He had, of course, known Queen Louise ever since her childhood in Mecklenburg and, although it was more than eleven years since he had partnered her to open the Coronation Ball at Frankfurt, he was gratified 'by the sweetness and tenderness' of her manner towards him.[12] Yet though 'received as an old friend' by the King and Queen, he noted that in Berlin the diplomats were generally kept 'at the greatest possible distance' from the court; Frederick William shared none of Frederick Augustus's liking for protracted formal entertainment. There were compensations: the stormy presence of Wilhelmine of Sagan in the Courland Palace along Unter den Linden; the good talk of Madame de Staël's salon; private concerts – and less laudable recreations – under the patronage of Prince Louis Ferdinand; and the attraction of Princess Ekaterina Dolgoruki, for Metternich had a weakness for Russian ladies with soulful countenances. But for much of the time he had to concentrate on encouraging the 'war party' (Hardenberg, Stein, Scharnhorst, Louis Ferdinand, and perhaps Queen Louise herself) and countering the efforts of the appeasers, Haugwitz and Lombard, who for the moment held the confidence of the King. His task was complicated by the fact that his objectives were not entirely those of Cobenzl: for, while Metternich sought to create a military alliance of Prussia, Austria and Russia, Cobenzl wished merely for a stable and neutralized Germany, inclined towards Austria and Russia rather than towards the French but still basically a guarantee of peace rather than of another war.

Yet the pace of events was set by neither Cobenzl nor Metternich, and certainly not by Haugwitz or Hardenberg. Every decision of importance was taken in Paris, and although once more Metternich was on friendly terms with his French colleague (Count Antoine Laforest), their conversational exchanges had little influence on Talleyrand. Early in 1804 monarchist sentiment was shocked by the abduction from Baden by French troops of the Duc d'Enghien and his subsequent execution; and in May 1804 the principle of legitimacy received a further blow when Consul Bonaparte was proclaimed Emperor of the French. Metternich in Berlin and Gentz in Vienna protested vigorously at Bonaparte's elevation and urged Cobenzl and Colloredo to withhold recognition of his new title.[13] But Cobenzl, wisely, chose to use recognition as a bargaining counter with Paris: he sought at first to gain Napoleon's consent to the conversion of the old elected German Empire into a hereditary state under the Habsburgs; and when this proposal was rejected, he substituted for it the proclamation of a specifically Austrian Empire comprising the Habsburg lands as defined in the Pragmatic Sanction of 1713. Emperor Francis assumed his new title in August 1804 (although he remained nominally Holy Roman Emperor of the old Germany until August 1806). For the moment, however, the Imperial status thus given to the traditional Archduchy of Austria was no more than an empty consolation prize. It was the French who had won the honours.

De la Rochefoucauld, now ambassador in Vienna, had sought to mollify Cobenzl by informing him that Napoleon's establishment of a French Empire would be 'the death blow to the Revolutionary Hydra'.[14] To Gentz, on the other hand, the subsequent coronation in the presence of the Pope saw 'the Revolution legitimized and even sanctified';[15] and Metternich, too, had no illusions. An empire was an amorphous institution without clearly defined territorial limits; with Holland, Italy and Switzerland already French satrapies, it seemed only a matter of time before the new Napoleonic eagles would cross the Rhine and establish a puppet administration to succeed the impromptu settlement made by the Imperial Recess. To Metternich the threat to the traditional European order of states was as great as in the days of the Jacobins.

His view, unpopular in Vienna, was shared by the Tsar of Russia.[16] Alexander had been subjected to a series of minor affronts by Napoleon despite the amicable understanding embodied in the Convention of 1801. The Tsar instructed his elderly ambassador, Maximilian Alopaeus, to collaborate as closely as possible with Metternich and he also sent personal envoys to Berlin in the hope of putting some spirit into the weak-kneed Prussian King. Metternich was kept informed of Russian policy, partly by Stadion (the Austrian ambassador in St Petersburg) and partly by Alexander's own couriers. There was a ridiculous incident when Metternich, knowing that an important letter from the Tsar to the King of Prussia was enclosed in a despatch for Alopaeus, arranged to visit the ambassador at an unusually late hour so as to be present when the despatch was opened. Not a sign of the letter was there to see. Convinced that his information was correct but unable to pass it on to Alopaeus, Metternich insisted that the ambassador should search for an enclosure and it was eventually found caught up in the folds of his dressing-gown. To add to the irony of the situation, the Tsar had changed his mind after sending the letter and its contents were therefore no longer of any value. It is hardly surprising that Alopaeus seems to have regarded Metternich with some suspicion.[17] Neither of them had any success in winning over Frederick William, nor did the Tsar's personal emissary, General Wintzingerode.

Meanwhile negotiations were continuing in London and St Petersburg for a Third Coalition and by the autumn of 1804 even Cobenzl and Colloredo had seen the need for a new alliance to curb French ambitions.[18] In November, Stadion in St Petersburg was accordingly authorized to conclude a secret military convention with the Russians, the main terms of which provided that, should there be another war with France, Austria would put 235,000 men into the field and the Russians would send an expeditionary force of 115,000 men to support them. It is clear that neither the Russians nor the Austrians had much faith in Metternich's ability to propel Frederick William on to the side of the angels; for the agreement also stipulated that Russia would intervene against Prussia should Frederick William ally with Napoleon and strike southwards towards Vienna. The Austrian authorities still lacked confidence in their army and showed a marked reluctance to commit themselves to military conversations with the Russians, each side believing that the other had deserted it in 1799. This irresolution in Vienna delayed the effective completion of the Coalition and it was not until the second week of August (1805) that Austria formally adhered to the alliance concluded between the Russians and British four months earlier. But thereafter events moved swiftly. In an effort to penetrate the Black Forest region before Napoleon was ready, the Austrians struck first and marched into Bavaria at the beginning of September. It was not until 25 September that Napoleon and the main French forces crossed the Rhine and by then General Mack's Austrian army was well-established along the Danube from Regensburg to Ulm. Were Prussia to be induced at once to join the Coalition, a formidable threat would develop to Napoleon's left flank. The key to victory lay in Berlin, if only Metternich could insert it in the lock.

He had, however, a virtually impossible task; the key did not fit.[19] There was nothing that Prussia believed she could gain from an Austrian alliance to equal Napoleon's tempting offer to cede Hanover. Haugwitz, as Metternich had written a year before, was 'totally devoted to the interests of France' and not even 'open to bribes any longer, for the French have seen to it that no one else can possibly overbid them.' Assurances given by Hardenberg in one conversation were contradicted by Haugwitz in the next. Exasperated, the Tsar threatened to send Russian troops into Prussian Poland and cajole Frederick William into partnership. The manoeuvre might well have had the opposite effect had not Napoleon, seeking to envelop Mack's army in Bavaria, sent a French force across Prussian territory at Ansbach. Infuriated by this cavalier disregard for his neutrality, Frederick William momentarily veered towards the policy urged on him by Hardenberg and Metternich, and invited Tsar Alexander to Berlin for personal consultation.

The Tsar arrived at Potsdam on 25 October and met Metternich for the first time four days later in Berlin.[20] The two men were, in time, to establish a close political relationship which survived until Alexander's death in 1825, and Metternich wrote an acute character sketch of the Tsar in his *Memoirs*. But in 1805 neither left sufficient impression on the other for any interesting record to be made of the encounter. Both were so conscious of the military emergency beyond Prussia's frontiers that they had no wish to fritter the hours in social pleasantry. It was fast becoming too late to intervene effectively in Bavaria. On 20 October General Mack, hopelessly outflanked by Murat and Soult, had surrendered to Napoleon at Ulm with twenty-seven thousand men; and while the Tsar and Metternich were negotiating in Berlin, the Russian commander Kutuzov was conducting a masterly but deep withdrawal from the River Inn in the Tyrol, to Krems on the Danube fifty miles west of Vienna. Yet on 3 November the Prussians at last reached an understanding with the Russians and Austrians: Frederick William undertook to propose a general peace settlement to France and, if Napoleon was not prepared to accept the Allied terms, to enter the war beside Russia and Austria. Provided that Prussia brought an army of 180,000 men into the field by 15 December, the Tsar pledged himself to seek the eventual cession by George III of Hanover to Prussia. Perhaps sensing the unreality of these engagements, Metternich put forward a supplementary article to the treaty by which the Prussians would have agreed to enter the war within forty-eight hours of any Austrian defeat which might jeopardize the safety of Vienna. But this pessimistic proposal was far too much for Haugwitz or for his royal master; and when, on 5 November, the Tsar left Potsdam for Kutuzov's headquarters (which were by then at Olmütz, in Moravia) he had to remain content with a mere treaty of armed mediation. It fell short of his expectations and, as Metternich feared, of Austria's needs.

There followed six weeks of disaster for Metternich and the policy he represented. The news which reached him in Berlin was far worse than he had anticipated. Only five days after the Tsar's departure, Cobenzl wrote to warn him that the fall of Vienna was imminent and it was small consolation to learn in the same letter that he had been awarded the Grand-Cross of St Stephen for his efforts in Berlin.[21] Murat's cavalry were at the gates of Vienna on 14 November and the French had occupied the city and its surrounding hills by the morning of 16 November. Although Frederick William of Prussia continued to feel himself bound by the Potsdam Treaty, Haugwitz had no intention of permitting his sovereign to ally himself with a corpse. It was not until the end of November that Haugwitz sought out Napoleon with the Prussian proposal for mediation. By then Napoleon himself was in Brno and

insisted on Haugwitz proceeding to Vienna where Talleyrand had come
to await, in Francis's own capital, the Austrian plea for peace. Haugwitz, too, was prepared to wait; and as soon as the news reached him of
the French victory at Austerlitz, he negotiated with Talleyrand a
treaty at Schönbrunn by which the Prussians ceded Ansbach and
Neuchâtel to France in return for the cherished prize of Hanover.
Haugwitz put his signature to the Treaty of Schönbrunn on 15
December, the very day by which, according to the Potsdam Treaty,
the Prussians should have been at war.[22] The whole episode reflected
little credit on Prussia; and it was a dismal beginning to the partnership
of Metternich and the Tsar.

But, by 15 December, all Austro-Russian collaboration had also come
to an end. It had virtually finished in the early afternoon of 2 December
when Tsar Alexander rode wretchedly eastwards from Austerlitz, the
tears coursing his cheeks as the snow began to fall over the plateau
where he had insisted on giving battle. The following night Napoleon
slept in Metternich's own room 'in M. de Kaunitz's handsome château'
(as he wrote to his brother, Joseph).[23] Earlier that day he had received
Prince Johann Liechtenstein, who had known the place in happier
times but who now sought to arrange a meeting between Napoleon and
Emperor Francis as a first step towards peace. Alexander and Kutuzov
retreated into Russian territory, for the Tsar still had two armies which
he had not committed to the campaign. But Austria was once more
defeated, and this time Francis had to accept far harsher terms than at
Campo-Formio or Lunéville. On 26 December a peace treaty was
signed at Pressburg (Bratislava) by which the Austrians lost the Tyrol
and Vorarlberg to Bavaria, such small dependencies as had survived in
western Germany to Württemberg and Baden, and all their territories
in Venetia, Istria and Dalmatia to Napoleon's puppet kingdom of Italy.
The Austrians, in addition, had to pay a considerable war indemnity
and recognize the elevation of Napoleon's south German allies (Bavaria,
Baden and Württemberg) to the status of kingdoms. The only consolation for Austria was a rectification of the Bavarian frontier which
allowed her to acquire Salzburg and Berchtesgaden.[24]

To St Petersburg or to Paris?

'I have aged thirty years', wrote Metternich to Gentz early in the New
Year. 'The world is lost, Europe is burning out, and only from its ashes
will a new order of existence arise.'[25] He found political life in Berlin
intolerable after the 'perfidy' of Haugwitz and the humiliations of
Austerlitz. For a few weeks, however, he seems to have clung to his old
policy, as though too shell-shocked to accept a change. In a memorandum he drew up in January 1806 he was still pressing the need for a

coalition of Austria, Prussia, Russia and Saxony, although it is true that he was now thinking apparently of a defensive Eastern bloc rather than any fundamentally offensive alliance.[26] He had hopes that Frederick William might refuse to ratify Haugwitz's Treaty of Schönbrunn and that the other Russian armies might redeem Alexander's disastrous failure in Moravia, but in those early months of 1806 there seemed little will to resist French demands anywhere in central Europe. The silence of acquiescence prevailed in Berlin, as it had two years before in Dresden.

Yet Metternich's personal standing in Vienna had been enhanced rather than diminished by the dismal anticlimax of the Third Coalition. For, in this crisis, the Emperor Francis determined to assert his own authority.[27] The scapegoats were Colloredo and Cobenzl rather than the diplomats who had sought to give vitality to the policy they pursued. Colloredo was dismissed five days before Austerlitz and Cobenzl's resignation was accepted on the day the Peace of Pressburg was concluded. The only person to whom Francis was prepared to listen was his brother, the Archduke Charles, who had fought with distinction in 1796 and 1799 and who, as commander of the southern army in the recent campaign, had at least avoided defeat and briefly come near to a victory. For three years the Archduke had urged the Emperor to give younger men posts of responsibility and free Austria from the creaking governmental machine set up by Colloredo; and now Francis not only made the Archduke generalissimo but fetched back Philip Stadion from St Petersburg to become, at forty-three, Austria's youngest Foreign Minister since Kaunitz. This appointment was doubly interesting for Metternich: he had worked closely with Stadion for the past three years; and his promotion was a victory for the 'non-Austrians', for Stadion's estates were in Swabia and he was the first specifically Germanic Count to be given responsibility for Austria's diplomatic affairs. His advancement improved the prospects for the career of that other 'foreigner', Clement Metternich.

He had not long to wait. In the third week of February he was informed that he was to succeed Stadion as ambassador in St Petersburg; and on 2 April he set off from Berlin by way of Dresden to Vienna for consultations. He found the prospect of serving in the Russian capital attractive, not least because the Tsar had lavished flattery on him when they had met in the previous October.[28] The appointment was welcomed in Russia: 'He has everything to ensure success', wrote the Vienna correspondent of a highly select St Petersburg newspaper.[29] There were, of course, some Russian aristocrats who wished for more details: the elder Nesselrode, for example, wrote to his son for information about the Metternichs and Charles Nesselrode, who had met them both in Dresden and in Berlin, willingly gave his father a candid pen-portrait. 'Metternich', he wrote on 25 April from the Hague, is certainly not lacking in wit. Indeed he has more of that quality than three-quarters of Their Excellencies in Vienna. When he wishes he is agreeable enough, good-looking, almost always in love; but he often appears a little absent-minded, a trait as dangerous in diplomacy as in romance. His wife is tiny, charming enough but not witty or endearing in any way. In general she has a very insipid nature, which has led to extra-conjugal associations, her husband finding compensation for himself from the illustrious Princess Dolgoruki.[30]

Society in St Petersburg must have awaited the coming of the Metternichs with lively apprehension.

It was, however, to be disappointed, for he never went to Russia. After Pressburg it was clearly essential to have a man of ability at the Austrian embassy in Paris. Stadion originally wished to send Philip Cobenzl, elder brother of the fallen Foreign Minister and himself a former ambassador to France. But Talleyrand indicated that Napoleon had no wish to see him once again in Paris. On 26 March Napoleon himself sent a note to Talleyrand 'to find out if there is not a Kaunitz to be sent here'.[31] Almost certainly Napoleon meant, not literally a member of the Kaunitz family, but someone who – like Kaunitz sixty years earlier – would use the Paris embassy as a pedestal from which he might step up to the Austrian Foreign Ministry, a Francophile in experience and conviction. But curious confusion followed Napoleon's suggestion. On 28 March the Austrian *chargé d'affaires*, Engelbert von Floret, reported a conversation with Talleyrand in which the French Foreign Minister had suggested a Prince Liechtenstein, a Prince Schwarzenberg, or 'a Kaunitz'.[32] Puzzled, Floret asked if he meant by that suggestion Prince Aloys von Kaunitz, the grandson of the great statesman, who had served as Austrian Minister in Naples. 'Yes', replied Talleyrand, 'he is a young man, a great name'. The suggestion caused some dismay in Vienna for Aloys von Kaunitz lacked the experience to hold such a key post. Napoleon himself would almost certainly have preferred Prince Johann Liechtenstein, but Stadion and his colleagues had convinced themselves that he wanted someone 'from the House of Kaunitz', and inevitably they turned to the brother-in-law of Prince Aloys, Clement Metternich, who was adept at trading on his wife's family name. His claims were supported in Paris both by de la Rochefoucauld and by Laforest (who, in January, had written to Talleyrand from Berlin and commented, a little dryly, on the goodwill Metternich had shown him since Pressburg). Exchanges between Paris and Vienna continued for more than two months before it was finally settled in the last week of June that Metternich would, indeed, go to Paris, although his appointment was officially dated 18 May.[33]

'This change in my destination, when I learned it, fell upon me like a thunderbolt', he wrote many years later in his *Memoirs*, and added,

'I resigned the position at St Petersburg with reluctance'.[34] Even at the time there were some who felt that they should commiserate with Metternich for his misfortune in being sent to such a blood-stained city rather than to St Petersburg. 'A soul so pure and elevated as yours ought never to find itself in contact with the source of so much crime and horror,' wrote Gentz, in his most nauseating style, that autumn.[35] But Metternich was elated by his appointment. His vanity was almost bursting all restraint: his services as ambassador had been sought by the Tsar of All the Russias and by the new Charlemagne, and he had nobly refused the friend in St Petersburg in order to tame the beast in Paris. 'I have completely outstripped all contemporaries among my colleagues,' he wrote to his wife on 28 June.[36] His letters to Eleonore ring with the vigour of earlier days, when she was at Austerlitz and he wooed her from Prague and Königswart. She is told almost all of the negotiations: how cross Bonaparte was at the delay in confirmation; how complimentary de la Rochefoucauld had been; how friendly everyone was in Vienna; and how he would receive ninety thousand guilders a year for so long as he was ambassador.[37] On one point only was Clement silent: he did not inform the old Chancellor's grand-daughter that the name Napoleon mentioned was not Metternich, but Kaunitz. Perhaps he did not know it.

AMBASSADOR TO NAPOLEON

The End of the Holy Roman Empire (1806)

Metternich's personal elation in the summer of 1806 was in marked contrast to the mood at court in Vienna. The Austrians had accepted the fact of a lost war when they signed the Peace of Pressburg in the last week of the old year; but the reality of defeat impinged only slowly upon their political consciousness in the following months. Gentz, observing Europe's affairs from Dresden, gloomily wrote: 'Everything is surely over now, for the little that remains can be so easily supplied in imagination that even the pleasure of surprise no longer remains to us.'[1] And in Vienna the Emperor Francis and Stadion were hardly less fatalistic.

Austria was in almost total eclipse that summer; and no effective authority seemed able to dispute with France the control of Central Europe. Technically the Russians remained in the field against Napoleon, but there was no arena of battle in which they could engage their armies, for with the Peace of Pressburg and the subsequent Franco-Prussian agreements a belt of non-belligerents straddled the continent from the Baltic to the Balkans. The British, of course, were also still at war and were by now masters of the seas; but on land they could do little more than irritate the French by pinpricks at the toe of the Italian peninsula. In southern Dalmatia the Austrians had handed over Cattaro (Kotor) to the Russian Admiral Senyavin; and there were strange happenings in the Adriatic where Senyavin and his wild Montenegrin allies besieged a French garrison in Dubrovnik. But although Napoleon was angered by the presence of the Russians at Cattaro and at Corfu (for a Russian force occupied the Ionian Islands early in 1806), these operations could hardly alter the general pattern of Europe's affairs. Napoleon was, as Metternich wrote to Gentz, 'the only man in Europe who wills and acts'.[2]

It was many centuries since a military conqueror had exercised such a plenitude of power on the continent. Austerlitz gave him a free hand to demolish the crumbling relics of mediaeval Germany. His intentions had been vaguely foreshadowed in the Peace of Pressburg, which contained an imprecise reference to some future 'Germanic Confederation'.

Throughout June reports circulated in Vienna that Napoleon intended to create a new political entity, the Confederation of the Rhine, by which all the southern and western German lands would be organized under French protection. When, in the second week of July, the final form of the Confederation became known, it was clear that Francis would have to renounce his title of Holy Roman Emperor or accept a resumption of hostilities. The rulers of Bavaria, Württemberg, Baden and eleven other petty German states ratified the Act creating the Confederation on 25 July in Munich. There were rumours that a general settlement was about to be made, for both the Russians and the British had representatives in Paris exploring the possibilities of peace. How could Francis have faced a new war for an empty dignity? On 6 August he formally renounced his title of Holy Roman Emperor, although retaining his Imperial status as Emperor of Austria.

The new ambassador to France played no part in these momentous events. On 2 July he wrote to his wife informing her that he hoped to be in Paris 'about the twentieth of the month';[3] but there was almost a fortnight's error in his estimated date of arrival. He left Vienna on the evening of 11 July.[4] Instead of going directly to Paris by way of Munich and Strasbourg, he had received permission to travel as far north as the Main and spend a few days in Frankfurt. He covered some seventy-five miles a day, passing through Linz, Schärding and Straubing to Regensburg and crossed the Jura to Wurzburg, eventually reaching Frankfurt on the night of 17–18 July. He remained there for three days, sorting out money matters with the family bankers (Mühlen), for the changes in Germany had led to considerable financial embarrassment, and his father was heavily in debt. When he left Frankfurt on the afternoon of Monday, 21 July, he was not able to take the shortest route, through Mainz and Metz to the Marne, but turned southwards for Strasbourg and reached the borders of metropolitan France at Kehl, two miles east of the city, in the small hours of 23 July. There, to his amazement and disgust, he found that the frontier had been closed for nine days to all foreigners coming from across the Rhine, including those with diplomatic passports. He was delayed at Strasbourg for a week, with little enough to do, while the pact establishing the Rhenish Confederation received final ratification. For a time he began to doubt if he was ever going to reach Paris, for he had been alerted to the danger of a new French attack on Austria by a message sent by courier from Stadion and he watched with apprehension the movement of troops and guns into Germany. But once Napoleon was assured of ratification, all border restrictions were removed. Metternich resumed his journey on 30 July and, travelling now as rapidly as he could, covered more than three hundred miles in three days. His carriage rumbled at last into Paris on the evening of Saturday, 2 August, three weeks and one day after he had set out from Vienna. The journey had been dispiriting; and he began his embassy in a cheerless frame of mind.

Austria's affairs had been safeguarded in these difficult weeks by General Baron von Vincent, a Lorrainer in the Emperor Francis's army, who had originally been sent to Paris on a military mission concerned with the evacuation of French troops from the Habsburg lands. He had shown himself an able diplomat and on 22 July, while Metternich was trundling towards Kehl, he had sustained with dignity a hectoring lecture from Napoleon on his Emperor's pretentious claims to sovereignty in Germany. He had also dined, on the day before Metternich's arrival, with Talleyrand and the British representative in the peace negotiations, Lord Yarmouth; and he was able to brief the ambassador on the prospects for a general settlement. The First Secretary was Engelbert von Floret, a Belgian by birth. He had served in Paris for several years and supplemented Vincent's information from his personal knowledge of the French political scene. So impressed was Metternich with Floret's acumen that he retained him for twenty years as a close adviser, 'my shadow' he was to call him in 1819. With men such as Vincent and Floret to bring him abreast of recent developments, Metternich was able to recover his self-esteem before presenting his credentials to Talleyrand and to Napoleon.

His first meeting with Talleyrand took place in the Foreign Minister's room in the Rue de Bac on 5 August.[5] It was a very ordinary affair. Each participant was interested in discovering what he could of the other's character. Talleyrand from long experience said little: Metternich from inclination said too much. Courtesies and small talk were exchanged with decorum. Talleyrand blandly declared his regret at the way in which Metternich had been delayed in Strasbourg. The ambassador, encouraged by such graciousness, began to show his hand. Although he disliked raising disagreeable topics, he explained, it seemed to him right to emphasize his sovereign's desire for complete fulfilment by the French of the terms agreed at Pressburg; and he suggested that they might return prisoners of war and, as a sign of goodwill, evacuate Braunau and the right bank of the Isonzo. So full of charm was Talleyrand that he disputed nothing, nor does he appear to have reminded the ambassador that the Austrians themselves had failed to observe all the stipulations of the Pressburg Peace, notably in allowing the Russians to establish themselves at Cattaro. Such things could wait. Metternich went away well pleased with himself: the Foreign Minister, he wrote, 'was amiable and obliging'.

In the next few days, however, it became clear that the French would support fair words with action only in return for concessions. Napoleon bluntly refused to accept Metternich's credentials, since they had been drafted in the name of 'the Roman Emperor of the German nation' as well as of 'the Austrian Emperor'. It was a delicate situation, made no easier for the ambassador by the fact that he was notified of Napoleon's objections only a few hours before setting out for his audience at St Cloud. He acted sensibly. Swallowing his pride, he decided to present himself purely in his capacity as ambassador of Austria; better this indignity than a breach over matters of protocol. Such an adjustment of principles represented a virtual recognition of the new order in Germany; but when, four days later, the news reached Paris that Francis had renounced his old Imperial title, Metternich's moderation won general approval from the other members of the diplomatic corps, some of whom affected to believe that such tiresome disputes could be settled only on the battlefield.

First meeting with Napoleon

Metternich was received by Napoleon at St Cloud on 10 August.[6] Despite his later attempts to embellish this meeting with the lustre of history, it was no more dramatic than his visit to the Rue de Bac on the previous Tuesday. He made a short speech on the need for reciprocal confidence; and the sentiments were so pure and noble that Napoleon fully agreed with them. It is probable that Napoleon found it difficult to take seriously a young aristocrat who appeared to carry himself with such empty arrogance. In his *Memoirs* Metternich complained that Napoleon, who was in the uniform of his own Guard, had received him wearing a hat, a mode of dress which the fastidious Rhinelander considered to show poor breeding; but he said nothing of this affront in the reports or letters which he wrote at the time and, although he told Eleonore that the court at St Cloud was 'impossibly pretentious', he seems to have been impressed by its brilliance. It was not until their second meeting that Metternich sensed the breadth of Napoleon's understanding; and it took even longer for the Emperor to perceive that beneath his brittle superficiality the ambassador, too, possessed a mind of quality. Perhaps it was only the intellectual stimulus of Paris that enabled Metternich to discover it for himself; for, although he had personally never doubted his abilities, others needed to be convinced of his capacity to succeed, and proof came from his response to the challenge of a hard assignment.

His task was, indeed, difficult. 'Napoleon ... no longer has any regard for our armed strength,'[7] he wrote to Stadion after his first audience at St Cloud. For the moment he could not assert himself, but only observe and warn. Soon, however, he sensed the conflicts and rivalries at court and set himself, with Floret's backing, to exploit them. Within a few days of his arrival he had dined with Lord Yarmouth and realized that, while there was little chance of peace between England

and France, the rumour which Yarmouth encouraged that Napoleon would support the return of Hanover from Prussia to George III was sufficient to put the anti-war party in Berlin into the saddle. The Prussians had already shown they liked the Confederation of the Rhine no more than did the Austrians; and they suspected Napoleon would be as willing to partition Prussia among their neighbours (including Russia) as Frederick the Great had been to share out Poland. Yet, in reality Napoleon preferred partnership with Prussia and, a week after his meeting with Metternich, proposed that the French Army which had concentrated in Germany during the negotiations over the Confederation should be withdrawn. He was therefore genuinely surprised when he learned from his ambassador in Berlin on 22 August that the Prussians had begun to mass troops on their western frontier. It was a development that Metternich, despite his low opinion of Prussia's leaders, had expected; and he continued to advise Stadion throughout September to discount any reports that the breach between France and Prussia would be healed. The Russians, who in August abandoned their half-hearted attempts at a settlement with France, supported Prussia. War followed on 7 October; and for once Austria remained a neutral observer.

Napoleon left St Cloud to join his army in the Rhineland on 25 September. He did not return to his capital for another ten months. Metternich had at first hoped the diplomats in Paris might follow the Grand Army, but Napoleon refused to encumber his camp with spectators whose sympathies were, as often as not, with his adversary. Talleyrand, however, was summoned to Mainz, since Napoleon rightly expected that he would soon need his Foreign Minister to negotiate peace with Prussia. There was little for Metternich to do in Paris. He reported, with some exaggeration, that the war was unpopular, and he rightly warned Vienna of Napoleon's sympathy with the Poles. But he seems to have heard of Prussia's defeat at Jena and Auerstadt on 14 October with mixed feelings. He genuinely feared Napoleon's power, but he had little love for the nation that had stood aside in the Austerlitz campaign. On 31 October the French secret police – who had by now begun to keep a careful eye on Metternich – noted with satisfaction 'the rejoicing' of the staff of the Austrian embassy at Prussia's humiliation; and there is no reason to doubt the authenticity of the police agent's report.[8]

The pleasures of Paris

The prolonged absence of Napoleon and Talleyrand enabled Metternich to establish himself in Parisian society. He had already, in the first month, seen most of the sights of the city and the surrounding countryside: sad memories of Marie Antoinette assailed him in the Place de la Concorde; he liked Malmaison, but was pained by the vandalism which a decade of neglect had inflicted on Versailles.[9] His letters to Eleonore, who was staying that summer in Dresden with her three children, dutifully recorded his impressions, including his amazement at the severe classical elegance of women's fashions ('for the most part they have no diamonds at all, or very few').[10] He began that autumn to go to the theatre and to exercise his wit in the salons; and he hired a box at the Opera. Eleonore and the children travelled to Paris in the middle of October, crossing southern Germany as the Grand Army was taking up its war stations for the campaign against Prussia. It was a remarkable journey of more than 550 miles and Eleonore's ability in organizing it without incident filled her husband with admiration: 'If you have an army to give to a commander,' he wrote to his old friend, Madame de Caumont, on 22 October, 'you must choose Madame de Metternich, who is afraid of nothing.'[11] The family joined him in the Hotel du Prince de Galles, at the corner of the Rue de Faubourg Saint Honoré and the Avenue Marigny. It had been built in 1768 as the residence of Marshal de Beauvau and was converted into a hotel in time to attract the tourists who flocked to Paris during the Peace of Amiens. Metternich found it 'detestable', cold, draughty and smoky; and he described its owner, M. Delpech, as 'the greatest scoundrel among the knaves who run hotels in Paris'.[12] In November the Metternichs took the lease of an attractive house in the Rue Grange Batelière, furnished it elegantly and soon acquired a reputation for the excellence of their cellar and kitchens.

Eleonore shared fully in the social life of Paris, accompanying Clement to the Opera Ball in December and the other spectacles of the season. On 8 February 1807 she was granted a formal audience with the Empress Josephine, the first ambassador's wife to be so honoured since the establishment of the Empire; and her husband sent a detailed report to Stadion that same day, noting with particular gratification that the ceremonial 'was the same as had been observed for the reception of Countess Starhemberg in 1761'.[13] But, although Clement was pleased to have his wife and family in Paris and proud of Eleonore's dignity and good sense, he was no more a figure of moral rectitude in France than in Saxony or in Prussia. At thirty-three he was still handsome and the women at court found him attractive. Portraits show his face as less flaccid than a few years earlier; dental trouble was beginning to draw his cheeks in slightly, giving the line of his mouth more emphasis and thereby suggesting greater resolution of character. His appearance was described in retrospect by Laura Junot, the most industrious scribbler among all his mistresses: 'Metternich was truly the grand gentleman at his most elegant,' she wrote, 'with a finely powdered head of fair hair, a knight of Malta's coat of red with black facings, and with courteous ways and an easy graciousness of manner.'[14] Like his father at the Frankfurt coronation festivities, he spent money liberally on good living. It was impossible not to notice his carefully groomed figure at a soirée or his carefully groomed horses under the chestnuts which stretched in those days from his residence to the city barrier at Chaillot; and when the spring came people saw and admired his equipage among the carriages which graced the Promenade de Longchamp.[15] With Napoleon and so many military paladins absent from the capital, he was lionized by a society in which mediocrity and execrable bad taste too often forced itself unchallenged to the top. His social ease and unruffled conversation brought an air of almost respectable permanence to what was essentially transitory. From the secret police reports, it seems as if his patronage of a gaming-club in the Rue de la Loi was in itself sufficient to transform a dubious enterprise into an exclusive institution; and at that time he had been in Paris for less than five months.[16] It was many decades since an ambassador had so rapidly achieved such social eminence.

He had several scandalous liaisons, partly through inclination and partly because it was expected of him. Were half the gossip true – and it almost certainly is not – it would seem that he avenged Austerlitz by cuckolding the Grand Army on a scale of appropriate magnificence. The most important of his conquests was Caroline Murat, Napoleon's youngest sister and his own coeval, who at first tended to despise him as an effete aristocrat. She had already tired of Murat, with whom she had little in common except an alarming propensity for histrionics and a costly taste for luxurious living. 'Caroline combined a pleasant exterior with uncommon powers of mind,' wrote Metternich himself in his 'gallery of celebrated contemporaries'. 'She exercised considerable power over her brother and it was she who cemented the family ties.'[17] It may be doubted if she had quite so much influence as he imagined, but the statement probably explains what was to him her greatest attraction. He failed to realize that she was a supreme mischief-maker, with a deep hatred of the Empress Josephine and all the Beauharnais family. He certainly received information from her, but it was rarely accurate and seldom of value. No doubt it was interesting for Stadion to learn within a month of the first night which Napoleon spent with Marie Walewska that 'the Emperor has a mistress in Warsaw'[18] and that Josephine was worried, but since Metternich was not able to let the Minister know the name, ranking or political connections of the new favourite, it was hard to see to what use the Austrians could put the report. On the other hand, he was able as early as July 1807 to inform Vienna of a possible separation in the Imperial family, and his knowledge of the background tensions among the Bonapartes was to assist him considerably a few years later.[19]

Neither Metternich nor Caroline cared deeply for each other; and in 1807 both were amusing themselves by supplementary extra-conjugal *amours* with the same family. Caroline's relations with the commandant of the Paris garrison, General Andoche Junot, so scandalized Napoleon on his return to St Cloud that he rebuked her and sent Junot himself to an army command in Bayonne; but Metternich's liaison with Laura Junot does not appear to have been discovered – at least by the secret police – until he was rash enough to accompany her to a well-known fortune teller in March 1808.[20] Caroline's vindictive jealousy made much of the affair for the next two years, ultimately endangering Metternich's own position and, indeed, Laura's life.

Laura Junot was twenty-three when Metternich first met her, apparently at a reception in the Junot residence in the Rue Boissy-d'Anglas early in 1807. She had married the courageous but choleric General seven years previously. Madame Junot was an indefatigable flirt, with dancing eyes and a good sense of humour; her husband, who was a couple of years older than Metternich, was devotedly loyal to Napoleon on whose reputation he had climbed to eminence since their first meeting at the siege of Toulon in 1793. Twice in his absence from the capital Napoleon had entrusted the General with command of the Paris garrison, a key position which made him the watchdog against conspiracy; and it is probable that Metternich originally cultivated the Junots in the belief that, like Caroline Murat, they would be able to furnish him with valuable information. But the General was far too bluff and engrossed in his own affairs to give anything away; and Laura was much too silly. By the time Junot was packed off to Spain, Metternich seems to have been infatuated; and by now he was an expert at consoling wives whose husbands were absent at the war. Laura herself has given picturesque details of her passionate romance with Metternich: hired cabs hurriedly changed to elude police agents; a grotto by the bridge at Neuilly; weeping, pleading and remorse; silent declarations of timeless devotion; such stuff as tears are jerked on. Perhaps it really was not at all like that, but so it seemed to Laura writing her account after many years of sentimental reminiscence.[21]

During Metternich's term as ambassador, the affair did not come to a crisis. Junot, defeated by Wellesley in Portugal in the summer of 1808 but allowed to return to France by the Convention of Cintra, passed a few months of Imperial displeasure and his wife suffered a mild nervous breakdown. Then, in January 1809, he was reinstated in Napoleon's favour and created Duke of Abrantés. Relations between the General and Laura improved about the same time, for she was pleased by the new title. Unfortunately, however, Metternich kept in contact with her. He seems always to have had an irresistible urge to send letters to his ex-mistresses; and this time the correspondence was to have a dramatic

C

sequel a year later. But by then Metternich was Foreign Minister in Vienna and Napoleon had his own reasons for hushing up the scandal.

Intrigues with Talleyrand (1807–8)

In 1807 all this was still in the future: the present was dominated by the newest triumphs of the Grand Army and by the remarkable meeting of Napoleon and Tsar Alexander at Tilsit. At the end of October 1806, Napoleon had completed the humiliation of Prussia, reviewing the Imperial Guard outside Frederick the Great's palace at Potsdam and occupying Berlin itself. Before Christmas he reached Warsaw and the Polish lands were at his disposal. In the second week of February an indecisive victory amid snow-squalls at Eylau postponed the defeat of Russia until the middle of June, when Ney thrust Bennigsen's army into the River Alle at Friedland. The Russians concluded an armistice on 21 June and four days later the two Emperors met for the first time on the famous raft in the river Niemen. There followed the dramatic diplomatic revolution of Tilsit by which not only did Russia and Prussia concede peace with France but the Tsar accepted an offer by Napoleon of apparent partnership in a Europe divided into a western and an eastern sphere of influence. The published terms of Tilsit were startling enough: although Russia lost only her military outposts on the Adriatic and in the Ionian Islands, Prussia surrendered her Polish territories to a Grand Duchy of Warsaw and her western provinces to a new Kingdom of Westphalia, ruled by Jerome Bonaparte, Napoleon's youngest brother. But the greatest significance of Tilsit was in what it implied rather than in the stipulations of the published agreements. The remaining states of central Germany hastened to join the Confederation of the Rhine, giving the French hegemony up to, and in some places beyond, the Elbe; and all south-eastern Europe apart from Constantinople and the Mediterranean coasts was left to the Russians. The real loser by Tilsit was therefore Austria, deprived of influence either in Germany or in the Balkans. It seemed to Stadion little short of a catastrophe.[22]

Metternich was more sanguine. He conceded that the position of Austria had been weakened by the Tilsit treaties and more especially by the growth of the Rhenish Confederation which, he wrote, 'embraces us on both sides' so that 'any war with France would begin at the same time on the banks of the Inn and of the Wieliczka' (in Galicia).[23] But he argued that the new order in Europe contained its own 'germs of destruction', not least because it was artificial and dependent 'on the life of one single human being'. Moreover he was convinced that Napoleon and Alexander would not long remain allies: the day when they would fall out was inevitable, he declared to Stadion on 19 August, 'and, according to my innermost feelings, much nearer than many people suppose'.[24] When that happened both France and Russia might be expected to turn to Vienna for an alliance and the Austrians would recover their political initiative.

There was, however, little sign that autumn of any improvement in the situation. On 9 August Talleyrand handed over the Foreign Ministry to Jean Baptiste de Champagny, hitherto a markedly syco-phantic Minister for Internal Affairs. Although Talleyrand remained an adviser on foreign policy, all routine matters were left to Champagny. Metternich found him far less accommodating than his predecessor and at many times personally antipathetic. The Austrian ambassador should not, thought Metternich, be subjected to overt surveillance by police agents; and when they began to question his servants about their master's movements, a strong protest was given to the French Foreign Ministry.[25] Meetings between Champagny and Metternich became more and more frigid: and the courier to Vienna carried long complaints of slights and affronts to Stadion, for when under strain Metternich tended to seek release by writing frequently and at great length.

Unfortunately for Metternich, he had to see much of Champagny in this autumn of 1807. There were still problems unresolved from the Treaty of Pressburg, among them the future of the French military bases at Braunau on the Inn and along the banks of the Isonzo (topics raised by Metternich at his first meeting with Talleyrand more than a year before). Protracted discussions went on throughout September and into October. On three occasions Metternich threatened to break off all negotiations. This particular tactic made no impression whatsoever on the French who were, in effect, sitting tenants well-satisfied with the existing situation. Eventually they agreed to evacuate Braunau, for by now they possessed many more effective bases in the German lands; but they would make no concessions over Italy. They insisted on re-taining a military corridor between the satellite Kingdom of Italy and Dalmatia, although Trieste was left in Austrian hands. These provisions were incorporated in a convention signed by Metternich at Fontaine-bleau on 10 October. He knew that his personal enemies in Vienna would make much of his failure to secure a more generous revision of the Pressburg settlement; and when he returned to the Rue Grange Batelière from Fontainebleau he spent eight hours in writing his apologia.[26] But it is hard to see how anyone could have achieved more: Austria was a toothless tiger.

In the following months Metternich made the most of such assets as Austria possessed and his personal prestige gradually rose both in Vienna and in Paris. Napoleon had written to the Tsar at the end of August suggesting that France and Russia should coerce Austria into a diplomatic breach with Britain and adhesion to the Continental System so as to close Trieste to British commerce. Metternich was prepared for Austria to give way to Napoleon over this matter, provided that there should first be negotiations aimed at establishing a general peace settlement in Europe. In these discussions both Metternich and Starhemberg, the Austrian ambassador in London, would be in a powerful position as the natural diplomatic mediators between the two contestants.[27] Exchanges continued for some months and, although in the end they were no more successful than the Yarmouth proposals of 1806, they did at least help to raise the status of Austrian policy.

Metternich himself was encouraged by the friendly approaches of Talleyrand, whom he met frequently in November and December. 'Austria is necessary for the existence of Europe,' Metternich reported that he had said on 12 November. 'I believe it also necessary for the maintenance of the social order and we must guarantee Austria intact, complete and basically a great power.'[28] It was gratifying to discover that there was an Austrophile faction at the French court. Although Metternich had no illusions about Talleyrand's integrity, he respected his intelligence and, indeed, learned much from his technique of statecraft. Stadion at one time was afraid that Metternich placed too much reliance on Talleyrand's word; but the ambassador insisted that he checked and counter-checked all the information which he gathered from conversations with the veteran statesman. 'Such men as M. de Talleyrand,' he explained in a letter to Stadion the following September, 'are like sharp-edged instruments with which it is dangerous to play, but for great evils drastic remedies are necessary and whoever has to treat them should not be afraid to use the instrument that cuts the best.'[29] From the end of 1807 the Austrians had an ally in Paris; and, it goes almost without saying, by the end of the following year they had a pensionary as well.

The close rapport between Metternich and Talleyrand was shown early in 1808. Napoleon arrived back at the Tuileries on the very first day of the New Year, after six weeks in Italy. That same evening he sent for Talleyrand and talked with him well into the night over grand ideas of world strategy. Other conferences followed in the next few days. At the end of the following week Talleyrand twice visited Metternich and indicated the general trend of Napoleon's thoughts. 'The Emperor nourishes two projects,' Metternich reported him as having said on 18 January, 'one rests on a sound basis, the other is romance. The first is a partition of Turkey, the second an expedition to the Indies.'[30] He advised Metternich to send a courier to Vienna with the information, so that Austria could decide whether or not to join in the dismemberment of the Turkish Empire. A long despatch embodying the substance of Talleyrand's conversations was on its way to Vienna some days before Napoleon raised the partition of Turkey at a private audience accorded to Metternich on 21 January.[31] Napoleon spoke vaguely of 'the just and geographical claims' of Austria on the Danube and Metternich, well primed by Talleyrand, received the Emperor's proposals with feigned surprise, sympathy and an apparently open mind. He had, in reality, already urged Stadion to go along with the French in this matter, even though neither he nor Talleyrand wanted to raise the Eastern Question, with all its delicate ramifications at such a time. 'We cannot save Turkey,' he wrote to Stadion on 18 January, 'and we must therefore join in the partition and seek to obtain as good a share of it as possible' and eight days later he added, 'Napoleon has provided us with far too precious a basis of discussion for us to let it slip'. The details could be settled later: what mattered was 'to take a firm hold of the thread'. The advice was sound: it might almost have been said by Talleyrand.[32]

Napoleon's proposals came to nothing, partly because his attention was soon concentrated on the Iberian Peninsula and partly because the preliminary negotiations between Russia and France showed such a conflict of interest between the two Tilsit allies that the whole project was put into cold storage. There was never any enthusiasm for the idea in Vienna, and one of Stadion's first reactions to Metternich's reports was to urge him to move forward step by step with the Russian envoy in Paris, Count Tolstoy.[33] The advice was, in fact, superfluous for Metternich had already sounded out Tolstoy, who informed St Petersburg of the Austrian's concern for the fate of Turkey in a despatch sent on 25 January. Metternich thereafter became – as he had been at Berlin – a strong advocate of a Russo-Austrian alliance, which he put forward as a formal proposal to Stadion in the last week of April. But Tsar Alexander was not yet prepared to risk a re-entry on the European stage; his armies were fully engaged in the wings – against the Swedes in Finland, against the Turks around the mouth of the Danube, and against the Persians in Transcaucasia. He had no desire for a second Austerlitz.

Verbal conflicts with Napoleon (1808)

On 2 April Napoleon left St Cloud for Bayonne and he did not return to his capital until the middle of August. Throughout these four and a half months he was occupied with the affairs of Spain, seeking both to repress a national insurrection and to secure for his brother Joseph a throne in Madrid. Once again Metternich was forced to observe a campaign from afar; but this time he was much more hostile to Napoleon than he had been eighteen months previously; and his messages to Vienna called for action, with some of the fire and spirit of student days. He seems to have been shocked by the casual way in which the Bonapartes sought to replace a Bourbon dynasty which was already obediently subservient to them. 'Peace does not exist with a revolutionary system,' he declared to Stadion at the end of April. 'Whether Robespierre declares eternal war against the châteaux, or Napoleon wages it against the Powers, the tyranny remains the same and the danger is only more general.'[34] He believed that once the Spanish affair had been settled, Napoleon would turn against the Habsburgs and sweep them from the throne. The patriotic resistance of the Spanish people and their success in securing the capitulation of Dupont's divisions at Baylen in July encouraged Metternich considerably. 'In moments of crisis,' he told Stadion, 'a government will always find great resources in the nation; it must arouse and make use of them'; and he began to urge the government in Vienna to preach a people's war, suggesting that it was essential to influence the press, distinguishing truth from falsehood and giving the lie to Napoleon's bulletins. In Berlin on the eve of the Austerlitz campaign, he had tried to alert Vienna to the need of propaganda: now he returned to the same theme, believing that Spain had shown how national consciousness could serve as a buttress for the oldest dynasty. 'Public opinion,' he wrote, 'is the most powerful medium of all. Like religion it penetrates into the darkest corners.'[35] The statement, as so often with Metternich, was more sententious than profound; but it was, perhaps, a little unusual in an aristocrat of such impeccably conservative principles.

Stadion needed little encouragement. He possessed a personal hatred of Napoleon, which Metternich never shared. Stadion was determined to wage a war of revenge on the French and to arouse national enthusiasm among all the German peoples for this crusade of liberation. He would have gone further than Metternich or the Emperor Francis wished, for he favoured decentralization of the cumbersome administrative machine in Austria, and emancipation of the peasantry from their remaining feudal obligations. But Stadion was a Foreign Minister, with no responsibility for domestic reforms; and little was done to change the climate of the Monarchy. Yet, Archduke Charles did reorganize army administration and began to modernize the tactical principles upon which were based its military operations; and Archduke John prepared a scheme for a people's militia (*Landwehr*), so as to provide Austria, the Czech lands and Hungary with a second reserve force, purely for home defence. The French ambassador in Vienna, Andreossi, began to send Napoleon reports of the Austrian army reforms at the end of May 1808, although throughout the summer he continued to emphasize their essentially defensive character.[36]

Metternich believed that another war with France was inevitable, but that it would be madness to provoke one before Austria's own forces were ready or before Austria could be assured of external support, preferably from Russia.[37] He was increasingly alarmed by the reactions of Champagny to the Austrian military reforms and to a number of incidents in Trieste and Bohemia, and also by the rumours which reached him of Napoleon's hostility; and he complained to both Talleyrand and Fouché (the Minister of Police) of press reports and official commentaries on Austria's alleged war preparations. His letters and despatches show that he awaited the return of Napoleon from the Pyrenees with some perturbation. He had good reason.

15 August 1808 was Napoleon's thirty-ninth birthday. It was celebrated as usual by a reception of the diplomatic corps to which, this year, additional importance was attached since the Emperor had only arrived back at St Cloud on the previous afternoon.[38] Napoleon always received the ambassadors accredited to him as though he were inspecting a guard of honour; he moved rapidly down the ranks, accepting and returning a few words of formal greeting. On this occasion he followed his usual practice, added a few additional remarks to Tolstoy on the Tsar's campaign in Finland, and turning to Metternich abruptly asked, 'Well, and is Austria arming much?' There followed the famous scene in which the Emperor sought, before all the diplomats, to expose the weakness of Austria's position and her isolation. With so many witnesses, there are several accounts of what was said by Napoleon (including two mutually contradictory ones by Metternich himself); but little note was taken of Metternich's replies. The ambassador claimed, in a despatch written two days later, that the conversation had continued for an hour and a quarter and that he had answered Napoleon's reproaches over Austria's military preparations by declaring, 'You may well believe, Sire, that if you have counted our soldiers, we have counted yours'. But the other diplomats do not seem to have heard this remark, or at least to have troubled to note it. They all agreed that it was a memorable occasion, and most of them assumed that war with Austria was nearer; and so, it appears, did the Paris Bourse, where prices slumped disastrously on the two following days.[39] But Tolstoy was shrewder: in the account of the reception which he sent to St Petersburg, he wrote that he did not share the general view of the inevitability of a war: 'All the methods which the Emperor Napoleon adopts towards Austria show his intention of obtaining by menace what circumstances will still not permit him to carry off at the point of a sword.' It was a sound assessment of the situation. Napoleon had proclaimed his brother King of Spain. The prestige of his family would not allow him to compromise with insurgents. To discipline Spain he would have to wage a genuine military campaign. For this he needed to despatch his veterans of the Grand Army from the German lands to the Iberian Peninsula. He dared not risk an Austrian war of revenge once he had denuded central Europe of troops. It was time to give the Habsburgs, and their arrogant young ambassador, a good fright.

The public audience of 15 August did, indeed, make a lasting impression on Metternich. Fifteen years later, when the Napoleonic Empire and its master were things of the past, he noted as the date came round again, that the day 'was still living in my memory'. But, at the time, the crisis seemed to pass as rapidly as it had come. On 20 August he visited Talleyrand, who had himself just been received in audience by Napoleon for the first time in several months. Talleyrand believed that there would be no war, although he admitted that he was puzzled by events. The Emperor's alarm, he suggested, was all the fault of listening too much to Champagny 'who does in twenty hours what the Emperor tells him to do in twenty-four' whereas he, Talleyrand, 'would always have taken exactly three weeks'.[40] It was not the whole truth, but it was a good enough story to ease the tension.

Five days later Napoleon accorded Metternich a private audience, once again at St Cloud. He was aggrieved rather than aggressive; and, as Metternich himself wrote, it was not so much a discussion between sovereign and envoy as 'a lovers' quarrel'.[41] Relations with Russia were so much more friendly, Napoleon said: the Tsar and he would exchange gifts and courtesies, whereas the Austrians were aloof and the Emperor Francis never mentioned him by name; small wonder that he was suspicious of military movements in Bohemia and Moravia. Metternich was as accommodating as he could be, for it was difficult to know how to react to such a maudlin interview. If Napoleon wanted a lasting peace or an alliance or the presentation of a few vases, then he declared himself ready to discuss such matters. But, for the moment, all Napoleon wanted was vague talk and friendly reassurance. It was a curious encounter. That evening the Court Theatre was presenting the first play since the Emperor's return; it was entitled – unfortunately perhaps – L'Assemblée de Famille; but for once the head of the Bonaparte family preferred the company of an ambassador to the charms of his favourite actresses. They were still talking together an hour after the play was supposed to have begun.[42]

By the end of the month, after further meetings with Talleyrand, Metternich felt that 'our differences with France are entirely over'. And so, for the moment, they were. But it was difficult in the following weeks to promote that amiability between the Emperors of France and Austria on which Napoleon appeared to set such store. On 2 September Metternich sounded out Talleyrand about the rumours of a forthcoming congress in Germany, and he thus heard for the first time of the projected meeting between Napoleon and Tsar Alexander at Erfurt.[43] Immediately he proposed that the Emperor Francis, too, should be invited to Erfurt, for 'Napoleon never ceases to tell me of the good relations he wants to establish with us'. Tactfully Talleyrand, who knew very well that Napoleon intended Erfurt to show the minimal influence of the Habsburgs in Germany, avoided a direct answer; he suggested that Metternich should write to Stadion and propose that, later in September, Francis might make a journey to Bohemia and suddenly cross the frontier to Erfurt. Bursting in on the Tsar and Napoleon, he might say, 'Here I am! I have come to see how my two friends are getting on'. Metternich seems to have been attracted by this scheme: he informed Stadion of it on the next day; and returned to the idea in a second letter eleven days later, although this time planning a more dignified entry for Francis – 'I am putting 400,000 troops and all my people armed into the balance of justice'.[44] Stadion, very sensibly, regarded Imperial gate-crashing as unworthy of a Habsburg. There was no guarantee that Francis would be allowed across the frontier in the first place and some risk that, even if he reached Erfurt, he would not be permitted to return.

To Metternich's chagrin he was not himself allowed by Napoleon to go to Erfurt. Superficially it was a dazzling occasion with everyone of importance in Germany present, even Goethe. Alexander had the doubtful pleasure of being conducted around the battlefield of Jena by its victor (who had, of course, at the time been his principal enemy). There were a series of balls and ornate receptions and thirty-two actors and actresses from the Théâtre Français, including Talma, mounted a heavy programme of classical tragedies. Politically Erfurt was less remarkable: although Napoleon felt confident that Russia would not take advantage of his Spanish embarrassments to turn against him, he could not secure a definite undertaking from Alexander of active operations against Austria. But the Congress certainly emphasized Austria's isolation. The two Emperors received General von Vincent as a personal emissary from Francis. An official artist commemorated the occasion on canvas. On one side of the salon stands Napoleon, flanked at a respectable distance by the Tsar and all the German princelings. Vincent, alone with bowed head, hands the French Emperor a letter. Behind a table between the two men stands Talleyrand, impassive and inscrutable, seeing everything and saying nothing. It catches the spirit of the encounter better than most such representations.[45]

On his return to Paris, Talleyrand revealed to Metternich as much of the secrets of Erfurt as he thought the ambassador should know. Metternich was encouraged to learn that the Tsar refused to be dragged into a war with Francis, but he was even more pleased by what he interpreted as signs of disaffection at the French court. He reported to Vienna that only the higher command of the army, 'Marshals wishing to become Archdukes', supported Napoleon in his hostility to Austria. Stadion was impressed, but not entirely convinced. He summoned Metternich back to Vienna for consultation. It was a good moment for the ambassador to make the journey. Napoleon left Paris for the army in Spain on 29 October; Metternich passed that unpleasantly familiar frontier barrier at Kehl twelve days later and reached the Austrian capital on 12 November.[46]

Preparing a war of revenge

He spent some five weeks in Vienna, not arriving back in Paris until New Year's Day. Stadion he found prepared to advocate war with France, either while Napoleon was still in Spain or as soon as the winter snows had melted in the Jura and the Tauern. He was supported by Baldacci (who was in effect, though not in name, minister of the interior) and by the Empress Maria Ludovica, who had become the third wife of Emperor Francis early in 1808. Being Italian by birth, she was enthusiastically German-patriot by adoption. The Emperor himself was reluctant to side with the war party so long as his brother, the Archduke Charles, insisted that the army was not yet ready for another tussle with the French and their satellites. Everyone knew that Austria's finances could not afford a war in 1809; and Stadion's very Viennese argument that the country would not be able to afford a war in 1810 or 1811 either, did not entirely carry conviction. The prospect of a British subsidy had more weight; but ultimately the decision over peace or war rested on the man who brought the latest intelligence from Paris.[47]

Metternich summarized his advice in three long memoranda, dated 4 December.[48] In the first of these he developed his thesis that Napoleon had lost the support of the French nation by the over-ambitious demands of his foreign policy; in the second he gave his reasons for believing that Russia would take no active part in operations against Austria; and in the third he maintained that, because of the campaign in Spain, Napoleon would only be able to concentrate 206,000 men for a war against Austria. Nearly half of these troops would be raised from the German states and the Duchy of Warsaw, and they might therefore be regarded as militarily unreliable. These arguments won over the Archduke Charles, perhaps against his better judgement. By March 1809 he hoped to put into the field more than 300,000 regulars and a quarter of a million reservists; and he counted on risings behind the French lines, notably in the Tyrol. On paper, the balance was in Austria's favour; and by the middle of the month it was agreed that war should follow in the spring. The immediate objective would be to destroy French primacy in central Europe; but its ultimate aim was the restoration of Habsburg authority and influence over the German lands and northern Italy. Lunéville, Pressburg and Erfurt called for vengeance.

Arrested by Napoleon

The last three months of Metternich's sojourn in Paris are riddled with ill-concealed dissimulation. The Austrians needed time to complete their diplomatic preparations: Baron Wessenberg was sent to Berlin in the vain hope that the Prussians might turn against the French; Prince Schwarzenberg was despatched to St Petersburg, where he was assured the Russians would avoid an open clash with the Austrian troops even if they formally declared war against them; and secret contact was also made with London. Most of these activities were well known to the French, and the secret police rarely let Metternich or the other members of the Paris embassy escape from their vigilance. On 10 January the police reports recorded that couriers passing through Strasbourg indicated a build-up of Austrian forces and that this intelligence was corroborated by remarks of Floret in Paris.[49] A fortnight later it was seen as ominous that Metternich turned the other cheek when members of the Russian embassy made slighting remarks over Austrian policy;[50] and on 25 February it was reported that Metternich was very reassuring, that he was dismissing all talk of war as the invention of the press, and that he had rented a country house at Clichy, three miles beyond the city boundaries.[51] When, on 7 March and 8 March, the police found he was selling his wine and horses, it was assumed war would not long be delayed.[52] On Palm Sunday the assiduous agents noted he had brought back for Eleonore 'a large branch of sacred box-wood', a gift which intrigued them as much as the fact they recorded it puzzles us.[53] But by then they were so alert to the unusual they would have jotted down any sneeze that had overcome the ambassador in public.

Such ubiquitous surveillance necessarily cramped Metternich's activities. He saw far less of Talleyrand, partly because Napoleon had at the end of January upbraided his former Foreign Minister for his double-dealing in one of those stormy audiences which so often accompanied his return from a campaign.[54] Metternich found Fouché of little assistance and he regretted the recall of Tolstoy to St Petersburg, for he could never achieve with his successor a similar degree of understanding, let alone of co-operation. But he was able to obtain (from an unspecified source who is generally assumed to have been Talleyrand) a detailed analysis of the disposition of French troops; and he forwarded this valuable information to Stadion by way of Dresden, for he had little confidence in the ability of the Vienna couriers to avoid interception. He continued to attend diplomatic receptions throughout January and February, although Napoleon had nothing to say to him, apart from enquiries over Eleonore's health.[55] But on 13 March Napoleon had a long conversation with Andreossi, his ambassador in Vienna, who confirmed verbally the assurance he had already given in writing that Austrian war preparations were nearly complete.[56] On 23 March a curt note from the Grand Chamberlain informed Metternich that 'His Majesty the Emperor and King would not receive him that evening'. In the Tuileries the Court Theatre was presenting *Romeo et Juliette*; and this time the entertainment was not delayed.[57]

Metternich waited in Paris for news that the Austrians had crossed the Inn. Now that war was near his spirits were low and he was apprehensive. The Austrian troops had arrested one of the couriers serving the French embassy in Vienna and, in consequence, his own messengers were harassed. On 10 April he sent a strange letter to Schwarzenberg in St Petersburg, indicating that he believed he would be cast into the citadel of Vincennes and perhaps even suffer the fate of the Duc d'Enghien, whose execution in the moat of the fortress had left such a strain of dishonour on the closing months of the Consulate. 'Nothing would surprise me now,' he wrote, not very convincingly, to Schwarzenberg; and in a farewell message to Stadion, written at four in the morning of 10 April, he was even gloomier. Declaring that he expected to be taken away and shot, he requested Stadion to arrange 'for a spiritual and diplomatic Requiem Mass [*sic*] to be said for such a sacrifice'.[58] Unless he feared arrest as a spy, it is difficult to understand his forebodings. They were, of course, completely unjustified.

Paris learned during the evening of 12 April that the Austrians had occupied Passau three days previously; and by the next morning Napoleon was on his way to Strasbourg and his fourth campaign against the Habsburgs. Metternich remained in the capital, unmolested; and Vincennes had no new prisoner in its dungeons. When it was reported that the Austrians had detained French diplomats in Vienna, Metternich was indeed placed formally under arrest. But it could hardly be called a burdensome restraint. 'My life in society continued in much the same way as before the breach in relations,' he admits in his autobiography.[59] He knew that, in time, he would have to leave the country but meanwhile he made careful plans. He decided that it would be safer for Eleonore and the family to live privately in Paris rather than undertake another wartime journey, especially as the Austrians were encouraging the subject peoples of the French Empire to emulate the Spanish and rise in revolt; and he arranged for personal servants and a secretary from the embassy to remain with the family. He was himself in no hurry to leave, partly because he was suffering from a painful attack of conjunctivitis, a form of discomfiture which frequently attacked him at moments of tension and strain. His departure was postponed until the last week of May.

In the afternoon of 25 May a long line of carriages, each drawn by four posthorses, waited in the Rue Grange Batelière. A silent crowd watched as two of the vehicles were packed high with baggage. Some distinguished Austrian travellers, detained in France by the outbreak of war, clambered aboard another carriage, and Prince Paul Esterhazy, the ambassador's personal attaché, entered the fourth. At four o'clock Metternich emerged. He said farewell to Eleonore – whom he was not to see again for ten months – and climbed the steps of the leading carriage, accompanied by Lieutenant Brouville of the *gendarmerie*, his official escort. Slowly the cavalcade pulled away, eighty hooves clattering noisily over the *pavés*, out through the waste land of eastern Paris to the Barrière de Pantin and at last to the wooded slopes above the Marne. At Chalons Metternich encountered the first group of Austrian officers, taken prisoner in the campaign; and at Strasbourg he was received by Empress Josephine, even though their two countries were at war. It was a strange end to an embassy; and no less uncertain than its beginning.[60]

COLLABORATION

The Wagram Campaign; and appointment as Foreign Minister (8 October 1809)

The war of 1809 lasted for only thirteen weeks and led once more to a peace settlement which humiliated the Habsburgs. It was therefore a disaster for those, like Stadion and Metternich, who had believed French exhaustion and Austrian ardour would speedily restore the old order in central Europe. Hopes of a major insurrection in Germany came to nothing, although the whole of the Tyrol answered Andreas Hofer's call to rise against the Bavarians and their French overlords. On 13 May the French entered Vienna and Napoleon took up residence at Schönbrunn, as in 1805. Yet this was not the story of Austerlitz over again. At the start of the campaign there were two main Austrian armies in the field, each commanded by a brother of the Emperor Francis: Archduke Charles brought his army back virtually intact from Regensburg along the left bank of the Danube to the Marchfeld, north of Vienna; and Archduke John, facing Eugene Beauharnais' 'Army of Italy', retreated in an orderly fashion from the Karawanken Mountains across Carinthia and Styria to Hungary where he joined forces with the local militia of the Hungarian Palatine, the Archduke Joseph (yet another brother). On 21–22 May Archduke Charles repulsed an attack by Napoleon in the Danubian plain around Aspern and Essling, only five miles from the centre of Vienna, gaining an impressive victory which he was unable to exploit because his troops were exhausted and he lacked pontoons. Although his brothers had little success – they were, in fact, defeated by Eugene at Gyor on 14 June – the fate of the whole campaign and perhaps even of the French Empire was in the balance for more than a month. Napoleon's Russian ally stood inactive along the Vistula as a third Austrian army engaged the Polish forces of the Grand-Duchy of Warsaw; he had expected more from Tsar Alexander than a mere watching brief. The news from Spain was bad, and there was a sudden outburst of activity in the English Channel, where the British bombarded French positions preparatory to a diversionary raid on the Scheldt estuary. Another defeat on the Danube, a second Aspern, could have forced Napoleon to pull his troops back from Vienna and might well have tempted Russia and Prussia to bring their armies into the field against him.

It was during these critical weeks, on 5 June, that Metternich completed his strange homecoming to Vienna.[1] He was still technically a prisoner and found the despised Champagny installed in the Hofburg and Andreossi acting as governor of the city. Metternich's father had been threatened with deportation to France, pending payment of a tribute by the Viennese to their conquerors, an order which Clement succeeded in having countermanded through the intervention of Berthier. He was only allowed to remain in the city for three days and was then interned in his mother's house near Schönbrunn. He twice declined suggestions that he might have an informal audience with Napoleon, who may well have considered using him as a peace emissary. There was considerable delay in arranging his transfer for the French diplomats still held by the Austrians and on one abortive journey to the outposts along the Danube his coach was damaged by cannon fire from an over-zealous Austrian battery. But, at last, on 2 July he was handed over to a Hungarian detachment near Komaron and by the following evening he was with the Emperor Francis and Stadion at Wolkersdorf, where Archduke Charles had established his headquarters.[2]

Two days later Metternich was by the side of the Emperor Francis as Oudinot, Eugene and Bernadotte moved their troops across the Danube and on to the open fields below Wagram. Gentz, who was at that time irritated by Metternich's overweening self-confidence, recorded in his diary a gently ironical description of Metternich watching the ebb and flow of battle through a long telescope he had somehow acquired and giving a running commentary on what he saw: 'Admirable! Incomparable! Our cavalry is attacking! Now we are going forward!' But Wagram unfortunately was not Valenciennes, and the Archduke Charles wanted more than the encouragement of someone who had once observed Coburg's martial peregrinations across the Flanders plain. By the afternoon of the second day's fighting it had become clear that only the arrival of the Archduke John with reinforcements could save the battle; and he was still ten miles to the east, along the road to Pressburg. As he realized his army had been defeated, the Emperor Francis turned to Metternich and said, 'We shall have much to repair.'[3] It was almost an understatement; by the end of the day – 6 July – Archduke Charles had only thirty-five thousand men capable of offering resistance.

The Emperor, Metternich and what was left of the army retired to Znaim (Znojmo) in Moravia, forty-five miles to the north-west. The Archduke considered there was little point in prolonging the war. Francis, who was always far less resolute off the field of battle than on it, could not make up his mind: he was, in particular, reluctant to conclude any settlement which would leave the Tyrolean insurgents of Andreas Hofer to the mercy of the French, for he had given a public assurance as recently as 29 May that the Tyrol would be reunited to the Monarchy. Now it seemed that, so far from recovering lost provinces, he would lose more territory – and perhaps even his throne. Stadion, though despondent, still believed that there might be some hope of maintaining the integrity of the Empire if Napoleon was alarmed by developments in Poland or by the long delayed British diversion in the west. Nevertheless, Stadion tendered his resignation, maintaining that he was too associated with the war party to obtain reasonable terms from the victorious French if peace talks were begun. Francis immediately offered the post of Foreign Minister to Metternich, for there was no-one else who seemed so eager to assume such responsibility. But Metternich was too shrewd to accept office without conditions.[4] He argued that Stadion's fall would be interpreted by the other powers as evidence that the Austrians wished for peace at any price; and he therefore proposed a compromise by which Stadion would remain nominally Foreign Minister until the end of the campaign, while Metternich himself would become a minister of state in attendance on the Emperor and would handle all negotiations with the French. Once peace was signed he would formally succeed Stadion. Both Francis and Stadion saw the merits of this scheme. Metternich duly accompanied the Emperor to western Hungary in the Imperial coach, taking the opportunity to lecture his captive audience on the current situation. ('I was convinced that on all important topics my views would always be in harmony with his.')[5] Francis took up residence in the castle of Totis, near Komaron: Stadion remained with the Archduke Charles. There were weary encounters with the French troops on 10–11 July, and on 12 July Charles sought an armistice. The Emperor promptly dismissed his brother from the post of Commander-in-Chief, replacing him by Prince Johann Liechtenstein, who made the first contact with Napoleon.* It was a sad end to the military career of the ablest soldier among the Habsburgs for many generations.

Liechtenstein found Napoleon aggressive and vindictive: he even demanded the abdication of Francis; and for a time it seemed as if the armistice might prove to be no more than a truce. Gradually Napoleon's mood mellowed, although he remained personally hostile to the Austrian Emperor. He agreed that there should be formal peace negotiations between his Foreign Minister, Champagny, and Metternich (whom he particularly asked to be appointed head of the Austrian delegation). But he made it clear he would insist on the cession of at least as much territory as in the Treaty of Pressburg and he laid down

---

* The unfortunate Liechtenstein had also been given the task of seeking peace terms with Napoleon after Austerlitz.

Metternich as a young diplomat

The Coronation of
Emperor Francis at Frankfurt, 1792

Princess Eleonore
von Kaunitz, Metternich's first wife

Metternich's audience with
Napoleon I at the Marcolini Palace,
Dresden 1813

Napoleon I at the battle of Wagram

Viscount Castlereagh, British Foreign Secretary 1812–22

pre-conditions for the talks, including demobilization of the reserves and reduction of the regular army to half its size. It is possible that Napoleon was in no hurry to make peace, for he was particularly worried by the equivocal attitude of the Russians to the Polish Question and highly suspicious of an arrangement by which the Austrians had surrendered Cracow to the Tsar's commanders rather than to the army of the Grand-Duchy of Warsaw. At last it was agreed that a peace conference would open at Altenburg, a dull little town south of Pressburg, on 15 August; but characteristically Champagny arrived late, and the talks did not begin until 18 August.[6]

They continued intermittently for five weeks and failed to produce a settlement. The fault was hardly Metternich's. With few assets, apart from the intuitive knowledge that Napoleon was uncertain about Russia's intentions, he maintained the dignity of the Monarchy, even arguing it was illogical to treat defeated Austria less generously than defeated Russia at Tilsit. He did not, however, have a free hand, for he was subject both to the truculent whims of Napoleon at Schönbrunn and to the sudden alternations of belligerency and despair at Komaron. He knew well enough the long-term objectives which he believed Austria should seek and made them clear to the Emperor Francis in a memorandum, dated 10 August: co-operation with France, membership of the Continental System, replacement of Russia as Napoleon's principal partner by Austria; a policy of 'tacking, wiping away the past, and collaboration'.[7] As a programme it showed admirable common sense, but it lacked nobility, and there were some at Komaron who would have preferred to risk total destruction of the Empire in another campaign rather than humble the dynasty by such a servile accommodation with the Bonapartist usurper. Nor was this the only proposal of Metternich which caused consternation at Komaron: six days after the talks began at Altenburg, the Emperor received from him another memorandum[8] suggesting that the Austrians and Prussians should support the restoration of a Polish state under a Polish ruler; and at one point in his disputes with Champagny he seems to have indicated that Austria would regard a resurrected Poland, under a native dynasty, as a potential ally. Such meddling in the Polish Question was far too dangerous for the liking of Francis or Stadion, to whom the Emperor was once more turning for advice. And in September Francis – who had the Habsburg failing of believing what he had most recently been told – began to ignore Metternich and sent two personal missions to Napoleon in Vienna, anxious if possible to secure peace on reasonable terms rather than permit the armistice to expire. Metternich was temporarily in eclipse.

The Altenburg talks were broken off in the last week in September and Metternich returned to Komaron, vexed that the Emperor had given plenary powers to Prince Liechtenstein to conclude a settlement.[9] Napoleon was becoming impatient and had begun to complain that Metternich was an insincere negotiator whose advice had contributed to the outbreak of the war. He thus played no part in the final talks in Vienna and Schönbrunn; and it was left to Prince Liechtenstein to sign, on 14 October, preliminaries of peace which conceded virtually all of Napoleon's territorial demands but at least allowed Francis to retain his throne. The terms were hard: the Austrians lost their share of Poland and their remaining Adriatic coastal region, parts of Carinthia and Croatia, the Slovene areas of Carniola, solidly German territories around Salzburg and Berchtesgaden, and a segment of Upper Austria near the Bavarian frontier. They had to pay an indemnity of eighty-five million francs (although their financial situation was desperate), to accept limitation of the army to 150,000 men, and to join the Continental System. The Tyrol remained unredeemed, despite the pledge Francis had given at the end of May, but Napoleon promised an amnesty for the Tyrolean rebels (which, in the event, saved neither Andreas Hofer nor his chief lieutenant, Mayr). The Schönbrunn Peace was a document to which Metternich – and, for that matter, Francis – did well not to attach their name: Prince Liechtenstein was, after all, in Metternich's eyes expendable.

A week before the conclusion of peace at Schönbrunn, Stadion formally resigned and on 8 October Metternich, who soon recovered his influence once he rejoined the court, was officially made Minister of the Imperial Household and of Foreign Affairs. Napoleon left Schönbrunn on 16 October and the French Army slowly began to evacuate the areas it had occupied. It was not until 28 November that Emperor Francis made his formal return to Vienna, where he was rapturously received.[10] A few hours later Metternich took up his duties in the Ballhausplatz, where Foreign Ministers had lived since the days of Kaunitz. It was to be the centre of his private and public empire until March 1848.

Negotiating the marriage of Marie Louise

The most pressing problem for Metternich continued to be relations with France. Champagny and Liechtenstein had agreed that the new ambassador to Paris should be Prince Charles Schwarzenberg and Metternich warmly approved of their choice. Schwarzenberg had already shown dignity and skill as the Emperor's representative in St Petersburg and he was a soldier for whom everyone felt respect. He did not have Metternich's subtlety and charm nor his contacts in Paris; but there were some who regarded the absence of these attributes with favour. He did, however, take back to France with him Engelbert

Floret, who was by now as gifted as anyone in interpreting the political scene at Napoleon's court. And, for the moment, the Austrians could also rely upon the influence of Eleonore Metternich, who was welcomed once more into Parisian society as soon as peace was made and for whose sound sense Napoleon himself showed an increasingly high regard. Floret and Eleonore von Metternich were now to play an important part in making possible Napoleon's second marriage, although the first discussions took place in Vienna.

Metternich had known of the persistent rumours that Napoleon would divorce Josephine and seek a new wife capable of bearing him a son ever since the Tilsit meeting. He had long considered that the most likely choice for a new Empress would be a Russian Grand-Duchess. The prospect of such a marriage filled him with dismay, partly because he believed it would perpetuate the division of Europe between two great Empires to the exclusion of Austria but also because he attached particular significance to the policy of matrimonial alliance, a traditional weapon of the Habsburgs. Napoleon's annoyance at Russian inactivity in the 1809 campaign, and at the marriage of the Tsar's most eligible sister to a German prince, gave Metternich hope; and even before the resumption of diplomatic relations between France and Austria, he aired the possibility of a dynastic link. Liechtenstein, apparently on his own initiative, had raised the subject with Champagny in September and had written about it, in general terms, both to the Emperor Francis and to Metternich. General Bubna, one of Francis's closest military confidants, had on Metternich's instructions mentioned the Archduchess Marie Louise in conversation at French headquarters in November; and Floret dropped ambiguous hints to Champagny about the same time. Two days after taking up residence in the Ballhaus Platz, Metternich himself raised the matter with Count Alexandre de Laborde, a French diplomat with Austrian connections who was returning to Paris after assisting Napoleon to improve relations between the two ex-enemy states. Metternich insisted that he alone was responsible for the idea of a marriage between Napoleon and the Archduchess and that he had not discussed the subject with Francis, but he claimed to have every confidence that the Emperor would willingly consent to his daughter's marriage. Laborde set out for Paris on the next day and remained an ardent and active supporter of the marriage project for the next five months.[11]

There are many tear-stained narratives of the marriage negotiations. For years a popular legend persisted of how the Emperor Francis, to save his dynasty, was forced to sacrifice his eldest daughter – just turned eighteen and loving only her Papa, her pet ducks and her whipped cream – to satisfy the demands of the forty-year-old Corsican Antichrist (for so the girl had been taught to regard her future husband). But it is clear the initiative came from the Austrians rather than from Napoleon, and Marie Louise was by no means distressed at being removed from her governesses and carried as a bride to Paris. The preliminary work in the French capital was undertaken by Floret, by Laborde and by Eleonore Metternich; for, although Schwarzenberg was responsible for the formal negotiations, he was far too slow and dignified to adapt himself to the changing situation in Paris and, from the letters and despatches of the period, he seems to have undertaken these duties with some distaste.[12] On the French side the principal champion (apart from Laborde) was Talleyrand, with whom Floret early established secret contact and who genuinely believed that France and Austria were natural allies. More surprisingly, once Napoleon had decided irrevocably for a divorce and had settled her at Malmaison, the Empress Josephine and her daughter worked for an Austrian marriage rather than any link with Russia or with one of the petty German dynasties, the only other possible families in which Napoleon might find a mother for the heir he desired.

Metternich's own account in the autobiographical fragment is picturesque but confused;[13] for, although in 1811 he was pleased to claim credit for the marriage, he wished in later years to put the responsibility firmly on the French. It all began, he maintains, at a masked ball given by Cambacérès (who had once been Second Consul and was now Arch-Chancellor). During the evening Eleonore, who had been especially invited, was approached by a figure 'whose disguise she immediately penetrated'; and as there can have been few dominos in Paris that night with an authoritative manner, stockily built and five feet two in height, this part of the tale at least is credible. Napoleon – 'for it was he' – led her into a private room and, after some trivial remarks, asked her if she thought the Archduchess Marie Louise would accept him in marriage. When Eleonore, very surprised at the proposal, made it clear that she believed the Archduchess would refuse, Napoleon urged her to write to her husband on the subject. This she declined to do, very properly suggesting that the Emperor should make contact with Metternich through Schwarzenberg; and it was by this means, according to Eleonore's husband, that Vienna came to hear how the French were once more seeking the hand of an Austrian Archduchess.

The operatic undertones of a masked ball and an Imperial suitor inadequately disguised make this curious story, at first reading, improbable. Cambacérès did indeed give such an entertainment as Metternich describes and it was attended by the cream of Paris society; but the ball was not held until 21 January 1810, and by then the marriage project had been widely discussed for several weeks.[14] There is little doubt Napoleon talked informally to Eleonore on the subject before authorizing an approach through Schwarzenberg to the Emperor

Francis; but the meeting appears to have taken place before Christmas, probably at a time when Eleonore was considering returning with her family to Vienna, a journey for which she required Napoleon's permission.[15] And before the end of the year, she had discussed an Austrian marriage with Josephine and Hortense Beauharnais as well.[16] Her correspondence with her husband shows she was in close touch with Laborde; and late in January Clement was prepared to incite her to a diplomatic indiscretion – the old ruse of a private letter allowed to fall into 'wrong' hands – in order to convince the French of the value attached by the Austrians to a Habsburg-Bonaparte marriage link.[17] Napoleon for the moment temporized. He was still awaiting reports from Caulaincourt in St Petersburg on his offer of a marriage with the Tsar's youngest sister, Anna (aged fifteen), a proposal over which Alexander was in no hurry to make up his mind. Throughout January the rival partisans of an Austrian or a Russian marriage intrigued and gossiped at the French court.

It was during these undignified exercises in marriage politics that the Junot affair reached an appropriate climax.[18] On the evening of 13 January – a day on which, significantly, both Schwarzenberg and Eleonore had written to Metternich describing the activities of the pro-Austrian group in the capital – a ball was held in the residence of Count Marescalchi, the Foreign Minister of the puppet kingdom of Italy, in the Rue d'Angoulême. At some point in the entertainment a female informant (masked, as usual, but probably Caroline Murat) told General Junot that if on his return home he opened his wife's desk he would find there some compromising trinkets and a packet of letters, tied together with pink ribbon. Junot angrily broke into his wife's desk, discovered what he was looking for, and charged his wife with infidelity. Beside himself with rage, he vowed at first that for this insult he would induce Napoleon to resume the war with Austria. Subsequently, with slightly more sense, he declared that as this was a personal matter he would challenge Metternich to a duel, which would be fought at Mainz in the middle of February. Meanwhile he contented himself with half-strangling Laura and attacking her with a pair of gilt scissors. Leaving 'a blood drenched wife, half-dead and cut to pieces by his own hands' – the words are Laura's, many years later – he immediately stormed off to let Eleonore von Metternich know of her husband's misconduct. But Eleonore was too accustomed to Clement's waywardness to join Junot in a display of temperament. 'The rôle of Othello ill becomes you,' she declared icily to the man whose affair with Caroline Murat had scandalized Napoleon less than three years previously; and following Junot back to his house in the Rue Boissy d'Anglais, she consoled Laura and left the unfortunate couple outwardly reconciled. A week later a cryptic note in the secret police files records that 'storm clouds' over the Junot household 'are dispersed'. Nothing more was heard of the duel at Mainz. On 2 February Junot was posted by Napoleon to Spain, and took his wife with him; and in November their second child was born. Eleonore was congratulated on her courage and tolerance both by Napoleon and by his sister, Pauline Borghese; and Metternich did not meet Laura again until the spring of 1814, nearly a year after Junot's death.

At the time Eleonore believed the melodramatic scene was caused by private jealousies. This may well have been the case, but a scandal of such a nature involving the Austrian Foreign Minister at that point in the marriage negotiations could easily have embarrassed Metternich's position and policy, especially if his wife had shown less indulgence towards his behaviour. As it was, the whole affair aroused considerable comment but the gossip was critical of Junot's excessive reaction far more than of Metternich. He was not unduly disturbed by the incident.

The pace of the marriage negotiations was speeded up rather than slowed down in the third week of January, probably because of pessimistic reports from Caulaincourt in St Petersburg. By 7 February Napoleon had decided on the Austrian marriage and Eleonore was able to indulge in a little self-congratulation, while letting her husband know there was no reason why he should not return to Paris for the wedding celebrations.[19] Marie Louise was married by proxy to Napoleon in the Capuchin chapel of the Vienna Hofburg on 11 March with her uncle, the Archduke Charles, deputizing for the man who had defeated him at Wagram. Two days later the guns of the Austrian capital thundered out in salute and all the bells pealed as the new Empress of the French began the long fortnight's journey to meet her husband. The people of Vienna, though not the great families, were pleased at the marriage: Austria still had something to offer Europe, if only a girl of eighteen. This was the type of diplomacy to which they were accustomed; even the marriage contract had precedent, since it followed clause by clause the document prepared for Marie Antoinette and the prince who was to become Louis XVI.

Marie Louise travelled to Compiègne, where Napoleon awaited her, by way of Munich and Strasbourg. She was accompanied across Germany by an impressive retinue which included her new sister-in-law, Caroline Murat, and Marshal Berthier who had Laborde with him as adviser and secretary. Metternich, too, was on the road westwards.[20] He left Vienna on 15 March but since it was felt to be impolitic for him to take the same route as the Imperial progress he journeyed by way of Nuremberg and Metz. He had announced his intention of going to France in a despatch to Schwarzenberg on 17 February, and the news had been ill-received in Paris, especially by Champagny who could not see any reason for a visit by the Austrian Foreign Minister now that

Napoleon had made the marriage he desired. It was emphasized – and Metternich publicly agreed – that he would come to France as a private traveller with two responsibilities: to escort his family home again; and to report to the Emperor Francis on the way in which his daughter carried her Imperial dignity. He was expected to stay in Paris for not more than six weeks: he remained there for six months.

A special mission to Paris (1809)

This 'special mission' to Napoleon's court is one of the most extraordinary episodes in Metternich's career. He had been Foreign Minister for barely half a year; he had many enemies among the Austrian aristocracy who distrusted him as an ambitious 'foreigner' who had sold his soul and his sovereign's daughter to the Corsican; and yet he risked a long separation from the centre of political life, even entrusting the day-to-day running of his department to a man of whose ability he can have had few illusions, his own father. That he chanced such a gamble is a sure sign of his self-confidence and his conviction that by the marriage he had made himself indispensable both to Francis and to Napoleon. Yet it also demonstrates the extent to which Paris was at that moment the capital of Europe, for there is little doubt he assumed he could obtain more for Austria by residence abroad than by controlling from Vienna the missions of Emperor Francis's representatives in St Petersburg, Berlin and other traditional courts. He hoped the nuptial bliss of a protracted honeymoon would enable him to modify the peace terms of Schönbrunn and in particular to recover a port on the Adriatic, for the loss of Fiume and Trieste was a hard blow to Austrian commerce. He believed that, while in Paris, he might mediate between Napoleon and the Pope (affronted by the divorce and the new marriage) and perhaps even preside over a conference to establish peace between France and Britain.[21]

Political realities fell far short of such dreams. He flattered Napoleon to excess, even proposing a toast at a banquet in the Tuileries to the 'future King of Rome'. In return for these attentions Metternich imagined himself favoured and petted as the Russian envoys had been at the time of Erfurt. But the concessions he gained for Austria were trivial: trading rights extended to long-established Austrian merchants in the Illyrian Provinces; a delay in payment of the war indemnity; restitution of some estates belonging to Germans in the Austrian service (including the Metternichs); and abrogation of those clauses in the Peace Treaty which had limited the Austrian Army to 150,000 men.*

* The removal of this particular disability was welcomed in Vienna as a sign of renewed independence, but it had always been superfluous since after their defeat the Austrians were unable to afford a military establishment of even this meagre size.

Metternich also concluded a preliminary commercial agreement with France, but when the authorities in Vienna heard of its terms they considered them so unfavourable that it was never ratified.

Nor was Metternich any more successful in his larger diplomatic projects. Napoleon brushed aside all offers of mediation with the Papacy: it was an institution for which he had scant regard, especially after thirteen Cardinals had absented themselves from the marriage service in Notre Dame on 2 April; he would not treat with such men. The prospect of peace with Britain aroused little interest in Paris, or indeed in London: it never got any further than a long memorandum from Gentz (which eventually reached the Foreign Office in June 1811) and some hints conveyed more speedily to England by a trusted intermediary between the British and Austrian governments, the former Hanoverian diplomat Count Hardenberg.[22] Once in September Napoleon did indeed hold out the prospect of treaty revision on the Adriatic littoral but only if Francis would cede Galicia to a new Polish Kingdom and join him in an anti-Russian alliance; and it was hard to determine if Napoleon really meant the proposal to be taken seriously or whether he was putting it forward, half-teasingly as he did from time to time, in order to test Austrian reaction and discourage any collaboration between Vienna and St Petersburg.[23] Galicia remained in Habsburg hands and 'Illyria', from Villach to Dubrovnik, continued to be administered as part of metropolitan France.

During this protracted stay in Paris Metternich had every opportunity of seeking to understand Napoleon and of working out what his next moves would be. These were the tasks he had set himself as ambassador in 1806, without conspicuous success; and they should now more properly have been left to Schwarzenberg and Floret. But Metternich was always curiously fascinated by Napoleon: in 1853 he claimed with some justice that he had enjoyed 'such long immediate contact as never existed between Napoleon and any other person not a Frenchman';[24] and, in an earlier essay of reminiscence, he declared in 1820 that 'conversation with him has always had for me a charm difficult to define'.[25] There developed between them some of the friendship of opposites; and it was perhaps made more sincere than either realized by the fact that each was essentially a pretender, Bonaparte to the dignity of an Imperial crown, Metternich to social primacy among the greater names of the old Empire. Occasionally this bond unexpectedly showed itself. Thus at St Cloud in September they consoled each other on the elevation of Bernadotte to the steps of the Swedish throne: 'You should have given more importance to remaining the only one,' said Metternich; 'You are right,' replied Napoleon, 'that consideration ... has often made me regret placing Murat on the throne of Naples'.[26] It was an admission he would have made to no other foreign statesman. At times one feels that Napoleon was laughing up his sleeve at Metternich, even while enjoying his company. It probably never occurred to him he might yet prove a formidable adversary.

Metternich's reports from Paris were no more accurate than his forecasts two years previously, apart from a rhapsodic despatch on 9 July announcing that the Empress was pregnant. He hopelessly exaggerated the influence which Marie Louise had acquired over her husband, possibly because he was anxious to prove to the Emperor Francis that his daughter's marriage was a masterly stroke for Austria's interests. He swallowed, but did not digest, every Balkan bait which Napoleon dangled in the hope of entangling Austria with Russia. Yet he did indeed observe much of Napoleon that summer although, as diplomatic observers sardonically noted, he spent even more hours with his sister, Caroline. He saw Napoleon in state, he saw him hunting and at the play, and he saw him in the constrained domesticity of St Cloud; but it is probable that during all these weeks in Paris there was only one night when he caught a glimpse of the real Bonaparte, rather than the actor who was playing the new Charlemagne. On 1 July Schwarzenberg gave a grand ball to celebrate the Imperial marriage and invited some fifteen hundred guests. No sooner had the first quadrille ended and the dancers taken partners for an *Anglaise* than a decorative garland caught fire in the gallery and the flames spread rapidly to the heavy draperies. Napoleon hurried Marie Louise out into the gardens and sent her back in the state coach to St Cloud; he then returned to the disaster and directed the fire-fighting until the small hours of the morning as though it were a military operation. Several guests perished in the blaze, including the ambassador's sister-in-law, Princess Pauline Schwarzenberg. It would have been an even worse tragedy but for Napoleon's presence of mind, especially as it was a Sunday night and the primitive fire-fighting force was at low strength. Eleonore von Metternich, who had been beside Princess Pauline watching their daughters dancing, had a narrow escape but was unharmed.[27] Among the injured, Metternich found Marie-Constance de Caumont, whom he had loved so idyllically at Mainz nineteen years before. He had hoped for a happier reunion.

Napoleon's Austrian lackey (1811)

When the autumn came Metternich was still in Paris, but in the last days of September Napoleon and Marie Louise went into residence at Fontainebleau, where there was good hunting by day and the court theatre in the evening. Napoleon gave Metternich a farewell audience before leaving St Cloud and presented him with a marble bust to add to the Gobelin tapestries and the gift of vases which he had been allowed to select for himself at Sèvres as long ago as the second week in April.

Metternich, Eleonore and the children set out for Vienna on 26 September but found, when they reached home at last, that the Emperor Francis was in Styria. It was therefore at Gräz on 12 October that Clement was able to hand his sovereign messages from Marie Louise and from the son-in-law who had wished to force his abdication a year before; and there was also a letter testifying to Napoleon's high regard for the Foreign Minister.[28]

He had every need of support, for his enemies had been gathering strength in the previous two months. There were those who complained, with good reason, that his father had been allowed to bumble around the Ballhausplatz far too long and that his presence there could only be explained on the assumption that Metternich's policy was so unsavoury he would trust no one else with its secrets. He had made no new friends by his behaviour in Paris and had lost some old ones: Stadion, who had supported him, was affronted by Metternich's failure to recover his estate at Chodenschloss in Württemberg, while securing recognition of his own father's claim to Ochsenhausen (the former abbey in Swabia granted to Francis George in 1803); the Liechtensteins, who had assisted Clement and Eleonore in their early years in Vienna, felt insulted at the way Prince Johann had been passed over once the Peace of Schönbrunn was concluded; and the Schwarzenbergs, another great family which had befriended him, resented the way in which the Foreign Minister had constantly upstaged the unfortunate ambassador in Paris. The Archdukes Charles and Joseph viewed with distaste the warmth of his collaboration with the former enemy; and the Empress Maria Ludovica complained that his protracted sojourn in France had shown irresponsible levity at such a grave moment in Austria's history. There had moreover, been a significant change in the inner councils of the government during his absence. He had collaborated well with Count O'Donnell, the Finance Minister; but O'Donnell dropped down dead on 4 May and was succeeded by the Oberstburggraf of Bohemia, Count Joseph Wallis, a hot-tempered lawyer of Scottish descent who knew nothing of money matters and hid his ignorance by displays of violent energy. Metternich had already clashed with Wallis *in absentia* over the abortive commercial treaty; and there were soon to be more storms around the conference tables, for Wallis (in contrast, here, to many of Metternich's other critics) believed that the Foreign Minister was pursuing a positive policy beyond Austria's resources.[29]

Metternich's intimate advisers were men of lesser standing. He could rely on Floret (whom he had left in Paris) and on Gentz, but the great publicist was at that time discredited, a despondent neurotic who had 'cried like a child' when he heard the bells pealing for Marie Louise's wedding. And he could also count among his supporters the Irish-born General Nugent, who had assisted him at Altenburg and who maintained close links with London; but although he was respected as a soldier, Nugent's foreign origin kept him out of the centre of affairs and he was soon to depart for England. Ultimately Metternich staked his future on two assets: his supposed understanding of Napoleon; and his ability to handle his own sovereign, the Emperor Francis. Like Richelieu before him and Bismarck after, his survival for a quarter of a century depended more than anything else upon the master and servant relationship.

Francis was not one of the greatest Habsburg rulers: he lacked high intelligence, imagination and personality. Ever since his childhood, wrote a British diplomat in 1811, he had been 'impressed with the idea of his own nullity, or rather imbecility, in matters of state'. This was an unduly harsh judgement. He was amiable, mildly indolent and gifted with remarkable patience. Some of his qualities are conveyed in the portrait which Sir Thomas Lawrence painted in 1818 and which hangs in the Waterloo Gallery at Windsor: he sits uneasily in uniform, sword by his side, left leg tautly perched on a stool rather than resting on it; his eyes are shrewd and alert but not pensive; and his mouth begins to curve in a diffident smile which he dares not make. He is waiting for someone to arrive, as so often in his reign, for he was accustomed to give a dozen audiences a day when in residence at the Hofburg. Once he had greeted Cobenzl with the weary observation, 'When I see you enter my study my heart sinks at the thought of all the business you are bringing with you.' Like most of his sayings, the remark was not profound but it was honest. So too were his idiosyncrasies: cooking toffee on the royal stove; greeting his subjects affably in the Prater in broad Viennese dialect. He was conscientious, but he liked as quiet a life as possible, preferably without having to think too deeply. Hence he sought continuity of people and policies, provided nothing diminished the absolutist duty which was to him the divine burden of kingship. It was this simple principle of authority which safeguarded his ministers against his tendency to agree with the last person who spoke to him and which hampered the intrigues of court factions; for on reflection he always chose the familiar to the unknown. At times this characteristic suggested duplicity and made for timid government. It explains his preference for a 'system' which encouraged spying, censorship and cumbersome repression; but, in the last resort, it also explains the loyalty which enabled Metternich to continue in office for so long.[30]

As he hastened from Vienna to Graz through the mists and mud of a wet October, Metternich was confident he could retain his Emperor's support; and he was right. Francis, a good family man and an affectionate father, was relieved to hear favourable news of his daughter's health, now that she was in the fourth month of pregnancy; and he listened approvingly as his Foreign Minister deftly outlined a policy in which Austria would benefit from the dynastic links to free herself from French restraint while showing benevolent neutrality towards Russia, Prussia and Britain.[31] At all costs, Metternich said again and again in those winter months, she must avoid a catastrophic war as Russia's partner. His father had foolishly encouraged Russian feelers for a secret alliance: the son would have nothing to do with it. He was prepared to be charmingly sociable at the Russian ambassador's receptions; he was indecorously eager to make love to Katharina Bagration, whom his enemies maintained had been sent by the Tsar to steal his political virtue; but he was by now too experienced to be drawn into a new anti-French alignment. Later he was even able to use the Russian approaches as a weapon against his enemies at court, for his spies intercepted a letter from Archduke Joseph to the Tsar's mother which, while not actually treasonable, showed the Archduke in a poor light and threw suspicion also on the Empress Maria Ludovica.[32] It was, of course, un-gentlemanly to present such evidence to the Emperor Francis but his years at Napoleon's court had tarnished Metternich's polished manners. If, in diplomatic exchanges, he had learned something from Talleyrand, he had also acquired some of Fouché's bland skill in profiting from others' frailties. As yet he was a pupil rather than a master in both crafts, but he was improving; and it was enough to discourage the opposition for another twelve months.

By the end of February 1811 Metternich was convinced the Tilsit alliance was a historical relic and France and Russia heading rapidly towards war. On the last day of the old year, Tsar Alexander had taken Russia out of the Continental System, for the attempt to isolate Britain economically from Europe was becoming increasingly burdensome to all Napoleon's partners. Three weeks later the French, as if in response, annexed Oldenburg, a duchy whose heir was married to the Tsar's favourite sister. Alexander thereupon began to bid for Polish support, much as Napoleon had done in the previous year; and at the end of February, again like Napoleon, he offered Austria generous terms in ex-change for the cession of Galicia. Francis was to have a free hand to break off the crumbling fringe of the Ottoman Empire (Serbia, Wallachia and part of Moldavia), thus acquiring control of the Danube from Linz to the Black Sea.[33] It was a momentous gesture on the part of the Tsar, especially as Russian troops had for five years been fighting the Turks in those same Roumanian lands which he was now ready to assign to Austria. But Metternich had set himself resolutely against any action which might exacerbate the French, and the Russian offer was turned aside. At the same time, he assured the Prussians and indirectly the British that Austria would remain neutral in any Franco-Russian conflict. He let London know, through the Hanoverian Hardenberg, that although the Austrians could not have official relations with the

British government, he sought a 'friendly understanding' between the
two countries; and, as a gesture of goodwill, he arranged for a banker
in Linz to hold money which could be used by escaped British prisoners
of war.[34] He was sensitive to the criticisms of Napoleon's enemies who
tended to imagine him as permanently prostrated in self-effacement
before the French Imperial throne: there was sufficient truth behind
such a caricature for it to sting.

Conditions in Austria in this spring and summer of 1811 were
wretched.[35] Although police powers over learned works had been relaxed in the previous year, a timid censorship, for which Metternich
was only partially responsible, forbade books or plays which might excite feelings against the French: it banned, for example, Schiller's
Wilhelm Tell since events in the Tyrol had made it tragically topical.
But there was more of which to complain than cultural stagnation.
Enforced membership of the Continental System and the absence of an
Austrian seaport robbed the people of minor comforts, such as tea and
coffee, for which the wines and scents of France were no substitute; and
even these luxuries were controlled by rigid customs regulations, as
Metternich learnt when Francis refused to permit him to import an
unusually large consignment of French wine. Manufacturers of glass and
leather goods found themselves deprived of export markets, although
there was a minor boom in Bohemia and Moravia where the textile in-
dustry, freed from English competition, flourished and where sugar-beet
began to replace the cane-sugar which it was no longer possible to
import. Yet even in those regions where there was nominal prosperity
the paper money in circulation was so worthless that it could purchase
almost nothing. In order to check inflation Wallis had issued 'redemp-
tion bonds' on 20 February and these now formed the sole legal tender;
but the measure was extremely unpopular, especially in Hungary, and
the army was placed on the alert at the end of February throughout the
Monarchy for fear of rioting. Wallis was universally unpopular, but he
retained the complete confidence of Francis until the spring of 1813 and
his position was therefore as secure as that of Metternich.*

The rigid separation of departmental responsibilities which the
Emperor Francis favoured meant that Metternich had far less influence
over Austria's internal affairs and economic policy than most foreign
observers believed at the time. He tried, on several occasions, to revive
the formal Council of State. This institution, he explained, would
'ensure for the monarch ... a higher degree of tranquillity and
security ... by associating with the Emperor ... one common deliber-
ative body'. It would also, although he did not mention it in his
memoranda, have allowed the councillors to band together against

---

* Perhaps at times Wallis was even more secure than Metternich, for the Empress and the
Archdukes made another attempt to unseat the Foreign Minister early in 1812.

Wallis or any other adviser who wished to pursue a strongly independent line; and it was probably for this reason that Francis ignored the proposal.[36] Metternich disliked Wallis's policy, partly on personal grounds but also because the tight control of funds made the army appear weak and therefore muffled Austria's voice in the affairs of Europe. In July 1811 Wallis countered a plan to augment the army with sixty thousand recruits as a first stage in re-armament with the simple and effective statement that there was no money with which to pay them. He was, of course, perfectly correct but it did not endear him to the Foreign Minister or to Field-Marshal Count Heinrich Bellegarde, the Saxon-born president of the War Council, who rapidly emerged as Metternich's closest political ally.[37] There was a fundamental difference of principle between the attitudes of Wallis, on the one hand, and Metternich and Bellegarde, on the other. He wanted a guarantee there would be no war until Austria's economy had recovered from past disasters; they wished to postpone another military campaign for as long as possible, but they also argued that if Napoleon sought assistance, Austria should be able to furnish an expeditionary corps in order to stake a claim for consideration in any future peace settlement.

Metternich kept consistently to this policy throughout 1811 and into the troubled early months of 1812. He had first outlined his political strategy in a memorandum to Francis on 17 January 1811:[38] neutrality in a Franco-Russian war was desirable, but impossible; if Austria was to recover her position as a Great Power, she must support the French since the Tsar 'did not have the remotest prospect of success'. Although there were Russophiles at court who hankered after the old Austerlitz coalition, each successive emergency in the following eighteen months was seen by Metternich as merely strengthening his argument; and by the end of November 1811 he was even claiming that only a military alliance with Napoleon would solve Austria's financial problems, since it would bring in its wake a French subsidy.

Ultimately, however, Austria's decision was taken on solely political grounds. After diplomatic exchanges between Berlin and Vienna in early December, the Prussians had decided they must either pledge support to Napoleon or face territorial extinction; and on 24 February 1812 King Frederick William III concluded an alliance with France, the terms of which were so humiliating that almost a quarter of the Prussian Officer Corps immediately resigned their commissions.[39] Metternich was determined to avoid such an abject capitulation and he saw to it that Schwarzenberg handled the negotiations in Paris shrewdly. Napoleon had originally asked for sixty thousand men, three times as many as in the Prussian contingent and considerably more than the Austrians were prepared to put in the field. Schwarzenberg was instructed to offer half that number and insist they should remain as 'an

auxiliary corps' under Austrian command. The French, anxious to complete their dispositions in case the Russians moved first, accepted the
proposal and, in rather vague terms, assured Austria of adequate territorial gains when the maps came to be re-drawn after the war: there
was talk of Silesia (which was Prussian) and of restitution of the Tyrol
(which was Bavarian) and once again a hint was dropped that Galicia
might be exchanged for the Illyrian Provinces. Such ready bargaining
seemed proof to Metternich he had recovered for Austria her freedom of
initiative and asserted her preferential rank among France's clients,
above Prussia and all the other German states.[40]

The French alliance was signed on 14 March and became known in
Vienna twelve days later. It was, Metternich explained, merely a
promise of armed neutrality; and he added, with characteristic lack of
modesty, that the terms were almost as good as those obtained by
Kaunitz in 1756, a contention which less partial analysts might legitimately doubt.[41] He was well-pleased: the British were privately assured
that, despite the exigencies of the moment, the Austrians would at heart
never cease to regard themselves as opponents of French ambitions; and
the Russians were given verbal assurances that, should war come, they
need not fear extensive participation by an Austrian force. There was
something coldly unheroic about Metternich's policy: he had changed
since the days when, as ambassador, he had stoked the fires of the war
party; but, then, so had Austria.

The Meeting of Napoleon and Emperor Francis at Dresden (1812)

Everyone knew in the spring that war with Russia could not long be
delayed. Yet there remained one last Napoleonic gesture, the triumph
before victory. Poor Frederick Augustus of Saxony was invited to be
host for an impressive display of pageantry and concentrated his tidy
mind on the arrangements with all the punctilio which he reserved in
happier days for horticulture. Napoleon left St Cloud with Marie
Louise on 9 May and after a week of dusty travel arrived in Dresden at
eleven at night on 16 May. The bells pealed and the cannon thundered
as they had when Marie Louise left Vienna in her bridal cavalcade two
years previously. Thirty-eight hours later she was reunited for the first
time since that day with the Emperor Francis and her step-mother,
Maria Ludovica. Metternich accompanied his sovereign to Dresden and
Eleonore was in attendance on the Empress, who so mistrusted Clement
that she seems to have been surprised to find his wife possessed both
'intelligence and tact'. Even the Metternichs were preferable to her
boorish stepson-in-law, on whom she bestowed the affection of an
iceberg.[42]

There was a week of festivities – banquets, an Opera gala, plays, hunting, fireworks – and innumerable formal receptions as the rulers of Germany paid homage to their new master in the presence of their old. Francis was surprised to find that his daughter seemed happy with the father of his grandson: 'Whatever she says,' he complained, 'I cannot stomach that creature'. He was momentarily tempted by a proposal from Napoleon that he should put himself at the head of Austria's troops and participate in the forthcoming campaign. But the idea aroused nothing but contempt from Maria Ludovica and was strongly opposed by Metternich, who had no wish to be thrown into such open hostility towards the Russians; and nothing more was heard of the suggestion.

Metternich, as ever, enjoyed Napoleon's company. They talked of the French craving for public applause and of political reforms which might come in the new Empire when the wars were ended; and Napoleon explained how he intended to advance that summer to Smolensk and wait for the Russians to sue for peace. Only once was there a strained note in their conversation, and this was when Napoleon questioned the size and nature of the troops which Schwarzenberg was now to lead on his southern flank; for the commander of the Grand Army found in their composition and character a certain lack of warlike spirit.[43] This was, indeed, so: and when Schwarzenberg arrived at Lemberg on 30 May to take command of the Auxiliary Corps he was horrified at the shortage of equipment and at the deficiencies in the nominal strength of several units. But Metternich was not prepared to admit these weaknesses to Napoleon. He gave him satisfactory assurances and, towards the end of the Dresden Congress, Caulaincourt noted that Napoleon was speaking of the Austrian Foreign Minister in friendly and generous terms. Metternich himself was less pleased; for he was uneasily conscious that, despite his expansive generosity, Napoleon said nothing about a subsidy nor did he clarify his intentions for the future of Galicia.[44]

Dresden was essentially a hollow spectacle, less ornate than Erfurt but no more fruitful. No one, except the guest of honour, found pleasure in the series of strained entertainments which served as a substitute for deliberation. On 29 May as Napoleon's coach sped eastwards into Silesia, where Davout and Murat awaited their marching orders, the princes quietly and unceremoniously crept back to reality. Francis and Metternich went to Prague and Eleonore hurried to Vienna before setting out with the family to spend the summer months in Baden. Only Marie Louise lingered on in Dresden, carried in a gondola along the Elbe, visiting the sacred grove of elm trees at Tharandt, until at last even these relaxations began to pall and she, too, crossed the frontier into Bohemia to spend what remained of June amid the tragically proud beauty of Prague. There, like everyone else, she awaited confidently the Imperial bulletins announcing victory in the East.

PEACE AND WAR

Metternich, the Empress and the Archduke Joseph

The prestige and influence of Austria reached their nadir at Dresden and remained low throughout the next six months. The Emperor Francis was made aware of the contempt in which his subjects held him by the sullen indifference of the people at Prague; and Metternich had few illusions about his own unpopularity. Emperor and Minister lingered for almost seven weeks in Bohemia, mostly at Teplitz (Teplice), and it was not until 26 July that Metternich arrived back in Vienna. Prolonged absence from the capital had the advantage of protecting him from interrogation by over-zealous diplomats, and his own position was so uncertain that he had good reason to remain in close attendance on Francis that summer.

To the Empress and the Archdukes, Metternich was little more than Bonaparte's flunkey. They resented the hold he had acquired over Francis and, with veterans of the war party of 1809, sought means to discredit him. But events within the Habsburg realm played directly into Metternich's hands. In May the worst constitutional crisis in recent Hungarian history came to a head, when the Diet refused to grant an extraordinary subsidy and rejected other financial reforms. Against the advice of his brother (the Palatine Archduke Joseph), Francis dissolved the Diet and sought to establish in Hungary a similar autocratic administration to the other parts of the Empire. The Palatine was indignant and barely troubled to hide his feelings. Rumour unfairly credited him with a wish to be crowned King of Hungary, and the secret police were urged to intercept his correspondence once again. On Metternich's return to Vienna they presented him with a valuable weapon for use in his contest with the members of the Imperial family: for they had found a letter written by the Archduke Joseph on 8 July to his sister-in-law, the Empress Maria Ludovica. Although it was not a particularly damaging document, it criticized the Emperor's policy in general and his treatment of Hungary in particular. Nor did the secret police limit their snooping to the Archduke's postbag. They intercepted confidential letters from Maria Ludovica to Countess Esterhazy, one of her ladies-

D

in-waiting, and to the heir to the throne, the nineteen-year-old Arch-duke Ferdinand.[1] None of these letters was politically indiscreet. They showed the Empress to be in a state of high nervous depression, irritated by the haughty manners of Marie Louise and by the insincerity of the Austrian court officials. They also contained domestic complaints about the Emperor: his insistence on making her take long walks in the summer heat of Bohemia; his liking for tedious coach drives along im-possible roads. It was hardly the material on which a plot is hatched; but Metternich was determined to make political mischief.

On 13 August he informed Francis that a liaison was beginning be-tween the Palatine Archduke and the Empress: it was not, as yet, a serious matter and he urged Francis to treat it lightly and show 'paternal understanding' of any weaknesses; he excused his presumption in raising such a delicate topic with assertions of his desire to safeguard the Emperor's marriage from all scandalous talk. A strong Emperor would have resented his Minister's interference, but not Francis. He listened to Metternich's advice and he read the letters: he would not banish Archduke Joseph from court, nor dismiss him from his Hungarian responsibilities for this would have brought to a head a grave political crisis; but he seems to have urged restraint on both his wife and his brother, and the anti-Metternich cabal was effectively broken up. The episode reflects credit on neither the Emperor nor his Minister, but it is a significant commentary on their interdependence. By such intrigues Richelieu had climbed to greatness in France two centuries earlier. Beneath his polished manner and easy fluency Metternich was acquiring a ruthlessness as hard as steel; from now on it would be no easy task to sever the links by which he held the Emperor's confidence.

Austrian policy during the Russian campaign

His diplomacy was as devious as his political manoeuvres. Throughout the summer and autumn of 1812 he behaved as if Austria and Russia were still good neighbours, and there was no disruption of diplomatic relations between the two Empires. He seemed, indeed, determined to emphasize his friendliness towards the Tsar. Assurances of goodwill were despatched to St Petersburg both in the Emperor's name and in Metternich's. He attended the Russian ambassador's private recitals and his daughter Marie, who was then sixteen, enjoyed the Russian embassy ball that season, as did the daughters of most of the great families. Metternich himself spent more time than ever with Katharina Bagration, even though her husband was commanding Russia's Second Army against Austria's nominal ally that summer.*

* The fact that General Bagration was mortally wounded at Borodino in September gave to their passionate relationship a poignant irony.

At times in Vienna there was an almost defiant contempt for reality.[2]

The Austrians also sought a closer understanding with Napoleon's most persistent enemy. Although there was still no formal diplomatic contact, Metternich treated the Hanoverian Hardenberg as if he were a British envoy and saw to it that London remained aware of his desire to assert Austria's independence. In General Nugent he had a particularly valuable intermediary.[3] Nugent had left Vienna for England on 21 April bearing a personal letter from Francis to the Prince Regent in which he explained the delicate position of his Empire. It was not until the first week in September that Nugent landed at Falmouth, for communications were extremely difficult in a continent at war. After eighteen weeks Francis's message had little value, although much of it was so amiably formal that passage of time neither increased nor diminished its relevancy. While Nugent was on his travels, Castlereagh had become Foreign Secretary and although no one – including Castlereagh himself – anticipated that he would have more than a few months tenure of the office, it was important to discover the new personalities beginning to emerge in Lord Liverpool's administration. In Metternich's name, Nugent urged the British to intensify their efforts in Spain; and there were somewhat haphazard suggestions that the Royal Navy might be interested in supporting a resistance movement against the French in the Illyrian Provinces. It was a confused situation in which Metternich seemed so intent on defeating his own policy that the British understandably regarded both Nugent and the man who had sent him with cool distrust. An *émigré* Irish Catholic from Westmeath was not the ideal person to allay Castlereagh's suspicions.

The elusive character of Austrian diplomacy was symptomatic of the uncertainties caused by the 1812 campaign. When the Grand Army crossed the Niemen on 24 June there was a pause in the affairs of the continent. News travelled slowly, and as Napoleon advanced across the scorching Polish plains he became as isolated from the administration of his Empire as if he had been a fleet commander at sea.[4] He established a staging-post in Vilna, the former capital of Lithuania, and six diplomatic envoys took up residence there together with Maret, who had succeeded Champagny as Foreign Minister in the spring of 1811; but this cumbersome method of conducting foreign policy worked poorly, and inevitably the restraint which France had in previous years imposed upon her allies was considerably relaxed. So long as Napoleon was west of Smolensk, couriers could reach Vilna from his headquarters in four or five days and complete the journey to Paris in under a fortnight; but once he began to penetrate farther towards Moscow communication became harder and information was rapidly outdated by events. It was then that rumour turned expectancy into fevered speculation, so that when winter came dramatically in the first week of November the whole fabric of the Napoleonic Empire shook with hope or with apprehension.

Although Vienna was only half as distant from the crucial battle zone as Paris it took even longer for the news to get through. Floret was among the diplomats at Vilna and he made every effort to keep Metternich posted with the truth, but there were inevitable delays: it was 4 October before Vienna heard that Napoleon had entered burning Moscow three weeks previously; and on 8 November, when he was struggling back through a blizzard to Smolensk, Metternich still regarded the collapse of Russia as imminent and was only anxious not to be left out of the negotiations when the Tsar sued for peace.[5] It was not until the start of the second week in December, when Napoleon had already abandoned what remained of the Grand Army and was hastening back across Poland to Dresden and Paris, that Metternich began to appreciate the catastrophe which had overtaken the great enterprise. His mind and his loyalties were so flexible that he rapidly adjusted his policy to the new circumstances.[6] In the next three months he cautiously steered Austria away from the French connection while, at the same time, avoiding premature collaboration with Russia or subsequently with Prussia. He was by now too chastened by experience to believe in a grand crusade of liberation and his objectives were limited. By exploiting every opportunity as it presented itself, he hoped to assert Austria's genuine independence and to recover her influence over Germany and central Europe. Despite his wearisome propensity for enunciating general principles, he was fundamentally a pragmatist and offered no ready-made design for the rest of the continent. There are few occasions in his career which show such restraint and sense of timing.

The essentials of his policy were contained in a despatch which he addressed to Floret, whom he wrongly assumed to be still at Vilna, on 9 December. It began by expressing mildly ironical surprise that the Tsar had determined to fight on after the loss of Moscow, but it proceeded to argue that events had made peace essential. Since the conquest of Russia was impossible and since it was unlikely Napoleon or Alexander could agree on the terms of a separate peace, Metternich proposed that Austria should seek to negotiate a general settlement acceptable to all the combatants. He maintained that she was well qualified for this task because of the links she had kept with other nations and because Napoleon could expect sympathetic understanding from the representatives of a dynasty with which he was connected by marriage. 'When our exalted master was informed of the evacuation of Moscow,' Metternich concluded, 'he summarized the essence of his reaction in these few words: "The hour has come when I can show the Emperor of the French who I am".' Metternich himself underlined this passage in the despatch and instructed Floret to be certain Maret should know of the Emperor's words. The menace latent in their ambiguity could hardly be ignored: 'Any commentary,' added Metternich drily, 'would only detract from their forcefulness'.[7]

Yet neither Maret nor Napoleon was impressed by the Austrian attempt at mediation. The Emperor Francis sent a personal letter to his son-in-law five days before Christmas in which he echoed Metternich's views, but without any apparent effect on French policy. On New Year's Eve Napoleon gave an audience in the Tuileries to Count Bubna, the new Austrian ambassador, at which he spoke of plans to resume the campaign against Russia once the spring had come and demanded that Austria should double the size of her auxiliary corps.[8] Napoleon seems to have misunderstood the purpose of Metternich's policy, assuming that the Austrians wanted peace because they were afraid Russia would otherwise overrun Germany, Poland and the Danubian lands. He failed to distinguish between alarm at a new invasion and desire for independence; he was prepared to allow Metternich to sound out the possibilities of a general settlement but he did not take it very seriously. Napoleon had encountered Metternich's longing to be a grand mediator in other years, and there seemed no reason why he should have any more success on this occasion. Metternich himself believed that 'Austria is strong through the exhaustion of the two other Imperial courts'; but Napoleon refused to admit he had suffered more than a temporary setback.[9] As a military commander he was far more interested in the future of Schwarzenberg's auxiliary corps. In 1812 it had effectively avoided the unseemliness of battle and the indelicacy of pursuit. The 1813 campaign would require a less fastidious approach to military operations.

Attempts at a General Settlement (1813)

Throughout the first four months of 1813 the Austrians pressed Napoleon to accept peace. In a series of conversations with the French ambassador, Metternich sought to convert the Franco-Austrian alliance into an instrument for ending the war: 'When it comes to anything which touches the soil of France,' he explained, 'Napoleon and the Empress's father, as grandfather of the successor to the (French) throne, must think alike.'[10] Already Metternich had in mind a negotiated settlement which would leave a Bonaparte-Habsburg dynasty secure in France and in Europe. This was to be a recurrent theme of Austrian policy for the remainder of the year; but Napoleon had so often paid lip-service to family sentiment in his approaches to Vienna that he remained indifferent to Metternich's words. He was still a man who spoke the language of war, and that winter he was immersed in administrative detail, improvising a Grand Army from half-trained conscripts; what, he kept wondering, was Schwarzenberg doing?

He learnt Schwarzenberg's intentions early in February, and the information was hardly pleasing. Count Bubna read to him a letter, nominally from the Emperor Francis but drafted by Metternich, in which the Austrians notified the French that, because of the changing situation in the East, it had become necessary for Schwarzenberg to withdraw the auxiliary corps to Cracow and conclude an armistice with the Russians.[11] Napoleon was too shocked by the news even to be angry with Bubna. It was the first totally independent act of foreign policy with which the Austrians had dared to confront him since their defeat at Wagram, and he was powerless to do anything about it. Schwarzenberg would defend Austria's frontiers against any invader but, having watched the drama of 1812 from the wings, he had no intention of taking the stage in its sequel.

Yet Metternich continued to acknowledge limits to his freedom of action. For a brief moment in the middle of January 1813 he considered the possibility of collaborating with Prussia as a 'third force' to impose a barrier between the French and Russian antagonists. The Prussian government was in a far more desperate situation than the Austrian: General Yorck's corps had defected to the Tsar's army at the end of December; and there was an imminent threat of a Russian invasion. The Prussian Chancellor, Karl von Hardenberg,* accordingly sent General von dem Knesebeck from Berlin on a diplomatic mission to Metternich. Knesebeck proposed a political and military alliance and an eventual division of Germany: a Prussian sphere of influence in the north and an Austrian in the south. It was a tempting offer, but it would have meant a final breach between Austria and France and the loss of Metternich's bargaining position. He preferred to remain on the sidelines as long as possible, and he even advised Knesebeck that Prussia should seek her own terms with Russia.[12] Austria was still not ready for war. Better a Russo-Prussian combination than an ineffectual pan-German alliance.

Meanwhile Metternich persevered with his efforts to secure a general settlement. He sent Baron Lebzeltern to Russian headquarters at Kalisch and Johann von Wessenberg to London. Neither envoy brought peace appreciably nearer. Lebzeltern did at least obtain from Tsar Alexander a vague statement of war aims: it was gratifying to discover that these included the restoration of Austria's lost territories, the expulsion of the French from Germany, and the resurrection of the old German Empire under Habsburg leadership; but there was no reason why at the moment Napoleon should accept any of these conditions. Wessenberg had less success. He even failed to gain acceptance into

* The Prussian Chancellor was a cousin of Count Hardenberg, the Hanoverian intermediary between Vienna and London. Metternich had first met Karl von Hardenberg in Berlin in 1803 (see p. 40).

London society. Castlereagh complained that Metternich was still totally submissive to French designs; and Lord Liverpool, the Prime Minister, wrote that 'Nothing could be more abject than the councils of Vienna at this time'.[13] Wellington was by now confident of final victory in Spain once the spring rains had ceased and, after twenty years of war, the British had no wish to scatter the laurels of triumph in a second Truce of Amiens.

There were good reasons why Wessenberg should be treated so coolly in London: Austrian policy, which had seemed excessively devious to Castlereagh during Nugent's visit, was as full of intrigues and counter-plots as a Goldoni comedy, although with far more sinister undertones. There was, for example, the case of the unfortunate Joseph Danelon, who had once been British Vice-Consul in Trieste, and now served as a courier for an unofficial British agent in Vienna, the Honourable John Harcourt King. Danelon, with a passport issued by Metternich, was waylaid by brigands on 25 February in Bohemia while travelling to St Petersburg with despatches for Castlereagh. Among the documents plundered at the time were letters from King rashly giving details of an insurrection planned for Easter in the Tyrol which would be stirred up by several of the patriots who had worked with Metternich in 1809 and which had the active support of the Archduke John. The British believed Metternich had at one time sympathized with the project and Nugent had certainly encouraged its extension to Dalmatia. But on the night of 7 March Metternich suddenly struck at the conspirators, using the information gained from Danelon's papers to justify his actions to the Emperor Francis. There were wholesale arrests and the Archduke John was banished from court and placed under surveillance; and one of Wessenberg's tasks in London was to demand the recall of the indiscreet King.[14] Small wonder that Britain and Austria tended to drift apart, or that the British representatives with the Tsar's army of liberation continued to regard every move made by Metternich in the summer of 1813 with apprehension and distrust.

Many Austrians, too, were puzzled and angered by his tardiness in aligning the Emperor Francis with the angels of retribution. Stadion openly refused to serve Austria so long as Metternich maintained his policy of appeasing the French and he was supported by Baron Baldacci, who had exercised considerable influence over Francis in earlier years. Some of Metternich's opponents went further than this: two officers were arrested at the end of February for planning to assassinate the Foreign Minister 'on his way back from a house to which he goes frequently' (as the French ambassador wrote, with exquisite tact, to Paris).[15] And there was more trouble in that same month from the Archduke Joseph, whose postbag had been profitably raided yet again. But the Emperor Francis was still heart and soul with his Minister.

Within a week of hearing of the alleged assassination plot, the Emperor created Metternich Grand-Chancellor of the Order of Maria Theresa, a post which no one had held since the death of Kaunitz. Stadion, Baldacci and the others had received their answer.

By the spring of 1813 both Francis and Metternich were alarmed by the trend of events in the German lands. The Prussians had allied with Russia at the end of February and declared war on France in mid-March. This development had been anticipated by Metternich and did not cause him particular concern. The man whose voice counted in Germany was not, however, Hardenberg but Stein, the Prussian reformer who had attached himself to Alexander's cause in 1812 and returned as the Tsar's administrator of the territories occupied by the Russian Army. To Metternich, Stein seemed to preach a gospel of revolution, inciting the German people to rise and fight a patriot's war against the French and against their own princes. A national crusade in the name of 'a vigorous and united Germany' was no less a menace to Habsburg authority than the doctrines which had permeated the universities of Strasbourg and Mainz so long ago. In 1809 Metternich had himself played with the fire of patriotic insurrection, although he had never kindled it with the enthusiasm of a Stadion or an Archduke John: but in 1813 the torches were in the hands of Stein and Tsar Alexander, and both Francis and Metternich feared they would brandish them with indiscriminate irresponsibility. A peace which preserved the German dynasties and the Napoleonic order west of the Rhine had become an urgent necessity. If British suspicion ruled out a general settlement, then it was essential for Austria to take the lead in negotiating a continental peace. 'Prolongation of war will soon threaten the existence of thrones, since it does not permit the sovereigns to devote themselves seriously to stamping down the Jacobin ferment, which grows daily,' wrote Francis to Napoleon early in April. It was a clear enough warning; but Napoleon had a different answer to the menace of popular revolt. On 15 April he left St Cloud for the Rhine and a new campaign in Germany. Marie Louise was appointed Regent in his absence: she was instructed to write to her father once a week, to send him details of military operations, and to assure him of his son-in-law's affection. 'Papa François', as Napoleon called the Austrian Emperor, had hoped for a different response.[16]

Slowly and reluctantly Metternich was moving towards armed intervention. Austria began to mobilize in early April: sixty-four thousand men concentrated in Bohemia guarded the frontier against invaders from either side; and another 100,000 reservists were ordered to report to their units before the beginning of May. The army was scarcely more ready for war than it had been a year before: there was a shortage of greatcoats and of boots; but there was a willing acceptance of the need for another campaign against the French, and echoes of the patriotic sentiments of 1809. Stadion and Baldacci joined Metternich in urging the issue of new paper money in order to finance the enlarged army, an inflationary measure against which Wallis rightly but vainly protested. Francis himself had considerable doubts over the wisdom of mobilization and of abandoning the appeasement of his son-in-law; and his fears were increased by the two early victories gained by Napoleon in the 1813 campaign, at Lützen on 2 May and at Bautzen on 20–21 May. Metternich, however, maintained the French successes restored a proper balance between the antagonists, and therefore improved prospects for a compromise peace.[17] After Lützen he sent Bubna to Napoleon's head-quarters near Dresden and Stadion (who was prepared to co-operate now that the army was mobilizing) to the Russo-Prussian headquarters at Görlitz, to the east of Dresden. At the same time he persuaded the Emperor Francis, with some difficulty, to show a resolution he did not possess and put himself at the head of his army in Bohemia. In the last week of May the Emperor left Vienna and three days later arrived at the castle of Gitschin (Jicin) where he was close to the battle zone and only eighty miles south-west of Napoleon at Dresden.

There were differences in the peace terms offered by Stadion at Görlitz and by Bubna at Dresden.[18] Stadion was instructed to inform the Tsar that ultimately Austria sought the surrender of all territory annexed by the French in Germany east of the Rhine, in Holland and in Italy as well as all Austrian possessions acquired since 1801: but as a minimal programme the Austrians would be content with the recovery of Illyria, dissolution of the Duchy of Warsaw, a new frontier with Bavaria, and a different status for the Confederation of the Rhine. Bubna, on the other hand, was to ask Napoleon for the surrender of the French possessions on the right bank of the Rhine, re-partition of the Grand-Duchy of Warsaw, the return to Austria of the Illyrian Provinces, frontier adjustments in Italy, and the placing of the Rhenish Confed-eration under an international protectorate.

Neither the Tsar nor Napoleon was prepared to accept Metternich's proposals for peace as they stood. This is hardly surprising, for they possessed a chameleon quality, especially over the future of the Rhenish Confederation, and any experienced diplomat would have regarded them with considerable mistrust. But the French and the Russo-Prussian allies wanted, if not peace, at least an armistice. So, for that matter, did the Austrian General Staff: Napoleon was short of cavalry horses and ammunition; the Russians and Prussians, twice defeated, needed to reorganize their armies; and Austrian mobilization had shown such weakness that the generals believed they could not take the field until the second week of July. When in the first days of June the French proposed to call a halt to all military operations, the offer was generally welcomed both for its own sake and as proof that Napoleon had for once begun a campaign which he could not bring to the boil. An armistice was concluded at Plaeswitz on 4 June and was to remain valid until 20 July. The continent was thus given six weeks in which to decide if it was to be peace, or war to the end. Metternich personally still hoped that the choice would be for peace, and believed it to be attainable; but there were others in the Austrian service – prominent among them Stadion – who were opposed to any settlement with France short of total victory, and they were prepared to commit Austria more firmly to the 'Good Cause' of anti-Bonapartism than Metternich desired.

Hitherto Metternich had entrusted all attempts at mediation to the diplomats, but it now became essential for him to be with the Emperor in Bohemia, which was at that moment the nerve centre of Europe. On 1 June he set out from Vienna for Gitschin, accompanied by Gentz: Baron Joseph von Hudelist was left in charge of the administration of the Austrian foreign service during the Minister's absence. After Bautzen the Tsar withdrew Russo-Prussian headquarters from Görlitz to Reichenbach (now known as Dzierzoniow) in Silesia, a town little more than fifty miles east of Gitschin; and during the armistice interlude all diplomatic activity was concentrated within a triangle formed by Dresden, Prague and Reichenbach and within which Gitschin was almost at the centre. Metternich confessed in a note to his daughter, Marie, that he was uneasy at the thought of the hundreds and thousands of troops ready and at arms in the hills beyond Gitschin Castle. But, if so, Metternich well disguised his inner feelings. He was what he had long sought to be, the arbiter of Europe; and the taste of power was sweet, even if it rested on an unshod army and the promissory notes of an inflated economy.[19]

The heightened sense of drama with which he was living necessitated, as on other occasions, a recipient of confidences. He found her, close at hand, in Wilhelmine of Sagan whom he had known since his days at the Saxon court. Wilhelmine possessed an impressive town palace in Prague and, more conveniently still, a small château at Ratiborzitz, on the slopes of the Sudeten mountains only a few miles north of Gitschin. That summer Wilhelmine became his principal mistress, and her personality continued to captivate him long after the armies had moved away from 'the Duchess of Sagan's paradise' in Bohemia: he maintained a regular correspondence with her throughout the second half of 1813 and for most of the following year, writing late into the night after days of tension and dispute. It is difficult to understand why, once absent from her, he remained bewitched. She was a woman of capricious temperament and there were moments when her whirl of ecstasy and passion imposed a burden on his literary conceits and patience. Love was the mainspring of her being, perhaps even her vocation; but it never breathed the warmth of understanding nor ultimately of trust. From his conversations with Gentz it is clear that Metternich had few illusions over Wilhelmine. Yet, though maddened time and again by the flicker of her fancy, he returned constantly to her flame. None of his other mistresses ever achieved such mastery of his will. But in those long midsummer days of 1813 it was pleasant enough to take advantage of her hospitality, supping at her table, or walking urbanely under the conifers of Ratiborzitz awaiting a summons to discuss peace with the Tsar or the Emperor of the French.[20]

Metternich had wished at an early stage to meet the French Foreign Minister and discover what sort of settlement Napoleon had in mind, but Maret was evasive. At the same time, however, Metternich had made personal contact with the Russians, both through Stadion and through the Tsar's sister, who was staying in Prague and was willing to serve as an intermediary. Alexander agreed to cross the Austrian frontier in the third week of June and spend some days at Count Colloredo's castle of Opotschna, which was not far from Ratiborzitz. Even in this serious hour for Europe, there was a touch of farce in the proceedings: for the Tsar, unable to resist the charms of the Duchess of Sagan, gave her twenty-four hours notice that he would pay her a visit, thereby narrowly missing an impromptu encounter with Metternich (who generously postponed his own trip to Ratiborzitz and lent Wilhelmine a valet as she was short of domestic staff).[21]

The Tsar and Metternich duly held their more formal conversations at Opotschna on 18–19 June.[22] They had not met since the feverish negotiations at Berlin which had preceded the Austerlitz disaster of 1805. Since then both their countries had suffered humiliations although, in the Tsar's eyes, all past failures were redeemed by the resolution which had carried his armies to victory after the loss of Moscow in the previous autumn. Metternich found Alexander at first suspected him 'of being totally on the side of the French' and the talks began coldly. Stadion had undertaken good preparatory work on the peace negotiations but his own prejudice against Metternich's old policy of appeasement may have intensified the Tsar's natural distrust of the man responsible for the Bonaparte-Habsburg marriage. He was obstinately set against any 'accommodated peace' with Napoleon.

There was, nevertheless, some general agreement. Four fundamental points, already discussed between Stadion and the Allies, were accepted as a basis for peace: the end of direct French military control of the Rhenish Confederation and the restoration of Hamburg and Lübeck as Free Cities; recovery of lost territory by Prussia; the return of the Illyrian Provinces to Austria; and the dissolution of the Grand-Duchy of Warsaw. If Napoleon had not agreed on these terms as a preliminary for a peace conference by 20 July Austria would join the Russo-

Prussian coalition in a renewal of the war and would insist on continuing hostilities until Napoleon was ready to concede the independence of Holland, Spain, and the Italian states and the dissolution of the Rhenish Confederation. These proposals, agreed verbally at Opotschna, were subsequently embodied in the Reichenbach Convention which was concluded by Austria, Prussia and Russia on 27 June.*

Metternich returned from Opotschna to find Karl von Hardenberg enjoying the beauty of Ratiborzitz, and the company of its chatelaine. But he barely had time to let the Prussian Minister know of his conversations with the Tsar, for an invitation to visit Dresden awaited him at Gitschin. He wrote immediately to Stadion at Reichenbach: 'You see that my evil star is calling me to Dresden . . . The conversation will lead to nothing.'[23] This pessimistic message was, however, for the Tsar's consumption. At heart Metternich was eager to win Napoleon over to a policy of common sense. The terms agreed at Opotschna were moderate: it should still have been possible to establish a continental peace, and perhaps even a peace with England, which would leave Napoleon on the throne of France and Marie Louise's son as his heir. Metternich set out for Dresden as early as possible on the morning of Thursday, 24 June; he had every confidence in the impression he would make upon Napoleon.

His arrival, however, was inauspicious. He reached Dresden on Friday afternoon, 25 June, but found to his annoyance that Napoleon was evidently in no hurry to receive him, for he had immediately left the city and ridden out to inspect troops at Koenigsbruck. An audience was duly arranged for Metternich with Napoleon at the Marcolini Palace after the morning parade on Saturday, 26 June. It began at a quarter to twelve and continued until half-past eight in the evening. King Frederick Augustus of Saxony arrived for a meeting with Napoleon that afternoon but, after a long wait in an antechamber of his own palace, he was sent away unreceived. By now the unfortunate King was resigned to such slights.

Audience with Napoleon at Dresden (June 1813)

The Dresden interview in the Marcolini Palace, like the scene at St Cloud in August 1808, is a set-piece enshrined in the Metternich legend.[24] But whereas at St Cloud there had been many witnesses, at Dresden what was said and done was known only to the two protagonists, and it is hard to separate reality from the later embellishments of Metternich's literary licence. We read of bluster and bombast and

* The Reichenbach Convention was signed by Stadion on behalf of the Emperor Francis and not by Metternich, who was in Dresden on 27 June. Metternich was thus able to maintain during the Dresden discussions that he had, as yet, concluded no formal engagement with the Allied powers; but the French were too experienced in such arts to be fooled by diplomatic casuistry.

affectionate reconciliation, of anxious marshals and ministers waiting outside, of a hat hurled angrily into a corner, and of prophecies from an unruffled Metternich of imminent disaster. 'At this decisive moment,' he wrote many years later, 'I saw myself as the representative of the whole society of Europe. Shall I say it? Napoleon seemed small to me.' For the sake of his reputation it would have been better not to 'say it', since at that point in his narrative our sympathies turn inevitably away from the arrogant career politician to the victor of Austerlitz and Wagram; but the remark was true in the sense that Metternich was seeking the general stability of the European order whereas by now Napoleon had become convinced that, once he began to surrender his conquests beyond the Rhine, the very existence of his throne was in danger. 'My reign will not outlast the day when I have ceased to be strong, and therefore to be feared.' Although the words may have been written into Napoleon's script retrospectively, the sentiment at least has the ring of authenticity.

Napoleon himself said jauntily after the interview that he had had a 'good fight' with Metternich: 'Thirteen times I threw the gauntlet down and thirteen times he picked it up again, but the last time it stayed in my hands'.[25] Both participants were therefore not unsatisfied at the outcome of the stormy debate, and one wishes more than ever that there was a reliable record of their verbal exchanges. Yet historically it matters little what was said and done at the famous confrontation: it was good theatre rather than decisive diplomacy. So long as Napoleon believed that he held half of Europe in his hands and could dictate from strength the agenda of a peace congress, genuine negotiation was out of the question. Once again, as in May 1812, there was a strange artificiality over the proceedings at Dresden; but this time they were ominously different in character.

Metternich stayed on in Dresden for another four days. He sent an express courier to Schwarzenberg, the Austrian Commander-in-Chief, to know how much longer it would take to complete mobilization; and was told that, with three weeks grace, the army could be augmented by another seventy-five thousand men. He sounded out Maret, Berthier, and other leading figures in Napoleon's entourage. Compromise proposals were at last handed to him on Tuesday afternoon, 29 June, but he turned them down and ordered his carriage for seven the next morning. As he was about to leave, he was summoned urgently to the Marcolini Palace. Napoleon walked with him around the neat gravelled paths of the garden, quietly discussing the possibility of a conference. At last they reached agreement and adjourned to the study, where Maret joined them. A note was hurriedly written and signed: the French would accept the armed mediation of the Austrians; peace talks would open between the belligerents in Prague on 10 July; and there

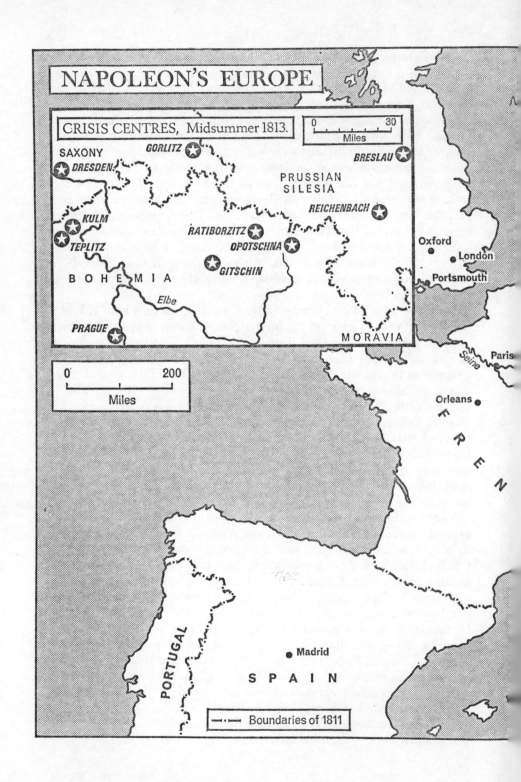

NAPOLEON'S EUROPE

CRISIS CENTRES, Midsummer 1813.

0   30
Miles

SAXONY
DRESDEN
GORLITZ
BRESLAU

PRUSSIAN
SILESIA

KULM
REICHENBACH

TEPLITZ
RATIBORZITZ
OPOTSCHNA

BOHEMIA
GITSCHIN

Elbe

PRAGUE
MORAVIA

Oxford
London
Portsmouth

Seine
Paris

Orleans

FREN

0   200
Miles

PORTUGAL

Madrid

SPAIN

—·—· Boundaries of 1811

RUSSIAN
EMPIRE

Baltic Sea

'th

a

Vilna

Tilsit

P R U S S I A

Berlin

GRAND DUCHY
OF
WARSAW

Vistula

Warsaw

CONFEDERATION

Brussels

Cologne

Leipzig

SAXONY

Dresden

Cracow

GALICIA

Erfurt

Coblenz

Gitschin

Frankfurt

Teplitz

Prague

Mainz

Würzburg

BOHEMIA
Königswart

Austerlitz

OF THE

Trier

MORAVIA

Rhine

Moselle

Meuse

Strasbourg

Stuttgart

Danube

Linz

Wagram

Pressburg

Marne

Chaumont

Rastatt

Munich

Melk

Vienna

Chatillon

Freiburg

Salzburg

AUSTRIAN

EMPIRE

Dijon

RHINE

B A V A R I A

Buda

Pest

Basle

SWITZERLAND

Innsbruck

TYROL

H U N G A R Y

KINGDOM

ILLYRIAN
PROVINCES

Milan

OF

Venice

ITALY

Po

DALMATIA

Danube

E

M

P

Adriatic Sea

OTTOMAN
EMPIRE

Elba

Rome

KINGDOM OF
NAPLES

Naples

Cattaro

Corfu

would be no military operations before 10 August. These conditions were very different from the proposals Metternich had discussed with the Tsar at Opotschna, but he was so anxious to preserve the Bonapartist state as a counterweight to Russia and Prussia in the new Europe that he signed them rather than set out for Gitschin empty-handed. Within an hour he had left Dresden. He was never to meet Napoleon again. 'It was a very friendly leave-taking', wrote Gentz in his diary on Metternich's return.[26]

The Abortive Conference of Prague and the Austrian Declaration of War (August 1813)

The Russians and Prussians were angry with the Austrian Minister. He had, on his own initiative, extended the Plaeswitz Armistice by three weeks, and the Dresden agreement seemed to make nonsense of the Opotschna talks and the Reichenbach Convention. Tsar Alexander's mistrust of Metternich speedily came to the surface once more. He excused his conduct on two counts: the need to convince Francis that everything had been attempted to reach an accommodation with his son-in-law and thus to avoid war; and the certainty that the Prague Conference would be a failure, but would help to weaken Napoleon since time was now on the side of the Allies.[27] Neither argument was sound, nor indeed sincere. Metternich still hoped, although with diminishing confidence, it would be possible to negotiate peace; and even obtained from Francis permission to drop the demand for restoration of the Illyrian Provinces if such a concession could win Napoleon to accept a general settlement. It made very little difference. Armand Caulaincourt, the chief French representative, did not arrive in Prague until 28 July and his instructions limited him to sounding out the Allied delegates. Napoleon refused to grant Caulaincourt authority to discuss the Reichenbach proposals, and the Conference therefore never technically met in a plenary session.[28] There were useful discussions between Metternich and Caulaincourt from which it became clear that he personally wished for peace, but believed that Napoleon would only negotiate when an Allied army was poised on the frontiers of metropolitan France. Thus paradoxically Caulaincourt, although as anxious as Francis and Metternich to safeguard the Bonapartist throne, completed their conversion to the war party. On 8 August Metternich presented him with a virtual ultimatum. No reply had been received by the night of 10–11 August. At midnight Metternich announced that the Conference was dissolved and ordered beacons to be lit on the hills around Prague to put Schwarzenberg's army on the alert. On 12 August Austria formally declared war on France; and within a few days the rival armies were locked in battle for the fifth time in a generation.

NEGOTIATING VALIANTLY

Allied disunity

The declaration of war in 1813 was interpreted by both the Russians and the Prussians as a defeat for Austrian policy. Metternich had set out from Vienna in June as the Grand Mediator, the saviour who would reconcile the sovereigns of East and West and restore a balance in the European state community. Now, nine weeks later, he became junior partner in a coalition against the French, overshadowed by the prestige of the Tsar and politically inconvenienced by bargains already struck by the Prussians and Russians with each other and with the British.* There was, in Alexander's eyes, no need any more to conciliate or cajole the Austrian leaders: they would fall in dutifully behind him on the triumphant march to Paris. And German nationalists, who were fully aware of Metternich's reservation towards liberal enthusiasm, confidently believed that as an ally he would at least recognize the ideal of a Fatherland: for was he not, like Heinrich vom Stein, a dispossessed Rhenish aristocrat? It was time for pan-German sentiment to show itself as more than a myth.

Metternich, however, saw things differently. The beacons on the hills were not for him a signal of failure, but of manoeuvre. He was prepared to associate Austria with the other Allies against Napoleon but he had no intention of becoming an instrument of Russian policy, nor of committing himself to Stein's nationalism. For over a week after the declaration of war he maintained contact with the French, refusing to give up hope that Caulaincourt or the Marshals would persuade their Emperor to join Austria in securing peace before hot-headed idealists swept away Europe's identity in a ferment of patriot zeal. Metternich successfully safeguarded the independence of Austrian policy at the very

* There were two principal agreements: the Russo-Prussian Treaty of Kalisch (February 1813), primarily a military alliance but containing vague provisions by which the King of Prussia would surrender some of his Polish lands to the Tsar and receive compensation within Germany, probably in the Rhineland and Saxony; and the Treaty of Reichenbach (14 June 1813) by which Britain provided a £2 million subsidy to Russia and Prussia, undertaking to support the restoration of Prussian territory as in 1806 in return for Prussian recognition of the integrity of Hanover.

beginning of the campaign. On 6 August the Tsar had reluctantly accepted the appointment of Schwarzenberg as supreme commander of the Allied armies; but eleven days later Alexander requested the post for himself. Metternich insisted on having Schwarzenberg's appointment confirmed and threatened that, if the Tsar persisted in seeking the high command, Austria would withdraw from all further participation in the campaign and leave the Allies to settle, as best they could, with Napoleon. There was even a possibility that Austria might place Schwarzenberg's army at the service of Napoleon, if he wished to impose a lasting peace on the Russians. The episode was a salutary warning to Alexander, but it did not make him feel any kinder towards Metternich.[1]

On paper all the military advantages lay with the Allied commanders. Their armies numbered in August 1813 more than 800,000 men – Austrians, Russians, Prussians and Swedes, who fought in northern Germany and were commanded by Bernadotte. Napoleon had mustered some 700,000 troops but many of them were raw conscripts and the loyalty of several contingents, notably the Bavarians and Saxons, was highly suspect. Rarely, however, has there been such lack of unity or such divided counsels as among the leaders of the Allied coalition in the seven months which followed Schwarzenberg's appointment. In earlier years Napoleon would have had no difficulty in exploiting their petty enmities and mistrust. Neither the Russians nor the Prussians treated Schwarzenberg with respect and he was plagued by interference from the Tsar and the Prussian commanders. Metternich was forced to negotiate day by day and step by step as the Allies moved forwards. He insisted that the three monarchs (Alexander, Frederick William III, and Francis) and their ministers should follow the armies across Germany and into France, for fear that otherwise all cohesion would come to an end and the Tsar be left supreme master of the Allied troops. It was, he confessed, as essential to keep an eye on friends as on enemies.[2]

Even so, there were bad moments when it looked as if the Allied will to hold together would prove as irresolute as in 1805. Alexander insisted on Schwarzenberg ordering a frontal assault on Dresden in the fourth week of August, against the advice of both Metternich and the Emperor Francis. They were so indignant with the Tsar that they declined to accompany him to the Racknitz Heights to observe the fall of the Saxon capital.[3] Their instinct was right: they were spared the alarming sight of the Old Guard sweeping down to the Elbe in a long dark line and snatching for Napoleon a victory which forced the Allies to fall back through the Erzegebirge and over the Austrian frontier. Momentarily there was a fear that Napoleon might strike towards Prague or towards Berlin, and the Russian command chafed at Schwarzenberg's indecision. But the French had not the resources to exploit their success at Dresden. On 29 August the reckless Vandamme brought the French First Corps to within five miles of the Allied headquarters at Teplitz. Among the Allied sovereigns only Frederick William of Prussia seems to have kept his head. While the Tsar and Metternich desperately sought reinforcements, Frederick William encouraged Ostermann to stand firm against Vandamme rather than fall back on the Elbe. And on the following day Kleist surprised Vandamme from the rear at Kulm, taking him prisoner and checking for all time Napoleon's thrust into the Austrian lands.* In later years Metternich looked back on Kulm as the decisive moment in the campaign, and it was certainly the one in which his own situation was most precarious. Vandamme's failure nullified the effects of the Battle of Dresden; but the Prussians insisted on regarding Kulm as primarily a triumph for their staff-work and enterprise, and it made Schwarzenberg's task as supreme commander no simpler. He was prepared to wait circumspectly in the hills along the Saxon-Bohemian frontier until Napoleon sued for peace or over-reached himself. Such caution was not popular with the Tsar or the Prussians.

It was only in the last week of September that Schwarzenberg began to move forward through western Saxony on Chemnitz and towards Leipzig. There was thus an interlude of four wet and dismal autumn weeks in which Metternich remained with the Allied monarchs at Teplitz. Militarily the situation was unpromising. The British ambassador to Russia, Lord Cathcart, explained the peculiar conditions of life in Teplitz when he wrote to Castlereagh on 7 September: 'In a residence where there are three sovereigns, three courts, three ministers, and three headquarters, there are of course many parties, many rumours, and great variety in stating the same matters of fact,' he said and added wearily, 'It is difficult to ascertain the truth.'⁴ But Metternich does not appear to have found Teplitz so disagreeable. He returned there many times after the wars had ended, and nearly always wrote nostalgically in his private letters of the crisis days in 1813.⁵

The truth was that, during this pause in the campaign, Metternich achieved considerable diplomatic success. The Tsar and the King of Prussia had been anxious to bind Emperor Francis to a formal alliance as soon as the Prague Conference broke down. Metternich, however, was cautious. He did not wish to commit Austria to any treaty which might rule out a negotiated peace with Napoleon; and he had no intention of accepting a programme for the future of Poland or the German lands which tied Austria's hands. He had his way. On 9 September Russia, Austria and Prussia signed three bilateral pacts, known collectively as the Teplitz Treaties. Outwardly they consisted of declarations of solidarity and mutual assistance; and the two agree-

---

* Napoleon personally considered a further assault on the Kulm-Teplitz region on 10 September, but abandoned the idea when he found the roads through the mountains too bad for his artillery.

ments with which Austria was concerned defined the principal war aim
as 're-establishment of a just equilibrium between the powers'. But the
significant clauses of the treaties were not published: Austria and
Prussia were to recover 'as closely as possible' the extent of territory each
possessed in 1805; the Confederation of the Rhine would be dissolved
and the middle German states accorded 'entire and absolute independence'; and the fate of the Grand-Duchy of Warsaw would be settled 'by
an amicable arrangement between the three courts'. No terms could
have been better devised for enabling Metternich to find room for
manoeuvre in later negotiations. He had shirked the issue over both
Poland and Germany, but he had said no word at all of Austrian intentions in Italy and the south. Both Hardenberg and Alexander believed they had brought the Austrians to heel. But Metternich knew
better. Writing to Hudelist on 1 October he explained: 'The difference
in the situation of the governments is this, that Russia orders Prussia
about at her pleasure, while we intend to manage Russia and will.'[6]

These problems were difficult enough: they were further complicated
by the unusual form of the coalition. Both Russia and Prussia had
political contacts with Britain and were benefiting from British subsidies. Cathcart was in attendance on Tsar Alexander at headquarters
throughout the 1813–14 campaign; and the British Minister to Prussia,
Sir Charles Stewart (Castlereagh's half-brother) enjoyed ready access
to Frederick William III and to Hardenberg, especially as he also held an
active military command in the Brandenburg Hussars. Although Cathcart and Stewart were often at cross-purposes, they made it clear to the
governments to whom they were accredited that no more money would
come from London if Britain's wishes were disregarded in shaping the
future of Europe. Metternich found they virtually imposed a power of
veto on proposals for a purely 'continental' territorial settlement. It was
difficult for Metternich to influence British policy: Cathcart and
Stewart treated him with suspicion; and Castlereagh in London could
not shake off his conviction that the Austrians were treacherous and
dissimulating. Poor Wessenberg was still cold-shouldered in London and
all his efforts to secure a British subsidy for Austria had come to nothing.
There was clearly a need to improve contact between the British and
Austrian governments. Metternich, for his part, had no wish to impede
possible negotiations with Napoleon by insisting on recognition of
Britain's 'maritime rights' and her championship of an independent
Netherlands; but, with Wellington's army ready to assail the ramparts
of the Pyrenees and carry the war into France itself, the Austrians could
no longer ignore Castlereagh's ideas on the shape of the new Europe.
And the wealth of the City of London remained a considerable attraction; for a generous subsidy would satisfy Wallis and all Metternich's
other critics in Vienna. It was worth signing a treaty of alliance with

Britain for the promise of a million pounds; it was even worth receiving a British ambassador, however assertive he might be, for another agitated voice in Teplitz could make little difference to the babel of conflicting opinion at headquarters. He might oppose Cathcart or Stewart or both. Perhaps, though this seemed unlikely, he would support the Austrian cause.[7]

The diplomat sent by Castlereagh to Teplitz early in September was so amiably ineffectual that he caused Metternich few worries. Lord Aberdeen at twenty-nine knew little of France and less of Germany; but he had all the right social graces. His talk was already rich in reminiscence and, when he wished, he could contrast the dining habits of the First Consul at Malmaison with those of Ali Pasha at Janina.[8] He was a dilettante classical archaeologist, who had excavated the Pnyx at Athens in a moment of philhellenic enthusiasm; and he still possessed all the buoyant confidence of youth. Unfortunately he was easily flattered by Metternich's attention. After fully two month's acquaintance with the Austrian Foreign Minister, Aberdeen sent back to London a letter of good advice: 'Do not think Metternich such a formidable personage, my dear Castlereagh,' he wrote. 'Living with him at all times, and in all situations, is it possible that I should not know him? If indeed he were the most subtle of all mankind, he might certainly impose on one little used to deceive, but this is not his character. He is, I repeat to you, not a very clever man.'[9]

Metternich, more succinctly, dubbed Aberdeen 'that dear simpleton of diplomacy.'[10] Within three weeks of their first encounter an Anglo-Austrian treaty was drafted and signed. Metternich gave a pledge that the Habsburg Empire would never conclude a separate peace: he was assured, in return, of the subsidy which he had sought. When, however, Aberdeen wished to discuss possible terms for a general settlement he found Metternich less forthcoming. Over the future of Italy he was darkly oracular and Aberdeen appears to have given him verbal concessions which Castlereagh had never authorized him to make, particularly over Naples and Sicily. There was talk in London of sending Castlereagh himself to give substance to British counsels; but it was nearly seventy years since a Secretary of State responsible for foreign affairs had left the United Kingdom for negotiations on the continent, and the cabinet was slow to make up its mind over such a novelty in constitutional practice. Castlereagh's health was poor and he had no wish to winter in Germany with all those foreign statesmen, certainly not before Christmas. Like Gladstone many years later, Castlereagh had confidence in Aberdeen's solidity of judgement; but it must be admitted that in those days there was little sign in him of that canny caution which Queen Victoria found so re-assuring in her Prime Minister of mid-century.

The Battle of Leipzig and the advance to the Rhine

In the first week of October the campaign moved north-westwards into Germany, with three Allied armies bearing down on Napoleon as he concentrated his troops at Leipzig. The Allies outnumbered the French by three to one, and it was clear by 12 October that a decisive battle was imminent. The three sovereigns, with their ministers and envoys, accompanied Schwarzenberg as ever. But the supreme commander was reluctant to order a simultaneous attack by the Allied columns on the city, fearing that the battle might turn into another Dresden. He was urged on by Blücher and by the Tsar. After a preliminary skirmish on 14 October, the main conflict began on 16 October and lasted, with considerable bursts of inactivity, for some sixty hours. Metternich watched its final stages from a distance, observing the movement of the columns as he had done at Wagram four years before. It was not until nightfall on 18 October that Napoleon, to avoid annihilation, ordered a retreat across the Pleisse River. By then, the Saxon troops had changed their allegiance, and the French were left alone to fall back across Germany.[11]

Emperor Francis did not doubt the triumph of his armies. On 20 October, from field headquarters in the village of Rotha, eight miles south of Leipzig, he published an order of the day which created Metternich a Prince. It was a gesture of gratitude for his 'wise direction' of foreign affairs.[12] The three Allied sovereigns then entered Leipzig in triumph. As their cavalcade passed through the centre of the city a pathetic figure bowed to them with contented resignation from the balcony of the Hotel de Prusse. It was Frederick Augustus, King of Saxony and nominal Grand Duke of Warsaw, anxious as ever to please those who held power in their hands. But his Imperial and royal brothers did not feel magnanimous. He had remained loyal to Napoleon too long, and they had other ideas on how his kingdom was to be administered. The King was treated as a prisoner of war and carried off to Berlin, where the people showed their patriotism by demonstrating against him in the streets. A Russian general was given control of his kingdom. It was an arrangement which would cause Metternich many hours of negotiation before order and legitimacy returned to Saxony.[13]

At the time Metternich had other thoughts in his mind. He was delighted with his new princely title, and did not hesitate to remind Hudelist in Vienna that the Imperial capital would no doubt wish to honour Schwarzenberg and himself on their return home. For the moment, smaller things pleased him. Years afterwards he would tell his grand-children how, on the day he was made a Prince, his valet had asked him earnestly, 'Will Your Highness put on the same suit as His Excellency wore yesterday?'[14] Perhaps because the campaign had begun so uncertainly at Dresden, Leipzig remained for him the greatest event in the war, far more memorable than the eventual fall of Paris. Tactically the Allied victory had shown no brilliance. The 'battle of the nations', as the Prussians liked to call Leipzig, was essentially an exercise in attrition, but its consequences were decisive. Now the path lay open across Germany to the banks of the Rhine. Bavaria had already changed sides and the puppet Kingdom of Westphalia collapsed. There was an unseemly dash for Frankfurt along roads deep in mud. Metternich had no wish for the old Empire to be restored in the German lands but, for the sake of Habsburg prestige, he was determined to assert Austrian primacy in the traditional Imperial city. He arrived there on the evening of 4 November and immediately set about arranging a grand ceremonial entry for the Emperor Francis on 6 November. The Tsar awaited Francis at the outskirts of the town and escorted him with deference to the coronation church.[15] Metternich was delighted: he had effectively made his point. Meanwhile what was left of Napoleon's army stood along the left bank of the Rhine, plagued by typhus and dispirited with precipitate retreat. The war was drawing wretchedly to an end.

But what end? All Germany was now in arms against the French; yet, to Metternich's alarm, the enemy seemed equally to be the petty German princes. It would be of no benefit to Austria if Stein and his unitary idea of a central German state replaced French primacy west of the Rhine; and Metternich resorted to some skilful bargaining in Frankfurt with the Bavarians and Wurtembergers in order to safeguard Austrian influence in southern and central Germany, thereby limiting Stein's power to the big cities and the sovereign states of the north (where, by now, the Prussians watched his activities with suspicion). It was harder to deal with other questions. Metternich, in Frankfurt, had by no means decided against Napoleon's rule in France. He continued to regret the failure to reach a compromise peace in the summer. On the eve of defeat at Leipzig, Napoleon had sent an emissary to his father-in-law with a tentative proposal for further negotiations, but the offer had been swept aside in the tide of battle and elation of victory. Now in November there seemed a further prospect of a settlement. Among the French diplomats who fell into Allied hands as the armies advanced across the German states was Baron de St Aignan, a brother-in-law of Caulaincourt. Metternich had conversations with St Aignan on 8 November and 9 November; and sent him as speedily as possible towards Paris with an offer of generous terms in the name of the Allies. France would be assured frontiers corresponding approximately to her territorial limits in 1797: Belgium and the entire left bank of the Rhine would thus remain within a Napoleonic French state.[16]

There is no doubt Metternich behaved with dubious honesty over the

Frankfurt Proposals. He consulted Tsar Alexander and his principal spokesman on foreign affairs, Karl Nesselrode; and he seems to have had support from Frederick William of Prussia and from Hardenberg. But he did not discuss St Aignan's mission with either Cathcart or Stewart, and the only British representative whose opinion he sought was Aberdeen. Technically, since Aberdeen was accredited to the Austrian court, this was a correct procedure; but Metternich took advantage of Aberdeen's inexperience to convince him that what was offered France fell within Castlereagh's instructions. Although Aberdeen complained that the Allies were not entitled to discuss maritime questions, he committed the British to tacit recognition of Antwerp as a French port; and he even gave St Aignan to understand that the British would allow France any commercial or navigational claims 'to which she could justly pretend'. Aberdeen was a sensitive man: he had ridden beside Metternich across the field of Leipzig soon after the battle and was horrified by what he saw; but, though he had a natural revulsion against the continuance of the war, he had no right to give British consent to the Proposals; and Metternich knew it.[17]

But Metternich was eager for Napoleon to accept the Frankfurt Proposals immediately as a basis for a settlement. They were the one means by which a powerful but not preponderant Bonapartist state could survive in Europe and help Austria to balance the Russo-Prussian combination, which he already found menacing over Polish and German affairs. To support St Aignan's mission he wrote privately to Caulaincourt on 10 November insisting that these were the most generous terms which could be obtained for France, that local French victories would not induce further concessions, and that delay would lead inevitably to harder conditions, especially once the Rhine was crossed by the invading armies.[18] He was, however, far from hopeful that Napoleon would see reason and accept the Proposals. On 23 November a note was received from Maret, dated 18 November, which avoided all reference to the conditions but suggested that talks might be opened in Mannheim. Metternich replied two days later, again insisting on the Frankfurt Proposals as a basis for discussion.[19] He was encouraged when news reached him that on 20 November Caulaincourt had succeeded Maret as Foreign Minister, for he had sensed at Prague an affinity of outlook with Caulaincourt and knew him to be a man of peace. Metternich was, however, by now beginning to lose some of the influence he had earlier possessed at Frankfurt, and Cathcart and Stewart were becoming alarmed at all they heard of Aberdeen's activities. It was only on 2 December that Caulaincourt, with Napoleon's approval, agreed to talks; but his answer did not reach Frankfurt until 5 December. By then the full storm had broken over Aberdeen's activities, and both the Tsar and Metternich were agreed that there had to be a British emissary at Allied headquarters who would speak with authority. General Pozzo di Borgo, a Corsican in Russian service, was sent to London on 6 December in the hope of persuading Castlereagh to come in person.* Meanwhile Caulaincourt was informed that no peace conference could begin until a British plenipotentiary had arrived from England.[20]

If Napoleon had hoped that Caulaincourt's reply to Metternich would win him a respite he was disappointed. Metternich believed in 'negotiating but while negotiating, advancing'. The Prussian generals and Tsar Alexander were obsessed with a desire to march directly on Paris by the shortest route across the middle Rhine. Schwarzenberg was reluctant to risk his main body of troops against the fortresses of Lorraine and his Chief-of-Staff, General Joseph Radetzky, proposed a plan by which the bulk of the Allied forces would advance across north-western Switzerland, through the Belfort Gap to the Langres Plateau and up the river Aube into Champagne and thence to Paris.[21] This plan was warmly supported by Metternich, not least because it would cut Napoleon's communications with northern Italy where a second Austrian army was contesting French control of Lombardy and Venetia. Radetzky's proposal was backed by Frederick William, on the understanding that Blücher would lead the 'Army of Silesia' forward through Nancy to the upper Marne, linking up with Schwarzenberg's army (which was twice as large as his force) in Champagne. The Tsar grudgingly accepted the Radetzky Plan at a conference in Frankfurt on 19 November. He appears, however, to have resented the dominance of Austro-Prussian planning in military operations, and his personal relations with Metternich deteriorated rapidly during December. Significantly, Nesselrode and most of the Tsar's suite did not agree with their master. 'There are some men who want to push as far as Paris,' Nesselrode wrote to his wife, 'but I only want to push as far as negotiations'.[22] The words might just as well have been Metternich's.

Accord with Castlereagh

The Allied armies crossed the Rhine on 22 December, the Austrians seizing Basle despite Swiss protestations of neutrality. Metternich himself left Frankfurt on 12 December and travelled to Freiburg in the Breisgau, spending Christmas and the New Year with his mother's relatives before moving to the new Allied headquarters in Basle on 12

* The principal purpose of Pozzo's mission was to secure British consent to the inclusion of discussions about subsidies and colonial conquests in the talks with the French; but he was also instructed to press for fuller representation of the British point of view. Castlereagh was appointed British plenipotentiary on 20 December and left London on 28 December, travelling by way of Harwich and the Hague. Icy fog delayed all communications by land and sea. The first two months of 1814 were colder in Western Europe than anyone could remember.

January. It was a difficult time for him. Wilhelmine of Sagan, bored in Vienna, poured out imaginary grievances in hasty letters haphazardly punctuated by a series of dashes; and he replied by every courier, writing at length with sympathy and understanding. Nor was hers the only Russian temperament to trouble him. Tsar Alexander became impatient with the progress of Schwarzenberg's troops and by the middle of January he could contain himself no longer. He was already quarrelling with Metternich over the peripheral questions of Saxony and Poland and there was strong disagreement over the future form of government in France itself, for while Alexander had plans for a new French monarchy under Bernadotte, the Austrians were toying with the possibility of a Regency under Marie Louise. It was, however, military matters that counted most with Alexander in these months. The thought of a triumphant entry into Paris drew him forward, as if in revenge for the fate of Moscow in 1812. 'Tsar Alexander,' wrote Metternich to Gentz on 13 January 1814, 'believes it is his duty to Moscow to blow up the Tuileries. They will not be blown up.'[23] The quarrels were too bitter for Alexander's mercurial temperament. On 16 January he left Allied headquarters at Basle to be with his troops. This was a political error of considerable magnitude, for it meant that the Tsar was not present when Castlereagh at last completed his grim journey from the Hague on 18 January. The British and Austrian Foreign Ministers were thus able to establish an accord which their mutual suspicion would have prevented had Russian influence been active.

The two men rapidly achieved a working partnership. 'I cannot praise Castlereagh enough,' wrote Metternich with rare enthusiasm after their first meeting: 'I get on with him as if we had spent all our lives together,' he told Wilhelmine on 21 January.[24] Castlereagh, although characteristically cautious, felt able to inform his colleagues in London some weeks later: 'The Austrian Minister is charged with more faults than belong to him'.[25] They agreed that a Bernadotte in the throne room of the Tuileries made nonsense of every principle of government for which they held respect. Castlereagh regarded the restoration of the Bourbons as the only logical alternative to Bonapartist rule; and although Metternich still hoped to save Napoleon's crown, he made it clear to Castlereagh that Austria would not support a Bonapartist solution of the dynastic question purely for family sentiment. To Castlereagh's relief Metternich was sympathetic over the future of the Netherlands and no longer held the extreme positions over the Rhine and over maritime rights which had so alarmed the English when reported by Aberdeen from Frankfurt. Clearly Castlereagh did not understand the complexities of the Polish or Saxon problems but, even on these issues, Metternich found some agreement between them. Stein was foolish enough to send a secret message, inevitably intercepted by the Austrians, which sought to warn Castlereagh against Metternich. It did not improve his standing with either Minister.[26]

In the last week of January Metternich and Castlereagh crossed into France and travelled to Langres for a conference with Alexander. The political divisions in the Allied camp were by now seriously hampering both the conduct of the war and the conclusion of a peace settlement. While the two statesmen were in Basle and the Tsar was in Langres, Caulaincourt waited in southern Lorraine at Lunéville to discover if the Allies really wished to talk peace. But they themselves were uncertain. The Tsar's war aims seemed to veer with every shift of the icy winds. It was impossible to reach an accommodation with him at Langres. During the long journey to Basle, Castlereagh had thought of himself as a mediator, but his natural sense of order inevitably inclined him towards Metternich's pragmatism rather than to the nebulous schemes of the Tsar. Neither could understand the psychological importance to Alexander of avenging the fall of Moscow; and had they been able to do so, it would not have commanded their sympathy. The one persistent theme in Alexander's rambling remarks at Langres was the need to press on with a military advance into the centre of France. Other considerations were, for the moment, beyond the compass of his mind: he did not object when Metternich first broached the possibility of a grand peace congress to be held eventually in Vienna; and he was ready to send a representative to negotiate with Caulaincourt, although he was not prepared to instruct him to show a co-operative attitude; but these were minor concessions for five days of discussion. Metternich even had to threaten, once more, that if Alexander did not accept the need for talks with Caulaincourt the Austrians would go it alone. The only consolation was the close identity between the British and Austrian points of view. 'Castlereagh behaves like an angel,' wrote Metternich to Schwarzenberg on 30 January.[27]

The Chatillon Conference and the Treaty of Chaumont

Talks with Caulaincourt began, at last, on 5 February in the small town of Chatillon, a neutral enclave on the upper Seine. Metternich had no intention of attending, for he was determined to remain at headquarters and keep watch on Alexander's activities. The chair at the Chatillon Conference was taken by Metternich's deputy, Count Stadion.[28] The British were officially represented by Cathcart, Stewart and Aberdeen, a trio never in harmony; but the opening sessions were also attended by Castlereagh as an observer. Ominously the Russian plenipotentiary was Count Andrei Razumovsky, one of the few diplomats in the Tsar's entourage who encouraged Alexander in his reluctance to negotiate with Napoleon. Caulaincourt made it clear at the early meetings of the

Conference that Napoleon was anxious for peace, and on 9 February even sent a private message to Metternich requesting an immediate armistice on the basis of the 1792 frontiers. But little progress could be made at Chatillon, since Razumovsky whenever pressed insisted that he had to await further instructions from the Tsar at headquarters. 'We are playing a comedy which is interesting only because of its platitudes,' wrote Stadion to Metternich in disgust soon after the Chatillon Conference opened.[29] He received scant sympathy from his Foreign Minister; for once even Metternich was too exhausted to carry his pen over the sheets of paper which had become his nightly substitute for relaxation in recent weeks. He scribbled a desperate reply to Stadion at three in the morning: 'I have just emerged from half a dozen conferences, I have spent the whole day writing, and I cannot go on.'[30]

Headquarters were by now in Troyes, ninety miles east of Paris, and relations between the Russians and Austrians had reached a point of crisis. Metternich sent urgently to Chatillon asking Castlereagh to return and attempt to reason with the Tsar; for Alexander was threatening, not merely to march directly on Paris as a conqueror, but to summon an Assembly of Notables once he had entered the city and permit them to choose the future ruler of France. To Metternich and to Castlereagh such a proceeding smacked of revolution. An appeal to popular will would undermine the sanctity of legitimacy and confound the prospects for a conservative settlement in Germany. Castlereagh pleaded with the Tsar and Metternich threatened yet again a separate peace with Napoleon.[31] But it was the French who this time ended the deadlock between the Allies. For Blücher and the Russians had followed too closely the Tsar's desire to march on Paris: on 11 February Napoleon defeated Blücher at Montmirail and, in a series of actions over the following days, destroyed a third of his army. A week later it was the turn of Schwarzenberg to suffer a repulse at Monterau. Troyes was hurriedly evacuated, and the Allies withdrew to the comparative safety of Chaumont, nearly fifty miles to the east.

Tsar Alexander, considerably shaken by these signs of French resilience, at last authorized Razumovsky to collaborate with Caulaincourt at Chatillon; and it began to seem as if there might yet be a compromise peace. But the victories had elated Napoleon as much as they had alarmed his enemies, and Caulaincourt was now instructed to accept no settlement which fell short of the Frankfurt Proposals. It was therefore the French who procrastinated, while Napoleon personally sent a letter to Francis on 21 February in which he spoke of the ease with which it would be possible to secure peace based upon the 'natural boundaries' of France. He also shrewdly commented on the Tsar's vindictiveness, seeking to widen the gap which Caulaincourt had seen in the relations between the Allied leaders. Neither Francis nor Metternich were to be caught by such a crude device.[32] Caulaincourt, on 25 February, was informed that he might have a fortnight in which to decide whether to accept a peace which restored the old pre-Revolutionary frontiers of France or to go on fighting to the end. Francis gave a dignified rejection to Napoleon's overture, emphasizing the Allied desire for peace on the basis of the 'ancient limits' of France.

Metternich continued to negotiate with the French throughout the first half of March. The campaign swung back in favour of the Allies when Schwarzenberg cautiously resumed his advance on 1 March. Eight days later Blücher avenged Montmirail by defeating Napoleon at Laon. But Metternich's advice to Caulaincourt did not change with the fortunes of war. On 3 March he appealed to the French in a series of rhetorical questions:[33] 'Are there no means to enlighten the Emperor about his situation? Is he irrevocably determined to leave his own fate and that of his son to the carriage of his last gun? Does he think that his courage and daring will protect him from being overwhelmed by superior forces? ... If the Austrian Emperor could cede the Tyrol in 1809 why cannot Napoleon cede Belgium in 1814?' But on 10 March Caulaincourt offered only a minor concession and it was clear that the Chatillon Conference was doomed. Even so Metternich tried yet again on 17 March:[34] 'Come to our headquarters on the day you are prepared to make the inevitable sacrifices for peace, but do not come as the champion of absurd projects. Matters are too serious for dream-world fiction without risking Napoleon's fate ... Austria still wishes to preserve a dynasty with which it is closely connected. Peace depends still upon your master: in a little while this will no longer be the case.'

While Metternich was treating Caulaincourt to lectures intended for Napoleon's hearing, Castlereagh sought to achieve some cohesion between the Allies in Chaumont.[35] A Treaty of General Alliance would, he thought, keep the powers together and at the same time demonstrate to Napoleon the Allied intention of imposing a united will on defeated France. On 9 March the four Allies signed the Treaty of Chaumont backdated to the beginning of the month: no separate peace; a settlement which would include independence for the Netherlands and for Switzerland, the establishment of a German confederacy of sovereign states, restitution of the old order (so far as was practicable) in Italy, and the return of the Bourbon dynasty to Spain. Ultimately of greater significance was the understanding that the four signatories would collaborate for twenty years after the ending of hostilities and that each would be prepared to place sixty thousand men in the field against a resurgent France. Europe thus acquired, almost casually and at a time when its leaders were divided by suspicion, its first charter of general security. It left great questions unresolved, notably the form of government in France and the future of the Polish lands, but it demonstrated that as long as Castlereagh was in control of British foreign policy there would be no polarization of the continent on an east-west axis.

At the time the Treaty of Chaumont made far less impact on the Allies than Castlereagh had hoped. It hardly brought them any closer together. There was a heated scene in Chaumont itself a week later, which stressed the tensions between the Austrians and their partners. Metternich, finding the Tsar reluctant to give Caulaincourt any further time, blamed the Russians for having obstructed the work of the Chatillon Conference in the previous month.[36] Frederick William declared that such accusations were treasonable; and the Tsar himself asked if it were true that Schwarzenberg had been ordered not to give battle to the French so long as there was any possibility of a settlement at Chatillon. Metternich wrote that night almost in despair to Stadion, who was still in Chatillon: 'You have no idea what sufferings the people at headquarters impose upon us! I cannot stand it much longer and the Emperor Francis is already ill. They are all mad and belong in the lunatic asylum.'[37] He was by now a tired man, for he had been engaged in diplomatic battles against Austria's enemies and some of her allies for the past six months. 'We are negotiating as valiantly as the army is fighting,' he declared in a note to Hudelist on 14 March.[38]

Yet, while victory was in sight for the army, Metternich had to concede partial defeat. In the third week of March he at last accepted the fact that Napoleon would not make peace, perhaps because he could not make peace. The Chatillon charade ended abruptly on 21 March, but it was followed by a week of military confusion in which the two principal opposing armies almost wheeled around each other. The Tsar, Frederick William and Schwarzenberg remained on the Marne, with Blücher covering their right flank; and Emperor Francis, Metternich, Hardenberg and Castlereagh were separated from the main command and forced to retire westwards, eventually finding refuge at Dijon on 24 March. It was a pleasant town, and Metternich and his companions remained there until the campaign ended with the fall of Paris on the last day of the month. They had the company of a Bourbon representative, Baron Vitrolles, and, although the absence of the Russian and Prussian monarchs delayed a formal decision in favour of restoring the traditional dynasty, by 28 March the Dijon group of Allies were at least prepared to drink a toast to King Louis XVIII.[39] There was a final desperate message from Napoleon offering to abdicate in favour of a Regency under Marie Louise, and conveyed to Francis by Wessenberg (who, unlucky as ever, had been captured by a French patrol). But the Emperor of Austria ignored his son-in-law's plea.[40] The Habsburg-Bonaparte union, brilliant as a comet to the end, had burnt itself out.

The war thus ended for Metternich quietly in Dijon. He could have journeyed to Paris as soon as the Russians and Prussians entered the city; like Castlereagh, he preferred to remain in the old Burgundian capital rather than share in the humiliation of the Parisians. Metternich was confident that Talleyrand, who had received the Tsar in Paris, would be able to restrain his more extravagant gestures. Once it was finally settled that France would take back the Bourbons, Metternich was prepared to set out from Dijon and resume his contest with Alexander over the character of the peace settlement. He was in no hurry: Dijon was as good a place as any in which to make sober calculations while the Tsar, 180 miles to the west, tasted a triumph that deluded him. Metternich let Alexander enjoy a week of exultation; but by 7 April his carriage was once more moving westwards towards Paris and all the turbulence of peacemaking.[41]

THE BUSINESS OF VICTORY

Napoleon is sent to Elba and Marie Louise returns to Austria

Metternich arrived in Paris from Dijon on 10 April, Easter Sunday, to find the city permeated by a curious sense of political disbelief. The Empire had fallen without a staggering military defeat and without a revolution. 'The town has a strange appearance. Everything is as quiet as if there had been no war,' he wrote to Wilhelmine of Sagan.[1] Although a sharp action took place at Montmartre it was not an Austerlitz or a Wagram in reverse and no one had struck impassioned attitudes on the barricades. Imperial authority merely withered away to unreality: it was autumn in springtime. Napoleon, surrounded by a remnant of the Old Guard, was still at Fontainebleau, where he had spent so many months since his second marriage. It is true that this time Marie Louise and his son were at Orléans, but they were not as yet out of touch: twelve letters passed between them in the first ten days of April. Yet what they said to each other mattered little, for the future was in other hands. The new dispensation was represented by a five-man provisional government, headed by Talleyrand and acting in the name of King Louis XVIII, whom the Senate had 'freely called to the throne of France' four days previously; but that well-meaning and slightly surprised gentleman was beyond the Channel, nursing a bad attack of gout at Hartwell in Buckinghamshire, and his brother the Comte d'Artois was delayed in Flanders and could not arrive until Tuesday in Easter Week. In the absence of the Bourbons effective sovereignty in Paris was improbably exercised by the Romanovs, as it had been ever since Tsar Alexander's ostentatious entry into the city on 31 March. It was a strange quirk of French history which had thrust into such eminence this 'Byzantine of the decadent period' (as Napoleon called him), and Metternich was far from happy at his elevation, but for the moment there was little he could do to hold him in restraint.

The Tsar's ascendancy was in part a direct consequence of Austrian policy. The Emperor Francis had wished so far as possible to remain in the shadows while acts of deposition were prepared for his son-in-law for, although he had no love for Napoleon, he was from time to time embarrassed by scruples of family sentiment. He had every intention of re-asserting parental control over his daughter and her son and he knew that he could count on Metternich to efface discreetly the record of the diplomatic marriage of 1810, that humiliating triumph which linked Emperor and Minister more closely than man and wife; but it suited Francis and Metternich for all formal negotiations with Napoleon's representative, Caulaincourt, to be entrusted by the Allied sovereigns to the Tsar of Russia. He alone should determine the fate of the fallen dynasty, at least in the records of public protocol. At first all had gone well enough. But Alexander, who in the enthusiasm of victory had seemed an appropriate instrument of retribution, was always prone to temper firm resolves with expansive magnanimity; and, by the time Metternich reached Paris, the negotiations had begun to show a generosity which alarmed him, and indeed Castlereagh as well.[2]

On 6 April Napoleon had signed an act of abdication in return for certain assurances conveyed by Caulaincourt from the Tsar in the name of the Allies. Napoleon and Marie Louise were each promised annuities of two million francs. He would be permitted to rule, in full Imperial sovereignty, the island principality of Elba. She was granted in perpetuity the Duchy of Parma, with Piacenza and Guastalla, these territories reverting on her death to their son, 'the King of Rome'. Napoleon regarded these terms as a humiliation and accepted them only with reluctance. Yet to the Austrians they seemed the height of folly. The Emperor Francis strongly objected to the proposal that his son-in-law should be given Elba, and he had little liking for any plan that left his daughter less than a hundred miles from her husband. Metternich agreed with him. To permit Napoleon a retreat so close to the mainland was, in his eyes, to invite a renewal of war within a couple of years.[3] He made his protest; but the Tsar was obdurate. The negotiations with Caulaincourt had been long and difficult, and Alexander had no intention of going back on his pledged word. Metternich did not wish to jeopardize relations with Russia by taking a stand on this issue when there were territorial questions of great moment to the Austrians still unresolved. He thought it essential to settle Napoleon's fate speedily; for only when he was out of the country would it be possible to conclude a preliminary peace with Bourbon France and begin work on the reconstruction of a European system. On 11 April, against his better judgement, Metternich agreed to the settlement with Napoleon. He and Stadion signed, on Austria's behalf, the document subsequently known as the Treaty of Fontainebleau. Napoleon, after an ineffectual attempt to poison himself, ratified the treaty on 14 April and six days later set out for Elba. He landed at Portoferraio on 4 May, the day after Louis XVIII at last returned to Paris.

By then, too, Marie Louise had left France, travelling not to her new

E

domain but to the palace she had regarded as her home in happier times, Schönbrunn. The decision that she should go to Vienna ran counter to her own desires, for there is little doubt that Marie Louise was still in love with Napoleon and wished to be allowed to take her son with her to Elba and to share her husband's misfortunes. This her father would never permit. She had received her first letter in many months from him when she returned to the Bishop's Palace at Orléans after Mass on Easter Day. It was ominously guarded: Francis wrote of 'his duties as Emperor' and of his need 'to accede to the wishes of the Allied sovereigns'.[4] Two days later Prince Paul Esterhazy brought her a happier message from Metternich: she had been assigned the Duchies of Parma, Piacenza and Guastalla; and she should now travel immediately to Rambouillet and meet her father there. The reunion took place on 16 April and for two hours father and daughter were left alone in conversation. Francis made it clear to her that it was impossible to join Napoleon or even to see him. She must travel first to Vienna with her son. When her health had recovered from the strain of these past months, she should go to Parma and perhaps then she might cross to Elba and visit her husband. Francis failed to understand his daughter's emotions; he could not bring himself to believe she cared for the man whom he had sent her to marry as an act of state. She received, at Rambouillet, courtesy calls from the Tsar and the King of Prussia. They found her crushed in spirit; but she was only twenty-two, her nerves were frayed, she could do nothing but obey her father.[5] On 23 April she left Rambouillet and on 2 May crossed the Rhine along the familiar route to Melk, with its great abbey above the Danube. The wheel had come full circle; and in Paris Metternich, who first set it in motion, turned in relief to problems less tarnished by past brilliance.

Italian problems (1814)

Metternich was faced by three main tasks that spring. He had to safeguard Austrian interests in the peace treaty with Bourbon France, taking particular care to reassert Habsburg primacy in the Italian peninsula. He had to modify any new settlement in Germany which might have led to the growth of Prussian influence at the expense of Austria's traditional rights. And, above all, he had to mobilize the diplomatic resources of Europe to prevent the temporary ascendancy of the Tsar from becoming a permanent menace to the stability of the continent. Each of these questions contained specific matters of dispute: the status of Lombardy and Venetia and their relationship to the Austrian Crown; the fate of Saxony, which was still under Russian administration; the garrisoning of Mainz, where the Prussian flag flew over Metternich's Rhenish homeland; the future of Cracow and the whole intractable problem of partitioned Poland. Not all these matters required early solution, and some would even benefit from the passage of time and the cooling of passions, but the problems of Italy were so acute that urgent decisions had to be taken. They were to occupy many of Metternich's working hours during the first half of May, although they remained unresolved long after he had left Paris for Vienna.

For Europe in general the campaign in Italy, like Wellington's in Spain, had been a sideshow fought, not against Napoleon in person, but against his stepson, Eugene Beauharnais, who as Viceroy held court in Milan. The Austrians however saw these operations differently. The Emperor Francis had been born in Florence when his father was Grand Duke of Tuscany, and he always felt a strong attachment to his Italian lands and titles. Their loss in 1805 was a greater personal blow to him than the formal demise of the Holy Roman Empire; and Metternich, assiduously attentive to his sovereign's predilections, had accordingly placed their recovery high on the list of military objectives when war was renewed with France in August 1813.[6] At first all had gone well: by the end of October the Austrians had not only recovered their position in Dalmatia, but had taken Trieste and Trento and were push-ing forwards towards Vicenza and the northern plains. But thereafter the inadequately equipped Austrian forces were bogged down by the winter weather, and their commanders, General Nugent and Marshal Bellegarde, had to look for support to the Italian people and even to Napoleon's puppet-king of Naples, Joachim Murat (who concluded an alliance with the Austrians in January 1814). These appeals to Italian national spirit proved an embarrassment to Metternich in Paris; and the swiftly changing loyalties of Murat delayed decisions on the future of Naples and Sicily until the beginning of 1815. It was a confused situation, made even worse by Castlereagh's inability to control the British commanding general in Sicily, Lord William Bentinck, a Whig nobleman inclined to dash off extempore proclamations of Italian liberty at the drop of a tambourine.[7]

The Italian campaign formally ended with the capitulation of Eugene Beauharnais on 16 April. As in Paris, a provisional government was chosen from the Senate of the Kingdom of Italy, and spokesmen were sent to the Allied commanders in Italy and the Allied sovereigns in France in the hope of negotiating independence for an Italian state, possibly ruled by a member of the House of Habsburg. But the pro-visional government in Milan, unlike its counterpart in Paris, had no exiled ruler to restore and, for that matter, no Talleyrand to guide it. Moreover while Austrian troops were still to the east of Milan, there was an outburst of mob violence in the narrow streets of the old city, and on 20 April Viceroy Eugene's former Finance Minister was seized and lynched.[8] The news of the outrage appeared to justify Metternich's contention that Milan was a hotbed of Italian Jacobinism: Austria had a duty to safeguard the natural order of society in Lombardy from the fever of anarchy. Hence, even before General Neipperg led the first Austrian units into Milan on 28 April, Metternich had gained tacit consent from his allies for the establishment of a frontier along the Ticino and the Po. It was left for Francis and his ministers to decide on the formal character of Austrian rule in Lombardy and Venetia; and counter the sentiment for national unity which had been stimulated by a war of liberation.*

On 6 May Metternich received a deputation from the Milanese Senate: he could give it little comfort.[9] A day later the Italians were granted an audience with Emperor Francis. They were heard courteously but left in no doubt of their position: 'You belong to me by right of conquest,' Francis told them bluntly.[10] In time, an autonomous Kingdom of Italy might, perhaps, be established under an Austrian archduke; but, for the moment, Lombardy and Venetia were to be ruled in the name of His Imperial and Apostolic Majesty the Emperor of Austria. Northern Italy was to be as much a Habsburg appendage as the Tyrol or the Croatian districts of Dalmatia and the Illyrian Provinces.

Metternich's thoughts on the Italian problem had, in fact, already gone much deeper than he was prepared to reveal to the Milanese deputation. He summarized them in a memorandum to Bellegarde sent from Paris to Milan on 15 May.[11] It is not in itself a remarkable document, for it is primarily a series of hastily drafted instructions to aid a military commander in a difficult position. But, apart from practical advice on the need to keep an eye on what was happening at Elba and on methods of cultivating the politically 'less corrupt' citizens of Venice, it defined in essence Metternich's whole approach to the Italian question and its basic assumptions remained valid for him a third of a century later.

The memorandum began with an uncompromising rejection of Italian claims. There was, he maintained, no genuine basis for a concept of Italian nationalism: the idea had been encouraged by non-Italians such as Napoleon, Murat, Bentinck and 'a few of our own people'. It was nonsense to talk of an Italian kingdom, for intensive local jealousies and rival interests had always kept the cities apart and rendered in-

---

* During Metternich's exile in London in 1848 it was reported to the then Prime Minister, Lord John Russell, that the former Chancellor was saying the annexation of Lombardy had been forced upon the Austrians by their allies against the wishes of Emperor Francis and of himself. (*Later Correspondence of Lord J. Russell*, volume 1, p. 335). Recent research – especially the studies of Professors Haas and Rath, cited in the bibliography – shows that Metternich's remarks were at best a considerable over-simplification, although it is no doubt true that the final decision to include Lombardy in the Austrian Empire was only taken in April 1814 and for defensive reasons rather than sheer territorial greed.

effectual all attempts at creating an integral unity. He believed in the political fragmentation of the peninsula as being both natural for the Italians and desirable for the Austrians. To counter Italian sentiment there would be an appeal to regional traditions and to local patriotism. 'We shall try to rekindle the Lombard spirit,' he informed Bellegarde. He was less sure of the future status of Venetia, and contented himself with the weak proposal that the Emperor would decide on the future of the Venetians when he had 'sounded the feelings and dispositions of his new Italian subjects'. But there could be no doubt of what was to happen in Milan: Emperor Francis would be proclaimed King of Lombardy and the ancient 'iron crown' of the Lombards symbolically incorporated in the Imperial coat-of-arms. Bellegarde speedily acted on these instructions. The façade of a provisional government was swept aside at the end of May; and annexation was formally proclaimed on 12 June. Baron Wessenberg, who had experienced so many frustrations as envoy to London in 1813, was given the equally thankless task of preparing a general survey of Lombardy and Venetia in order to determine how best the Italian provinces could be assimilated to the Germanic core of the Empire. The first round in Metternich's long contest with Italian nationalism had ended in a clear victory for the Austrians. It could hardly have been otherwise.

The first Peace of Paris (1814)

The German and Polish Questions defied so swift a solution, for they involved the vital interests of two of the other major Allied powers, Prussia and Russia. Castlereagh had at first hoped that it would be possible to conclude a general settlement for the whole of Europe before mid-summer, but Metternich was never so sanguine. He argued that it was impossible to reach agreement over Poland in Paris, which was already a centre of Polish expatriates, and without some accord over Poland little progress could be made on the German problem, for if Prussia were to lose some of her Polish lands she would require compensation further west. There was good sense in this contention, especially since Tsar Alexander ostentatiously cultivated the company of several prominent Polish exiles. Two attempts were, however, made to settle these matters while the Allied statesmen were still in Paris, the initiative coming on each occasion from the principal spokesman of Prussia, Prince Hardenberg.[12] On 29 April he proposed a settlement which would have given Prussia the whole of Saxony and the left bank of the Rhine. Russia would secure most of the Duchy of Warsaw, but not the Prussian fortress of Thorn nor the former Austrian districts around Cracow and Tarnopol, which would be retroceded to Emperor Francis. Bavaria and Baden would receive additional territory in Germany;

Austria was assured of her north Italian acquisition, together with the
Tyrol, 'Illyria' and the rest of Dalmatia; and a federal constitution
would bind the German states loosely together. Metternich had no
reason to like these proposals: he was suspicious of any suggestion which
the Prussians might make for a German federation, especially so long as
the fortress of Mainz remained in Prussian hands. But Hardenberg's
scheme did not trouble him for more than a few hours. The Tsar would
have nothing to do with it, nor did he find any more acceptable a modified version which was presented for discussion at a meeting in Metternich's rooms on 21 May. Alexander maintained that a formal treaty of
peace should first be made with Bourbon France; only later would the
Allies negotiate over the major problems of European reconstruction.
Metternich, Hardenberg and Castlereagh accepted this procedure, perhaps with relief. It was easier to draw the boundaries of France than to
revive old antagonisms by raising once more the spectre of a partitioned
Poland.

'The peace to be made with France could only be regarded from one
of two standpoints,' Metternich wrote later in his *Memoirs*.[13] 'Either it
would be dictated by the spirit of revenge or it would be inspired by the
need to establish as perfect as possible a political equilibrium between
the powers.' The victors were determined to show moderation and
generosity towards the French, not for reasons of sentiment or in a spirit
of reconciliation, but because without a just peace there was no hope of
building up the Bourbons as a safeguard against the ideals of the Revolution and a revival of Bonapartism. Even though in retrospect the
settlement seems surprisingly lenient, it was necessary for Metternich to
speak firmly to Talleyrand over the French frontier in the north,
emphasizing that Austria fully supported Britain's insistence that King
Louis should renounce all claims to Flanders and Brabant, an area
where the French may have hoped to exploit the memory of past disappointments in order to disrupt the Austrian's accord with Castlereagh.
But, apart from this problem and difficulties over the frontier in Savoy,
the negotiations were conducted amicably. The treaty, which was subsequently known as the First Peace of Paris, was signed on 30 May. The
French surrendered all claims over the Netherlands (including Belgium),
Germany, Switzerland, Italy and Malta, and ceded certain colonial
possessions to Britain and Spain. The boundaries of France were fixed
at those of 1792, with the addition of Chambery and Annecy, as well as
of the old Papal enclave of Avignon. No limitations were imposed on the
size of the French Army, no reparations were claimed: the French were
allowed to retain the art treasures which Napoleon had brought as
trophies of war to the Louvre and were spared the costly humiliation of
having to maintain an army of occupation. Metternich was well pleased
with the settlement. He congratulated himself on its magnanimity,

which was in marked contrast to the territorial amputations and monetary greed shown in the treaties imposed on Austria during the years of disaster.[14]

Now the state of war was legally ended there was no longer any reason why the Allied sovereigns and statesmen should remain in France, and all of them were anxious to leave. There was still much work to be done and, as Castlereagh wrote to Lord Liverpool, it was difficult 'for a man to work hard in such a town as Paris'.[15] Military reviews, grand balls and gala performances followed each other in an unending round of sublimated festivity. Metternich, who always enjoyed the trivia of social duty, missed few of the formal entertainments; and Wrede, the chief Bavarian spokesman, complained that so much time was spent 'eating, drinking, dancing and seeing the sights and the women' that 'business does not move forward as one would desire'.[16] If this criticism was intended to censure Metternich, it was not entirely fair. Inevitably he met Laura Junot again and permitted himself a few hours of candle-lit sentimentality; and it was impossible for him to shake off Wilhelmine of Sagan, who arrived in Paris on 8 May accompanied by two of her sisters; but he worked that spring with rare diligence and concentration, and there was no sign of the tendency to linger in the French capital which had provoked so much derisive speculation four years before. He had, in fact, his own reasons for getting away from Paris at the earliest opportunity: 'I follow the Emperor of Russia to England,' he wrote back to Hudelist in Vienna on 24 May. 'This present place ... is too much under the influence of wretched Polish Frenchmen and French Poles.'[17] London, he believed, would be a better city in which to settle the Polish Question; in a few months a Congress in Vienna could clear up any outstanding business, under his own chairmanship. A fortnight later he travelled to the Channel coast and embarked on a ship for the first time in twenty years. It proved a stormy crossing, but he had high hopes of London; and the fact that he was soon followed across the Channel by the ubiquitous Sagan did not lower his spirits.[18]

Metternich's visit to England (June – July 1814)

The visit to England failed to settle the Polish Question, or indeed any other major problem. It was dominated by social festivities and London was no more suited for the business of diplomacy than Paris. England that summer was bright with revelry, at least in the southern counties. Stage-coaches were decked with laurel leaves. There were illuminated transparencies in the London streets and the downfall of French tyranny was celebrated by an excess of patriotic drunkenness. Originally it had been intended to invite the Tsar alone to share in this collective rejoicing, for Alexander had become a legendary hero of the English people after Napoleon's retreat from Moscow. But from Paris Castlereagh advised the Prince Regent to 'dilate the libation to Russia' by extending the invitation to the Emperor of Austria and the King of Prussia as well as their ministers and generals. Frederick William accepted promptly, for it was gratifying to bask in the sun of victory after so many winters of disapprobation; but Francis refused to cross the Channel. He was genuinely eager to return to Vienna and hated organized festivity. Moreover he had no wish to compete with the Tsar for the plaudits of an English mob. Neither Metternich nor Stadion could persuade him to change his mind. Metternich was instructed to represent his sovereign; and, lest the Prince Regent should be piqued at Francis's absence, he was authorized to invest the Regent with the Order of the Golden Fleece, a distinction never before granted to a Protestant Prince.[19]

The four weeks he spent in England were a considerable personal triumph for Metternich, as Gentz noted at the time. Although Castlereagh had frequently let his colleagues know of his sympathy for Austrian policy and of the loyal support which he gained from Metternich at Chaumont and in Paris, there remained a strong antipathy in London to a schemer who had married off his sovereign's daughter to Bonaparte. By tact, sound political instinct and outright flattery he soon won favour at court and in society: 'the wisest of ministers,' purred the Prince Regent contentedly after an obsequious display of deference.[20] While the Tsar antagonized even the Whig Opposition by gratuitous insults to his host and a monumental display of bad manners, few could find fault with the representative of the Emperor of Austria, and Francis rose vicariously in the public esteem through the good sense of his Minister. It had been a wise decision to return to Vienna.

Naturally Metternich attracted far less public attention than Alexander and Frederick William or, indeed, than the military commanders. It was noted at the time that the most popular figures were the old Prussian Hussar, Marshal Blücher, and the Cossack commander, Hetman Platow. But Metternich had his full share of honours. On 14 June he followed the Prince Regent and the two sovereigns to Oxford. There was a banquet that night under the Italianate dome of the Radcliffe Camera and on the following morning Lord Grenville, as Chancellor to the University, bestowed honorary degrees on the visiting dignitaries in the Sheldonian Theatre. An anonymous contemporary account describes how 'Dr Phillimore, the regius professor of civil law, presented himself in the arena, and it having been proposed and agreed to that the degree of Doctor of Civil Law should be conferred on Prince Metternich, Count Lieven and Field-Marshal Blücher, Dr Phillimore attended by the bedel retired to the Divinity School and soon returned, introducing these favourites of the people' – an appellation infrequently accorded to the new Doctor.[21] There followed, at one o'clock, a meal described as breakfast and served in All Souls College, and in the afternoon the Mayor bestowed the Freedom of the City on those whom the university had already honoured. They all dined that evening at Christ Church and, while the Tsar and the King of Prussia drove out to Blenheim Palace, Metternich ended the day with the rare delights of a ball in Oxford Town Hall.*

Three nights later he was one of seven hundred guests who attended the famous victory banquet at the Guildhall in London.[22] It was 18 June and many of his neighbours on the dais of honour were to meet again a year hence on a ridge near Brussels, but for the moment they assumed that the wars were over and gave their attention to a 'dinner as sumptuous as expense or skill could make it' (for it cost the City of London £20,000). There was a magnificent turtle from the West Indies and a huge baron of beef which, with the royal standard flying incongruously from its loins, was borne in procession the length of the hall, master carvers and cooks in attendance. Three places to Metternich's right sat the Countess Dorothea Lieven, wife of the Russian ambassador. He was to know her well a few years later, but there is no evidence that on this occasion either made any impression on the other. Both were primarily concerned with the rift between the Tsar and the Prince Regent who, as the Countess noted, maintained throughout the banquet 'a haughty silence' towards Alexander and his exasperating sister, the Grand Duchess Catherine. Metternich was well-pleased to see evidence of the growing antipathy between the British and Russian royal families and, on the day following the Guildhall banquet, wrote to Emperor Francis describing the Tsar's ill-humour and the depth of his disillusionment with the Regent; it would have been far better for the Russian royalty, Clement concluded sententiously, if the Tsar and his sister had never undertaken the present visit. Alexander had, indeed, discredited himself more rapidly than Metternich had dared to hope when he was in Paris. 'A vain, silly fellow' was the verdict of Lord Grey as reported by Creevey, and if a Whig could think of the Tsar in such terms, the opinion of the Tories in the government was even less charitable.[23] Only Frederick William still seemed magnetized by Alexander's personality, and his subservience was offset by the obvious hostility to Russian policy of his chief minister, Hardenberg. There was no doubt that the Tsar had lost the pre-eminence which so alarmed Metternich in April; and his discomfiture was Austria's gain.

* It was only in Oxford that Metternich was honoured by both city and university. He had been granted the Freedom of the City of Vienna in October 1813 but he never received an honorary degree from any German or Austrian university, although he was elected a member of many academic and scientific societies in the Monarchy. He received a doctorate from the University of Pavia in April 1816.

Although Alexander's erratic behaviour prevented the settlement of any important questions, there had been much talk between the four Foreign Ministers both at private meetings and at more formal sessions under Castlereagh's chairmanship.[24] There was activity, too, on behalf of the smaller European states, with Metternich secretly encouraging the unofficial representative of discredited Saxony to sound out Castlereagh on the German problem. And there was an improbable encounter in London between Metternich and Cardinal Consalvi, the Papal Secretary of State, who was the first prince of the Church to visit England since the Elizabethan Reformation. Little was achieved by any of these meetings: some progress over the future character of the United Netherlands; a compromise which left Mainz to the, as yet non-existent, German Confederation; and an assurance that Britain and Austria would not forget the claims of the Pope to temporal authority in central Italy. It was an unimpressive record for four weeks of consultation. But at least the Ministers had agreed on the next step towards European reconstruction. Everything would be decided at the congress which the Peace of Paris had promised for Vienna. On the eve of the Oxford visit the four Ministers had accepted Castlereagh's proposal that the congress would open on 15 August. The Tsar, however, had immediately rejected the date as far too early and insisted that he must return to Russia before undertaking further negotiations. Neither Metternich nor Castlereagh liked this change of plan, suspecting that the Russians wished to consolidate their hold on Poland and Saxony before the fate of these lands was placed on the agenda of the congress. But reluctantly it was agreed to postpone the opening of the congress until 1 October, provided that the 'Big Four' met in September to settle procedural questions and provided that, in the intervening three months, no change was made in the status of the areas under Russian or Prussian military occupation. The Tsar was prepared to accept both these conditions, but Castlereagh and Metternich remained uneasy: a Russian army of half a million men was quartered in the eastern borderlands of Europe, and there seemed no reason why the Tsar should trouble to negotiate about Poland when he had troops in each of the Polish cities.

Alexander left Dover to begin the long journey back to St Petersburg on 27 June. Although Metternich was anxious to return to Vienna and prepare for the congress, he stayed another week in London and held some desultory conversations with Castlereagh.[25] When eventually he reached Paris he found himself delayed by an unexpected crisis. News had come from Vienna that Marie Louise was on her way to Aix-les-Bains in Savoy to take a cure for a weakness in her lungs. Aix was on the French frontier; and Louis XVIII saw in the 'Duchess of Parma's' movements a possible Bonapartist plot, even though Aix was separated from Elba by the Alps and the Ligurian Sea. Metternich duly reported

French fears to her father: 'The journey of the French Empress (*sic*) has created here an altogether unfavourable sensation. The King is seriously disconcerted.'[26] Metternich had to assure Louis and his Foreign Minister, Talleyrand, that the Austrians were convinced there was no danger in the unfortunate woman's movements. The Emperor Francis had, in fact, taken the precaution of keeping her son at Schönbrunn; and, at Schwarzenberg's suggestion, ordered General Neipperg to cross the Alps from Milan and serve as a personal aide to his daughter. Neipperg was a dashing cavalry officer of considerable charm and enterprise and, before the end of September, had become Marie Louise's lover. There had been no need for Louis xviii's alarm; the incident underlined for Metternich the Bourbon sense of insecurity. He was not impressed by what he had seen of the French Restoration, and, in his vanity, identified Talleyrand with the imperfections of the system he served. This was a mistake: for, whatever might be said of his masters, Talleyrand himself had forgotten nothing and was still learning as much as he needed to know.

Metternich at last returned to Austria in the middle of July. He joined his family in Baden, near Vienna, on 18 July and on the following day made a triumphant entry into the capital. Outside his residence in the Ballhausplatz, a choir and orchestra awaited him. He was greeted by Beethoven's 'Prometheus Overture' and a cantata specially composed for the occasion by Kinsky to words by Weith. It began modestly enough: 'Hail to thee, great Prince, whose prudent wisdom guided the royal course.' By the third stanza it had warmed to its theme and found 'the whole world blessing such mature counsel'. Tripping heavily across dithyrambic heights it reached the ultimate splendour – 'History holds Thee up to Posterity as a Model among Great Men'.[27]

The sentiment was not unfamiliar and the invocation rang with distinctly liturgical undertones; but Metternich savoured the incense of adulation with the contentment of one who had never doubted his right to be numbered among the illustrious. He was accustomed to less rapturous homecomings to Vienna.

VIENNA

The gathering of the Congress (September 1814)

The people of Vienna had been surprised to learn in June that Emperor Francis was to be host to the peacemakers. Perhaps they had even been a little disconcerted; for this was a new rôle for the Habsburgs and a new experience for their city. In the past Vienna was regarded as too distant from Western Europe to serve as a centre of international diplomacy, and although envoys had waited on Kaunitz in the great days of Maria Theresa, dignitaries were accustomed to travelling abroad for major conferences or assemblies of monarchs, to France or Holland, Westphalia or Saxony. But the marches and counter-marches of Napoleon's armies had foreshortened the continent and life was being transformed for the Viennese more rapidly than they appreciated. The wars made Vienna look to the west, even if two French occupations had barely disturbed the narrowly parochial felicity of its citizens. Now in 1814 a cavalcade of sovereigns and statesmen was about to descend on the city, and it was by no means clear how they were to be accommodated, how their business was to be conducted, or how their retinues were to be fed and foddered through the winter months. There was no formal invitation, merely an announcement that the Congress would open on 1 October. The heads of five reigning dynasties and of 216 princely families flocked to Vienna, as Blücher put it, 'like peasants to a country fair'. The city was wretchedly crowded and prices soared with a false inflation. Metternich might scribble off a note to Eleonore on the delights of having 'all Europe in my antechamber';[1] but not everyone in Vienna could share his enthusiasm for such exalted constriction nor bestow hospitality with such random largesse.

Outwardly Vienna was an ideal setting for a great Congress. Austrian Baroque made life a vast theatre of pageants and fantasy. The palaces of Fischer von Erlach and Lukas von Hildebrandt in sacrificing nature to perspective created an illusion of luxuriant excess and unassailable authority. The statesmen could meet formally against a backcloth of marble and malachite, with twisted columns rising to some apocalyptic vision on a patinated dome; or they could move at ease through Rococo salons rich in flagrant eccentricity of ornament. They had the promise of good music and good talk, the assurance of elegance and coquetry from a galaxy of princesses. If drawing-room diplomacy had too many ears it was always possible to seek the discretion of the great town houses where massive wooden gates shut out the world and, from high windows, crystal chandeliers cast a calming luminescence over cobbled courtyards. Despite the bustle and confusion in the narrow streets of the old town, Vienna was never oppressively urban. The chestnut avenues of the Prater were filled morning and afternoon with riders and carriages, for the Imperial stables of the Hofburg alone housed fourteen hundred horses, provided by Francis for his guests. And they could escape easily enough to the open country. Beyond the city limits to the south and west rose up a crescent of hills, visible from each of the Baroque palaces and etching the horizon with the terraced geometry of vineyards until the high land merged into the dark mass of the *Wienerwald* and lungs stifled by overheated rooms caught the transient breath of pinewood from distant mountain slopes. If peace were to be attained by pleasure, as the Prince de Ligne predicted soon after the Congress opened, there was no city in Europe better suited for its pursuit than Vienna.

The diaries and memoirs of the time record a formidable succession of social delights.[2] There was a 'Festivals Committee' of court dignitaries who worked out from week to week a series of grand diversions and entertainments; and at times it seems as though no other committee at the Congress laboured so diligently. Its work was supplemented by the great families and the socially ambitious, until one feels that the day of mourning on the anniversary of Louis XVI's execution must have been as beneficial for the living as the dead. Poor Francis disliked gala occasions and public spectacle but he was a conscientious sovereign and he fulfilled his duties as host on a magnificent scale, spending the equivalent of £5 million sterling by modern reckoning on entertaining his guests. The tedium of the Congress was relieved for him only by the doubtful compensation of reading each morning detailed reports from Baron Hager's police agents on who had been where with whom and what they were writing in their private correspondence, for the interception of letters remained a craft in which the Austrians had no equals.

But if the Emperor gained little from his hospitality, Metternich delighted in every festivity. His detractors, both Austrian and foreign, blamed him for turning a solemn conference of peace into a protracted apotheosis of hedonism, thus bringing the Congress into a disrepute which it has never entirely lived down. 'He is the best master-of-ceremonies in the world,' said the Tsar, and qualified this testimonial by the thought that 'it would be hard to find a worse minister'.[3] Talleyrand complained testily that Metternich held 'aloof inertia to be a kind of superior genius'.[4] And Wilhelm von Humboldt wrote to his wife: 'All that interests Metternich is arranging entertainments and tableaux vivants for the Court. He is quite capable of keeping a couple of ambassadors waiting, while he watches his daughter dance and chats amiably with the ladies. Only trifles are serious for him; and serious business he treats as a trifle.' Sir Edward Cooke, Castlereagh's principal adviser in the first weeks of the Congress, wasted few words on the man: 'most intolerably loose and giddy with women,' he commented tersely.[5]

There was justice in these complaints, and Metternich's incorrigible nonchalance in the last quarter of 1814 irritated even such a loyal colleague as Gentz. Talleyrand's estimate that Metternich spent three-quarters of his time at social festivities is not far off the mark. He knew he shone in society and made every effort to burnish his image. But it is facile to suggest Metternich deliberately allowed the Congress to drag on from one grand reception to another so that he could play out some private comedy of manners. There was a sound reason for procrastination: he needed time desperately if he were to break up the Russo-Prussian entente and ensure that the Tsar did not establish in Eastern and Central Europe a primacy no less overbearing than Napoleon had enjoyed. The chronicle of Metternich's activities during the six months the sovereigns were in Vienna is not always edifying; at times it lost public policy in private entanglement; but in the end it is a record of triumph rather than of failure.

Conflicts of interests

Metternich had hoped originally that it might be possible to settle some outstanding problems before the formal opening of the Congress and, more particularly, before the rulers of Russia and Prussia arrived in Vienna. He continued to spend most of August and the first half of September at Baden; the town was quieter and cooler than Vienna, and only two hours distant by carriage. When, on 14 September, he heard that the chief Allied ministers had completed their journeys, he rode into Vienna and urged them to adjourn to Baden for preliminary conferences. But the preparations for housing the deputations were so haphazard that the ministers had no wish to move out of the capital, preferring to concentrate on achieving some order out of the happy confusion around them. They were able to hold four meetings in the first week after their arrival but found no one had clear ideas on procedure. There were marked differences of approach, especially between Castlereagh and the Russians, but by 23 September they had at least agreed on a basic protocol. Major territorial decisions would be taken by the four Allied powers (Austria, Britain, Prussia and Russia) and submitted to the French and Spanish for approval, before being sent to the whole Congress for ratification. A separate committee of the five leading German states would draft a constitution for a German Confederation, and arrangements for the future work of the Congress would be determined by the 'Big Six' (the four principal Allies together with France and Spain). It was also agreed that this inner council needed a secretary who would draft all protocols and general statements. There seemed no man more versed in the affairs of Europe than Gentz, and on the evening of 23 September he was informed by Nesselrode that the ministers had nominated him 'by acclamation their Secretary'. The appointment pleased Metternich, for it would clearly strengthen his own influence on the conduct of business. The two men knew each other's minds; they had corresponded regularly over the previous year; and they had discussed public – and often private – affairs almost every day since the Prince's return from Paris.[6]

On that same Friday (23 September) Talleyrand arrived in Vienna, very quietly: on the following Sunday Tsar Alexander made his entry, very ostentatiously. Their coming immediately disrupted the work of the ministers. Talleyrand objected to the exclusion of France from the counsels of Europe and to the way in which the 'Big Four' were perpetuating a wartime alliance, despite the substitution of the Bourbons for the Bonapartes in Paris. He argued that they had no right to settle outstanding matters in committee before convening the full Congress, and he was supported by the Spanish representative, Don Pedro Labrador. There was a stormy meeting on the afternoon of 30 September.[7] That night Gentz noted in his diary: 'The intervention of Talleyrand and Labrador has hopelessly ruined all our plans. They protested against the procedure we have adopted; they gave us a dressing-down which lasted for two hours; it is a scene I shall never forget.' When the meeting broke up Gentz, highly ruffled, walked with Metternich in the gardens of the Prince's villa on the Rennweg. To Gentz' surprise, he did not seem unduly concerned by the embarrassing position in which Talleyrand's trenchant attack had placed the former allies. He was chiefly interested in preparations for a grand fête which he planned to give in the Rennweg on 18 October, the first anniversary of the victory at Leipzig. It was all rather exasperating for a conscientious First Secretary. Subsequently the spokesmen of Sweden and Portugal claimed an equal status with France and Spain; and at a meeting on 8 October it was agreed that the 'Big Six' should be replaced by a 'Preliminary Committee of the Eight'. Four days later the Eight published their first public declaration: the opening of the Congress was postponed until 1 November.

Talleyrand's sallies did not entirely displease Metternich. He had no intention of allowing decisions to be taken by the Congress as a body, but he did not object to procedural wrangles if they gave him a month's

grace in which to take stock of Alexander and seek to fathom the
depths of his policy. For, in Metternich's eyes, the Tsar was still the
greatest obstacle to a settlement. He had received such adulation in St
Petersburg that his self-confidence, gradually deflated in Paris and
London, was now fully restored. No one, as yet, knew precisely what he
wanted in Poland: there was talk of a Polish kingdom, with a liberal
constitution and linked with Russia through the person of the sovereign;
but over the centuries the territorial limits of Poland have been more
amorphous than those of any other European state, and it was not clear
where Alexander, in the intoxication of victory, wished to draw the
kingdom's newest boundaries. Nor was it certain what fate he had in
mind for the unfortunate King of Saxony who, by his tardiness in
deserting Napoleon, was conveniently held to have forfeited his
possessions.

Alexander's temperament made him at all times a difficult person
with whom to negotiate. In Vienna his attitude towards any problem
became even more unpredictable because of the peculiar character of
the Russian delegation.[8] The principal plenipotentiary was Karl
Nesselrode but it is significant that he received, not ministerial rank, but
the lesser designation of 'State Secretary for Foreign Affairs'. The Tsar
turned more readily for advice to one of the heterogeneous group of
specialists whose presence brought confusion to the conference table.
Some had been in Alexander's confidence for many years: Prince Adam
Czartoryski, friend of the Tsar for a quarter of a century and former
Foreign Minister, drafted most of the memoranda on Polish affairs,
without reference to Nesselrode. Stein, to Metternich's disgust, continued to advise the Tsar in German questions. Pozzo di Borgo, a
Corsican who hated the Bonapartes and had been in Russian service
since 1805, was summoned to Vienna as an expert on France, but he
was consulted less than contemporaries believed, partly because he was
bitterly opposed to Alexander's Polish policy. All these members of the
Russian delegation were familiar figures and Metternich was able to
make allowance for their influence on the Tsar, even if at times it was
difficult to determine which servant was currently in his master's favour.
It was the unknown newcomer, John Capodistrias, whom Metternich
came most rapidly to distrust, sensing that the thirty-eight-year-old
Corfiote was a natural antagonist.* He showed a disconcerting sympathy for liberal constitutionalism; and, although Metternich was
pleased to find that, like Pozzo, he opposed Alexander's Polish projects,

* John Capodistrias (1776–1831) was a member of one of the old families of Corfu. He
began to work for the Russians in 1800 when a naval squadron occupied the Ionian Islands,
and he formally entered the Russian diplomatic service in 1809. The Tsar had used him on
a special mission to Switzerland in 1813–14. In 1815 he was made State Secretary for Foreign
Affairs and shared the direction of Russian foreign policy with Nesselrode until 1822.

Emperor Francis of Austria
by Sir Thomas Lawrence (see p. 81)

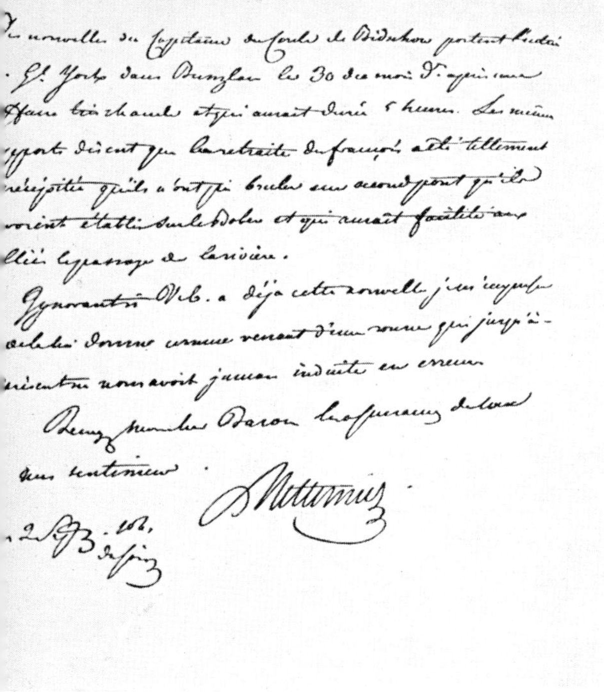

[A handwritten letter in French script appears in the upper left of the page, ending with a signature "Metternich"]

Letter from Metternich to the
Prussian Chancellor, Hardenberg,
September 1813

(*right*)
Frederick William III of Prussia

Tsar Alexander, Emperor Francis and King Frederick William III
give thanks after the battle of Leipzig, 1813

Emperor Francis returns to Vienna from Paris, June 1814

Victory banquet of the City of London in the Guildhall, June 1814 with the Prince Regent, Tsar Alexander, Frederick William of Prussia and Metternich seated at the high table

he feared that a Greek in the Tsar's entourage might at any time disturb the delicate balance of power in the Balkan peninsula. Capodistrias had such a subtle mind it was never clear what advice he would tender to Alexander.

There remained, too, uncertainty over Frederick William of Prussia. As if to emphasize the bonds linking St Petersburg and Berlin, he had ridden beside the Tsar in a joint solemn entry into Vienna. Six months earlier he had similarly accompanied Alexander into Paris, and the tactless parallel was not lost on the Viennese, who amused themselves for weeks with ironic pleasantries at Frederick William's expense.[9] But the Austrian foreign service took the friendship of the two sovereigns more seriously. It was assumed that since Prussia was guaranteed territories as extensive as those held in 1805, the Tsar and the King must have concluded a secret compact by which Prussia would receive Saxony (which was still under Russian administration) in return for renouncing her former Polish provinces, which would be incorporated in the new Polish kingdom. Metternich was faced by a double dilemma. He had no desire to see Russian garrisons deep in Central Europe or a Prussian army in Dresden, astride Bohemia's vulnerable northern frontier; and yet he had no wish to alienate the Prussians since he believed a durable settlement in Germany depended on Austro-Prussian collaboration. Similarly, he could not tempt Frederick William with compensation in the Rhineland, not only because this ran counter to his own inclinations but also because it would have stirred up the dormant antagonism of his critics at home, particularly in the Stadion circle; and yet he had little hope of direct personal negotiations with the Tsar, who by now distrusted him so deeply that he suspected duplicity in every proposal he made.

Characteristically Metternich took refuge in evasion. He left Castlereagh, who had no direct interests in Poland or Saxony and with whom he was still on good terms, to sound out Alexander and make sense of Prussian policy. Meanwhile he gave his mind to other matters. Some of these, as Gentz had already discovered, were totally frivolous; but there were still important decisions to be taken over Italy, a region where delay weakened rather than strengthened Austria's position. While Castlereagh had a series of strained discussions with the Tsar, Metternich attended to reports from Milan, Venice and the other cities of the peninsula.

These tactics achieved little. The Tsar insisted to Castlereagh he was the real arbiter of Poland's future since he had half a million men in the country, occupying every Polish town and village. He indicated that he had every intention of retaining all the former Grand-Duchy of Warsaw except for a small area in the north-west, which he would return to Prussia; and he made it clear that he did not propose to return to the Austrians any of the territory which had passed to the Habsburgs in the Polish partitions.[10] Finding Alexander obstinately immutable, Castlereagh concentrated on improving the relations between Prussia and Austria; and in this effort, at least, he gained some success. Meanwhile, Metternich's interest in the Italian Question had proved no more than spasmodic. He was willing to accept sound advice from Marshal Bellegarde on ways of placating Italian sentiment and on 9 October he even suggested to Emperor Francis that La Scala in Milan might be subsidized by the Austrian state so as to show the Italians how their new masters appreciated their cultural heritage. But Francis was ominously unresponsive.[11] He felt as strongly about Italy as Stadion about Germany; and he was by no means convinced that, as yet, Metternich was entirely sound on Italian questions, for he was still backing Murat in Naples and had received Eugene Beauharnais – the *ci-devant* Viceroy', as Gentz described him – almost as soon as he arrived in Vienna. Metternich's one consistent rule of action was to avoid a clash with the Emperor and, perceiving Francis' sensitivity to Italian issues, he discreetly lost interest in Lombardy and Venetia and turned his attention to Genoa. Here, in fact, the statesmen made some headway; and the incorporation of the city in Sardinia-Piedmont was approved by the Committee of Eight in a rare interlude of accord during the third week of November.[12]

There was no such interlude over Poland and Saxony. By the middle of October Castlereagh had made sufficient progress in his conversations with the Prussian Chancellor, Hardenberg, for a joint approach to be made to the Tsar. Metternich let Hardenberg know he was prepared to offer concessions in Saxony, provided Alexander could be restrained in Poland. It was agreed that Metternich should present to the Tsar three possible solutions of the Polish Question: a genuinely independent state, a rump Poland as in 1791, or a return to the partitioned boundaries of 1795. Metternich was granted an audience with the Tsar on the afternoon of 24 October to inform him of this joint plan of action.[13]

It was a bad moment to choose for an approach to the Tsar and Metternich was the worst of all possible emissaries. Throughout the past week Alexander had been peevishly petulant and, only the previous day, had set all Vienna gossiping after a stormy interview with Talleyrand. Part of his ill-humour had physical origins – he was suffering from recurrent bouts of erysipelas of the leg – but much was believed to spring from sheer pique, for he was not cutting such a figure in Viennese society as he had expected. He was at times childishly jealous of Metternich, and his ire was mischievously fanned by Katharina Bagration who was currently his principal mistress and who was furious with Clement for having succumbed to the wiles of her rival, Wilhelmine of Sagan.* The pettiness of the Tsar's temperament provoked comment during the celebrations of the anniversary of Leipzig, on 18 October. He had proceeded to Metternich's grand ball directly from a military reception given by Emperor Francis at the *Lusthaus* in the Prater and then went out of his way to let his fellow-guests know of his preference for soldierly company: 'The ball is fine. The ballroom is attractive and magnificent,' he had said, 'but there is always too much diplomacy around, and I don't like hypocrisy. I see too many diplomats here, and these people bore me.'[14] And now, only six days later, he was expected to receive his late host and hear what those tiresome diplomats proposed to do with the provinces which his glorious army had conquered. The afternoon held promise of a lively meeting.

Metternich was, of course, accustomed to Imperial tantrums. He had met Napoleon's outbursts with calm and dignity, eyebrows rising un-evenly in deprecation but never lifting his voice above a condescending drawl. But this time he, too, was under strain: Eleonore was giving another ball that night, more intimate than the previous week's but hardly less exhausting; and Wilhelmine was becoming so anxious for her Russian estates that she had begun to court the Tsar once more and found him readily bewitched by her charms. Clement was incensed by this treachery and spent much of the morning pouring out his troubles to Gentz and Wessenberg, who called on other matters. It was hard to focus the mind on Poland: and when Alexander spoke at length on his beneficence towards the Polish Kingdom, Metternich could not resist pricking his illusions by suggesting that Austria was as well able as Russia to create an independent Poland. The remark stung the Tsar: 'You are the only man in Austria who would dare to oppose me in such rebellious terms,' he shouted.[15] The latent quarrel had come to the surface at last.

The Prince tried to calm down Alexander but it was impossible to transact business with him. After two hours of empty verbiage, he left the audience declaring he would never again seek a private conversation with the Tsar; and that night he sent a written report to Francis in which he likened Alexander's language to Napoleon's and discounted the 'ridiculous idea' that he felt a personal antagonism towards the Tsar. He then joined his guests at the Rennweg. The King of Denmark

* At the end of 1813 Wilhelmine of Sagan had left Bohemia for Vienna and had taken over one wing of the Palais Palm in the Schenkenstrasse. After her visit to Paris and London in the summer of 1814 she returned to the same apartments. By chance the opposite wing of the Palais Palm was occupied by the Princess Bagration. The proximity of the two ladies, who had detested each other for the past twelve years, had already caused amusement in Vienna, not least to Eleonore von Metternich (see, for examples, Maria Ullrichova, *Clemens Metternich Wilhelmine von Sagan, Ein Briefwechsel*, p. 141 and p. 203). The Palais Palm was only a few hundred yards from Metternich's official residence in the Ballhausplatz and from Alexander's rooms in the Hofburg, (see the map on p. 296 below).

was there, the Duke of Coburg, the Duke of Weimar, Eugene Beau-harnais, but not the Tsar nor Wilhelmine of Sagan. In the small hours of the morning he gave 'all the details of his famous and sad conver-sation with the Emperor of Russia' to Gentz, and soon rumour was embellishing it throughout Vienna. Talleyrand reported, with ill-concealed glee to Louis xviii, that Alexander had 'used language so violent that, had it been addressed to one of his servants, it would have been extraordinary'. The original purpose of Metternich's audience with the Tsar seemed to be forgotten: a police agent reported to Hager on 26 October that the Polish nobles who had come to the Congress 'are for ever very restless over their fate'; and small wonder.[16]

There was no doubt Metternich's own position was now in jeopardy. Three weeks ago the people of Vienna were still amused by the circus of festivities going on around them; there had even been a 'People's Fête' in the Augarten on 6 October with rulers and commonalty cheer-ing a balloonist who drifted over the Danube wasteland in a basket decked with the flags of the Allied nations.[17] But now there were angry complaints at the cost of living and ironic badinage at who was paying for these frivolities.[18] There seemed little likelihood of the Congress opening on 1 November and Metternich's old political enemies had once more come together; there was talk of Stadion and Schwarzenberg taking over his duties and adopting a firmer line over the German and Polish Questions. Nor was it clear how far his quarrel with the Tsar weakened his position. Soon after their stormy meeting Alexander, with Frederick William obediently to heel, accompanied Francis on a short state visit to Hungary and spent much of the journey urging him to dismiss his Foreign Minister and find an Austrian statesman less 'rebellious' in temperament.[19] But Francis was not the man to be swayed by Alexander's gusts of prejudice and it seems likely that, with his dry sense of humour, he was enjoying the contest between his im-perious guest and a Minister who, on occasions, over-reached himself. Alexander was told he had always felt it was wisest for Foreign Ministers to do business with other Foreign Ministers and diplomats rather than with a monarch. Someone noticed Francis return from Pest well pleased with himself; and Hager's agents reported that Alexander had gone straight to Katharina Bagration and remained closeted with her for three and a half hours. Discreet enquiries next morning revealed they had talked politics, intermittently;[20] but the Princess said that over Poland 'he will not listen to reason'.

Yet Metternich was not unduly troubled by reports of his growing unpopularity. He felt confident of Francis's support and went ahead with plans for the next great entertainment on the Rennweg, a fancy-dress ball to be held on 8 November to which all the sovereigns, princes, archdukes and everyone of distinction or grace were invited. But he had taken advantage of the monarchs' absence to confer with the other leading ministers 'on ways of setting the Congress in motion'. None of them wanted to see the lesser plenipotentiaries take the initiative, if only because nobody had the faintest idea of the rules governing this particular diplomatic game; but could the Four Powers postpone a plenary session any longer? The First Secretary did not doubt they could and should, so long as there were divisions among them: 'I talked a great deal,' Gentz noted in his diary after a conference on 29 October, 'I have killed the idea of the Congress'.[21] But it was agreed that, in order to show progress was being made, a three-man commission would begin to examine the credentials of representatives from the smaller states. When this extensive labour had been completed, the Committee of Eight might formulate proposals on how precisely the Congress would come into being. Meanwhile confidential discussions and occasional meetings of committees would continue. Already Talleyrand was speaking sardonically of 'the Congress that was not a congress'.[22]

The Allies fail to agree

The failure to get down to business had a curious effect on social life in the city. Despite the fever of festivity, Vienna was full of self-important delegates who liked to give the impression they knew the inner secrets of the Big Four. Invariably their tales were scandalous or pessimistic, or both. The gloom spread to the Viennese themselves. At the beginning of November a report on the mood of his capital was prepared by Hager's agents for Emperor Francis: 'Public opinion with regard to the Congress is still bad,' it began. 'Everywhere people are saying that there is no agreement . . . and that everything points towards a general war, the outbreak of which will not long be delayed.' The rumours of war reached London and threw Castlereagh's colleagues into despair, for no one in Britain was interested in the fate of Poland and Saxony; and they also reached Elba, where memory stirred with interest at familiar names, and maps were spread on card-tables in a tiny palace on the hillside.[23] But matters were not yet so serious. The Powers might talk big and rattle their sabres if that was the surest way of reaching a settlement; but none of them wanted the expense and uncertainties of another campaign, especially in the depth of winter. Metternich sensed this, and so did Talleyrand; 'Too frightened to fight each other, too stupid to agree,' he noted with acid impatience; but not everyone had the nerve to observe the scene with such Olympian detachment. Hastily the Festivals Committee proposed a mediaeval carousel for 23 November; its preparation would keep the hotheads out of mischief. And there were other attractions, too; Signorina Emilie Bigottini would dance in the ballet *Nina* at the *Kärntnertortheater*; and Beethoven would conduct a concert of his own music on a weekday rather than the traditional Sunday, out of respect for the sabbatarian prejudices of the British delegation. Beethoven had such strong admirers and such staunch critics that this event, too, could be relied on as a conversational distraction from more menacing topics.[24]

But, despite *Nina*, despite the Seventh Symphony, despite caparisoned horses in the Spanish Riding School, November remained a month of political crisis and December was little better. On 7 November Hardenberg informed Metternich he had been ordered by Frederick William, in the Tsar's presence, to break off all confidential negotiations with Castlereagh over Saxony and Poland; and that evening it was learned in Vienna that Russia had surrendered responsibility for the administration of Saxony to the Prussian Army.[25] If this action was intended to force Metternich's hand it failed; Gentz was far more alarmed at what he termed 'Prussia's act of treachery' than the Prince. For eleven days Metternich made no response; he then reminded Hardenberg that Austria could support Prussian expansion in Saxony only if the Tsar gave concessions over Poland, and he therefore proposed that Hardenberg himself should seek to influence Alexander. But Hardenberg could make little progress: on 2 December he informed Metternich that, as a gesture of goodwill, Alexander was prepared to recognize Thorn and Cracow as 'Free Cities' but he insisted on retaining the rest of Poland as a satellite kingdom, and he still maintained the whole of Saxony should be incorporated in Prussia.[26]

This concession was not enough to satisfy Metternich. The German Committee had run into difficulties, the Bavarians refusing to join any German Confederation which did not include an independent Saxony. When, on 10 December, Metternich replied to Hardenberg's note, he pointed out that, if Prussia wished to participate in a Germanic league, she could not alienate the other German states by her policy over Saxony. He therefore proposed a division of Saxony, which would cede some territory to Prussia but retain Dresden and Leipzig in an independent kingdom ruled by Frederick Augustus. And this time he sent a copy of the proposals to Talleyrand, who had not as yet been admitted to the inner conference of the Big Four, although he was technically a member of the Committee of Eight.[27]

Talleyrand had been waiting for two months for this chance to intervene. He was a warm champion of the King of Saxony and therefore bound to oppose Prussian designs, but he immediately lifted the dispute to a higher plane of law. In a memorandum dated 19 December he argued that the fate of Saxony could not be discussed in terms of territorial compensation nor solely as part of the political balance within Germany (although he conceded this to be an important issue).[28] Since Frederick Augustus was the legitimate representative of a long-established dynasty, he could not be deposed or deprived of his inheritance because brother sovereigns who coveted his lands disapproved of an act of policy he had mistakenly undertaken. It was 'contrary to justice and reason' for Prussia to state what she would take and what she would hand over to the King of Saxony: it was for the lawful king himself to declare what he was prepared to yield to the Prussians. By thus invoking the sanctity of legitimate kingship Talleyrand struck a shrewd blow at the whole basis of the discussions in Vienna. Legitimacy was, in one respect at least, an awkward doctrine for Metternich to accept, because it would be impossible for him to continue recognition of Murat's claims in Naples, but his attitude towards the affairs of southern Italy was by no means rigid and he was already beginning to suspect a Murat dynasty of becoming the favoured instrument of Italian patriotism against Austria. He was willing to sacrifice Murat for French backing in the contest over Saxony.[29]

In the last fortnight of December Metternich and Castlereagh brought Talleyrand more and more into the affairs of the Congress until at the very end of the year it was proposed the French representative should henceforth participate in all conferences of the Big Four. The Prussians did not like this development but the Russians acquiesced, largely because Alexander was during that Christmas undergoing one of 'the periodic evolutions of his mind', as Metternich said later (with considerable insight). He began to despise the task of peacemaking as an exercise in sordid bargaining and his spirit became elevated by a sense of mystic exaltation. On 10 December his behaviour was still so frigid that he was barely speaking to Emperor Francis, let alone to Metternich; by 15 December he was so well-disposed towards Francis that he insisted on inviting him for two long discussions. His mood, noted the ever-vigilant police agents, changed from gloom to hope. There is no reason to suppose this transformation owed anything to Talleyrand's activity or Metternich's inactivity. But it made him naturally receptive to any talk of legitimate kingship. He was looking on himself once more as the elect of God: might it not be possible that Frederick Augustus of Saxony, too, was a King worthy in the sight of the Lord? Alexander's attitude towards Metternich did not change; but he became suddenly less interested in Saxony and even in Poland and more concerned with the fate of Orthodox Christians under the infidel Sultan. It was a tiresome topic to raise at such a time, especially for the Austrians, but at least it made a settlement of the Polish-Saxon dispute easier.[30]

For, in the course of his conversations with Francis, Alexander indicated that he was prepared to retrocede to Austria all the region around Tarnopol in southern Poland and repeated his willingness for Thorn and Cracow to be created Free Cities. The Prussians sensed they were isolated and spoke tactlessly of war. The New Year opened in a slightly unreal sense of crisis. Talleyrand achieved a diplomatic triumph by concluding a secret defensive alliance between France, Britain and Austria, but it was not really necessary and within two days of its conclusion Castlereagh was writing to his Prime Minister, 'The alarm of war is over'. The Prussians continued for three weeks to press for the whole of Saxony, offering Frederick Augustus a newly created kingdom on the middle Rhine; but the Russians were by now supporting them much less actively, and by the second week of February agreement had been reached. Poland was once more partitioned: Austria retained Galicia and Tarnopol; Prussia recovered Poznania including the towns of Posen and Thorn; and the rest of Napoleon's Grand-Duchy of Warsaw became a Kingdom of Poland ruled by the Tsar of Russia. Cracow was set up as a Free City. In Germany three-fifths of Saxony, including Dresden and Leipzig, was restored to Frederick Augustus; the remaining two-fifths was ceded to Prussia who also obtained much of the left bank of the Rhine and Westphalia. There was still much work to be done in committee, and Frederick Augustus was brought to Pressburg (Bratislava) for belated consultation early in March; but the worst disputes were over.[31]

The Tsar was not the only prominent figure at Vienna to feel disillusioned with the proceedings of the Congress. Gentz wrote in his diary at the end of 1814: 'The appearance of public affairs is depressing, not as in other times because of the massive and terrifying cloud hanging over our heads but because of the mediocrity and ineptitude of almost all our public figures.'[32] On 12 January he gave a dinner-party in his rooms in the Seilergasse and won praise from his distinguished guests, but he could not shake off his weary cynicism. 'It was a curious business,' he wrote afterwards, 'I contributed almost nothing to the conversation. Metternich and Talleyrand held forth in their usual way; while I sensed as never before the futility of human endeavour, the failings of men who hold the fate of the world in their hands . . . the fine-sounding nonsense of these gentlemen enveloped my mind in a fog of unreality.'[33] The delights of the Congress-which-had-never-met were beginning to pall. The Festivals Committee had listed no less than sixteen grand fêtes on the social calendar for January, to say nothing of sleighing parties and other diversions. It was fortunate that Lent began on 8 February, although awkward that Ash Wednesday should have been Wilhelmine of Sagan's birthday; a gift of faience vases from Metternich was not inappropriate;[34] forty days of abstinence had never been so essential for salvation.

But they were forty days of hard work and fresh alarms. Metternich was engrossed in the affairs of the German Committee, where the representatives of Württemberg were making difficulties over surrendering rights to a Federal Diet, and the Swiss Committee to which every one of the nineteen cantons had sent a delegation. There were conferences over abolition of the slave trade and over freedom of navigation on the Rhine and its tributaries. Before Castlereagh returned to England in February Metternich had agreed with him that the Bourbons must return to Naples; but no one was sure how to get rid of Murat, who was said to be raising a fine army in southern Italy. The days when foreign observers could complain that Clement never rose from his bed until ten in the morning were over, and the Palais Palm saw him infrequently. There were so many deputations for him to receive: the Catholics of Frankfurt; the Jews of Bremen and Strasbourg and Lübeck and then, for good measure, the Jews of Frankfurt as well; princes of the old Germany, pressing for a restoration of the Empire rather than a Germanic Confederation; the corporation of the Knights of Swabia; the corporation of the Knights of the Wettcrau; spokesmen for the publishing trade of Augsburg, anxious that the copyright value of the printed word should be appreciated in this monstrous talking-house of Vienna.[35] And there were reports to be studied from agents at home and abroad: the length of time that Marie Louise had walked in the gardens of Schönbrunn; the visits made by Eugene Beauharnais in Vienna; how many of Tsar Alexander's entourage had joined the Society of Philomuses of Athens; why the Grand-Duke of Baden was displeased; what they were saying in Stuttgart about Saxony; what they were saying in Luxembourg about the newly proclaimed King of the Netherlands; what they were saying in Paris about everything and everybody. And time had to be found for talks with Joseph von Pilat, who had once been Metternich's secretary and now edited the *Österreichischer Beobachter*, for he could be relied on to know what Stadion and Schwarzenberg would be thinking tomorrow – and that was a topic of permanent interest to Metternich.[36]

News of Napoleon's escape from Elba and its effect on the Congress

Yet, despite his complicated network of agents and informers, the most startling news of those early months in 1815 took him completely by surprise.[37] On the evening of Monday, 6 March, Metternich received in his official residence Talleyrand, Nesselrode, Hardenberg and the Duke of Wellington, who had succeeded Castlereagh as British plenipotentiary in February. A deputation was due to leave for Pressburg on Wednesday to inform the King of Saxony of the fate of his lands; there was much to discuss, and the meeting did not break up until three o'clock on the Tuesday morning. Metternich retired to bed, with orders that he was not to be disturbed. At six he was, nevertheless, awoken by a messenger who brought a despatch marked 'Urgent' from the consul at Genoa. Metternich put it beside his bed, without opening the envelope, and tried again to go to sleep. It was impossible: he had been disturbed and he was restless. At half-past seven he abandoned the attempt and opened the despatch. It said that Napoleon had disappeared from Elba. The Prince reacted promptly to the news. Within half an hour he was with the Emperor Francis. At a quarter-past eight he saw the Tsar and at half-past eight the King of Prussia. By ten o'clock all the leading ministers were gathered in his study, and couriers were on their way to the army corps of each of the Allied powers with orders to place themselves on the alert. The Austrians were concentrated in Lombardy-Venetia, the Prussians in central Germany, the Russians in Poland and there was a small British force in Belgium. Metternich himself thought they would soon be marching back along the road to Paris once more; and although Wellington and Talleyrand maintained that Napoleon would make for the Italian coast rather than for France, most observers agreed with him. Napoleon had indeed landed between Fréjus and Antibes on the first of the month and was already in Grenoble, heading for Lyons; but, in Vienna, it was not known he had actually established himself on French soil until 11 March.

At first the news of Napoleon's flight from Elba made little difference to the work of the Congress. It caused a burst of activity on the part of the so-called 'mediatized' princes of Germany. Encouraged by Stadion, they pressed Francis to have himself once more proclaimed Emperor of a German Reich in order to forestall any Napoleonic gestures on the Rhine. But Francis never took panic decisions without consulting his Foreign Minister, and Metternich insisted that an attempt to resuscitate the Holy Roman Empire would alienate the Prussians and cause a new breach between the Allies at a moment when unity was essential.[38] The news also influenced the attitude of the King of Saxony. On the afternoon of 8 March Metternich, Wellington and Talleyrand travelled down the Danube to Pressburg and met Frederick Augustus in the citadel where Napoleon had dictated peace in 1805. It was an unsatisfactory encounter; for now that Napoleon was apparently challenging the whole settlement, Frederick Augustus was not prepared to accept the arbitrary award of two-fifths of his territory to the Prussians. But there was little he could do except procrastinate. He was without friends, for Talleyrand was far too concerned with dissociating the French people from Napoleon's enterprise to take a stand as champion of the rights of Saxony. As soon as the three statesmen returned to Vienna, the Prussians were authorized to annex the area provisionally assigned to them and to continue occupation of the rest of Saxony until Frederick Augustus came to his senses. He eventually gave his consent to the transfer of territory on 6 April.[39]

The Big Five were in no mood for compromise or evasion. On 13 March the Committee of the Eight issued a declaration publicly indicting 'Napoleon Bonaparte' as an outlaw and 'disturber of world repose'. Four days later Vienna received reports that French regiments were defecting to their old master as he thrust towards his former capital. That evening, as Wilhelmine of Sagan was holding a grand reception in the Palais Palm, rumours began to circulate that Paris had already welcomed back Napoleon. Gentz, who was among Wilhelmine's guests, noted that the report caused 'general consternation'.[40] News had, for once, anticipated events since it was only on 20 March that Napoleon arrived in Paris, but the rumours had a beneficial effect on the statesmen in Vienna, steeling their resolve to remain united in the face of the common menace. Work began next morning on creating a new treaty of grand alliance, which was published on 25 March. The Austrians, British, Prussians and Russians pledged themselves to supply 150,000 men each to defend the new frontiers of Europe from Napoleon, and they invited Louis XVIII and the smaller powers of Europe to associate themselves with the treaty and co-operate in the forthcoming campaign. There was by now little evidence of a rift between Napoleon's old enemies.[41]

Outwardly the Tsar and Metternich were reconciled. At the end of March a Russian diplomat arrived in Vienna from Paris with a con-ciliatory message from Napoleon for Alexander and a copy of the secret triple alliance made by Metternich, Castlereagh and Talleyrand against the Prussians and Russians twelve weeks previously.[42] It had been left in the French archives when Louis XVIII fled the capital. Privately the Tsar was angry at the revelation, although he had sus-pected there was such an understanding soon after it was concluded. But Napoleon's attempt to exploit his temperamental instability failed. Magnanimously the Tsar declined to make an issue of this apparent proof of treachery. There was a touching scene in Alexander's wing of the Hofburg when the Tsar sent for Metternich and presented him with the document which Napoleon had forwarded from Paris. 'Let us kiss and let all be forgotten,' he said, according to Metternich. 'Let us never mention this incident again and let us attend to more serious matters,' he said, according to the Prussian Stein, who was also present. Peace had to be concluded and a new war won at the same time.[43]

Life in Vienna lost some of its glamour that spring as the army commanders departed and the diplomats concentrated on getting some order into the proceedings of the Congress. The boundaries of the Kingdom of the Netherlands were hurriedly fixed, proposals for a loose confederation of Swiss cantons were accepted by the Committee of the Eight, formal treaties delineated frontiers in Poland and provided a constitution and a guarantee of independence for the Republic of Cracow; and, from mid-March onwards, a Special Committee of eight plenipotentiaries and twenty-five secretaries began drafting a Final Act

of the Congress, a definitive statement which would summarize the
results of all their labours. There was, indeed, a new sense of urgency,
unfamiliar to Vienna.[44] Compromises were reached over abolition of
the slave trade (prompted, perhaps, by Napoleon's formal pronouncement against the institution on his return to Paris) and over the rights
of the Jewish communities in Germany. The committees on river
navigation and on regulation of diplomatic rank completed their tasks
by early May. There were only two problems of major concern to
Metternich which continued to defy solution: Italy and Germany.

The return of Napoleon brought the Italian Question to a point of
crisis.[45] On the day before Napoleon landed in France Hudelist had
drawn Metternich's attention to an agitation being carried on throughout central Italy by Murat's agents, and it seemed to the Austrians that
Murat's activities could not be unrelated to the main enterprise of
Napoleon (although, in fact, Murat was acting in foolhardy isolation).
On 30 March Murat issued a dramatic appeal from Rimini calling on
the people of the peninsula to rise up and liberate Italian soil. Emperor
Francis responded by two proclamations: on 2 April Austria formally
assumed responsibility for the administration of Parma, Piacenza and
Guastalla, nominally possessions of Marie Louise; and on 7 April the
new Lombardo-Venetian Kingdom was officially instituted in Vienna.
Fighting broke out between Austrian units in central Italy and Murat's
Neapolitan army; and on 18 April Metternich announced that Austria
considered herself at war with Naples. The campaign was over in a
month. On 3 May a sharp battle at Tolentino, on the eastern slopes of
the Appennines south-west of Ancona, led to Murat's defeat. Naples
was captured on 22 May and Murat fled to France, where Napoleon
refused to receive him. All Italy east of the Ticino and south of the Alps
was at Metternich's disposal by the beginning of June. Although willing
to restore the 'legitimate' Bourbon King, Ferdinand, to the throne of
the Two Sicilies, Metternich postponed the final political settlement of
Italy until after the diplomats had finished their work in Vienna. For
several months he was attracted by the idea of an Italian Confederation,
a loose union of the states of the peninsula under Austria's tutelage and
protection, but he was in no hurry to show his hand. When in October
Murat rashly landed in Calabria and raised a lone flag of insurrection,
it was convenient to leave responsibility for his capture and execution
to the restored Bourbons, especially as Caroline Murat – for whom
Metternich retained some affection – had found sanctuary at Hainburg,
not thirty miles from Vienna. With 'King Joachim' dead and his cause
discredited, Italy could wait until Metternich had sounded other minds
on the prospects for a confederation. There was no longer any hurry.

The affairs of Germany had no such dramatic climax.[46] Throughout
the winter months Prussian and Austrian representatives on the German

Committee had been preparing constitutional schemes, each of them a variation on a loosely federal theme. They were hampered by opposition from three groups: the liberal patriots, who wished for a genuinely effective central government in Germany; the dispossessed princes, eager for safeguards of ancient privileges; and the smaller ruling dynasties who feared that any federal union would imply a greater loss of sovereignty than under the old Empire. Eventually, in the third week of May, the Committee adopted a scheme jointly sponsored by Metternich and Hardenberg, the ninth constitutional draft submitted to it in five months: a Federal Diet was to be established at Frankfurt under Austrian presidency, and there was to be no other executive body. The sovereign rights of the thirty-eight members were limited only by restraints on the contracting of foreign alliances and by a pledge that each ruler would grant to his subjects a constitution based on a system of Estates.* Preparation of fundamental laws for the Confederation and the establishment of further federal institutions was, on Metternich's suggestion, reserved for later consideration by delegates to the Diet. Some of the members of the German Committee were suspicious of even these modest innovations. There were ten long conferences at the end of May and the beginning of June before the draft was formally incorporated in the 'Federal Act', which was signed by most of the German states on 8 June.

With Germany, as with Italy, Metternich had thus postponed decisions on an effective co-ordinating body until he had tested the reality of German national feeling. Although Stadion and his supporters criticized him for having failed to secure a German Imperial Crown for Francis, the Prince was well-pleased with his efforts. As president of the Confederation, Francis had potentially more authority over the German lands than any Habsburg Emperor since the Thirty Years War. The new Diet at Frankfurt could echo Austria's voice far more clearly than the archaic institution at Regensburg under the old system. Even though Prussia now spanned Germany from Rhine to Oder, the real Prime Minister of the German lands in the first years of the Diet was Metternich rather than Hardenberg or a patriot enthusiast thrown up by the war of liberation. And most of the German spokesmen in Vienna recognized his achievement. On 6 June one of Hager's agents noted: 'The ministers and representatives of the German

---

* Article XIII of the Federal Act provided for the establishment of a common constitutional system in the German states. It was, however, ambiguous and caused disputes between rival German parties for many years. The Article said: 'In allen deutschen Staaten wird eine landständische Verfassung stattfinden.' The noun Verfassung was commonly understood by the liberals, especially in Prussia, to mean 'parliamentary constitution'. But Metternich insisted that the use of the epithet landständische implied revival of a system of Estates and not a full parliamentary system; and his interpretation of the clause's phraseology appears to have been justified.

princes sent to the Congress continue to sing the praises of Prince
Metternich . . . They admire the tact and circumspection with which he
has handled the German Committee.'[47] It was a far cry from the complaints and cabals of November; only those who had seen Germany as
something nobler than a congeries of princely states left Vienna
disappointed.

The Final Act of the Treaty of Vienna (June 1815)

By the end of May Vienna was emptying rapidly. The aristocratic riff-
raff of Europe had scurried away like frightened rabbits once Napoleon
had reached Paris when, as one of their number wrote; 'A thousand
candles seemed in a single instant to have been extinguished'.[48] The
Duke of Wellington, too, had left early; for on 29 March he had ridden
off to take command of an army in the Low Countries, leaving British
interests to be represented in the final phase of negotiation by the Earl
of Clancarty, a loyal admirer of Castlereagh, sober and industrious.
Tsar Alexander and Frederick William of Prussia stayed on until 26
May, before setting out for their armies; and even Emperor Francis left
his capital on 27 May, ready to lead Schwarzenberg's troops westwards
into France once more. There were few festivities in the city that spring,
although the weather was superb for weeks on end. Gentz, whose taste
was always for the theatre or the ballet, contented himself at Whitsun
with an evening watching marionettes. Police agents who had tailed
Katharina Bagration for nine months now had nothing to report except
the sinister line of creditors waiting at her door; only Wilhelmine of
Sagan continued to the end to supply morsels of scandal, thanks largely
to the imbecility of Castlereagh's half-brother, Lord Charles Stewart.
Metternich celebrated his forty-second birthday on 15 May with nothing more ornate than a family dinner-party, in his garden on the
Rennweg. His private life was almost blameless, not only because of the
endless conferences, but because he was gripped by a tantalizing passion
for Countess Julie Zichy-Festetics, the beautiful and pious wife of the
Minister of the Interior, a woman of such sublime moral excellence that
she had moved poor Frederick William to tears of frustrated adoration.[49]
Talleyrand was still in Vienna, and Hardenberg and Humboldt; and
Nesselrode did not leave until 8 June. Occasionally they dined together
and played whist deep into the night hours, but the superficial frivolity
of earlier months seemed by now as remote as Elba. As they waited for
the last rites of a Congress that had never really come into being, their
minds were on other matters; for along the French frontier with Belgium
Napoleon's newest army was also waiting, hardened veterans and raw
romantics looking out towards Charleroi and the road to Brussels.
    On 9 June the final draft of a treaty embodying all decisions taken at

Vienna was ready. That night there was a solemn ceremony in the state-rooms on the Ballhausplatz. The plenipotentiaries of Austria, Britain, France, Portugal, Prussia, Russia and Sweden initialled the treaty 'in the name of the holy and indivisible Trinity'. But the Congress was not yet over and, indeed, for some diplomats it was only now beginning. There was one last great procedural problem; the representatives of the smaller powers wished to place their signatures on the Final Act and convey a copy of the treaty to their archives. The document comprised 121 articles and each of these had to be transcribed laboriously by hand. Throughout the following week twenty-six secretaries, spurred on by Gentz, were engaged in copying out the clauses one by one, and until they had finished their work the Congress remained in suspended inanimation. At last on 19 June the task was done. Once more the diplomats gathered in the Ballhausplatz at nine o'clock in the evening. By midnight they had all added their signatures; and Gentz could write thankfully in his diary: 'Definitive closing of the Congress, after a duration of nine full months. Slept in town.'[50]

Metternich did not wait for the completion of this tedious exercise. At one in the morning of Tuesday, 13 June, he set out once more on his travels, his carriage heading westwards towards the armies on the Rhine. But he was spared the exertions of another campaign. On Sunday, 18 June, Napoleon was defeated at Waterloo. The news did not reach Vienna until the following Sunday and by then no one of importance remained in the city. Even the weather had broken.[51]

DABBLING IN THE
SHIFTING SAND

The Second Treaty of Paris; the Holy Alliance; and the Quadruple Alliance
(1815)

By the middle of July 1815 the Allies were once more established in Paris and Louis xviii was giving thanks for the historically rare experience of a second Restoration. This time he owed his precipitate return almost entirely to the initiative of Wellington; for the Waterloo campaign had ended without the Austrian or Russian armies going into action and although the Prussians celebrated their share in the victory with menacing attitudes, the British had the opportunity of settling the dynastic question before the Tsar or anyone else could propose an alternative to the Bourbons. Not that the Duke had particular confidence in Louis xviii; he merely thought that it was better for Europe's security that Alexander and Frederick William should be received by the legitimate King rather than, as in 1814, by the impromptu spokesman of a provisional administration. 'The establishment of any other government than the King's in France must inevitably lead to new and endless wars,' Wellington declared firmly; and his partners in the coalition could only acquiesce in his decision. Metternich, although aware of the unpopularity of the *émigrés*, at heart agreed with him and had already written to Talleyrand urging the speedy return of Louis to his capital.[1]

Metternich was, however, in low spirits, partly on grounds of public policy and partly for private concerns. The cheers of '*Vive Henri IV*' and '*Vive le Roi*' which he heard in Paris seemed hollow and he distrusted the professed allegiance to the new order of men like Fouché and Lafayette. He had heard the news of Waterloo while in Heidelberg, and on the same day he received a letter from Marie, his eldest daughter, which disquieted him; for it informed him how, on 15 June, she and her brother and sister had narrowly escaped drowning when a bridge collapsed at Baden, where the family had gone on holiday while her mother awaited the birth of their seventh child.[2] He was worried at his enforced absence at such a time and he found the spectacle of Paris under Allied occupation strangely disturbing. On 13 July he wrote at length to Marie.[3] He told her of the English soldiery encamped beneath his windows on the Champs Elysees, of the odd sensation of finding himself once more in his old box at the Opera 'as if I had been eight years younger', and of the visit he had made to Blücher at his head-quarters in St Cloud: 'He and his staff smoke where we have seen the court in full dress. The army tailors have established themselves where they had the theatre.' From the balcony he looked towards the towers of Paris which he and Marie knew so well and the senselessness of human endeavour swept over him in a rare mood of humility. 'This city and this sun,' he wrote, 'will still greet each other when there will be nothing but memories of Napoleon, of Blücher and of my own self. The un-changing laws of nature . . . will always be the same, while we wretched creatures who think so much of ourselves, live only to make a little show by our endless activity, by our dabbling in the mud or in the shifting sand.' It is a curious letter, in part nostalgic for the fallen Empire but weary in anticipation of yet more months of public celebration and private dispute.

All the familiar faces were there in Paris: the trinity of sovereigns; Talleyrand, with his serpent's mouth and quizzing smile of irony; Castlereagh, very tall, very courteous and at times very bored; Capodistrias, the Corfiote in the Tsar's service, small and wiry, dark eyes flashing with almost Arabian fire; Nesselrode, gently arrogant and easily flustered; Hardenberg, sadly isolated in a silent world of deafness; and Don Pedro Labrador, a caricature of Spanish temperament, whom no one but himself took seriously. And most of the diplomats and many of the generals, too, had been in Vienna. In the wings, as ever, were Wilhelmine of Sagan and Katharina Bagration, who had come post-haste from Austria as soon as a generous gift from an unknown source allowed her to leave the Schenkenstrasse without embarrassment. Gentz, who had never visited Paris before, found it delightful: on one occasion he succeeded in seeing a play and a ballet at different theatres on the same evening; and Metternich was pleased to go with him to the museums and the boutiques in the Palais Royal.[4] But for the most part, as an indifferent summer gave way to a gloriously fine autumn, the gaiety of Paris was subdued with uncertainty; the ritual ceremonial of receptions, balls and dinners was endured rather than enjoyed. 'Paris is curious to observe,' sighed Metternich to Marie, 'people do not know in the least what they want.'

In 1814 the first Peace of Paris had been signed five weeks after Napoleon's abdication: in 1815 peacemaking dragged on for 133 days, a third as long again as the military emergency which had made it necessary. The difficulty this time was over the chastisement of France. The Prussians wished to impose harsh terms including the surrender of

F

Alsace and Lorraine, and the rulers of the Netherlands and Bavaria were also thinking of territorial compensation for the alarm along their frontiers. The Russians, on the other hand, would have been content with a monetary indemnity and a pledge of good behaviour. Castlereagh resisted all demands for the dismemberment of France, for he regarded a stable government in Paris as an essential counterweight to a militaristic Prussia. And Metternich, who began by thinking in terms of demilitarizing the French frontier, soon came to agree with him. Together they succeeded in winning the support of the Tsar for a compromise settlement which would restrict France to the boundaries of 1790 rather than to those of 1792, as in the first Treaty of Paris. The negotiations were hampered by the determined hostility of the smaller German states and of Prussia, who were encouraged by fiercely anti-French articles in the British press, a constant embarrassment for Castlereagh and an irritant to Gentz and Metternich.[5] Moreover so long as Talleyrand was in office he absolutely refused to consider surrendering any of the 'sacred soil' of France and it was only when he was succeeded by the more pliable Duc de Richelieu* in the last week of September that progress was made towards a treaty.

Nor was this the only vexatious problem. There were disputes over the size of the indemnity to be raised from the French, over the form and duration of Allied military occupation, and over the restitution of art treasures. The Parisians were particularly angered at this insistence on the return of all works of art brought to the city by Napoleon from other lands and permitted to remain in French possession by the treaty of 1814. The King of the Netherlands wanted Dutch and Flemish masters restored to the galleries of Holland and Belgium, and there were treasures from Florence and Rome on which the Grand-Duke of Tuscany and the Pope had legitimate claims. Metternich was personally interested in the four bronze Byzantine horses which Napoleon had brought from the basilica of St Mark's in Venice and placed on his Arc de Triomphe du Carrousel; for Metternich believed that their return would be a conciliatory gesture to the Venetians from their Austrian masters. When the Austrians came to remove the four horses, there was an angry scene with the Paris crowd and the situation was not made any easier by some English tourists who wished to chip souvenirs from the horses once they were lowered to the ground.[6] The Tsar, having no pictures or statues to recover (for the loot of Moscow was abandoned in the retreat), regarded all these operations as a need-

* The Duc de Richelieu (1766–1822) headed the French government from September 1815 to December 1818 and again from February 1820 to December 1821. As an *émigré* in Russia he had been entrusted by Tsar Alexander 1 with the governorship of Odessa and played a considerable part in developing the commercial potential of the port. He had a close personal knowledge of all the leading members of the Russian diplomatic service, but this by no means inclined him to support them.

less humiliation inflicted on Louis xviii, and his protests at the heavy-handed action of Prussian soldiery in the Louvre strained his friendship with Frederick William.

The Tsar, however, was mainly concerned with more spiritual matters. The religious enthusiasm which had illumined his soul so disconcertingly at the start of the year had grown in intensity until he came to believe that lasting peace depended not on paper guarantees but on a sacred treaty binding all sovereigns in faith and charity. He therefore proposed a 'Holy Alliance' of monarchs pledged 'to take for their sole guide the precepts of the Christian religion'. Alexander wished the Emperor of Austria and the King of Prussia to sign the document in the first instance, thereby setting Europe an example of Christian union. Frederick William iii, who had a typically Hohenzollern conviction that he was the adjutant of the Almighty, accepted the draft alliance readily enough, but Francis was perplexed. He was convinced the Tsar was mad, and Metternich agreed with him. They did not object to Alexander's exhortations to Christian benevolence but they distrusted a document which sought to translate mystic pietism into the language of diplomacy, and they were disturbed by sentiments in the original draft which clearly suggested that the old order of relations between states needed to be fundamentally changed. Yet, as Castlereagh reported to Lord Liverpool, Metternich 'was unwilling to thwart the Emperor of Russia in a conception which, however wild, might save him and the rest of the world much trouble as long as it should last. In short, seeing no retreat, after making some verbal alterations the Emperor of Austria agreed to sign it.'⁷

These changes in the Tsar's proposals were made by Metternich, rather than by Francis, and completely transformed the character of the alliance; the religious element was unimpaired but, whereas Alexander's draft implied penitence for past imperfection, Metternich's amendments emphasized the false presumptions of the revolutionary epoch and identified 'the exalted truths of the eternal religion' with a conservative philosophy of orderly government and the discipline of law. The revised draft was accepted by the Tsar, either because he did not realize the significance of Metternich's modifications or (as seems possible) because he was already emerging from the religious ecstasy of the original declaration. In this form the Holy Alliance was duly signed by Alexander, Francis and Frederick William iii on 26 September and subsequently by every monarch in Europe except for the Pope (who could not associate himself with the religious pledges of heretics and schismatics), the King of England (whose government conjured up insurmountable constitutional difficulties) and the Sultan (who, as an infidel, was not invited). As soon as he had put his name to the Alliance the Tsar set out for home, glad, as he told his sister, to be 'away from that accursed Paris'.[8] And the diplomats resumed the more familiar task of preparing a treaty of peace.

It was signed, at last, on 20 November. France ceded two fortresses to the Netherlands, Saarlouis and Saarbrucken to Prussia, Landau to the German Confederation and small areas along her frontier to Switzerland, Bavaria and Sardinia-Piedmont. She also agreed to a war indemnity of seven hundred million francs, of which more than one-fifth was assigned to Austria, and to pay for the maintenance of an Allied army of occupation in seventeen fortresses along the northern and eastern boundaries of the kingdom for a period of at least three years, possibly five. Finally it was stipulated that all Napoleon's artistic trophies of war were to be restored to their original owners. On the same day that this second Treaty of Paris was signed, the four partners in the coalition against Napoleon renewed the Quadruple Alliance of Chaumont, binding themselves to joint action if the French attacked the new frontiers or permitted a Bonapartist restoration and pledging themselves to consult together if any French administration were threatened by revolution. The greatest innovation in this treaty was, however, contained in its sixth article: Britain, Austria, Prussia and Russia agreed that, from time to time, their spokesmen on foreign affairs should meet in conference over matters of European concern. It was from this clause, inserted mainly on the initiative of Castlereagh but strongly supported by Metternich, that the so-called 'Congress System' of 1818 to 1822 came into being. 'New needs,' wrote Metternich ponderously, 'always create new forms.'[9]

Retrospect of the Peace Settlement

Six days later he left Paris, heading south-eastwards for Italy. The task of peacemaking was over and he received congratulations from his friends in Vienna, from the Emperor and from his family. Even his father, who thought Clement unsound on the rights of German princes, gave the final settlement his blessing. Metternich himself was as pleased as any of the statesmen with the result of their common labours. He had arrived in Paris full of gloom at the pretensions of the Prussians and uncertain of the Tsar's policy; but the Prussian urge for retribution had been effectively controlled and, as he remarked to Castlereagh, he had found Alexander 'of late friendly and reasonable on all points'.[10] His own statecraft had seen to it that the 'loud-sounding nothing' of the Holy Alliance echoed conservative sentiment rather than the emotional excitement of Alexander's idealism. And after wars which had twice ended with the occupation of Vienna, it was agreeable for the Austrians to receive an indemnity rather than be obliged to pay one and to have an army maintained at French expense on French soil. Yet although the new treaty provided greater security against fresh aggression than its predecessor it was not harsh and did not perpetuate a sense of injustice. There was every reason for hoping that France, too, would contribute to the new harmony of the European Concert once the Duc de Richelieu had shown that the King's government had the confidence of the French people; and the credentials of a Richelieu seemed to Metternich gratifyingly unsullied after eighteen months of Talleyrand's statecraft.

Metternich could also congratulate himself (and frequently did so) on the general result of a year of peacemaking for the House of Habsburg. Austria recovered all the territory she had lost since the outbreak of war with revolutionary France except for Belgium, some small enclaves in southern Germany (the most important of which was the Breisgau) and part of western Galicia, acquired only during the Polish Partitions. As compensation for these losses Austria received back Lombardy and the Tyrol and was allowed to absorb Venetia, Istria and Dalmatia (which had been in Habsburg hands from 1797 to 1805 by grace of Bonaparte) and to retain Salzburg, another territorial prize bestowed by Napoleon. In 1815 the Austrian Empire was almost half as large again as when Metternich became Foreign Minister and was second in population only to Russia among the states of Europe; the double-headed eagle of the Imperial coat-of-arms flew over cities as far apart as Milan and Lvov, Prague and Dubrovnik, Innsbruck and Brasov. Metternich's 'Austria' comprised all of the present-day republics of Austria, Hungary and Czechoslovakia, half of Roumania, over a third of Yugoslavia, almost a fifth of Italy and a sixth of Poland, and a large segment of the Soviet Ukraine. Moreover Habsburg influence extended throughout the German confederation and was paramount in the dynastic dependencies of the Italian peninsula. Critics might question the strategic wisdom of having to guard the line of the Dniester and the Po or of including lands north of the Carpathians and south of the Alps in the same defensive unit; and there were some who argued that Metternich should have concentrated on the territorial domination of Germany by the Habsburgs rather than on Italy and the Adriatic. But he believed the Habsburg Empire was a necessity to Europe only in so far as it represented a supranational order spanning the central lands of the continent. Were the Habsburgs to become a narrowly Germanic dynasty they would be distinguished from the Hohenzollerns and the Wittelsbachs solely by the memory of a universal Empire. The settlement of 1815 gave the Habsburg Empire a purpose; it became, in Castlereagh's words, 'the great hinge upon which the fate of Europe must ultimately depend'.[11] If the hinge was rusty, the fault was hardly Metternich's.

The greatest change in the character of the Empire was the responsibilities it had assumed in Italy. Lombardy had been a Habsburg province since 1714 and so had Mantua, while the Grand-Duchy of Tuscany had passed to the Habsburgs in 1737 on the death of the last member of the House of Medici; and the whole peninsula was traditionally a sphere of Habsburg influence. But until the end of the eighteenth century Austrian power in Italy was subject to four restraints: the Venetian hold on the Adriatic; the temporal authority of the Pope; the Spanish proclivities of the Bourbons in Naples and Sicily; and the occasional assertions of independence shown by the Savoyard rulers of Sardinia-Piedmont. The Napoleonic upheavals destroyed this pattern of government and by 1815 only the House of Savoy in Turin and, to a lesser extent, the Papacy was free from dependence on Metternich and the Austrian Army. Francis was titular King of Lombardy-Venetia, his brother was Grand-Duke of Tuscany, his daughter reigned in Parma, his cousin in Modena; and a secret treaty allowed the Austrians to retain garrisons in Naples and bound King Ferdinand not to introduce a liberal constitution in his lands. Moreover, although the Pope had recovered all his former territories, the Austrians now had the right to station troops at Ferrara and Comacchio in the Romagna and, as the fate of Murat had shown, could speedily move a considerable army southwards to maintain order. Metternich therefore believed he possessed the military power to impose as strict a surveillance on the Italian peninsula as Napoleon had exercised over Germany in his heyday. Basically he was interested not so much in territorial aggrandizement as in defence against the dangerous teachings of Italian nationalism and against the appeal of French ideas to a people who shared their Latin heritage. He was genuinely convinced Austria had something to offer: orderly government and security in place of intrigue and revolutionary anarchy. It was a point of view from which no events could shift him throughout all his years of power. Yet although the Italian Question loomed large in his plans for the future, Metternich had never set foot in any of the cities of the peninsula, nor did he know much of its peoples. His decision to travel southwards as soon as he had completed his work in Paris was significant. The visit was long overdue.

First visit to Italy (December 1815–April 1816)

He arrived in Venice on 4 December after a journey of eight days, three of which he spent in Geneva. As he explained in a letter to his mother, he had avoided Turin 'so as not to encounter the Court' and saw nothing of Milan 'except the hotel at which I stopped'.[12] Emperor Francis had preceded him by three days and received a genuinely enthusiastic welcome in Venice, partly because the port was suffering from economic stagnation and it was hoped something would now be done to stimulate trade. Francis was delighted to be greeted so warmly. His concept of the relationship between ruler and ruled was always disconcertingly unsophisticated and he responded to Venetian friendliness with a sympathy lacking in his general attitude towards the Italians. Metternich, on the other hand, was unimpressed by his introduction to Venice. There was in those days no causeway linking the city with the mainland, and the ceremonial *bucintoro* which conveyed the Prince and Floret across the lagoon from Mestre was caught in a wintry squall as it entered the Grand Canal and they landed at the Piazzetta cold and wet. Closer acquaintance did not change his opinion of the place. 'Venice resembles one vast ruin,' he wrote to his mother; and he informed Hudelist in Vienna that he thought the city was like a grandiose palace whose owner had been forced by poverty to live in a hut beside the monument of former glory.[13] Yet although Venice in December did not appeal to him, he was as satisfied as the Emperor with the loyalty of the Venetians to their new masters; and he accepted the need for reform of the harbour administration and for cutting port taxes. After a generation of wars and instability the Venetians asked for little more; commerce was of greater concern to them than forms of government in 1815.

It was otherwise in Lombardy. Metternich travelled to Milan on 18 December with his family, who had come south to winter in Italy. But they can have seen little of him that Christmas. He was busy with preparations for the solemn entry which the King of Lombardy-Venetia was to make into his capital on New Year's Eve, and he spent most of the week in political discussions with Marshal Bellegarde and with a number of Lombard dignitaries. They were afraid that Milan, which had enjoyed a privileged status under Eugene Beauharnais, 'might degenerate to a poor provincial town' and become 'a Brünn or Gräz and thus sink behind Turin and Florence'.[14] Metternich was as certain as in May 1814 of the need to re-kindle the Lombard spirit, although the doubts which he had earlier held over Venetia were now removed. Before Francis arrived he drafted a long memorandum in which he urged the Emperor to appoint a Viceroy with real authority and establish an autonomous Italian Chancery and a Supreme Court of Justice for Lombardy-Venetia: 'These lands,' he said, 'must be governed here and the governments here must then let themselves be represented in Vienna.'[15] But although Metternich and Bellegarde might plead for institutions acceptable to Italian sentiment, Francis had no desire to accord to his Italian territories a different status from the other lands of the Monarchy. Moreover when Francis made his entry into the city the Milanese showed no enthusiasm for their stolidly unromantic sovereign and he was disappointed at his reception. 'In Venice,' he said, 'I was among my children, in Milan I saw only subjects.'[16] Metternich's rare gesture of liberalism achieved little. Francis acknowledged receipt of the memorandum and failed to take any decision on what should be done in Italy. The study of detailed reports was always for him a passable substitute for action.

The Emperor and Metternich remained in northern Italy until the spring. For Francis these four months were a period of worry and sorrow: the health of his third wife, the Empress Maria Ludovica, failed rapidly and she succumbed to rheumatic fever early in April while in residence at Verona. Metternich, who was himself suffering from chronic inflammation of the eyelids, was endlessly busy. He tried to control the foreign policy of the Empire from Milan, although he left much of the formal work of diplomacy to Hudelist in Vienna, with whom he maintained a close correspondence. He also exchanged letters regularly with Gentz, who was highly critical of much that he was trying to do in Italy.[17] Inevitably the affairs of the peninsula were uppermost in Metternich's mind, but there was a crisis early in the year over Germany to which he was forced to give urgent attention. A serious dispute arose between Austria and Bavaria, whose ruler refused to give up his claim to Salzburg and the valley of the Upper Inn and threatened a civil war within Germany over delimitation of the frontier with the Grand-Duchy of Baden. The Prince-Royal of Bavaria was summoned to Milan and a compromise over both these questions was worked out at long conferences with Metternich: a treaty, signed at Munich in April, compensated the Bavarians for the loss of territories to Austria by concessions in the Rhineland. The crisis had more far-reaching effects than Metternich appreciated at the time. Uncertainty over Bavaria's attitude postponed the first meeting of the new German Diet in Frankfurt for over a year and thereby increased liberal-patriotic restlessness in the German lands. At the same time, Metternich's opponents in Vienna, who were sensitive to every vibration of German politics, began to criticize the Prince's decision to remain for so long in Italy. Yet, provided he did not drive Francis too hard on the Italian Question, there was no real threat of an effective cabal being organized against him. The illness and death of the Empress removed a formidable enemy of his policy; and Stadion, his most dangerous rival, was fully occupied that winter in trying to establish some order in the financial administration of the Empire.

There were, however, moments in January and February when it seemed as if Italy might cause his downfall. He continued to urge Francis to recognize that Lombardy-Venetia merited different treatment from the other regions of the Empire, but there was a powerful party in the Emperor's immediate circle, headed by Counts Saurau and Lazansky, which insisted the newly constituted Kingdom should be Germanized as rapidly as possible. Francis could not make up his mind:

he respected his Minister's judgement and was conscious of all he had achieved at the Congress and in Paris; but his own sentiments were nearer to the centralist ideas of Saurau and Lazansky. He prevaricated and referred all Metternich's proposals to Vienna, writing personally to Count Wallis, the Prince's critic of earlier years, who remained a minister without portfolio. Eventually, in March, Francis took his decision: he nominated Archduke Anton, the fifth of his seven brothers, as Viceroy; and agreed to set up a Supreme Court of Justice in Verona. He would not authorize the establishment of an Italian Chancellery although he was prepared to allow Italians to serve in the Lombardo-Venetian administration rather than to entrust it entirely to 'Germans'. At the same time he believed he had established a balance in Milan itself between the 'Italianizing' and 'Germanizing' parties: General Bubna, who was sympathetic to Metternich's policy of concessions, was appointed military commander in the city; but Count Saurau was made the civil governor.[18]

Metternich's views on Italy hardened perceptibly in March and April. There were three main reasons for his change of outlook: the obvious hostility of the Emperor to his earlier liberal impulses; the refusal of the Piedmontese to collaborate with him in creating a confederated Italian league, under Austrian protection; and reports from agents and envoys throughout Italy on the activities of secret patriotic societies. By the spring his policy had become far more negative and repressive. The establishment, under Austrian auspices, of a common postal system for the Italian states increased the influence of his police spies; and in May he warmly supported the formation of a Central Observation Agency in Milan, a police intelligence bureau to sift information on nationalist conspiracies throughout the peninsula.[19] He had not, however, abandoned his hopes of decentralizing the Empire. In May he travelled with Francis to Trieste and Laibach (as Ljubljana was then called) and tested the loyalty of the Emperor's southern Slav subjects in the former Illyrian Provinces. He duly proposed the creation of an Illyro-Dalmatian Kingdom in which the Slovenes and Croats would enjoy a measure of autonomy (and which would be a valuable Slavonic counter-weight to Hungarian patriotic ambitions). But once more Francis rejected his advice.[20] When, on 3 August 1816, a Kingdom of Illyria was proclaimed it did not include Dalmatia or any of the Croatian lands; nor did it hold out much prospect of home rule for the southern Slavs. Francis would not play with constitutional reform for the sake of his Foreign Minister.

Metternich arrived back in Vienna on 28 May. He had been away for almost a year, he was tired, and his health remained poor that summer: there was constant irritation of the eyes and, within a fortnight of his return, he was confined to bed for several days with a bout of fever. His main pre-occupation for the rest of the year was uncongenial; the Empire was threatened with bankruptcy and he had to spend long hours in conference with Stadion and Gentz evolving schemes for a National Bank and for issuing a new form of metal currency.[21] He was troubled by reports of student unrest in Germany and conspiratorial cells in southern Italy and he exaggerated the significance of radical demonstrations in London in November and December. Most of the year he spent quietly in Vienna, giving small dinner-parties on the Rennweg, at some of which his father would hold forth earnestly on the ills of Germany. The Prince was pleased when, at the end of October, Emperor Francis married for the fourth time. The new Empress was Princess Caroline Augusta of Bavaria, daughter of Maximilian of Zweibrucken who, nearly thirty years before, had been his patron at Strasbourg. The marriage improved relations between the Empire and the southern German states, which had been strained earlier in the year over the problem of the Bavarian frontiers. And there was another echo of his youth that summer when, in July, the Emperor unexpectedly presented him with the estate of Johannisberg, the former Benedictine abbey on the right bank of the Rhine, rich in vines and already famous for the quality of its Riesling wine.[22] Johannisberg, which had belonged to Marshal Kellermann in Napoleon's time, made the Metternichs once more Rhenish landowners; and the estate was only twenty-five miles south-east of Clement's birthplace at Coblenz. He did not have an opportunity to visit Johannisberg that year but he was gratified at this evidence of the Emperor's confidence and pleased to have a foothold on the hills of the Rhine.

His personal life was, however, saddened in the second half of 1816 by the illness of Julie Zichy-Festetics, a saintly creature of rare beauty to whom he felt drawn by a spiritual love, a woman who, as he said later, had 'descended upon earth but to pass over it like the spring'.[23] He had written love letters to her and once he gave her a ring as a symbol of the union of two souls bound in sympathy, but she remained loyal to her husband and it is unlikely she ever became Metternich's mistress. Few were aware of the bond between them. Before her death – which took place on 18 November 1816 – Countess Julie saw to it that all his letters to her were burnt and the ring broken. The ashes of the letters and the broken ring were later brought to him in a casket tied with black ribbon. Two years afterwards he wrote: 'My life ended there. I had neither the desire nor the will to live after that. My soul was shattered in pieces and I had no heart left.'[24] He was, in 1816, forty-three years old and he lived to be eighty-six; but there is no doubt he was deeply moved by the fortitude with which she had faced death and the devotion she had shown to their strangely spiritual attachment. The literary world of his youth was peopled by noble heroes hardened through the sorrows of a tragic love, and now he felt at one with them. Even Gentz, with the true romantic's eye for portent, noted that on the morning Vienna heard the news of her death, the sun passed in eclipse over the city;[25] and he had known her only as a distant luminary of virtue.

It is difficult to assess the lasting effect of Countess Julie's death on Metternich. Certainly it ran deeper than mere maudlin romance. He became more conscious of his religious obligations and, although conformist piety was a characteristic of court life under the new Empress, it is probable his assertions of faith were largely a testimony to the Countess's example. It is unusual to find him, in the following August, mentioning in a letter to Nesselrode that he 'read one or two chapters of the Bible every day' and considered himself 'a believer' where 'twenty years ago profound and sustained investigation of the scriptures' could have turned him into an atheist.[26] He did not become a moral bigot; but, in his later years, he was no longer satisfied with the sensualism he had found in his earlier affairs of the heart; he looked for a more elevating experience, a union of mind as much as of body. In 1820 Stewart, the British ambassador, remarked to Castlereagh that at some point between the Congresses of Vienna and Troppau Metternich had shed his incorrigible frivolity.[27] Countess Julie left a wound on his spirit which memory deepened rather than healed.

Second visit to Italy and proposals of reform (1817)

There was little change in his public life that winter. Day after day he studied reports from Italy and Germany. He was worried at the incompetence of the restored governments in the peninsula and alarmed by Saurau's heavy-handed administration in Milan. He even tried, unsuccessfully, to have Saurau appointed ambassador in Madrid.[28] The Diet in Frankfurt was making little progress and some of the German princes seemed more closely wedded to liberal constitutionalism than was warranted by the temper of the times. He was particularly alarmed by the actions of the Grand Duke of Saxe-Weimar, who had granted his subjects a constitution in May 1816, and who was hailed in the unfettered German press as an example to all the other sovereigns of the Confederation. Nor was Metternich satisfied with Hardenberg's ability to check liberal sentiment in the Prussian Rhineland and he did all he could to strengthen the influence of Prince Wittgenstein, the Minister of Police, whom no one could suspect of sympathy with new ideas (or, indeed, ideas of any kind). Metternich also distrusted the Tsar's constitutional experiments in the puppet Kingdom of Poland; they had, he felt, a bad effect not only on 'Austrian' Poles in Galicia but on such German states as Württemberg and Saxony, which were responsive to Alexander's enthusiasms.

It was at this moment that Metternich, rather unexpectedly, established a personal link with the Württemberg court. His sister Pauline, a homely spinster of forty-five, was married in February 1817 to Prince Ferdinand of Württemberg, an uncle of the King. But although his brother-in-law maintained an amiable correspondence with Metternich, he soon found Prince Ferdinand counted for little in the politics of Stuttgart. He was, however, appointed Governor of Mainz by the Grand-Duke of Hesse and thus acquired a position of dignified responsibility conveniently near to Johannisberg. So Pauline, too, returned to the vine slopes and fortress towns of their childhood.

Metternich had hoped to pay a visit to his German estate in the summer of 1817: he was prevented from doing so by the fortunes of the Habsburg dynasty and the nagging affairs of Italy. The Emperor's youngest daughter, Leopoldine, was betrothed early in the year to Crown Prince Dom Pedro of Portugal and Brazil, who with other members of the House of Braganza was still in Rio de Janeiro, where the family had taken refuge from Napoleon in 1807. It was arranged that, like her sister Marie Louise, Leopoldine would be married by proxy in Vienna and then escorted with dignity out of the Empire. Metternich, who was not without experience of such matters, was appointed by Francis as Leopoldine's custodian and commissioner. He was to remain in attendance on her while she journeyed to Leghorn where she would be met by a Portuguese naval squadron bound for South America. At the same time Metternich was to report on conditions in Italy and seek the opinion of Austrian officials in the north on the future development of the Lombardo-Venetian Kingdom.

He set out from Vienna on 5 June, accompanied once more by Floret and this time by Hudelist and his personal physician, Frederick Jäger, an eye specialist. They expected to arrive back in Vienna by mid-July, but the sailing of the Portuguese squadron was postponed because of a revolt at Pernambuco and it was September before Metternich returned to the capital.[29] The long delay enabled him to see far more of Italy than on his previous visit, although he abandoned a projected journey to Rome when it became clear that Pope Pius VII had no wish to receive the Austrian Foreign Minister so long as Church government in Lombardy-Venetia was supervised by the authorities in Milan. He visited Venice, Padua, Ferrara and Pisa, stayed for over a month in Florence, and spent a fortnight taking the waters at Lucca. In rhapsodic letters to his wife and daughter he described the delights of the cities, the colour of the countryside and the friendliness of the Tucsan people. 'Venice seen in December', he discovered, 'and Venice seen in June are two different cities'; and he informed Eleonore that, 'It would be difficult to give you any idea of the impression which Florence must make on all who love things of beauty and grandeur . . .

The climate is divine ... The early morning, the evening and the night are as it will probably be one day in Paradise.'[30] From his bedroom at Massa, where he stopped briefly in midsummer, he admired the endless expanse of sand beside the still waters of the Mediterranean; and one day in July he travelled further south and saw the rocky silhouette of Elba across the Tuscan Sea: 'I couldn't see that island without thinking of my rude awakening on 5 March 1815,' he told Eleonore, inadvertently antedating by two days the news of Napoleon's flight.[31]

Not all of Metternich's visit was spent in such touristic pleasures. He inspected marble quarries at Carrara and the construction of a strategic road to the Ligurian coast. With Floret and Hudelist in attendance, he tried to keep in touch with the affairs of the continent; and it was from Florence that he wrote a strange despatch to the Austrian ambassador in St Petersburg urging him to alert the Russian Court to the menace of radical religious sects in central Europe. But for most of the time Metternich and his companions were seeking to discover why there was still such political dissatisfaction in the peninsula. They had long talks with the military and civil governors of Milan and Venice at a meeting in Verona early in September; and Metternich was disquieted by much that he heard.[32] Little had been done to meet his earlier proposals: the Viceroy, appointed eighteen months previously, had not as yet arrived to assume his responsibilities; and the people of Milan and Venice were becoming tired of a Germanic administration which promised more than it could fulfil. Political life in the rest of the peninsula was more corrupt, more priest-ridden and more vindictive than in Lombardy-Venetia; but already Austrian officials were worried by the way in which dissidents, in Lombardy and elsewhere, were looking hopefully towards Turin for patronage of the national cause. General Bubna, who had an almost fatherly solicitude for the welfare of the Lombards, let Metternich know he did not trust the attitude of the House of Savoy; and the Prince shared his doubts to the full.[33] Both men still genuinely believed that, by wise government and a sensible regard for cultural and historic traditions, it was possible to win over the people of Lombardy and Venetia. But time was running out. On 29 August Metternich wrote to the Emperor from Lucca informing him that he was preparing a report on the problems of Italy. He would make one more plea for recognition of Italian national sentiment.[34]

Metternich arrived back in Vienna on the evening of 12 September. He was immediately thrown into the midst of preparations for the marriage of his daughter, Marie, to Count Joseph Esterhazy. The wedding took place on 15 September but the strain of the journey and the excitement at his home was too much for the Prince: he felt ill during the wedding reception in the Kaunitz Palace on the Ballhaus-platz, retired prematurely to his private rooms and was indisposed for several days, apparently with an attack of haemorrhoids.[35] The wedding and the enforced rest delayed work on his Italian report, and he was still awaiting memoranda from Tito Manzi, an experienced Italian civil servant whom he had commissioned to gather information for him.[36] At the same time he decided to broaden the scope of his proposals; he would outline changes, not merely in Lombardy-Venetia, but in the administration of the Empire as a whole, thus countering the criticism that the Italians were being favoured at the expense of the other nationalities. Once before, in the summer of 1811, he had urged Francis to create a Council of Empire and a cabinet of ministers; but his suggestions were ignored and the Empire continued to be administered by clumsy supervisory bodies of Francis's nominees. Now he had fewer enemies at court and his prestige was far weightier than six years before. But it was a bold decision for, to the great families, he was still an outsider; and internal reforms went far beyond the responsibilities of his department. Everyone knew the machinery of government needed to be serviced and even the Emperor conceded it was not functioning efficiently. It did not, however, follow that a Rhinelander with an enthusiasm for Italy, a man who had never seen the eastern lands of the Monarchy, possessed any right to be heard on such matters.

Most of Metternich's proposals were embodied in three documents dated 27 October 1817: an explanatory letter to the Emperor; a scheme for the interior organization of the Empire; and a special report on Italy.[37] He also submitted a further memorandum on Italy a week later. The changes he proposed were far from revolutionary, for he knew that he must proceed with caution. They were all limited to the executive sphere of government: he rejected the notion of creating a central representative body as absurd, although he subsequently claimed to have suggested an assembly of delegates nominated from the provincial Estates, a *Reichsrat*. He recommended the setting up of a Ministry of Justice and the appointment of a supreme Minister of the Interior whose work would be assisted by four Chancellors: for Bohemia and Moravia and Galicia; for Upper and Lower Austria, Styria, the Tyrol and Salzburg; for Illyria and Dalmatia; and for Lombardy-Venetia (which, significantly, he called 'Italy'). The Chancellors were to pay due regard to the national characteristics of their regions, while emphasizing unity through diversity. He deferred until a later date all consideration of changes in the status of Hungary and Transylvania, although he appears to have thought that as the responsibilities of the new creations increased with the passage of time, so the privileges of the Hungarian Palatinate would gradually wither away. This was an unwarranted assumption.

Metternich's programme of reform was the only serious attempt he made to revise the structure of government during the reign of Francis. On 24 December 1817 the Emperor published a Patent which incorporated some of his ideas.[38] But in substance, and even more in spirit, the Patent fell short of his proposals. The preamble emphasized the need for uniformity and centralization whereas Metternich had stressed the importance of safeguarding regional interests. Three Chancelleries were created, not four: Illyria was attached to the Austrian provinces, although since Francis never actually appointed an Austro-Illyrian Chancellor, the character of this institution was of little significance. There was, indeed, to be a Minister of the Interior: Count Saurau, for whom Metternich scarcely felt admiration, was brought from Milan to fill the post. No mention was made in the Patent of a Ministry of Justice but Count Wallis – another former opponent of Metternich – was made president of a department for ensuring orderly administration of the laws. The Patent showed that Francis would not admit any need for concessions to national consciousness. He ignored any suggestion of a council of nominated delegates. Metternich declared in an autobiographical note that Francis had 'put into a drawer' his scheme for a central assembly. He also said the Emperor mentioned the project to him in 1827 and again two months before his death; but nothing was done, and Austria had to wait for its *Reichsrat* until after the disasters of 1848.[39]

Yet in one respect at least Metternich appeared to have been successful. He at last gained recognition of the principle that Lombardy-Venetia was no mere geographical expansion of German Austria. The Kingdom was to have, not only a Chancellery in Vienna, but a Chancellor who was an Italian, Count Mellerio; and the language of administration, education and law was to be Italian rather than German. Nor was this all. Since Archduke Anton had decided, after twenty months of hesitation, he had no desire to settle in Italy, his brother Rainer was appointed Viceroy: it was agreed he would take up residence in Milan in the following spring and would hold court alternately in the Lombard capital and in Venice. In his letters Metternich made the most of these concessions: he insisted there was 'much more than meets the eye' in the changes of administration.[40] Perhaps he genuinely believed it; but, if so, he was soon to be disillusioned. The Viceroy was permitted no freedom of political initiative: he might patronize La Scala, smile benignly on charities, lay out ornamental gardens at Monza; but peremptory messages from the Emperor reminded him of the need to adhere to the 'forms and usages of his ancestors'.[41] Had Metternich felt sincerely attached to a policy of reconciliation in Italy, he should at some point in 1818 have tendered his resignation to Francis. But there was little likelihood of such an

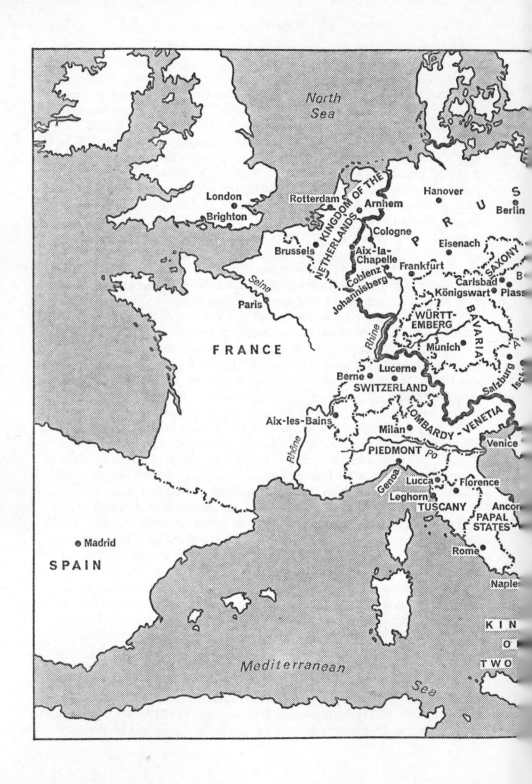

METTERNICH'S EUROPE

━━━━ German Confederation

0 ————————— 200
Miles

Baltic Sea

S I A

Vistula

KINGDOM OF
POLAND

R U S S I A

Münchengrätz
M I A
Troppau
Olmütz ●
R. ● Brno
R I A
Vienna

Cracow ●

Lemberg ●

G A L I C I A

MORAVIA
Pressburg
Komarom

Czernowitz ●

AUSTRIAN

Baden
Graz
ibach

H U N G A R Y

Budapest

EMPIRE

BANAT

*Black
Sea*

ILLYRIAN
PROVINCES

O T T O M A N

Danube

driatic Sea

M
E
LIES

Corfu

I O N I A N   Is.

E M P I R E

*Aegean
Sea*

Athens ●

GREECE

Navarino ●

uncharacteristic action. He enjoyed the game of power and its rewards too much to risk a precipitate end to his career for the sake of the Lombards. Moreover Italy was only one area of activity. Before the end of 1817 his attention had been drawn dramatically to Germany and the problems of safeguarding the European system from the rash enthusiasm of the young. For the next two years the affairs of Italy and the Adriatic provinces held a lowly place in his order of business. By the time he turned once more to the south, he no longer had anything constructive to offer, and throughout the peninsula his name had become synonymous with a code of repression.

AIX AND CARLSBAD

German problems (1817)

On 18 October 1817, several hundred students organized a meeting at Eisenach in the Grand-Duchy of Weimar in order to celebrate the tercentenary of the Lutheran Reformation and the fourth anniversary of the battle of Leipzig. From Eisenach they marched in an orderly procession to the Castle of the Wartburg, where Luther had found sanctuary in 1521. There they sang the Luther hymn, *Ein' feste Burg*, and listened to speeches in honour of the national war of liberation against Napoleon. They drank toasts to Luther and, for good measure, to the Grand-Duke of Weimar as well. There was some heady denunciation of the shackles of tyranny and a small group of students lit a bonfire on which they threw a copy of the Final Act of the Congress of Vienna and some books and pamphlets which they considered to be reactionary in tone or character. Other demonstrators added to the flames such obnoxious symbols of the old order as a powdered wig and a corporal's swagger cane. The students themselves defied contemporary fashion by having long hair and beards on their chins and by wearing short black coats with high collars to their shirts. They were not, however, a revolutionary mob; and, in the evening, they formed up in a disciplined body, lit torches from the embers of the fire and marched back to Eisenach, where some ended the day by attending a service in a Lutheran church. Most of them came from the University of Jena, where they had received encouragement from their professors, but there were some from Berlin and from places as distant as Kiel and Königsberg. The Grand-Duke of Weimar was said not only to have given permission for the double celebration, but to have ensured that the students could find board and lodging.[1]

The 'Wartburg Festival' was characteristic of the confused idealism in Germany during the post-war decade; the young were uncertain whom to praise and whom to damn. It was a movement far less radical than the riot which Metternich had witnessed at Strasbourg in 1789, but it sent a shiver of apprehension through the German courts and excited comment abroad. The French Prime Minister, Richelieu, anxiously

asked Metternich if he thought the affair marked the outbreak of a
German revolution; and Hardenberg hurried south from Berlin for a
personal investigation of the outrage.[2] The Austrian Minister in
Dresden sent to Vienna his version of what had happened and claimed
to have 'counted thirty professors' and more than eight hundred
students taking part 'in this Jacobin orgy'.[3] Metternich was not
entirely displeased by the news from Eisenach, although he authorized
Gentz to write a savage attack on the Festival for the *Österreichischer
Beobachter*. It confirmed the warnings the Prince had sent to the German
capitals on the dangerous enthusiasm for 'the Fatherland' which was
firing the hearts of the younger generation now that the foreign wars
were over. Earlier that year, in July, he had pressed for the establishment of a central bureau of information which would protect Europe
from conspiracy in much the same way as the intelligence network in
Milan was upholding the stability of Italy; but his proposals had
encountered heavy opposition from Castlereagh, and he abandoned the
idea. Although he perceived that the students were too muddled to
form a serious menace, the Wartburg Festival inevitably turned his
attention to German affairs once more.

Not that Germany was ever far from his thoughts. For more than
two years envoys and agents had kept watch on the *Burschenschaften*,
the student societies which sprang up in sixteen German universities
to encourage the personal virtues of sobriety and chastity and the
political ideal of nationalism. The movement had begun in June 1815
at Jena itself and, from his information, Metternich had already
singled out the Grand-Duchy of Weimar as a haven of misplaced liberal
sentiment and expressed fears that Berlin would become a centre of
German Jacobinism. It was gratifying to have one's prophecies vindic-
ated, although he was never inclined to doubt the accuracy of his
assumptions. In October and November 1817 his agents sent detailed
accounts of all that was happening in other universities: they told him
of rowdy scenes at Göttingen, of disturbances in Breslau, and of trouble
in Mainz. It is probable that they did not always bother to distinguish
clearly between students revelling in the new wine harvest and patriots
fired by loftier ideals. But the distinction mattered little to Metternich.
He had no desire to analyse too deeply the cause of all the commotion.
The reports merely fed his preconceived opinions: disorder was the
fault of Russian agents and of the unsettling legacy of the Lutheran
Reformation; or it resulted from the casual way in which the rulers of
Germany dabbled in liberal constitutions. If there was to be political
progress in Germany it must be handled with care and restraint, either
by the Diet in Frankfurt or by the German rulers acting together in
concert.[4]

Yet his field of action was no more solely limited to Germany than it had been to Austria or Italy. Although his methods were devious, his prime principle of policy remained simple and unsophisticated: he wished to strengthen the sense of unity and order among the European Great Powers. If he could convince Tsar Alexander and King Frederick William of the dangers of neo-Jacobinism in Germany, he would ensure his hold on the affairs of the continent and, at the same time, destroy the three principal threats to the stability of the German Confederation. Alexander could bring Anstett, his representative in Frankfurt, to heel. Frederick William, as the chief Protestant ruler in Germany, could reassert the traditional teaching of the Lutheran Church on political obedience. And once Prussia, Russia and Austria were seen to be acting together, the other German Princes would dutifully fall in behind them. Metternich was confident he could control the Prussians through his contacts with Wittgenstein, the Minister of Police in Berlin; but, as ever, the difficulty was that no one could predict the response of the Tsar to any item of political information. So long as the principal Russian spokesman on foreign affairs was Capodistrias, rather than Nesselrode, there was little hope of winning Alexander back to a conservative philosophy of government. Cautiously in the early months of 1818 Metternich began to sound out Russian opinion through the Austrian ambassador in St Petersburg; and, although as yet Alexander's faith in his Corfiote adviser seemed undiminished, it was at least clear he wished for another meeting of sovereigns in congress. It was a sign of concern for Europe which encouraged Metternich, even if the Tsar seemed to be thinking of a rather more comprehensive gathering than he desired.[5]

Other aspects of Russian diplomatic activity remained less satisfactory. Rumour, for example, credited the Russians with a plan for purchasing from the Spanish government one of the Balearic Islands in order to possess a naval base in the Mediterranean. Yet, although both Castlereagh and Metternich continued to look with suspicion for many months at Russian intrigues in Madrid, nothing more sinister appeared in Spanish waters than a squadron of old Russian vessels on sale to the naval authorities in Cadiz.[6] More disturbing was the renewed Russian interest in Serbia, the Danubian Principalities and Greece; for neither the Austrians nor the British wanted the Eastern Question to be reopened at a time when so much was uncertain in western and southern Europe. Alexander's erratic policy at both ends of the Mediterranean emphasized to Metternich the value of the Anglo-Austrian entente. With uncertainty in St Petersburg and Berlin, the friendship which he had formed with Castlereagh after Leipzig remained Metternich's one reliable political association.

The British government, and even more the House of Commons, were never prepared to accept Metternich at his face value, despite the

Prince Regent's high opinion of him. But, although Lord Liverpool still cautioned Castlereagh over Metternich's subtlety, there were not as yet any fundamental disagreements between the two Foreign Ministers.[7] It was Castlereagh who proposed, in March 1818, that there should be a congress later in the year, as envisaged in the Quadruple Alliance Treaty of 1815; but it was Metternich who took up the proposal and insisted on limiting the form of the conference so as to avoid the presence of the Tsar's protegés in Spain or among the German princes. By the end of April it had been agreed that the signatories of the Quadruple Alliance, together with representatives of France, should meet in the autumn. Their prime task was to end the military occupation imposed upon the French in 1815 but they had also to review the progress towards an international order, for which the statesmen had begun their search three years before in Paris. This time it was accepted that they should meet in Aix-la-Chapelle (Aachen).[8] They had considered and rejected Dusseldorf or Mannheim, and Capodistrias had suggested Basle but Metternich was not going to risk a conference in a city 'to which all the Jacobins of France and Germany might flock'.[9] Aix-la-Chapelle, with the Prussian Army firmly in control along the frontier, was a far more suitable place in his eyes. Moreover, as an ancient capital of the *Reich*, its name was pleasantly redolent of Habsburg glory.

Preparations for the Aix Congress

Nearly six months elapsed between the decision to hold the conference at Aix and the actual gathering of sovereigns and plenipotentiaries in Westphalia. Much of the time was spent in tedious disputes over the general nature of the agenda and even over who was to be invited. The Russians persisted in seeking the admission of spokesmen for the Spaniards and for the German courts, but without success; and in London Castlereagh had to use considerable tact to discourage the Prince Regent from leading the British delegation in person. For most of the summer months Metternich was occupied with routine matters of administration and remained in Vienna, accompanying his family out to Baden when the weather became oppressively warm.

He was suffering that summer from rheumatic tension in the muscles of the back and he was advised in July by one of his personal physicians, Dr Staudenheim, to travel up to Bohemia and take the waters at Carlsbad (Karlovy Vary). For a month he submitted to a strict regimen. 'I go to bed at ten-thirty and get up at six', he informed his wife,[10] 'Everybody is at the fountains by half-past six: we lunch at ten; we dine at three, and we do not take supper.' Carlsbad had the advantage of being only some thirty-five miles away from his *château* at Königswart and he planned to visit his estate once his lumbago had improved. But it was hard to escape from the attractions of the spa. The town was full of visitors. He had a pleasant meeting with Marshal Blücher and an inconclusive interview with John Capodistrias.[11] Not even the delights of Carlsbad could overcome his distrust of the Corfiote expatriate, and he parted from him convinced that he was less attached than the Tsar to the maintenance of the existing order in Europe. In later years he maintained that Capodistrias was even then thinking only of the liberation of Greece from Turkish rule, but it is difficult to see any evidence for this assumption.

Inevitably there were happier ways of relaxation in a spa of such Rococo splendour. While in Florence during the previous summer Metternich had attended a private concert where he was enchanted by the voice of Angelica Catalani, the opera singer.* He had introduced her to the musical salons of Vienna in the late spring of 1818; and in July she consulted Dr Staudenheim who immediately prescribed a month of the Carlsbad waters as a guarantee of recuperation. She travelled to Bohemia with her husband shortly before Metternich completed his own cure. Her ailments, which do not seem to have been particularly severe, did not prevent her from singing in a concert accompanied by an amateur orchestra in which the violins were led by a Saxon colonel and the cellos by a Prussian general. Metternich was delighted; he amused himself by presenting her to Goethe (of whom her husband, at least, does not appear to have heard) and to Wilhelmine of Sagan, with whom she had little in common apart from Metternich himself. His own relations with Wilhelmine had been frigidly correct since the Vienna Congress and her presence in Carlsbad was entirely fortuitous; she was not even a patient of Dr Staudenheim.[19]

It was while he was in Bohemia that Metternich heard of the illness and death of his father, at the age of seventy-two. Since he was then awaiting the arrival of Capodistrias, he did not travel back to Vienna but he made arrangements for the eventual interment of his father's remains at Königswart, the only family property to have survived the Revolutionary Wars without changing hands. In letters to his mother and his wife and in a formal message to the Emperor, Metternich showed a proper sense of filial duty. He was, as ever, sustained by an imperturbable egocentricity: 'My poor father', he wrote to his mother,[13] 'will at least carry from this world the consolation that I have never given him a moment's vexation, and that has been for me the most agreeable thought of my life. He cannot refuse me his blessing, and I will take care to merit it.' His mother, with whom Clement had a

---

* On 20 June 1817, Metternich wrote enthusiastically to his wife about the impression made on him by Catalani's voice: '*Assurément, si la Sainte Vierge se mêle aux choeurs des bienheureux, elle doit chanter comme cette femme, qui n'est pas vierge*'. (*Mémoires*, III, p. 28).

more natural affinity, lived on for another ten years in Vienna.

He continued to plan arrangements for the Aix conference while at Carlsbad and Königswart. At one moment in August he suggested that he might travel to Paris and meet Castlereagh and Wellington for preliminary talks.[14] He did not believe that Paul Esterhazy,* the ambassador in London, was correctly stating his views to the British government; and he had worked out a complicated plan for parallel meetings of the Allied ambassadors in Paris so as to keep Pozzo di Borgo, the 'liberal-minded' Corsican who represented the Tsar at the French court, from influencing his master at Aix. But Castlereagh failed to appreciate the merits of such devious diplomacy and rightly feared the effect on Russia and Prussia of an overt display of Anglo-Austrian concord. Neither Castlereagh nor Metternich went to Paris, although Castlereagh had useful talks with the Duc de Richelieu in Spa before crossing into Westphalia. Pozzo di Borgo, who may well have picked up rumours of Metternich's abortive plan, duly set out early for Aix and arrived ahead of the Tsar, who made a leisurely progress through Brandenburg.

Metternich, too, was in no hurry to reach Aix. He travelled from Königswart to Frankfurt in the last days of August, and spent a week trying to induce the Diet of the German Confederation to take decisions over what were largely procedural matters. He succeeded in obtaining the backing of the Diet for a military organization of federal forces, an essential preliminary to the proposed evacuation of France and a clear assertion by the Diet of sovereign powers which were still being called in question by the spokesmen of some south German states. In a letter to Eleonore on 11 September, he described his efforts at the Diet with customary hyperbole: 'My stay here has been crowned with great success. I came to Frankfurt like the Messiah saving sinners. The Diet took on a new appearance as soon as I began to busy myself with its affairs.'[15]

He enjoyed being fêted in the Rhineland that autumn. On 13 September he visited Coblenz for the first time in a quarter of a century and was surprised by its growth; and at last he had the opportunity to inspect Johannisberg and to admire the magnificent view of the Rhine from the terrace. On a clear day it was possible to see twenty miles of the river, he informed his wife, 'and when there is a mist the stream is so broad that it touches the horizon as though it were the sea'. As

* Paul Esterhazy's private life was in a confused state that summer and he was heavily in debt. Any other Foreign Minister would probably have recalled him but he had been a protégé of Metternich for more than ten years and was brother-in-law to his daughter, Marie. Moreover he was an especial favourite of the Prince Regent, for whom Metternich always showed an exaggerated regard. Paul Esterhazy remained in the London embassy until 1842; he appears to have been the only ambassador ever accredited to four successive British monarchs.

on his Italian journeys, his letters show a limpid sensitivity to land-scape.[16]

The Emperor Francis arrived at Mainz on 23 September and was entertained at Johannisberg. Together they travelled slowly down the left bank of the river through Bonn – 'Nothing is as charming as the situation of Bonn' – to Cologne. There was some hostility in the Rhineland towards Protestant Prussia and this sentiment encouraged popular demonstrations of support for a Catholic Emperor. Even Metternich claims to have been embraced by strangers in the streets. In Cologne his six-horse carriage and the line of coaches which accompanied him were understandably mistaken for the Emperor's own retinue, and he was given an Imperial welcome in unmuted diapason. So deafening were the bells of the city that neither he nor Gentz could make themselves heard as they tried to explain that this was merely the cavalcade of a Foreign Minister and that the Emperor would make his entry later in the morning. Although Metternich maintained he was 'furious' at the muddle and confusion in Cologne, it is clear he was in general pleased at receiving obsequious respect in a part of Germany where his father had always taken such care to cut a fine figure.[17] Politically, too, the triumphal progress of Emperor and Minister to Aix was gratifying. Respect for the dynasty ran deeper than at the Frankfurt coronations of 1790 or 1792 and Habsburg primacy along the middle Rhine evoked a more impressive acknowledgement in 1818 than in the closing century of the old Empire. By contrast the arrival of the King of Prussia and of the Tsar was attended by what appeared to be no more than gestures of formal ceremonial.

The Congress of Aix-la-Chapelle (1818)

The summit meeting of Aix-la-Chapelle, which Metternich himself termed a 'Congress', was the first European conference of sovereigns and statesmen to assemble under normal conditions of peace rather than in the immediate aftermath of war. It was therefore important for those who believed in a system of round-table diplomacy that it should be seen to have succeeded; and there were special correspondents from the newspapers of the leading capital cities to keep the reading public informed of what was happening (another innovation). In contrast to the Russian delegation, Metternich had prepared for the conference with care, and he was not disappointed. He had with him Gentz, as a public relations man, and two of his most experienced collaborators, Lebzeltern and Floret. Moreover, he had repeated on several occasions his insistence that the congress should concern itself solely with ending the military tutelage of the French and with means for maintaining the unity of the Great Powers.[18]

This clarity of purpose, no less marked in Castlereagh's instructions than in Metternich's, helped to complete the formal work of the congress in record time. Within eleven days of the opening session the statesmen were agreed on a treaty for withdrawing occupation forces from France and for payment of the remaining portions of the war indemnity. 'I have never seen a prettier little congress,' wrote Metternich in mid-October,[19] 'It will not cause me any unpleasantness, I assure you.' He was, it must be admitted, a little over-optimistic, for the business of the congress dragged on for another month, but there was none of the tension which had marred the first half of the assembly in Vienna. The Tsar put forward a number of idealistic projects, some of which were warmly backed by the Prussians: there was talk of a protective union of all governments against revolution; a plea for disarmament; and a suggestion that a European Army might be established, with Wellington as Commander-in-Chief and Brussels as his headquarters.[20] But Castlereagh and Metternich succeeded in convincing the Tsar that such detailed proposals were premature and that it was wiser to insist on the 'moral solidarity of the Alliance'. The four signatories of the Alliance of 1815 concluded a secret protocol reaffirming its validity in case of revolutionary changes in Paris; but, so as to complete the European system, a formal invitation was extended to Louis xviii to associate his kingdom with pledges upholding the peace of the continent. France was no longer to be blackballed from the club of the Great Powers; she had recovered the position which Talleyrand attained for her, under different circumstances, in Vienna before the Hundred Days.

Outwardly there seemed complete harmony between the views of Metternich and Castlereagh, even though the British Foreign Minister was obliged to warn his Austrian colleague that henceforth decisions on foreign affairs would require the approval of the cabinet in London and he could not exercise such autocratic powers as at Chaumont or in Vienna. But already the German problem had induced Metternich to assume a right of intervention in the internal affairs of another independent power in defence of the conservative order; and this was a doctrine which it was impossible for Castlereagh or any Foreign Secretary publicly to uphold, however much he might sympathize with it. For on 14 November Metternich sent a confidential letter with two supplementary memoranda to Wittgenstein for the attention of the King of Prussia warning him of the revolutionary dangers which would threaten his monarchy and the whole of Germany if Frederick William fulfilled the promise he had made in May 1815 of granting his subjects a constitution.[21] At the same time Metternich drew attention to the dangers of uninhibited political discussion at the universities, of the menace of patriotic gymnastic societies, and of the need to restrain the press. Metternich was sounding the first blast of the intellectual counter-revolution. As yet it remained muted and the contents of his message were known to only a few Prussian ministers, but it was a portent of which Frederick William soon saw the significance.

Little of these inner thoughts disturbed the work of the congress. Life in Aix proceeded at a decorous pace. At one time Gentz believed five thousand visitors would flock to the city for the congress; and he foresaw, with some despondency, a repetition in miniature of the pleasures of the Vienna assembly.[22] He need not have worried. The town was crowded with onlookers and with champions of good causes; even Robert Owen came to observe the masters of Europe in conference, vainly seeking in conversation with Gentz to awaken consciousness of the social question. But there was none of the frivolity of Vienna. There were concerts and there were balls and receptions but on a far smaller scale than in 1814–15 and, at times, the principal participants in the Congress were content to play whist through the evening hours. Some of the background lobbying was important: the statesmen and sovereigns still had a conscience over the slave trade; and there was a significant luncheon party on 12 November when Metternich made himself agreeable to Carl and Solomon Rothschild who were upholding the civil rights of the Jews in Germany and spreading the influence of their banking-house at the same time: but the formal work of the Congress was as limited as Metternich had intended it to be.[23] Gentz drew up an official declaration at the close of the Congress which proclaimed the virtues of 'justice, moderation and concord'.[24] They were happy abstractions which could mean much, or nothing. It was better not to seek definitions.

To the Austrian delegation the most surprising development at Aix was the change in attitude of the Tsar. Metternich was quick to notice that, after the first few days, he was no longer interested in Pozzo di Borgo's proposals, nor so willing to listen to the honeyed phrases of Capodistrias. The temper of the students in Germany and the possibility that radical dissidence might even contaminate his own soldiery had put him on guard against liberal ideas. To the public he showed once more that gracious and kindly dignity which had charmed the German princesses at Erfurt exactly ten years before. He flirted innocently enough with Marie Esterhazy who, to her father's pride and her husband's admiration, was the social delight of the ballrooms that autumn. She was flattered to be invited to lead polonaises with the Tsar of All the Russias, as any young wife would have been; but, remembering the tensions of the Vienna Congress, she was surprised at his affability. 'It struck me as wholly amusing', Marie wrote to her mother, 'to see Papa one evening arm in arm with the Tsar.' The quarrels of Vienna were forgotten in an ecstasy of reconciliation. 'We have found one another again, as in 1813,' Metternich told Eleonore; and politically, too, they were drawing closer together.[25]

Dorothea Lieven

At Aix, also, he 'found' Dorothea Lieven, a discovery which for many years seemed of greater moment to him than any event at the Congress itself. They had met formally in England in 1814 but she appears to have thought him 'cold and unapproachable'; and it was only at the Nesselrodes's reception on 22 October 1818 that the 'man of ice' began to melt. She was, at the time, thirty-two years old and the wife of the Russian ambassador in London. Although born in Riga she was hardly less German in origin than Metternich (or, indeed, than Nesselrode) for her father, Baron Benckendorff, came from a Junker family with estates in Estonia and her mother was a Württemberger. Both the Lievens were Lutheran, with little understanding of the Orthodox mysticism which, from time to time, influenced Russian public policy. The Countess – she became Princess Lieven only in 1826 – was educated at the Smolny Convent and introduced to the unrealities of life at the Russian court. In later years she recalled how, at the age of twelve, she had played blind man's buff with Tsar Paul, Marshal Suvorov and the last King of Poland; and it was a game which she never really abandoned when she emerged into the world of politics. She was a social snob who would intrigue with any statesman careless enough to fall for the dark vivacity of her eyes or for that ballerina silhouette of angular face and swan neck. Men as different as the Prince Regent, Castlereagh and the Duke of Wellington enjoyed her company. She had introduced the waltz to England; and she was a talented pianist. Above all, she was a brilliant listener tempting those who talked to her to reveal heart and mind by the sympathetic perspicacity of her silence, although a malicious wit and possessive jealousy made her a treacherous friend. In time she was to become the confidante of Canning (who at first detested her) and of Grey, Palmerston and Guizot for, as she once wrote to Metternich, 'I quite like prime ministers'; but the earliest and most intense of her political friendships was the one which began at Aix that October night when she induced the Austrian Foreign Minister to talk to her about Napoleon, a topic of which he never wearied. She rarely chose a wrong conversational gambit.[26]

It was a strange relationship. Metternich was at first hopelessly infatuated with the Countess – or, perhaps more accurately, with the image of what he imagined his 'dearest Dorothea' to be. Although after the Congress of Aix broke up he followed her to Brussels for a few days, they saw each other for no more than a fortnight in all during

1818 and then not again until 1821, when they had the spare moments of a crowded week in Hanover for their private meetings. Inevitably their friendship matured through correspondence, and they exchanged some four hundred letters in the course of eight years before mutual affection turned sour.[27] They wrote to each other as though entering pages in a diary, evening after evening, with the free range of a long conversation. She was always conscious of posterity snooping over her shoulder; and perhaps she welcomed its presence there. He was less inhibited: improbable protestations of devotion mingle with impossible flights of metaphysic; deceptively candid passages of autobiography are interspersed with staggeringly complacent self-analysis. She fed him with the political gossip of London and Brighton; and in return he told her of what he liked and whom he despised, of his love of music and gardens, his daily routine in Vienna, his affection for his family, his early romances, the silliness of Wilhelmine of Sagan, and the spirituality of Julie Zichy-Festetics (whom he could not bring himself to mention by name). 'I have never been unfaithful', he explained in a letter written from his birthplace on 1 December 1818. 'The woman whom I love is the only one in the world for me.' He would not write politics to Dorothea 'for two reasons. The first is that with you I have something better to do, and the second is that I am too happy to have found someone with whom I can talk of love, friendship, reason – all of which are worth more than politics.'[28]

Week by week throughout that winter he revealed his character to her: 'My soul is strong and upright and my words are true, always and on every occasion' ... 'I believe that each day must add to your conviction that I am a person apart from my fellow men'.... 'There is never indecision in my step. I go straight to the objective and am sure of reaching it'. ... 'My friend, you are in love today with a kind of barrier. It has been placed where it is to stop those who run too hard and in the wrong direction'.... 'I have twenty defects but presumption is not among them.'[29] Once at least he seems to have written with an ironic smile: his old enemy, Count Wallis, dropped down dead in November 1818, and the event seemed worthy of comment: 'For several years now,' he wrote, 'I have made a singular observation. It is that men who are diametrically opposed to me die. The reason is quite simple. These men are mad and it is the mad who die'.[30] We do not know if, when she received such confidences, Dorothea Lieven laughed with Metternich or at him, but the healthy acidity of her letters suggests a likely reaction to his more preposterous essays in vanity. She was a woman of few illusions, except perhaps about her own importance. Their passion, which warmed both their hearts that first winter, became by the following summer a natural intimacy of the mind rather than a romance sustained at fever heat. Ultimately what she loved about Metternich was the sense of clandestine power which the relationship gave to her; and, for all his early pledges of timeless adoration, what came to matter for him were the letters themselves rather than the recipient. She was a mirror reflecting those qualities of resolution and infallibility which he wrote into his correspondence because he could not find them in himself.

Third visit to Italy (1819) and the assassination of Kotzebue

All this, however, lay in the future; and, as he travelled back from Brussels to Aix and up the Rhine through the short days of a mild December, his feelings for the Countess were as sincere as any emotion he had felt in his youth. Even Munich, 'a city I detest', did not lower his spirits unduly despite the presence there of Capodistrias, towards whom his sentiments had not changed.[31] He arrived back in Vienna late at night on 11 December in such a state of confusion that he upset his daughter, Leontine, aged seven, by greeting her as Hermine, aged three – an incident which so impressed him that he reported it by letter both to Marie Esterhazy and Dorothea Lieven.[32] He had seen little of the younger members of his family in recent years, for he had been away from Vienna for months at a time ever since 1813. Nor was he able to spend much time in their company now. The Tsar had so shed his Austrophobia that he was paying a private visit to Vienna that Christmas and Metternich thought it essential he should make himself agreeable to his re-discovered friend by entertaining him to lunch. And there were long hours spent in the Chancellery studying reports of unrest in Italy and of fiery meetings in German universities. Moreover already in October plans had been made for another grand progress of Emperor Francis through the Italian peninsula and Metternich knew he would have to accompany his master south as before. He set out only twelve weeks after his return from Brussels; and it was to be another six months before he saw his garden on the Rennweg again.

This third journey in Italy took him once more to Verona, Florence, Leghorn and Pisa, but he also visited for the first time Rome and Naples, and from Florence southwards he was accompanied by his favourite daughter, Marie Esterhazy, and her husband. He fell yet again under the spell of the Italian cities and countryside. Naples was more beautiful and on a vaster scale than he had imagined and he was awed by the majesty of Vesuvius. Rome, too, surprised him. He had expected the city to be 'old and sombre' but he found it 'ancient and superb, resplendent and eternally new'.[33] Yet there were reservations. The Holy Week ceremonies stirred all the latent contempt of his former rationalism: 'I admit that I do not understand how a Protestant becomes a Catholic in Rome', he wrote to Eleonore. 'Rome is like some splendid theatre with very bad actors.'[34] And to Gentz, who was worried over the divisive tendencies of German Protestantism, he replied, 'From the summit of the Quirinale I cannot take Dr Martin Luther to task'.[35] His opinion of the Italian people was not changed by what he saw: 'The Italian makes much noise but takes no action. . . . Hatred never shows itself against a thing but always against a person. Hence in Italy detestation exists between province and province, town and town, family and family, one individual and another.'[36] Nothing could disturb his old conviction that the Italian provinces of the Empire could be brought to accept Austrian rule if only appeals were made to 'the Lombard spirit'. He was disappointed by the practical effects of Viceregal administration in Lombardy-Venetia and in June he sent a note of ironic despair to his wife: 'I do not believe there are two things less alike than Germany and Italy, and yet our sages in Vienna want, cost what it may, to make Germans out of the Italians. Well, they'll succeed marvellously.'[37] But this time he proposed no new solution for the Italian problem. The whole visit was overshadowed by bad news from Germany, where the situation had become so serious that he cut short his sojourn in Lombardy-Venetia and hurried directly to Bohemia, for a meeting with Frederick William III at Teplitz.

On 23 March 1819, August Kotzebue, the German dramatist and agent of the Russian intelligence service, was murdered in Mannheim by a fanatical student of theology from Jena, Karl Sand.[38] The assassination caused even more widespread alarm than the Wartburg Festival, of which it was seen as an almost inevitable consequence. Kotzebue enjoyed an international reputation – it was an adaptation of one of his plays that Jane Austen selected for the amateur theatricals in *Mansfield Park*. Young Germans hated him for having mocked the student movement and they believed it was mainly through his reports that the Tsar abandoned 'liberalism' and recovered his belief in autocracy. Gentz, whose criticisms of the young patriots had been even sharper than those of Kotzebue, went in fear of his life, dashing off almost hysterical letters to Rome.[39] But Metternich, although complaining that 'the world had been in fuller health in 1789 . . . than today', reacted slowly to the news from Mannheim. He sought to restrain Gentz and to have the articles in the *Beobachter* toned down; for he maintained that he had warned often enough and that it was essential for other German governments to take the opportunity to set their house in order. He hoped, in particular, that the Kotzebue affair would mark the end of Prussia's flirtation with constitutionalism and would see the triumph of Wittgenstein.[40]

Metternich's attitude was confused. He was uncertain if he should treat the crime at Mannheim as an excuse for disciplining the universities or as a means for asserting Austria's will in the Federal Diet against the weakness of individual German rulers. At first he thought it would be sufficient to induce the Diet in Frankfurt to impose police regulations on the universities rather than to interfere in any way with the educational curriculum. But Gentz was against half-measures and, with some reason, had no confidence in the ability of the Diet to settle any matter whatsoever. He persisted in prodding Metternich into action: it was irritating to despatch detailed memoranda on German unrest and to receive in reply a courteous acknowledgement, some weary platitudes, and a rhapsody on the marvels of plant-life in Rome; nor does the promise that, 'as a botanist', he would be sent a few 'precious seeds' appear to have mollified him.[41] Gentz enlisted the support of the conservative writer, Adam Müller, an old friend who was serving as Austrian consul general in Leipzig. Together they urged Metternich to secure the appointment of controllers for each university and to initiate a purge of professorial chairs, possibly by transferring the more outspoken academics to posts in the government service, where they would be effectively muzzled. Nor would this be sufficient. It was essential to encourage the teaching of natural science rather than 'philosophical and critical studies' for, as Gentz wrote, 'any-one may philosophise and criticise ... as he pleases, but positive sciences have to be learned. If the younger generation chooses real learning once again, it will be capable of intellectual subordination without which academic life is merely a prelude to the wild anarchy in which all politics today revolves'.[42] This argument, at least, made sense to Metternich who distrusted other men's philosophies and always fancied himself as a scientist *manqué*.

By mid-June, ten weeks after receiving Gentz's first entreaties in Rome, Metternich had decided on a course of action. In a letter to Gentz from Perugia on 17 June he minimized the danger from the students: 'I have never feared that the Revolution could be produced within the universities', he wrote, 'but I feel convinced that a whole generation of revolutionaries is being bred there.' In order to ensure tranquillity in Germany control must be exercised over what was printed and read: 'Today the greatest evil – and therefore the most immediate – is the press.'[43] But unrest in the universities was a symptom rather than a cause of the general malaise in Germany. A committee of ministers in Frankfurt had failed to propose any policy for maintaining order through the Diet. If the German governments would not act, the Austrians would have to assume the initiative. He therefore proposed an informal conference of the principal representatives of the German states in Carlsbad, where he would once more take the waters in July and August. Provided that Prussia collaborated with Austria, agreement could be reached for a uniform course of action against revolutionary German nationalism. Before the ministers arrived in

Carlsbad, Metternich therefore arranged an audience with Frederick William at Teplitz, the King of Prussia's favourite spa, which was only fifty miles north-east of Carlsbad, in the Sudeten Mountains.

At Teplitz and Carlsbad (July–August 1819)

Metternich arrived at Teplitz on 27 July. He found himself in the same room that he had occupied in 1813 when he signed the treaty of alliance with Prussia and Russia against Napoleon, and he prepared for his encounter with the King by writing a self-congratulatory letter of reminiscence to Eleonore.[44] Then he had been the junior partner in the alliance; now he enjoyed a prestige which enabled him to dictate his terms. As if to emphasize the urgency of action, news reached him of an abortive assassination attempt on the Chief Minister of Nassau, Ibell. Frederick William abased himself wretchedly before the prophet who had warned Prussia of the menace of liberalism at Aix. 'Everything you foresaw has taken place', the King admitted. Metternich roundly castigated the Prussian administration: sympathizers with the revolutionary conspiracy were 'without doubt to be found in the highest ranks of your Majesty's servants'. Provided that Frederick William was prepared to give his confidence only to reliable ministers, such as Wittgenstein and his friends, Austria would safeguard the Prussian state machine; but it was to be understood that the King would undertake never 'to introduce any representation of the people into your kingdom, which is less fitted for it than any other'. Frederick William, who had in his time been browbeaten by Napoleon and browbeaten by the Tsar, meekly accepted both remonstrance and advice. Weak and indecisive government in Berlin was, he explained, all the fault of Hardenberg and his associates. He urged Metternich to negotiate with the Prussian ministers here in Teplitz: 'Do try, above all, to get these people to commit themselves in writing,' he added pathetically.[45]

They did. On 1 August Hardenberg and Metternich put their signatures to the Convention of Teplitz by which Prussia and Austria agreed on a common course of action at the informal meeting of ministers in Carlsbad and at a subsequent conference in Vienna. At Carlsbad decisions would be taken over freedom of the press, control of university teaching, and methods of investigating the revolutionary movement. The Vienna Conference would settle outstanding questions over the nature of the German Confederation and would interpret, in a conservative spirit, Article XIII with its pledge that each sovereign state would have an assembly. The Carlsbad meetings opened on 6 August and continued until the end of the month, but there was so little objection to Metternich's programme that the ministers could

G

well have concluded their work in a few days. Metternich enjoyed a
triumph as yet unparalleled in his career: each state had the right
to veto any publication of more than twenty pages printed anywhere
within the Confederation; each university was to be kept under
surveillance by a representative of the Confederation with power to
enforce discipline and prohibit dangerous lectures; and all revolutionary
activity was to be reported to a Central Commission, established in
Mainz. Three weeks later, without debate, the Diet in Frankfurt
unanimously approved the Carlsbad Decrees; and the ministers of the
German states began to prepare for the Vienna Conference, which was
to open at the end of November.[46]

By modern standards of repression, the Carlsbad Decrees seem
innocuous. Although permitting public authorities to interfere in the
universities, they did not impose rigid conformity and it could be
argued that there was greater academic freedom in Berlin and Jena
during the years of the Mainz Commission than at any time in the
middle third of the present century. But the Carlsbad Decrees meant
the end of the *Burschenschaften* and all the muddled dreams of unity
which had fired the enthusiasm of students ever since the Battle of
Leipzig. The Decrees were received with dismay and contempt in
many universities and were assailed by public figures outside Germany.
Tsar Alexander, inconsistent as ever, let Metternich know that he
disapproved of the measures. They were condemned in the House of
Commons and in the columns of *The Times* which, reported the
Austrian *chargé d'affaires* to Metternich, 'has become even more seditious
and Jacobin than the *Morning Chronicle*'. The Prince Regent, whose
Hanoverian connection gave him a peculiar interest in the German
agitation, warmly approved of Metternich's policy; but Castlereagh,
who was sensitive to feeling in parliament, tactfully informed the
Austrians that 'we are always pleased to see evil germs destroyed,
without the power to give our approbation openly'.[47] Metternich
was disappointed not to receive the public backing of his British and
Russian allies for the steps he had taken against 'the German revolution', but it did not lessen his sense of achievement. He had become 'a
moral power in Germany', if not in Europe.

The Carlsbad Conference was, indeed, a landmark in his public
life. He enjoyed the sense of triumph when the assembled diplomats
deferentially thanked him for the prescience with which, 'while still
on the other side of the Alps', he 'recognized the real cause of the
evil'.[48] He genuinely believed that he had established Habsburg
primacy over all the other German dynasties and revived the old
Reich in spirit. It is significant that he chose to share his elation by letter
not with Dorothea Lieven but with Eleonore, who had known the past
in all its uncertainty. On 1 September he wrote to her from Carlsbad:[49]

'Three weeks of work at Carlsbad has resulted in something that thirty years of revolution could never produce. For the first time there will appear a group of anti-revolutionary measures, correct and peremptory. What I have wanted to do since 1813 and what that infernal Tsar Alexander has always spoiled, I have now pulled off because he was not present here. At last I have been able to follow for once all my ideas, to put forward all my principles of public order, supported by a body of thirty million men (or fifty, if we count all the non-German Austrians) ... If the Emperor doubts that he is Emperor of Germany, he is mistaken.'

'MY FRIENDS THE SPIDERS'

The Vienna Conference on German Affairs (1819–20)

From Carlsbad Metternich was glad to escape to Königswart for a week of rest and reflection amid the 'tranquillity and peace' of the Bohemian forests and mountains. Now that the excitement of the ministerial meeting was over, his own mood became as autumnal as the golden beeches of his parkland caught in September sunlight. Although still glowing with satisfaction, he was mournfully conscious of the fleetingness of his achievements, the failure to create something lasting. He gave orders for a column bearing his name to be erected beside a new bridge on the estate. 'I have had the misfortune,' he wrote, 'to belong to the revolutionary epoch. This age, like all other human follies, will pass. Happy are those who will have learned to remain upright amid the ruin of several generations ... Fate has laid upon me in part the duty of restraining, so far as my powers permit, a generation whose destiny seems to be that of losing itself upon a slope which will surely lead to its ruin.'[1] The political battles of the German Confederation lacked the glamour of earlier contests; it was to be a long and vexatious winter.

There were good grounds for his fatalistic despondency. Teplitz and Carlsbad were successes won almost too easily to be true; and in the weeks preceding the Vienna Conference the rulers of southern Germany became increasingly unhappy at the prospect of indefinite subjection to the double yoke of Austria and Prussia. At Carlsbad the bogey of a German revolution had stampeded the ministers of nine German states into surrendering their right of independent political development; but once they returned to their capitals it was inevitable they should have second thoughts. The German Confederation had, after all, been established by an international congress. It could be argued that changes in its character were the responsibility of all members of the Quadruple Alliance and not merely of the governments in Vienna and Berlin. If this were the case, then why were there no British or Russian representatives at the Vienna Conference?

So at least reasoned King William of Württemberg; and, convinced of the need to safeguard the sovereignty of the lesser German states, he duly appealed for support at the forthcoming conference to his brother-in-law, the Tsar.[2] For a few weeks at the end of 1819 it looked as if Metternich might be embarrassed by the arrival of a Russian delegation for his exclusively Germanic gathering. But the danger soon passed. Although Capodistrias sympathized with the King's plea and made vigorous representations to the Tsar on his behalf, Alexander would not commit himself irrevocably to intervention in German affairs. He turned elsewhere for advice. Castlereagh, when sounded out by Lieven, declined to claim a seat for Britain at any conference table concerned solely with the Confederation, and the Tsar was reluctant to make a unilateral protest. Lebzeltern, the Austrian ambassador in St Petersburg, had no difficulty in satisfying Alexander that Metternich's German policy was a practical application of principles implicit in the Holy Alliance. Moreover, both Lebzeltern and Metternich played on Nesselrode's resentment of Capodistrias' influence, skilfully exploiting for their own ends the jealousy and suspicion of rival factions in the Russian capital.[3] These pressures were sufficient to restrain the Tsar. He instructed Capodistrias to indicate his active interest in what was determined at Vienna, but not to provoke any crisis which might harm the growing intimacy of the two Empires. The Russians made a cautionary growl rather than the snarl of anger which Metternich had, at one time, feared.

He had, however, other troubles. By now he regretted the speed with which the German Committee had completed its task in 1815. He wished to limit both popular sovereignty in the German states and the jurisdiction of the Federal Diet in Frankfurt; and he hoped to create a permanent council of ministers which, meeting in Vienna under his presidency, would determine what matters might profitably be discussed by the Diet. All such attempts to limit and control princely authority ran into heavy opposition from the spokesmen of Württemberg and Bavaria. They continued to insist that a comprehensive revision of the federal structure could be determined only with the assent of the four Great Power guarantors, sensing that Metternich had no desire for a congress which would have permitted Russia once more a voice in German affairs. He gave up all idea of fundamental reforms and even accepted a stipulation that no federal institution, whether council of Ministers or Diet, had the right to force a government to rescind its constitution.

But, though the conference dragged on until the spring of 1820, the south German representatives could not extort any further concessions, and the 'Final Act of the Vienna Conference' was an ominously reactionary document.[4] It subordinated the Federal Diet to executive decisions taken by the princes or by their ministers in joint consultation. No attempt was made to repeal the controversial Article XIII, but it was modified by the virtually meaningless pronouncement that a promise to bestow a constitution in no sense limited the sovereignty of the ruler in whose name the pledge was given. It was resolved that there could be no unfettered discussion on 'matters of public security' in a representative chamber anywhere within the Confederation and that a King or Prince whose authority was challenged by his subjects might appeal for federal aid against a presumptuous legislature. Hence, for twenty years, the political life of the German states was condemned to docile tranquillity and the ideal of a unified Fatherland faded into a pipe-dream of nebulous romanticism. 'One word spoken by Austria will now count as inviolable law throughout Germany,' wrote Metternich triumphantly as the conference broke up.[5] So pleased was he with the form of the 'Final Act' he even convinced himself there was no need for a permanent council in Vienna, and therefore forgot he had ever wanted one.

Family sorrows

He had found the conference an infernal bore. While it was in session he was forced to check his preference for peripatetic administration; and he remained in Vienna from the middle of September 1819 until the end of the following May. His letters are full of complaint: the tedium of long dinners, the tiresome interference with a normal way of life. Every time he held a grand ball, his library had to be transformed into a buffet, with tables for thirty-two guests fitted in beneath the fifteen thousand volumes 'on their fine mahogany shelves which stretch from floor to ceiling'. And he could never be sure what to do about the Canova *Venus* in the centre of the room: 'It upsets the arrangements a little,' he explained.[6] 'The statue is eminently modest from in front; but you cannot say the same about the hinder parts.' But the most irritating feature of the conference was the way it absorbed all the short daylight hours, retaining him in his study or the salons of the Chancellery. 'I really hunger and thirst for my garden on the Rennweg,' he wrote at the end of February. 'I have not set foot in it for a whole month. It is true that my rooms are full of the finest blooms from my greenhouses, but they are not the only things that delight me. I need fresh air and sunshine; I am a child of the light and must have brilliant light to be able to live.'[7]

Although he insisted he could enjoy 'only a few hours of leisure' during the conference, there were moments that winter when he seems to have done little except read and write or amuse himself with the 'astronomical clocks and scientific instruments' which littered his study. He was happiest delving in books of travel or science. 'I have a bad habit of reading for half an hour – or an hour – before going to sleep, although generally I read nothing to do with my work,' he wrote to Dorothea Lieven a week before Christmas. 'The ordinary novel does not interest me; I always find it inferior to my own experiences. Dramatic situations strike me as contrived and, as soon as I look at the title, I cannot help turning to the last page where someone gets married or kills themselves. Then it only remains for me to say *Amen*, and as far as I am concerned the novel is digested.'[8] Naturally he could not resist studies in contemporary history, provided that they portrayed him favourably; and he found a three-hour perusal of Koch's narrative of the 1814 campaign particularly gratifying because, upon reflection, he could not think of any occasion when he personally had made an error or fallen short of his duty. That night he stayed awake until five in the morning, his 'mind full of 1814'.[9]

There was, indeed, something pathetic in his pre-occupation with the past. It is as if he were convinced that, at forty-six, his years of constructive labour were over. He had reached a stage of ironic detachment where he admired diplomatic expertise rather than the nobility of purpose which inspired, from time to time, a man like Alexander. There is a curiously revealing passage in a rambling letter which he wrote that April, at a moment of worry and sorrow:

I am beginning to understand the world better. I believe that if flies are eaten by spiders it is because they die too young and therefore have no experience, not knowing a spider's web when they see one . . . Spiders indeed interest me. I watch them frequently; they are the best barometers and, apart from their ugliness, the most charming little creatures, always busy and arranging their homes with the greatest neatness in the world.[10]

In part he allowed his mind to dwell on such trivialities in order to escape from the gloom which enveloped his private life that spring. His daughter Clementine had celebrated her fifteenth birthday while he was at Carlsbad. He had thought her plain as a child, but on his return from Bohemia he was impressed by her delicate beauty and he commissioned Sir Thomas Lawrence to paint her portrait, as though filled with a presentiment of disaster. Early in the New Year she developed bouts of fever and by the middle of March he had summoned six specialists, characteristically insisting on joining them in consultation and adding his knowledge to their experience. She was tubercular and there was nothing that could be done. Hour by hour, as he sat at the wearisome conference, he sought to hide his grief. She lived long enough to see the completed portrait, which arrived from Florence on 1 May.[11] Five days later she was dead. 'I have, fortunately, the gift of keeping my feelings to myself, even when my heart is half-broken,' her father wrote when it was all over. 'I soon get back to business, which makes a barrier between me and myself.' The Vienna Conference ended on 15 May –

his forty-seventh birthday – and hurriedly he got away to Bohemia. Despite his outward show of insincere affectation, Metternich was a man of deep family sensitivity and a father fond of his children (who always reciprocated his affection). He journeyed to Prague with an aching heart, hoping to find comfort and serenity in the changelessness of the Bohemian woodlands.

But it was not to be. Within ten weeks a second tragedy burdened him with fresh sorrow. His love for his eldest daughter, Marie Esterhazy, was the warmest of all his emotions.[12] She was so close to him in temperament that, as he said, 'there was no need for me to tell her what I was thinking for she always guessed it, knowing me better than I knew myself.' Marie had been unwell even before Clementine's death. At first her father hoped that her sickness was a sign of pregnancy, but by midsummer she had begun to show the merciless frailty of a consumptive, and he was summoned back from Carlsbad to her bedside at Baden, a town which the family loved so well that they had persuaded him to purchase a small house there only a year before. He knew as soon as he saw Marie there was little hope. She died on 20 July, a day when he was so engrossed in work that he had to spend six hours in the council chamber and another eight in the Chancellery. 'From now on,' he wrote, 'duty will supersede for me the joy of living.' The loss of two daughters in less than three months made him fear for the health of his remaining children, Victor, a young dandy of seventeen, and the two girls, Leontine and Hermine. Metternich was certain that there was something evil in the climate of Vienna. Ought the family to seek the sunshine and warm winters of Italy, he wondered? But he dared not advise Eleonore and the children to take up residence in a land where there was such active hostility towards the government he represented. Instead she chose to emigrate to France and set up a new home for the family in Paris.[13] By the end of September Clement was alone with his memories in the villa on the Rennweg; his wife's cousin, Countess Flore von Wrbna-Kagenegg, took charge of the household administration.

Revolts in Spain and Italy (1820)

'In the midst of such anguish,' Metternich sighed a few days after Marie's death, 'the World bears down on my shoulders with problems of insupportable weight'.[14] Half Europe did, indeed, seem wrapped in conspiracy in 1820. It was the year of the *Carbonari* in Italy and southern France, and of mutinies in the garrison at Cadiz and in a crack regiment of the Russian Imperial Guard. In February Arthur Thistlewood's radicals in Cato Street plotted to murder the British cabinet, and the Duc de Berri was assassinated outside the Paris Opera. In March the Spanish insurgents in Madrid compelled Ferdinand VII to restore the liberal constitution of 1812, a charter which inspired rebellion from Oporto to Palermo before the summer was out. Week after week reports of unrest reached Metternich from agents throughout the continent: only Germany remained undisturbed.

At first it seemed as though Spain posed the greatest problems. Tsar Alexander, who had made a point of patronizing Ferdinand VII, was all fire and flame when he heard of the liberal successes in Madrid. Metternich was in a quandary: he could no more accept in principle the overthrow of the existing order in Spain than in Germany or Italy; but he was realist enough to recognize that Austria had no interest whatsoever in the political condition of the Iberian peninsula. The ideal of the Alliance might demand intervention, as Capodistrias was quick to point out; but common sense was against it, and found a vigorous champion in Castlereagh. Late in April the Russians formally proposed joint action to free Ferdinand from the restraints imposed upon him by the constitutionalists.[15] But the thought of some Russian Duke of Brunswick leading an army of retribution across Europe to Madrid aroused scant enthusiasm in Vienna and positive hostility in London, where people had strong views on forays beyond the Pyrenees, especially if they involved the French. Britain would never support intervention in Spain. Desperately Metternich looked for a compromise and at the end of May he thought he had found one: he would agree with the Tsar on the need for solidarity against revolution and, at the same time, accept Wellington's verdict that military intervention in Spain was undesirable and impracticable.[16] This solution seemed to Metternich a wise exercise in sympathetic inactivity, well calculated to allow him to go on sheltering behind high-sounding platitudes until the Tsar Quixote and his Corfiote Sancho Panza had found windmills elsewhere to charge. Unfortunately Metternich could not foresee what would happen so soon in Naples.

'No Italians have the energy to revolt in the long six months of summer,' he had written confidently from Florence in July 1819.[17] He was wrong, for almost exactly a year later General Guglielmo Pepe placed himself at the head of a rebellious cavalry squadron in the Neapolitan Army and forced a terrified King Ferdinand to issue a constitution similar to the one granted by his nephew and namesake in Madrid. The news of Pepe's revolt reached Vienna on 15 July and fetched Metternich back to the Chancellery from poor Marie's bedside in Baden. He was surprised and puzzled by the first reports from Naples, for he had genuinely believed conditions in southern Italy to be materially better than for many years.[18] But he at once appreciated that a Neapolitan revolution was potentially a greater danger for Austria's future than student troubles in Germany or a mutiny in Spain; for Naples was the largest Italian kingdom, bound to Austria by a special relationship. Should Pepe's rebellion succeed, Habsburg primacy in the peninsula, to which Metternich had attached such importance in 1814–15, would be challenged by a movement which was both liberal and nationalistic. Moreover, at the back of his mind, there was always a fear that the spirit of revolt would spread beyond the Alps. Even though later reports indicated that the leaders in Naples were moderate Muratists rather than radical *Carbonari*, he was far from re-assured and sounded out his allies.

Castlereagh had no doubt what should be done. This was an Austrian emergency and an Austrian army must at once be sent south to deal with it.[19] But the Russians and the French argued that Naples, like Spain, was a revolutionary challenge to the European system and should be condemned jointly by the Great Powers even if, for practical reasons, the suppression of the revolt was left to Austria. Metternich was cautious: he did not want to lose the support of the British, but neither did he want to commit Austria's limited military forces in the south while leaving Central Europe free for Russian intrigue and a possible restoration of the close relationship between the Tsar and Frederick William. He therefore proposed a joint conference of ambassadors to meet in Vienna at the end of August. The Tsar, on the other hand, thought that the time had come for another congress of sovereigns. He had already undertaken to meet Emperor Francis to discuss the Spanish Revolution at Troppau (Opava) in Austrian Silesia; and in September he proposed that Frederick William and Hardenberg should also be invited to Troppau and approaches made to the British and French. Metternich felt at this stage that he was losing the diplomatic initiative, but he agreed to the Troppau meeting, though with some misgivings at the thought of finding Prussia once more in the Tsar's pocket. He also distrusted French policy, which made much of the links between the Bourbons of Paris and the Bourbons of Naples. For a time he suspected that there might be a Franco-Russian entente or even a latter-day Tilsit, though with Russia as the dominant partner. Since he could not rely on the British Parliament for support, such an alliance would leave Austria isolated. His fears were increased by Castlereagh's refusal to be associated with joint action over Naples and by his insistence on sending an observer, rather than a representative, to Troppau; but they were slightly allayed when the French, offended by Alexander's high-handed manner, announced that they, too, would despatch a mere observer to the congress. Clearly it was to be primarily a gathering of the three Eastern autocrats and their ministers.

Metternich prepared for Troppau as carefully as for Aix-la-Chapelle.[20] He was in no hurry to settle the affairs of Naples since his reports suggested the revolutionaries were falling out among themselves; and he therefore wished to use the congress as an arena for the Great-Power contest, a game he always delighted in playing. His sole aim was to secure mastery of Alexander's mind, dominating him as he had Frederick William at Teplitz, and thereby displacing Capodistrias. Gentz defined the Austrian objective with his usual clarity: 'Our task may be summed up in one word: Capodistrias.'[21] Remove the Corfiote and all Alexander's dangerous impulses would be placed under restraint. Metternich carefully cultivated the friendship of the principal British and French observers, Lord Stewart (Castlereagh's half-brother) and the Marquis de Caraman. Both men were ambassadors in Vienna and were inclined to purr with delight at the slightest flattery. At the same time Metternich instructed Lebzeltern to keep close to Alexander and play constantly on his fears of conspiracy and revolution; and Frederick William was treated once more to kindly advice on Prussia's internal problems which, being a simple man, he does not seem to have resented.

Yet, strangely enough, Metternich approached the Troppau Congress in a mood of uncertainty and even despair. He was sleeping badly and on 15 August, Napoleon's birthday, he noted: 'Today is the Feast of the great exile. If he were still on the throne and there was only he in the world, how happy it would make me.'*[22] And it was on 6 October, a few days before leaving Vienna, that Metternich wrote to Dorothea Lieven one of his most frequently quoted letters: 'My life has coincided with a wretched epoch. I came into the world too soon or too late; today I know I can do nothing. Earlier I should have enjoyed the pleasures of my age; later I should have helped in reconstruction. Now I spend my life in propping up buildings mouldering in decay. I ought to have been born in 1900 and to have had the twentieth century before me.'[23]

The Congress of Troppau (1820)

He was needlessly pessimistic: Troppau proved as much a personal triumph as Teplitz. He reached the Silesian capital on 19 October, a day ahead of the Tsar. Within a few hours of Alexander's arrival he was granted an audience and found him graciously amenable.[24] 'Between 1813 and 1820, seven years have elapsed,' said the Tsar, 'but to me these seven years have been as long as a century. In 1820 I would in no circumstances do what I did in 1813. You have not changed but I have. You have nothing with which to reproach yourself, but I cannot say the same for myself.' It was a good beginning and Capodistrias, whom Metternich saw on the next day, was so bland and con-

---

* Sentimental nostalgia does not seem to have influenced Metternich when, on 13 July 1821, he heard news of 'the great exile's' death ten weeks previously. He advised Francis I not to pay public respect to the memory of his son-in-law, but he conceded that it would be appropriate for Napoleon's son to go into mourning.

ciliatory that a statesman of lesser experience might reasonably have
assumed the business of the Congress would be settled in a week.
But Metternich, well accustomed to parrying diplomacy, was not
deceived: 'I attacked his past; and he condemned it. I outlined the
future as I saw it; he agreed entirely with me. Eventually I started to
laugh; and he laughed too. I believe that had I wept, he would have
burst into a flood of tears.'[25] Gentz, who at Troppau was more than
ever in Metternich's confidence, cautioned the Prince against the
Corfiote's veiled liberal sentiment. He needed no such prompting: in
the previous year Capodistrias had visited England and stayed with the
Lievens, and Dorothea had let Clement know of the universal popularity
which he had won by a persuasive tongue and the glamour of his
personality. Metternich did not doubt that 'the pseudo-Saint John of
the Apocalypse', as he dubbed him, was a formidable adversary.[26]

At the first full session of the Congress, on 23 October, Metternich
proposed that, as a general principle, powers should never intervene in
the internal affairs of other states unless their domestic troubles exerted
an influence beyond their frontiers. He implied that, since what had
happened in Naples concerned the Austrians, they possessed a right to
act while their allies, who were distant from the peninsula, did not.
This doctrine momentarily stymied the Russians. A Prussian memorandum six days later disconcerted them further by showing what
an abject dummy Frederick William had become on the knee of his
Austrian ventriloquist. But by 2 November Capodistrias had rallied
and thought of an answer. It was not original. Intervention, he maintained, depended on the need to sustain the settlement of 1815 rather
than on any right of self-defence, and it could therefore be justified
only in the name of the Allies. Before troops marched on Naples there
must be an attempt at mediation and a solemn Allied declaration that,
when the revolutionary movement was suppressed, it would be succeeded by a government pledged to uphold the 'dual freedoms' of
national independence and political liberty. He had in mind, he
explained, something 'on the model of the French Charter' of 1814, a
document of which 'all enlightened men' could approve. For three hours
Metternich had to listen to Capodistrias as he ranged 'into all the
labyrinths of his general views . . . upon the construction of the governments of empires and nations'; and, reported Stewart to Castlereagh, it
left him 'extremely low and out of spirits'. He always resented other
statesmen expounding general principles in his presence.[27]

Yet Metternich was, at heart, far less disturbed by Capodistrias
and his ingenious juggling with political abstractions than Stewart
believed. He certainly displayed appropriately ruffled feelings for
the benefit of Nesselrode, who begged him 'in Heaven's name to wait'
and do nothing rash.[28] But in reality Metternich and Gentz never let

the situation get out of control. Metternich counted on the Tsar, whom he rightly saw had been impressed by his consistent prophecies of pending disasters over the previous five years. Now he piled on the pressure. Lebzeltern, briefed by Gentz, sought out the Tsar and explained that the Russian proposals were too vague for political action; and Metternich found a slightly unexpected ally in his sister Pauline, who was related to the Tsar by marriage, and happened to come over to Troppau for three days, making herself agreeable to Alexander at a time when everyone was finding the social delights of Silesia in winter distinctly limited. The Tsar gave way gracefully. At the end of the first week in November he instructed Capodistrias to accept a compromise: if intervention were necessary it would be carried out in Naples on behalf of the Holy Alliance, but without reference to the 'dual freedoms' or any other proposed measure of reconstruction. Outwardly it was not a complete victory for Metternich since Capodistrias was authorized to draft the protocol defining the 'beneficent intentions' of the congress; but, although Metternich took a risk in leaving Capodistrias with the right to draw up such an important document, he could at least disclaim responsibility for phrases in it which might alienate Castlereagh or the French.[29]

The 'Preliminary Protocol' of Troppau was, indeed, cumbersome. It announced the intention of the Allied powers 'to bring back to the bosom of the Alliance' states which had endangered the security of their neighbours by an 'illegal' change in the form of government. It also proposed that Allied representatives should accompany an army of occupation into Naples and invited King Ferdinand to meet his brother sovereigns in Laibach to discuss the future of his kingdom. Stewart, as Metternich anticipated, protested at such a doctrine of interference in the internal affairs of the smaller states of Europe and Castlereagh subsequently declared that the Protocol assumed 'a moral responsibility of administering a general European Police' which was contrary to British notions of international law.[30] But Metternich refused to regard British hostility as anything more than a gesture towards parliamentary opinion and Paul Esterhazy, the ambassador in London, lent support to this interpretation: 'Castlereagh is like a great lover of music, who is at Church,' he wrote. 'He wishes to applaud, but he dare not.'[31] Moreover, although Metternich always set much store by Castlereagh's friendship, he could not risk endangering his personal entente with the Tsar for the sake of Britain's diplomatic sensitivities. And by the end of November he had every reason to believe Alexander was showing towards him a confidence he denied to either Nesselrode or Capodistrias. He had already gained his main objective, although he could never be sure that the Tsar would not veer back to the wiles of the subtle Corfiote.

The Austrians and Russians decided to remain at Troppau until they had heard if Ferdinand would come to Laibach. The weather in Silesia throughout November and December was abominable. The municipal authorities were perplexed; they had exhausted their imagination in October by erecting a triumphal arch in anticipation of the happy results which would follow the gathering of such a distinguished company in their midst. By 1 December the streets were so impassable that Metternich described them as 'chocolate ice'. Someone had the happy idea of spreading wooden planks for the great figures to tread; but they were so narrow that they produced new problems of etiquette.[32] When the Tsar met a lady coming in the opposite direction his sense of gallantry and her instincts of monarchical respect invariably meant that both stepped aside and floundered in the mud: 'Cruikshank would find in these incidents material for innumerable caricatures,' wrote Metternich, with a certain waspish glee. There was little else amusing in such a dead town. The diplomats met for talk or whist evening after evening. Never before had Metternich come to know the Tsar so well. One night, as they sat drinking tea, Metternich commented that he found it hard to work with Capodistrias: 'He never understands me,' he complained. 'I have often taken him to task over that,' replied Alexander, 'It is because he always feels you have hidden thoughts.' Metternich enjoyed the novelty of Russian tea and Tsarist sympathy. 'Oh, if only that aromatic brew could make Capodistrias reasonable,' he wrote at the end of a letter on 15 December. 'Heavens alive, what a mass of tea I would send for from China!'[33]

That same night Metternich put the finishing touches to a long document of eight thousand words which he had prepared for the Tsar.[34] He called it a 'profession of political faith' and it is, in essence, a manifesto of conservative principles designed to convince Alexander that the party of order could rest its beliefs on teachings of more lasting validity than the liberal idealists, who had for so long sought to interpret for him the will of the Almighty. It is basically a shallow essay in political philosophy, pretentiously wrapping the commonplace in an impressively analytical style learned long ago at the University of Strasbourg; but it is an interesting revelation of what Metternich thought he believed at the zenith of his diplomatic career.

The European society in which they lived, Metternich began, was in a state of flux. In every country there were some men well disposed towards political change, but most people were observers who wanted 'a tranquillity which has already ceased to exist, and of which even the first elements seem to be lost'. During the preceding three centuries there had been greater progress in human endeavour than in human wisdom and this was particularly the case in France where a nation

quick to understand ideas found itself too civilized to temper intellectual
novelties with the caution of experience. There had, in consequence,
emerged 'the presumptuous man', a being who was steeped in the
values of private judgement, independent in his beliefs and individualistic in his principles of behaviour. 'Knowledge seems to have come by
inspiration.' It was inevitable political institutions should decay
for reasons 'so closely linked with the nature of things that no human
foresight could have held them in check': but it was at least possible for
wise governments to control the process of change in order to protect
society from 'the scenes of horror' associated with the French Revolution and arising from the false doctrines of presumptuous individualism.
Napoleon had at first restrained anarchy by his military despotism
although the Jacobin contagion had broken through into Germany,
Italy and Spain as a form of patriotism. Moreover the 'return of the
usurper' in 1815 had the gravest political consequences: 'In a hundred
days Bonaparte destroyed the work of the fourteen years in which he
had exercised authority. He let loose the revolution which he had come
to France to subdue. He brought men's minds back, not to the 18th
Brumaire, but to the principles which the Constituent Assembly had
adopted in its wanton blindness.' Since 1815 Prussia had tolerated
secret societies and some of the German princes had betrayed their
own order.

Metternich then proceeded to analyze the evils of the day and to
suggest a course of future action. Society was endangered by the most
presumptuous of its classes, those who lay between the aristocracy and
the people – financiers, men of letters, lawyers, civil administrators,
teachers and professors. This middle class, jealously coveting power,
agitated for constitutional reform although what was meant by the
demand varied between 'pure monarchies' and states where there was
already a form of representation. Using 'the scourge of a free press'
this class sought to destroy everything which 'through the centuries has
achieved the right to claim respect and allegiance from human beings'.
Governments must resist the temptation to make concessions to violent
factions, although they might 'progressively develop institutions by
legal means', free from hasty passion. 'The hostile party is divided into
two groups', he explained, 'the levellers and the doctrinaires.' The
levellers were more to be feared in moments of crisis: the doctrinaires,
'devotees of abstract ideas ill-suited to real needs', were not men of
action but their insidious influence was dangerous in the deceptive
calm which precedes a political thunderstorm. The sovereigns of
Europe knew their duty: they must protect the purity of religion from
the vision of foolish sectarians; they must reduce the doctrinaires to
silence and control the press; they must be just but strong; they must
suppress conspiratorial groups, 'that gangrene of Society'; but above

all they must unite in a league to defend the social order against those who would disturb public tranquillity by their attacks.

This manifesto was essentially a product of long evenings at Troppau and it caught the spirit of the place, the time and the conflicts of the moment. In part it was a weapon for use against Capodistrias who, in Metternich's eyes, possessed all the presumptuous idealism of the doctrinaire liberal. The 'Profession of Faith' was a far more subtle document than any of the memoranda with which Metternich had bombarded the King of Prussia. Although it contained no direct criticisms of Russia's past policy, there were within it arguments and examples to make the Tsar doubt the wisdom of his constitutional gestures in Poland and to show him the folly of patronizing reformist ideas abroad or religious enthusiasm nearer home. Metternich knew his man, and spoke the language which the author of the Holy Alliance would understand, even if it showed heavily Teutonic undertones. He preached an anti-revolutionary crusade with a moral fervour well calculated to appeal to Alexander's latent religiosity. It was a powerful Advent sermon, and not without effect on the penitent to whom it was addressed.

The Congress of Laibach (1821)

The Congress of Troppau formally dispersed in the third week of December when it was learned that Ferdinand would, indeed, be able to leave Naples and make the journey to Laibach. Frederick William, who was perfectly content to entrust the ordering of Italy to Metternich, saw no point in setting out for another congress where nobody was interested in his problems, and he very sensibly went home to Berlin. The Russians and Austrians, with attendant British and French observers, travelled south over Christmas week and the New Year, relieved to get away from the mud and slush of Troppau and pass a few festive days in Vienna before discovering the comforts of a second provincial capital.[35] Metternich was the first to arrive in Laibach. He left Troppau on Christmas morning, arrived in Vienna forty-eight hours later and then set out for Laibach on the afternoon of New Year's Day, 1821. The weather was bitterly cold in Styria but it improved once he reached the Slovene uplands of Carniola and by 7 January, when the other statesmen had completed their journeys, the climate seemed refreshingly mild after endless weeks in Silesia and they were glad to have moved their meeting place three hundred miles to the south. Laibach was a pleasant city, a baroque façade standing out against a backcloth of snow-covered mountains; and it even possessed an opera house where they mounted two of Rossini's recent compositions. Almost, it seemed to Metternich, he was in Italy, that land for which he felt such mixed emotions of wonder and contempt.[36]

Metternich (standing on the left) at an informal session of the Congress of Vienna. Talleyrand is seated second from right

A ball at Princess Metternich's, late 1814. 1. Emperor Francis. 2. Empress Maria Ludovica of Austria. 3. Prince von Leuchtenberg. 4. Tsar Alexander 1. 5. Queen of Bavaria. 6. King Frederick William III of Prussia. 7. Crown Prince of Bavaria. 8. Baron von Tettenborn. 9. Prince de Ligne. 10. Princess Eleonore von Metternich. 11. King Maximilian of Bavaria. 12. Castlereagh. 13. Baron Stein. 14. Metternich. 15. Talleyrand. 16. Humboldt. 17 Prince von Hardenberg

(*left*)
Dorothea Lieven

Metternich's daughter, Clementine
painted by Lawrence shortly
before her death

Princess Melanie Zichy-Ferraris,
Metternich's third wife

Emperor Ferdinand

Metternich's summer residence on
the Rennweg, Vienna, 1815–45

Metternich dominated the affairs of Laibach to a greater extent than at any of the other congresses.[37] He had found in Count Ruffo, the Neapolitan ambassador in Vienna, a puppet spokesman for King Ferdinand, prepared to read speeches which were drafted by Gentz and Metternich and which explained with dubious casuistry why the King felt bound to abandon the constitution he had sworn only a few weeks before never to violate. Capodistrias fought a rearguard action, not because he cared for Naples, but because he hated Metternich. He vainly sought British or French mediation, but could never quite decide for what purpose. Metternich watched his efforts with amused disdain: 'Capodistrias writhes like a devil in holy water, but he really is in holy water and can do nothing,' he said. The Tsar gave his Minister no support and the British were most unhelpful; for, while they made a show of protest, Castlereagh assured his former partners that he still believed 'in the cordiality and harmony of the Alliance' and did not doubt 'the purity of (their) intentions'. On 30 January the constitutionalist Foreign Minister of Naples was fetched from Görz, where he had been detained for nearly four weeks, to hear Metternich announce that Austria, as the representative of Europe, would restore orderly government in the Kingdom of the Two Sicilies. On 6 February the Austrian Army headed southwards across the Po: it entered the city of Naples seven weeks later. Had it not been for Metternich's determination to use the Neapolitan Revolution as a foil in his contest with the Russians, the whole affair would have been speedily settled seven months before (and two congresses back). But, then, he would never have become the accepted arbiter of Europe. He had reached his prime and he delighted in his ascendancy, even if his motives lacked at times the purest sublimity of purpose.

The Congress of Laibach was formally adjourned on 28 February after representatives of the Allied powers had agreed that there should be another meeting at Florence in September 1822.[38] Metternich had no wish for all the sovereigns and statesmen to disperse until it was clear what would happen in Italy; and the Russians and Austrians remained in Laibach throughout March and April and well into May. There were difficulties over inducing King Ferdinand to return to Naples where he feared for his personal safety; and at times Metternich found the Tsar over-eager to carry out some of the propositions which he had put forward in the 'Profession of Faith'. It was not easy to present sound reasons why, if there was a universal danger from constitutionalists, the French should not be authorized to enter Spain and march on Madrid as the Austrians were marching on Naples. Metternich fell back on the bogey of a massive French-inspired conspiracy, with secret headquarters in Paris, which, he informed the Tsar, made French intentions so uncertain that it was as well not to give them the

opportunity of acting as Europe's agents in the chastisement of the
Spanish. It would be far better to defer the Spanish problem for the
congress of 1822. The Tsar dutifully accepted Metternich's advice.[39]

By the middle of March the statesmen in Laibach were faced by a
new problem. Early on 12 March Metternich was awoken with news
that a military revolt had broken out among garrisons of the Piedmontese Army in Turin and Alessandria; liberals were calling for a
constitution and for a war against Austria on behalf of the Neapolitans.[40]
Metternich responded quickly, as he had done when bad news arrived
that other March morning five years before. He hastened now, as then,
to inform Emperor Francis and the Tsar; and in the course of the day it
was decided that eighty thousand troops should at once be ordered
from Vienna to the plains of Lombardy and that a force of ninety
thousand Russians would be concentrated in reserve along the Austrian
frontier. The Tsar was most impressed by the news from Piedmont and
had to be restrained from precipitate action. 'Now I understand why
the Lord has kept me here until this moment,' he declared. 'How
much gratitude do I owe Him, for so arranging things that I was still
together with my allies.' Metternich does not appear to have been
entirely surprised by the news, perhaps because he was well informed of
the activities of the Italian secret societies and recognized that once the
main Austrian forces were committed in southern Italy, it was tempting
for the liberals to threaten the Austrian flank in Lombardy. Gentz,
on the other hand, wrote in his dairy on 14 March: 'This unexpected
blow struck me very hard, as it did all of us. . . . The important decision
of this evening, principally the march of 90,000 Russians, has lifted me
up completely.'[41] Europe should see how great was the unanimity
between the Austrian and Russian courts; and Metternich himself was
not displeased to have this opportunity of hunting out Carbonarist
sympathizers in the north of the peninsula at a time when the southern
revolutionaries were under pressure. His fear had always been that
Austria would not have the men available for a double emergency, but
his Russian policy had relieved him of this nightmare. 'Order' was
restored in Turin by the second week in April.

Metternich appointed Chancellor (25 May 1821)

The Piedmontese Revolt and Metternich's response to it stirred up
opposition among his old critics in Vienna. Stadion, as Minister of
Finance, was beside himself. It had been possible to finance the
campaign in southern Italy only with the help of a loan from the
Rothschilds; and now there was to be another war in the north. 'For
the love of God, how is this to be paid for?' Stadion wrote despairingly
to Metternich on 8 April. 'With this manner of doing things, all

responsibility on my part ceases,' he added.[42] Moreover, he was seriously alarmed at the possibility of Russian involvement so deep in Europe: was it in Austria's interest to have such a large force of Russians deployed along her frontier? And would it not have been possible to discipline the Neapolitans and Piedmontese without a concentration of military power? There was a strain of irony in his letters.

Metternich replied to Stadion's repeated criticisms in two long despatches from Laibach, dated 21 April and 22 April.[43] Patiently he explained that the intervention of Russia was intended only as a threat and demonstration to Europe that the two largest powers in Europe were prepared to act in concert against radicalism. He was not alarmed by the movement of Russian troops on the Austrian frontier: 'If I were not master of making them retreat just as we have made them advance, do you think we would ever have set them in motion?', he asked scornfully. And he rejected the complaint that the military operations would impose an additional financial burden: Piedmont and Naples would have to pay for the privilege of having the Austrian Army suppress their revolutions. His only fear was that not enough had as yet been done to stamp out the revolutionary evil. 'An immense good has been achieved,' he said in his most portentous manner; 'but it does no more than assure us of a chance that we may continue to exist. We must not delude ourselves: we have taken only a single step towards this possibility.' These were gloomy words. Perhaps they were intended merely to check the optimistic exuberance which assailed some of his colleagues in moments of success; but throughout the previous year he had tended to look at the world through fatalistic eyes and he may well have believed every word he wrote. If this was his mood after restoring the Empire's predominance in the Italian peninsula then the outlook for Austria was black indeed.

Yet there were consolations. He had enjoyed springtime in the Slovene countryside, taking long excursions with Nesselrode to the mountains and lakes; and there had been pleasant evenings at the opera, with a performance of *La Cenerentola* winning high praise from his pen.[44] He travelled back to Vienna in the fourth week of May across the Wurzen Pass and along the valleys of Carinthia. As he neared the capital he learned from the newspapers of new honours bestowed on him. On 25 May he was created Court Chancellor and Chancellor of State, a rank held only by Kaunitz among his predecessors.[45] It was a pleasant surprise for him and he recognized at once that it broadened his sphere of responsibility. But what pleased him most was the purely diplomatic achievement of the congresses: the three autocratic courts of Vienna, Berlin and St Petersburg were as closely linked together as at any time since 1813. He did not actively seek to limit or to destroy the Quintuple

Alliance, but if five-power unity proved impracticable because of the vagaries of the British or of the French, then he could at least rely upon the goodwill of his immediate neighbours.

Back in Vienna he was obsessed once more with the image which had first entered his mind in the previous spring. 'I have the feeling,' he wrote, 'that I am in the middle of a web which I am spinning in the style of my friends the spiders, whom I like because I have admired them so often.' In this web he believed he held the Tsar and all his Ministers. 'A net of this kind,' he continued, 'is good to behold, woven with artistry, and strong enough to withstand a light attack, even if it cannot survive a mighty gust of wind.'[46]

It was a fragile creation, as he readily admitted; and already a gale was beginning to blow around the Greek islands. 'A spider's web' around 'buildings mouldering in decay' suggests insubstantial triumph. At times he seems to have delighted in the very hopelessness of his mission.

POWER'S FOREMOST PARASITE

The Greeks pose the Eastern Question

While Austrian armies were suppressing the revolts in Naples and Piedmont disconcerting news reached the sovereigns and diplomats assembled at Laibach. On 17 March 1821 they learned that a fortnight previously one of the Tsar's *aides-de-camp*, Prince Alexander Ypsilanti, had crossed the River Pruth into Moldavia with some followers and raised a revolt against the Turks and their vassal rulers in Jassy and Bucharest. Within a month this information was followed by reports that, in the Peloponnese, the Archbishop of Patras had solemnly blessed the cause of Christian rebellion against the Sultan's government. Thus in the spring of 1821 the Greeks dramatically re-opened the 'Eastern Question', a problem which remained central to Europe's diplomacy for the rest of Metternich's life and which continued to defy solution for more than half a century after his death.[1]

The Eastern Question was first posed in its modern form in 1774 when, by the Treaty of Kutchuk-Kainardji, Catherine the Great gained a foothold for Russia on the Black Sea. At the same time the treaty conceded maritime trading rights to the Russians and an ill-defined protectorate over 'those who served . . . a Russo-Greek Church' which was to be built in Constantinople. Subsequent wars with Turkey enabled the Russians to extend their frontier to the river Dniester in 1792 and the river Pruth and the Danube delta in 1812. The Austrians watched this southward thrust of the Russians with concern. The Ottoman Sultans, long the masters of the middle and lower Danube, were traditional enemies of the Habsburgs, but from 1768 onwards the Austrians supported the territorial integrity of Turkey, except for a brief moment of aberration at the end of Joseph II's reign. Metternich, who by background and temperament looked to the West and to the South, had always endorsed this policy. Like Maria Theresa before and Bismarck after, he regarded the Balkans as a barren area of mountain and swamp inhabited by the overspill of Asia. He had no particular liking for the Ottoman system of administration but he saw the existence of the Turkish Empire as a barrier to Russian expansion and a denial of dangerously presumptuous sentiments of national patriotism. In 1815 Gentz had written prophetically: 'The end of the Turkish monarchy could be survived by the Austrian for but a short time';[2] and Metternich agreed with him. Hence, throughout the experiments in congress diplomacy, the Austrians had deliberately ignored south-eastern Europe, hoping Alexander's interest in other regions on the continent would induce the Russians also to keep the Eastern Question closed.

It had not always been easy. There was an awkward moment at Vienna in 1815 when Castlereagh proposed a comprehensive guarantee of the integrity of the Ottoman lands and Nesselrode responded with a memorandum claiming for Russia a protectorate over all Christians under the Sultan's rule; but Napoleon's return from Elba put a stop to such speculative diplomacy and in the years that followed nobody seemed anxious to revive the topic. Then, too, there had been problems raised by the Serbian struggle for autonomy under Miloš Obrenović, a development inevitably sending tremors of response through the Slav minorities in southern Hungary; and Metternich had long regarded with suspicion the *Philike Hetairia*, a Greek secret society which was founded at Odessa in 1814 but which had cells among Greek merchants in Venice and Trieste. Nor could Metternich forget that Capodistrias was a Greek by origin or ignore Alexander's right, as Tsar of All the Russias, to act as sole spiritual and political guardian of true Orthodoxy. Neither Metternich nor Gentz believed the Eastern Question would remain indefinitely quiescent, but both were surprised by the timing and manner of its reawakening. By precipitating a revolt on the lower Danube while the rulers of Russia and Austria were in conference, Ypsilanti had committed a major error of political judgement.

Ypsilanti was personally known to Metternich and to most of the members of the Laibach Congress for, as a general in the Tsar's service, he had come in 1815 to Vienna, where his gaiety had provided succulent tales for the gossips.[3] In advancing into Moldavia, Ypsilanti genuinely believed he could rely on the Tsar's sympathy and let it be understood that Alexander was patron of a crusade to liberate the Greeks. The Tsar, however, speedily denounced Ypsilanti's rash action, as much from his own detestation of revolt as from Metternich's prompting; and at first Metternich was inclined to dismiss the whole affair as a trifle. 'So far as the Greek revolution is concerned, let it go,' he wrote airily to Stadion on 26 March. A month later he was more restrained: 'In the past six weeks,' he wrote on 20 April, 'we have ended two wars and stifled two revolutions. It is to be hoped that the third revolution, which has broken out in the East, will be no more successful.' And by 6 May he had become angry and apprehensive, convinced that the Greek conspirators endangered the peace and unity of Europe: 'The complications which may arise in the East defy all calculation. Perhaps it is of little importance. Over there, away beyond our eastern frontiers, three or four hundred thousand individuals are hanged, slaughtered or impaled; and that hardly counts!'[4]

Whether Metternich was writing with callous malevolence or in irony it is difficult to say; but there is no doubt he wished the Turks to restore order swiftly and without Russian intervention. His early education had spurned the classics: he knew some Latin, and was prepared when in the Forum or on the Capitol to mourn the grandeur of Rome; but he knew no Greek, and the visions that uplifted the Philhellenes were always denied to him. English Tories like Aberdeen and Eldon were stirred by a struggle Homeric in its tragic endlessness: but not so Metternich. For him a Greek patriot was little more than an Aegean species of Jacobin, a half-savage challenging his legitimate ruler and worthy of no more consideration than the liberals of Naples or Piedmont. He was consistent; he was logical; and he prided himself on being down to earth ('*terre à terre*').

The Tsar never saw the affairs of Greece in such stark clarity.[5] So long as he was at Laibach he was prepared to accept most of Metternich's arguments. Together they had conjured up a mysterious central committee of revolutionaries which met in darkest Paris to inspire and control insurgent unrest throughout the continent; and it was no doubt comforting to find in Ypsilanti's conspiracy merely one more attempt at 'frustrating ... the Christian principles proclaimed by the Holy Alliance'. Before returning to Russia Alexander even pledged himself not to take action in the Balkans without prior consultation among the Allied powers. But the world looked different from St Petersburg, where the Admiralty spire thrust a minatory finger to the heavens and the massive dome of the Kazan Cathedral testified to the compass of Orthodoxy. Moreover, the very character of the Greek rebellion had changed. Ypsilanti's ill-considered expedition was defeated by the resentful apathy of Roumanian peasants and the skill of the Turkish soldiery; but the rising in the Peloponnese had spread to Greek communities throughout the Ottoman Empire and aroused such fanatical hatred between Moslem and Christian that a political revolt was rapidly becoming a holy war. On Easter Sunday the Turks hanged the Patriarch of Constantinople outside his cathedral, and executed several auxiliary bishops beside him. Such an affront to Orthodoxy offended Alexander's deep sense of religious duty. Although he assured the Austrians in July that he would hold fast to the pledges he had given at Laibach, his position was becoming difficult. The Turks murdered Russian sailors and heaped insults on Stroganov, the Russian ambassador, who was forced to flee for his life from Constantinople. How, Alexander asked Metternich pathetically, could he be expected to ignore such constant provocation?[6]

Metternich knew there was a powerful war party in St Petersburg and he sensed the Tsar was personally isolated. He feared Alexander might again experience some apocalyptic change of mood and set out on a crusade against the Turks from which no argument or remonstrance would deflect him. In letter after letter Metternich built up a bogey of mass conspiracy and Emperor Francis aided him, warning his brother sovereign that a war against Turkey would play into the hands of 'people who do not believe in any God and who respect neither His laws nor the laws of Man'. By contrast Capodistrias, vigorously championing his compatriots, saw to it that Alexander was informed of every instance of Turkish brutality and of every movement of Turkish troops along Russia's Bessarabian frontier. Metternich thought the crisis so grave in August he abandoned plans to visit Johannisberg – a hard decision, for Dorothea Lieven was on holiday at Wiesbaden, twenty miles away – and contented himself with a few days' rest in Baden, where memories of Marie bore heavily upon him. His messages to St Petersburg were, however, not unfruitful; for in August Alexander explained to Capodistrias he could not go to war with Turkey since action of this kind was what 'the Paris directing committee' most desired.[7]

By September Metternich thought it safe to assume the seasons were too advanced for a military campaign in the Balkans that year; but his relief was tempered with anxiety for the following spring. If war were to be averted, he needed a more positive policy than the medley of warnings and appeals upon which he had relied throughout the summer, and he turned again to the statesman who over eight years had shown the warmest personal regard for him, Castlereagh. The tension of the summer months proved there was little difference in diplomatic strategy between the attitudes of Austria and Britain to the Greek revolt. Castlereagh was prepared to offer greater sympathy to the Greeks than his Austrian colleague but he had consistently urged restraint, both in St Petersburg and Constantinople. He had even written personally to the Tsar, stressing the need to maintain 'the European system' against 'that organized spirit of insurrection which is systematically propagating itself throughout Europe'. Yet although Castlereagh made it clear he would preach Allied solidarity to ensure inaction, Metternich very rightly doubted if he was prepared to accept the ideological doctrines of Troppau and Laibach. Clearly if there were to be genuine Anglo-Austrian collaboration, the time was ripe for Metternich to meet Castlereagh once more. As he wrote to Lebzeltern: 'It is . . . necessary for me to know a little about the English; their role is extremely influential in the European-Russo-Turko-Greek affair.'[8]

Metternich meets George IV and Castlereagh in Hanover (October 1821)

The opportunity for such a meeting came in the late autumn when George IV undertook a state visit to his Hanoverian kingdom, with the British Foreign Secretary in attendance. Tentative arrangements were made for the King and Castlereagh to extend their German journey and to spend a few days in Vienna, but George was at the time suffering from gout and Lady Conyngham, and he, felt too fatigued to travel farther than Hanover. It was accordingly proposed that Metternich should come up from Vienna and join them; and he duly set out on the afternoon of Sunday, 13 October, reaching Hanover on the following Sunday morning. To his surprise and pleasure he was joined later in the day by Dorothea Lieven, to whom King George had sent a special invitation. Her husband had been recalled to St Petersburg for consultation and was unable to reach Hanover until 28 October, a few hours before the King, Castlereagh and Metternich began their homeward journeys.[9] Nobody seems to have missed the Count particularly, although Dorothea took care in her private letters to explain he had been delayed by circumstances beyond anyone's control.

George IV was in one of his most petulant and perverse moods in Hanover. He was pleased at the loyalty shown by his German subjects but bored by their solemn and conventional way of life. Metternich received a warm welcome. King George lavished praise on him, informing all who cared to listen that the Austrian Chancellor was the peer of Minos, Themistocles, Cato, Caesar, Gustavus Adolphus, Marlborough, Pitt and Wellington. 'I do not remember ever having been embraced with such tenderness and I have never in all my life heard so many pretty things said about me,' reported Metternich, adding that the King rolled off the great names of history 'as if he were saying a litany of saints'. For once the flattery was almost too much even for Metternich, who was mildly embarrassed by the King's sustained verbal attacks on Lord Liverpool and all his ministers except the Marquis of Londonderry (as Castlereagh had now become).* It should be added that Metternich's contempt for the 'appalling outburst' did not prevent him from intriguing with Dorothea Lieven to see if it were possible to secure Castlereagh's succession to the English premiership.

The King was so incensed at the alleged slights inflicted on him by the Liverpool Government that he said little to Metternich about the affairs of Europe, but the Chancellor and Castlereagh were able to have

---

* Viscount Castlereagh succeeded his father as second Marquis of Londonderry on 8 April 1821. Since the new title was still in the peerage of Ireland and not of the United Kingdom, he did not have to give up his seat in Parliament and he remained Leader of the House of Commons until his death. Throughout this chapter reference will be made to him as 'Castlereagh' rather than as 'Londonderry'.

some profitable conversations. The parliamentary Opposition at West-minster had, for more than five years, used Austria's failure to repay the loans of 1795 and 1797 as a stick with which to beat an unpopular Foreign Minister.[10] The debt, with interest, now stood at nearly £20 million and neither the British nor the Austrian governments expected such a large amount to be discharged in its entirety. Metternich realized that, if there was to be closer diplomatic collaboration between London and Vienna, he must provide Castlereagh with a promise of token settlement, if nothing more; but he was hampered by a threat from Stadion that he would resign as Minister of Finance rather than accept inroads on his small reserve of florins. While Castlereagh indicated that he was willing to reduce the British claim to £4 million, Metternich dared not accept a compromise without reference back to Vienna, and the most he could offer Castlereagh was an assurance, which he could pass on to his parliamentary critics, that 'a negotiation was still in progress' and that there were grounds for hope. Both men regarded the long dispute over the loan as a particularly tiresome distraction which they would have preferred to ignore.

Fortunately they found it easier to make progress over the principal topic of discussion, the Eastern Question. They agreed on the need to distinguish between rights which Russia might legitimately claim from Turkey as based on earlier treaties and demands put forward by the Greek rebels and their sympathizers. The Russians were entitled to seek the restoration of Greek churches and guarantees of the liberties of the Orthodox Church; they might also seek the establishment of a reformed administration in the Danubian principalities of Moldavia and Wallachia, for the Turks had conceded the right of the Russians to protect the Sultan's Christian subjects living in these sensitive provinces along the Russian frontier; but there could be no recognition of the political existence of a Greek nation and certainly no encouragement for Capodistrias' schemes of an autonomous Greek state. Britain and Austria would continue to urge the Tsar not to go to war, although placing emphasis on different points so as to avoid any appearance of a hostile combination against Russia. At the same time their repre-sentatives in Constantinople would warn the Sultan against excessive brutality and advise the Turkish government to fulfil its treaty obliga-tions. This programme of action was neither inspiring nor noble in intention, but it showed the working of Metternich's mind at its best, clarifying the essentials of an intricate problem and suggesting practic-able measures to forestall a crisis. He was always more impressive in handling the details of diplomatic negotiation than in enunciating the abstract pseudo-philosophy of which he was so proud.

The Fall of Capodistrias

Everyone left Hanover well content: George IV, elated by such rare proximity to high politics, let it be known he intended to join his brother sovereigns at the projected congress in Florence the following autumn; Castlereagh thought he had won the Chancellor back to the British doctrine of non-intervention and away from the menacing tone of the Troppau Protocol; and Metternich, for his part, believed he had reached full accord with the only British statesman for whom he held high regard. The Hanover meeting, he declared, had given him 'the advantage of being able to prove to Russia how far one can go with England when one understands her language'.[11] Yet Metternich began to wonder if it would even be necessary to put joint pressure on the Russians. Before setting out for home the two ministers spoke briefly to Count Lieven, who had come straight from the Tsar and who assured them that Alexander intended to maintain the peace of Europe. The Chancellor gained the impression that in Russia 'there are now two parties', the Metternichers and the Capodistrians, appellations which he considered 'not exactly flattering'. 'These two Parties,' he explained in a letter, 'are as opposed to each other as the Right and the Left in France. Since Tsar Alexander is a Metternicher, that party is on top; as to the other, one can leave it to its fate.' Small wonder that when he returned to Vienna Metternich sent instructions to Lebzeltern that he should avoid Capodistrias as much as possible and deal only with Nesselrode.[12]

Metternich travelled back from Hanover in better spirits than for many years, a change of mood for which Dorothea Lieven was, no doubt, in part responsible. Even the German students now seemed infantile rather than menacing and he was amused at the respect shown to him by the 'Jacobins' of Frankfurt. Everything was so peaceful that he stopped for three or four days in Johannisberg before setting out on the familiar drive across Bavaria and down the Danube. He had some difficult exchanges with Stadion over repayment of the loan from Britain but he extricated himself by the simple expedient of doing nothing. Although there was disturbing news from Piedmont and from Lombardy (where the Carbonarist agitation had won over a number of distinguished Italian families), Metternich retained high optimism for the closing weeks of the old year.[13] He was convinced the European order had survived a concerted challenge of revolution and the experience had strengthened rather than weakened the Alliance.

In these assumptions he was deluding himself. British objectives in the Eastern Crisis were far more limited than he appreciated. One of Castlereagh's main concerns was the possibility that a Russo-Turkish war might lead to increased Russian naval activity in the Mediterranean, a menace which the Admiralty had taken seriously since 1805 when Admiral Senyavin's squadron operated in the southern Adriatic; and Metternich was always confused over the influence of naval strategy on British official thinking. Moreover, while Castlereagh agreed with Metternich that the Alliance should 'exist in full force' as far as the Eastern Question was concerned, nothing was said at Hanover about Spain or Italy, the areas where the attitude of the Alliance powers had most disturbed British sensitivities in the previous winter. The weakness of the Anglo-Austrian entente did not become apparent for several months, but Metternich's complacent over-simplification of Russian politics was to confound him even before Christmas. For, not for the first time, he had too easily dismissed the influence of the 'Capodistrians' and the resilience of their leader. There was no guarantee Alexander would remain attached to any one faction in the Russian capital, as Metternich knew full well; and by the end of the year the Tsar had ceased to be a 'Metternicher' – if, indeed, he had ever been one at all.

Yet it was hard to know precisely what Alexander wanted. Although both Castlereagh and Metternich sent reasoned appeals to St Petersburg, the Tsar maintained an ominous silence. Capodistrias, on the other hand, sent a series of aggressive notes to Vienna over the Christmas period and well into the New Year; and, with the Turks obstinately refusing all concessions, Metternich began once more to fear the imminence of war. Then, suddenly, on 19 February the Tsar came down on the side of the angels: he informed Lebzeltern he was weary of the exchange of notes between Vienna and St Petersburg and he proposed to send Dmitri Tatischev, who had been Russian ambassador at Madrid, to the Austrian capital for direct talks with Metternich. Tatischev arrived in Vienna on 6 March and, after their first conversation, Metternich was convinced Capodistrias had at last been finally exposed and defeated. This time he was right.[14]

The Russians could hardly have chosen a worse spokesman. Tatischev was conceited and ambitious. He thought himself so versatile that he would make rings around Metternich and he did not bother to hide his jealous contempt of Capodistrias and all he stood for. The background to the mission was characteristically Russian. Tatischev had been given a dual set of instructions: according to Capodistrias, he was to claim a Russian protectorate over all the Sultan's Christian subjects and the right to negotiate for Greek autonomy within the Ottoman Empire; but he was also told by the Tsar that he was not, under any circumstances, to risk a breach in the unity of the Allies. There followed six weeks of almost farcical negotiations in which Metternich, with little difficulty, convinced the Russian that his instructions from Capodistrias were inappropriate and that the Tsar's wishes could only be fulfilled by permitting the Austrian Chancellor to speak for the Alliance and deal directly with the Turks. It was one of Metternich's easier victories.

By the beginning of April Metternich had obtained almost all he wanted.[15] He was drafting Tatischev's despatches for Capodistrias and for the Tsar, while the Russian was congratulating himself on the extent to which he had been lionized by Viennese society. On 19 April the Tsar was informed, in a letter ostensibly from the Emperor Francis, that if Turkey refused to accept Russian demands based on existing treaties, Austria would break off diplomatic relations with the Sultan as a sign of solidarity, provided the other Allied powers would follow suit. This was a safe assurance for Austria to give, since Metternich knew well enough Castlereagh would never be allowed by the force of parliamentary opinion in London to participate in such a 'pro-Russian' step. But the Tsar was impressed by Francis's gesture of support: he agreed that the Allies should co-ordinate their policies over the Eastern Question by means of a series of ministerial conferences to be held in Vienna during June and July pending the meeting of the proposed congress in the autumn. Soon more gratifying news arrived from St Petersburg. On 25 June Capodistrias was granted indefinite leave of absence and departed for Switzerland: it was the end of his services to Russia, if not to Greece. 'The reign of Capodistrias is over,' Metternich wrote exactly a month after the Russian minister's fall. 'It is a long time since I first gave battle to him but I have always stuck to my guns and pressed forward. Capodistrias is a clumsy general but a crafty one.'[16]

Intervention in Spain?

Metternich's satisfaction at the fall of his old rival was, however, muted. He had not as yet extricated himself from what he assumed to be the final snare laid by the Corfiote. For almost two years the Alliance had turned a blind eye to events in Spain: now they suddenly became so pressing that they could no longer be ignored. At the end of April 1822 the Russians proposed that, in accordance with the Troppau Protocol, the Allied powers should intervene in Spain in order to free King Ferdinand from the restraints imposed upon him by the liberal revolutionaries. The Tsar drew the attention of his brother sovereigns to an appeal sent by Ferdinand to his uncle, the King of Naples, in February; and Alexander proposed 'formation of a European Army to which each of the Allies would furnish a contingent, and whose aim should be to crush out the centre of revolutions in Spain or anywhere else where it could go'. The Russians, he added, could provide an expeditionary force immediately: 'The deplorable events in the East would be no obstacle since Russia had sufficient troops to make her rights respected there and at the same time to fulfil her duties towards the Alliance.'[17]

This proposal was 'utter nonsense', Metternich wrote privately to Lebzeltern as soon as he heard of it.[18] At first he believed the Tsar's unexpected solicitude for the Spanish Bourbons had been prompted by Capodistrias in the hope it would induce the other powers to give Russia a free hand in the East rather than have 'the Cossack hordes' thrusting deeper into Western Europe. This assessment of Russian policy was, perhaps, unduly subtle; it is more likely that the initiative came from Nesselrode and the Tsar himself (as the British believed at the time) and that it was intended to cover a diplomatic retreat over the Eastern Question by reverting to the sacred principles of the Holy Alliance and the interventionist doctrines of Troppau. The thought of renewed diplomatic wrangling over Spain made Metternich profoundly uneasy: he had already received a note from Castlereagh warning him the British could never agree to withdrawal of their ambassador from Constantinople; and, although he had expected this response, he feared that by resurrecting the Spanish Question at a time of such uncertainty in the East the Tsar would stampede Castlereagh into opposition to the Alliance and undo the good work of the Hanover meeting. If he was to keep the general policy of Europe under his control he needed the support of Britain more than ever at the forthcoming congress in order to check Russian predominance. As so often before and after, he played for time. Officially he informed the Russians nothing could be done about the Tsar's proposal until the matter had been discussed with the British and French, and he suggested that there was a risk of exposing the King of Spain to fresh dangers by precipitate action. Reports of turmoil in Madrid during June and July added weight to his remarks; but, at the same time, made a solution of the Spanish problem more urgent.

Metternich placed all his hopes on Castlereagh personally, knowing he was the only member of the British government with a sense of European unity. It seemed to him essential for Castlereagh himself to attend the congress, which was now to meet in Verona rather than in Florence so as to keep it more directly under Austrian management. But in a letter of 6 June Metternich suggested King George and Castlereagh should come direct to Vienna, where the major problems of Europe would be discussed: the Italian Question could be reserved for the Verona meeting, to which the British government need not send a representative if it wished to dissociate itself from these matters. He begged Castlereagh to make the journey, at least to Vienna, so as to complete the rout of the Tsar: 'What force Russian policy has lost in the East, it will attempt to regain by greater activity in the West,' Metternich said. 'If you fail me, I shall be alone and the battle will become uneven. God has blessed me with sufficient courage not to decline the contest; but I do not find the issues to be well balanced if I alone must sustain what should be contested by the two cabinets who understand each other best, given the uniformity of their political views.'[19]

It was difficult for Castlereagh to decline so pressing an invitation, but the political life of London was extremely complicated that summer and he could not send an immediate acceptance back to Metternich. The government had no wish for the King to associate himself with the European autocrats and, after the customary display of pique and bad manners, he was induced to undertake a state visit to Edinburgh rather than go to Vienna. Castlereagh himself was weary from a long parliamentary session and would have preferred to rest at his house in Kent, leaving British representation to his half-brother, Stewart, or to Wellington. He cautiously sought to discover what were Metternich's real attitudes towards Spain and Turkey. The Chancellor's reply was long-winded, high-sounding and uninformative; for he was so uncertain of the nature of Russian policy without Capodistrias that he could not commit himself. Clearly it was essential the British representative should be a man of prestige and experience at such a moment of transition: congress diplomacy, lacking any institutional basis, depended to an excessive degree on personalities and the relationship between one individual and another. On 29 July Castlereagh at last let Metternich know that, 'should no unforeseen events arise', he would set out from London on 15 August and, after spending a few days sounding out the French government in Paris, would continue to Vienna, where he planned to arrive at the end of the first week in September. He would thus have plenty of time to settle 'numerous and very important' subjects with Metternich before the coming of the Russians and Prussians.[20]

It was not to be. On 9 August Wellington and George IV had conversations with Castlereagh and, independently of each other, realized he was suffering from a mental breakdown: on 12 August he cut his throat with a penknife. Eight days later the 'terrible news' of Castlereagh's suicide reached Metternich. He genuinely grieved for the death of a friend and yet, characteristically, he was also concerned with the significance of the event for his own position and policy. 'It is a great misfortune,' he declared. 'The man is irreplaceable, especially for me ... Castlereagh was the only person in his country who had experience in foreign affairs. He had learned to understand me. Now it will be several years before someone else can give me the same degree of confidence.' On 25 August Metternich urgently requested that Wellington should be sent as Britain's representative, since he alone among his countrymen approached Castlereagh in world stature. But, although the despatch of Wellington had already been discussed in London, it was not possible to settle such matters speedily; and their solution was made no easier by the fact that the Duke was forced to take to his bed with a high fever.[21]

There was an interlude of over a month between the death of Castlereagh and the appointment of George Canning as his successor. Dorothea Lieven's letters supplied Metternich with a vivid commentary on the political game in London, where Lord Liverpool had considerable difficulty in overcoming George IV's prejudice against accepting Canning as a Secretary of State. Unfortunately Dorothea Lieven and the Austrian ambassador, Paul Esterhazy, also disliked and distrusted Canning and took every opportunity to warn Metternich of his 'ambition and lack of principles'.[22] But at first Canning's appointment seemed to make little difference. Within forty-eight hours of his arrival at the Foreign Office, one at least of Metternich's wishes was granted: on 17 September Wellington set out for Paris and Vienna as Britain's spokesman. He arrived in the Austrian capital twelve days later.[23] Yet, though Wellington bore with him the instructions Castlereagh had drafted for his own use, he was no substitute for an experienced Foreign Secretary. Poor Castlereagh had intended to amplify his instructions after preliminary talks revealed Metternich's line of conduct; but the Duke possessed no such freedom of manoeuvre, nor did he have the gift of reading diplomatic riddles and posing ones of his own. He might watch, he might warn, he might advise; but, though he did not always approve of the government's attitude, he could never initiate policy. That prerogative was now in the hands of Canning – a man who, at the end of August, had declared it was England's duty to be 'a spectatress' rather than a participant in the struggles on the continent.[24]

Metternich did not wait for Wellington's arrival before modifying his own policy. All his fine talk of opposing the Russians, if necessary alone, perished with Castlereagh. When Tsar Alexander and his horde of ministers and advisers descended on Vienna in mid-September, they found the Chancellor conciliatory and unexpectedly amenable.[25] For once he positively welcomed Nesselrode's ideas on how the forthcoming congress should be run. There was no difficulty in determining the agenda. Technically the Italian problem had still to head the list, for it was agreed at Laibach that a conference would be summoned in 1822 specifically to review the political affairs of the peninsula. But, by the late autumn, the Spanish Question had become so immediately menacing that it warranted high priority in discussion. Spain was gripped by a civil war, with an insurgent 'Regency' established in Catalonia and calling for the liberation of the 'captive King' by foreign intervention. But who would 'rescue' Ferdinand from the constitution he had been induced to grant? In the spring Metternich had discouraged the Tsar from sending an army across Europe because of the effect it would have on the British and the French. Now it seemed likely that the French would themselves cross the Pyrenees and re-tread the route to Madrid. The prospect of independent action by France in

Spain inevitably drew the Austrians and Russians together once more, not necessarily to oppose the march of French troops but to ensure that what was done should be in the name of the European Alliance rather than for the greater glory of the House of Bourbon.

If, however, there was to be Austro-Russian collaboration over Spain the two Empires could not risk friction by discussing the future of Greece. For the first quarter of the year the Eastern Question had dominated international affairs and even as late as July Castlereagh considered it to be the outstanding problem of the moment; now it was virtually ignored. Before leaving Vienna Nesselrode proposed the Turks should either negotiate with the Great Powers a guarantee of toleration for their Greek subjects or 'by a series of actions' show they intended to respect the Orthodox faith. But no other gesture was made over Greek affairs either at Vienna or during the subsequent congress. The question was relegated to the position which Spain had occupied during the conference at Laibach. 'At Verona,' Gentz later explained with disingenuous suavity, 'it was a matter of courtesy not to mention difficulties in Turkey.'[26]

Not all of Metternich's attention was given to such fine points of diplomacy. While the statesmen were discussing what not to discuss, Metternich was engaged in the final stage of a business transaction of significance to himself personally and to the Austrian state. Since his first meeting with the brothers Rothschild in Aix in 1819, the fortunes of the Jewish banking-house had prospered. Solomon von Rothschild settled in Vienna in 1820, while his brother James established himself in Paris. A second brother, Karl, followed the Austrian Army to Naples and a third brother, Nathan, moved to London. Only the eldest Rothschild of his generation, Amschel, remained in Frankfurt, where he had been a generous host to Metternich as he was travelling home from the Hanover meeting.[27]

The Rothschild brothers were accorded consular rank by the Austrian Emperor and they placed at Metternich's disposal the extremely speedy courier service on which they relied for information. They assisted Stadion with a loan to the Austrian Exchequer in 1820 and financed military operations in southern Italy in 1821; and they also made themselves popular in Viennese society by guaranteeing the solvency of the Court Theatre at the Kärntnertor. By the autumn of 1822 Solomon Rothschild had thus built up for himself a position of considerable influence within Austria, and indeed with the whole German Confederation. He exchanged frequent visits with Gentz – on whom he bestowed gifts with liberality – and he had easy access to Metternich. It only remained to place the relationship between Chancellor and banker on a proper commercial basis. On 23 September 1822, Metternich obtained a personal loan of 900,000 *gulden* from Solomon Roths-

H

child, repayable over twelve years at five per cent interest. Six days later an Imperial decree raised all five Rothschild brothers to the Austrian nobility, with the rank of Barons. Subsequently Solomon von Rothschild accepted responsibility for Metternich's personal expenditure throughout the Verona Congress; and a six-million-pound loan to Russia, negotiated while the Tsar was in Verona, won for Solomon and for James the coveted ribbon of the Order of Vladimir, tactfully decanonized for the occasion. Rarely has the diplomatic world rotated with so many deserving good turns.

The Congress of Verona (1822)

Metternich, comfortably freed from immediate monetary embarrassment, made a leisurely journey from Vienna to Verona.[28] He travelled to the Tyrol for a few days of relaxation, although since his companions included Lebzeltern, Nesselrode and Pozzo di Borgo, it was not intended that he should pass the time in happy idleness. At Innsbruck he was joined by his son Victor (who was to serve as an attaché at Verona) and by the Lievens. The whole party arrived at Verona on 12 October, eight days before the opening of the Congress, in a mood of holiday gaiety which promised well for their deliberations.

Outwardly Verona was a more impressive gathering than any conference since 1815.[29] Emperor Francis, Tsar Alexander and King Frederick William III were once more present and so, too, were all the rulers of Italy, except the Pope. The French delegation was headed by the Vicomte de Montmorency, the Foreign Minister, and by Chateaubriand (who did not reach Italy until the second week of the Congress). The great writer was at the time ambassador in London; and if, in Verona, he showed a tiresomely apt propensity for Shakespearean allusion, who can blame him? As a social occasion the Congress was a great success. Some twenty ambassadors were present, one cardinal, fifteen ministers and two Barons von Rothschild. A magnificent banquet was held in the Roman amphitheatre; Rossini conducted performances of his own operas, with Angelica Catalini as the leading soprano; the Duchess of Parma, once Empress of the French, defeated the victor of Salamanca and Waterloo at the card-table; and the Tsar amused himself with the new Marchioness of Londonderry, over-plump wife to Castlereagh's over-ambitious half-brother. Night after night Dorothea Lieven entertained on a generous scale so that, though the Russians tended to snub her, Metternich could inform his wife by letter that 'the Lievens' salon resembles ours at Vienna'.[30] There was at times an odd nostalgia for past splendours.

Yet somehow all this brilliance failed to win the sympathy of Europe. The Philhellenes in particular were aggrieved. A deputation of Greek patriots, pledged to inform the statesmen that their nation would never be reconciled to a settlement in which they had no part, was intercepted by the Austrian authorities and turned back at Ancona.[31] Byron voiced their anger and disillusionment in the bitter satire of *The Age of Bronze*:

> Strange sight this Congress! destined to unite
> All that's incongruous, all that's opposite.
> I speak not of the sovereigns – they're alike,
> As common coin as ever mint could strike;
> But those who sway the puppets, pull the strings,
> Have more of motley than their heavy kings.
> Jews, authors, generals, charlatans, combine,
> While Europe wonders at the vast design;
> There Metternich, power's foremost parasite,
> Cajoles; there Wellington forgets to fight;
> There Chateaubriand forms new books of martyrs;
> And subtle Gauls intrigue for stupid Tartars.[32]

It was a damning indictment of congress diplomacy, but not without justification. Wellington had advised Canning while still in Vienna that the conference would 'turn almost entirely upon the affairs of Spain', and he was right. Very little was said of Italy, the original reason for bringing the sovereigns together; it was merely agreed that, with the improvement in political conditions, the Austrian occupation forces could be gradually withdrawn from Piedmont and reduced in size in Naples. Otherwise, from the first full session of the Congress until the drafting of the final protocol, the Spanish Question dominated every discussion.

Metternich played a smaller rôle at Verona than Byron's satire assigned to him. Before the Congress formally opened he sent a confidential note to the Russians and Prussians proposing that the three autocracies should concert moral action against the Spanish liberals in order to prevent the French from embarking on a military expedition across the Pyrenees. But there was little response and the initiative passed inevitably to the French delegates. The key speech at the Congress was delivered by Montmorency who wished to know what material support the French might expect from the Allies if it became necessary for them to enter Spain. Tsar Alexander, anxious to counter any French moves, at once offered to send 150,000 men to assist in the operation. Metternich was aghast, fearing they would have to travel either across Germany or through Italy for embarkation in Naples. The French firmly rejected the Tsar's offer, but even this development did not entirely please the Austrian Chancellor for he had become convinced Montmorency – and to a far greater extent Chateaubriand – was using the language of the Alliance to hide a desire for French freedom of action. Metternich's chief concern, however, was with the reaction of the British. Canning disliked congress diplomacy and it was not until the fourth week in September that he sent Wellington authority to proceed from Vienna to Verona as British plenipotentiary. On 30 October the Duke made it plain that Canning would stand resolutely by the doctrine of non-intervention in Spain: he asserted that 'such an interference appeared to be an unnecessary assumption of responsibility'.[33] Throughout November Metternich tried to lessen the gap between Britain and his three other allies. He suggested that the four powers should let the French know they had their moral support in seeking to free King Ferdinand from the political restraints imposed upon him; but Wellington would not associate himself with a joint declaration or with separate notes which seemed to condone intervention. Eventually on 19 November the delegates of Austria, Russia, Prussia and France signed a protocol offering the French assistance against the Spanish liberals provided the government in Paris could prove the situation in Spain had deteriorated to a point where military action was justified. On the following day Wellington insisted on a formal record of Britain's disapproval of any such step.[34]

Wellington himself left Verona on 30 November, for the Congress was virtually over. He was soon followed by the principal French delegates. Metternich watched their departure with disquiet: he had come to regard Chateaubriand as a dangerously individualistic nationalist, and it was with marked displeasure that he learned early in the New Year of Chateaubriand's appointment as Foreign Minister in succession to Montmorency.[35] Although the French claimed they wished to do in Spain after Verona what Austria had done in Naples after Troppau and Laibach, Metternich distrusted their intentions. A march on Madrid seemed to him to reverse the verdict of 1814, a view not unnaturally shared by Wellington. At heart the Austrian Chancellor would have preferred to ignore the troubles of the Iberian peninsula entirely; but had he done so, he might well have been faced by a Franco-Russian combination and this was a danger which, with Britain's policy so anti-European, he could not afford.

Metternich and the Russians lingered on in Verona until 18 December. They then spent nine days in Venice, where the Tsar was given a colourful and impressive reception. After Christmas Metternich escorted the Tsar to Innsbruck and the frontier, solicitous to the end for his comfort and entertainment. Now it was Russia's friendship on which he counted.[36] For, although he hoped the breach with Britain would be no more lasting than after Troppau, he had few illusions over Canning's pride in insularity. Metternich would never abandon his almost mystic faith in the virtues of 'the Alliance' and in the value of diplomacy by congress; but he was realist enough to appreciate that, for the immediate future, the three autocracies of Russia, Prussia and Austria shared a concern over the principles of conservative order for which they could expect little backing either from a parliamentary Britain or from an opportunist France. Who had ensnared whom in the spider's web?

THE SHADOW OF ECLIPSE

The limits of Austro-Russian collaboration

Metternich returned to Vienna at the end of the first week in January 1823, having spent a few days in Munich after the Tsar's departure. He remained in the capital until the middle of September, when he accompanied Francis eastwards for another meeting with Alexander. That spring he celebrated his fiftieth birthday and, although he had regained some of the zest for living lost in the tragic summer of 1820, the strain of office was beginning to bear heavily upon him. A few years earlier he used to enjoy the incessant journeys across the continent: the racing wheels of coaches thundering past groups of peasants gaping by the roadside; small town burgomasters attendant as on royalty; leisure hours in which to collect bric-à-brac, or climb a mountain, or wander through ruins; and the changes in landscape which, now and again, so touched his eye that he would ask an artist in his retinue to capture on canvas its contours and pigmentation for later delight. But after the Verona Congress he travelled much less, partly because of the endless paper work retaining him in the Chancellery, but also because his health suffered from night halts in draughty rooms and the constant buffeting of carriage springs along the roads. He was seriously ill during his journey east that autumn and he tended thereafter to find excuses for postponing trips which he would have willingly undertaken in other times. Yet, despite his illness, his private life was happier: Eleonore and his family returned to Vienna from Paris in May and stayed in Austria for most of the remaining months of the year; and he shone once more in Viennese society, where hostesses continued to vie with each other as patrons of private musical entertainments.

Politically, however, he found the year 1823 vexatious. A French army crossed the Pyrenees in the spring and marched south to Madrid with scant regard for Austrian advice or the 'moral solidarity' of the Alliance. Across the Channel Canning flourished jauntily in diplomatic isolation, undisturbed by Metternich's attempts to intrigue with his sovereign and to alert Wellington to his colleague's folly.[1] In Rome

Pope Pius VII died and, at the subsequent conclave, Cardinal della Genga (Leo XII) was elected against the wishes of Metternich, who thought him too sympathetic towards the French Bourbons.[2] Sad cavalcades of shackled prisoners were conveyed from Venice to the grim Moravian fortress of the Spielberg, on the hills west of Austerlitz – an eloquent commentary on the Austrian failure to re-kindle that 'Lombard spirit' of which the Chancellor had once written at such length.[3] There was trouble, too, in Germany where the governments of Bavaria and Württemberg persisted in showing a distressing independence of mind in foreign affairs. A formal complaint was received from Stuttgart that, in excluding the smaller states from the Congress of Verona, the three Allied autocracies had usurped 'the heritage of influence in Europe arrogated to himself by Napoleon'. Metternich so resented this accusation that for several months he broke off all official contact between the Austrian and Württemberger courts; and the Mainz Commission was induced to suppress that eminently respectable gazette, the *Stuttgart Beobachter*, for daring to publish an article critical of the Verona deliberations.[4]

During these disturbing months Metternich frequently made an outward show of contentment with Austro-Russian relations. Here, at least, was true friendship. The Eastern Question remained dormant and Strangford, the British ambassador in Constantinople, was skilfully wearing down Turkish opposition to diplomatic negotiations with the Russians. Although there was always a danger some foray in Greece would make the question active once more, for the moment it was still an issue over which Russia and Austria could collaborate and even, through Strangford, maintain some contact with the Foreign Office in London. But Metternich was realist enough to be apprehensive over Russia's future policy. In a letter which he wrote to Eleonore shortly before her return to Vienna, he showed that exasperating complacency which was with him always a sign that he needed re-assurance: 'That I should have succeeded in creating such harmonious understanding between Tsar Alexander and ourselves verges on the miraculous,' he wrote, but he added 'When you consider from what opposite points the two empires set out in order to reach such harmony, it seems like a dream.'[5]

With Nesselrode in charge of foreign affairs at St Petersburg and Capodistrias in Switzerland, the dream appeared at least to possess substance. But did it? Metternich knew Nesselrode too well to be sure of his constancy. In May the Chancellor complained to Lebzeltern that Nesselrode's character was so weak he let 'himself be led by a predilection for individuals without scrutiny as to what they offer of real value'.[6] It was a just criticism, although it could be argued this very defect enabled Metternich to gain mastery over Nesselrode's policy whenever they met. The danger which Metternich feared that spring was represented by the activities of 'the infernal intriguer' General Pozzo di Borgo, who was still Russian ambassador in Paris. Should the Tsar and Nesselrode follow Pozzo's advice, then it seemed to Metternich his efforts to oust Capodistrias would have been in vain. Throughout the summer and autumn of 1823 – and, indeed, for long after – Metternich and Lebzeltern did all they could to discredit Pozzo at St Petersburg.[7] Tactically this was a grave error on Metternich's part. Alexander was astute enough to realize the Austrians were seeking, for a second time, to poison his mind against a chosen adviser; and all his old suspicions of Metternich began once more to come to the surface. For the moment, however, it seemed to matter little. In September the French ambassador in St Petersburg told Chateaubriand that Austria was still 'the strongest crutch' on which the Tsar and Nesselrode could rest.[8] Metternich himself looked forward with some confidence to the meeting between Francis and Alexander, which had been arranged for the late autumn. There was, he knew, a risk the Russians would re-open the Eastern Question, but he believed he could once more charm Alexander into agreeable passivity.

The meeting was to be held at Czernowitz (Chernovtsy), the most eastern town in the Habsburg Empire, on the banks of the upper Pruth, barely ten miles from the Russian frontier.[9] In the last week of September Metternich accordingly travelled eastwards, past Teschen and through the unfamiliar poverty of eastern Galicia, depressed by all he saw. On 27 September he reached Przemysl and immediately developed a high temperature. Next day he struggled on to Lemberg (Lvov), still 170 miles north-west of his destination. He was able to go no farther; and for nearly a month he remained at Lemberg, racked by what appears to have been rheumatic fever. At first the Emperor Francis hovered round his bedside, seeking to distract him with gossip. The Chancellor was forced to choose a junior diplomat from his retinue, Count Andreas von Mercy, as his personal spokesman at Czernowitz. Later he described to Eleonore what happened: 'When it was settled that I could not accompany His Majesty ... and I had chosen Mercy as my deputy, I sent him to inform the Emperor. With his customary good humour the Emperor then said to Mercy, "Well, that will be a splendid piece of business! I only know these affairs superficially; you have only known them since yesterday. Between us we shall indeed cut a fine figure. If it will not work out, I will fetch Tsar Alexander to see Metternich; and he will get farther ahead with him in half-an-hour than the two of us would in a week".'[10] There was laughter all round; Francis had, at times, a typically Austrian reaction to any crisis.

The conference did not, in fact, 'work out' well. Alexander avoided

the indignity of a pilgrimage to Metternich's sickbed, although Nesselrode travelled up from Czernowitz and the two ministers held desultory
discussions. Probably no more would have been achieved, even if
Metternich's health had not given way. By now Canning had recognized
the Greek insurgents as belligerents and it was no longer possible to
go on treating the revolt as an isolated episode. The European Great
Powers would have to intervene, by diplomatic pressure or as a last
resort by armed mediation. The Austrians insisted that the Turks
were gradually making the concessions which Russia demanded as
guarantees for the Orthodox Church and the future of the Danubian
principalities; but Alexander was becoming impatient. At Czernowitz
he suggested a congress might be held in St Petersburg to settle the
Eastern Question, although as yet he did not formally propose summoning such a gathering. This was, for Metternich, an awkward development. So long as congresses met within the Habsburg orbit, no one
championed diplomacy by conference more warmly than the Austrian
Chancellor. But a congress in the Russian capital was a different
matter. Who would hold the reins? The Tsar? Nesselrode? Perhaps
even the one man who seemed to have a clear sense of direction,
Pozzo di Borgo? Metternich would not openly oppose a congress, but
he urged on Lebzeltern a policy of masterly procrastination. It was a
miserably negative expedient for a minister who claimed to be leading
Europe.

Fortunately for Metternich the Tsar overplayed his hand at the
beginning of the following year (1824). He invited the Great Powers
to send representatives to a conference in St Petersburg which would
force the Turks to accept a settlement of the Eastern Question favourable to Russia. At the same time he proposed the creation of three
autonomous Greek principalities, guaranteed by the five Great Powers
of Europe, and enjoying a status similar to that of Moldavia, Wallachia
and Serbia. As Metternich immediately perceived, the one proposal
inevitably weakened the effectiveness of the other; for no government
in Europe, apart from the Russian, could tolerate such a re-arrangement
of the Balkan map and the conference was therefore condemned to
impotence before it had ever come together. Yet there was sufficient
matter here to keep any gathering of diplomats talking for many
months and it might always be possible to divert the Tsar into accepting
a less drastic solution. Metternich accordingly welcomed the proposed
ambassadorial conference and he did not reject the idea of a full
congress at a later date.[11] He was particularly interested in the attitude
of the British. If fear for England's trade in the Levant tempted Canning back into the European Concert, Austria could well find an ally:
but if Canning – 'that scourge of the world' – remained unshakeably
incorrigible, then it was far better for the Tsar to be held in partnership

with Austria than stampeded into precipitate action by outright opposition. The possibility of an Anglo-Russian accord which would leave Austria isolated seemed too remote to Metternich for consideration. He was, after all, still in regular correspondence with Dorothea Lieven, whose husband would have to handle such a negotiation; and it had been Dorothea who first revealed to him the full iniquities of Canning's statecraft.

Metternich was reasonably content with the diplomatic exchanges over Greece throughout 1824. Many of them were little more than elaborate exercises in shadow-boxing; and this was a game at which both he and Canning were adept. Alexander, for his part, blamed Canning for every delay, partly because the British hesitated for several months before indicating they would not participate in any congress at St Petersburg. Canning's final excuse for ordering the British ambassador not to attend the conferences was the hostility aroused among both Turks and Greeks when the Russian proposal of principalities was made public in a Paris newspaper at the end of May. The Russians were convinced Canning had himself leaked the information to the French press and they treated the British Foreign Secretary thereafter with frigid reserve. But Canning had no contacts among the French journalists, unlike Metternich who frequently boasted of his ability to have 'inspired' articles inserted in the newspapers of Paris (and, indeed, London). By the end of the year the Tsar had become so irritated at Canning's persistent refusal to enter a congress that he sent a curt message to London putting an end to 'all further deliberation between Russia and England on the relations with Turkey and on the pacification of Greece'.[12] Metternich was certain Canning's manoeuvres, aided by the indiscretions of the French press, had confirmed his own ascendancy over the Tsar's will to act. Many months were to pass before he realized that this assumption was unjustified and that Alexander had once more come to distrust the earnest exhortations of his Austrian mentor.

Problems within the Austrian Empire

Long before the end of 1824 Metternich was complaining of how 'that wretched Eastern Question' prevented him from concentrating his mind on more pressing problems.[13] There were, as ever, unresolved doubts over the future of Italy and the German Confederation. Nor was it clear how the national balance within the Empire itself might wisely be maintained. After three years as Chancellor, Metternich was finding it increasingly difficult to separate his responsibilities in foreign affairs from his obligation, as principal minister of the Habsburg Emperor, to bolster up a system of government in the realm he had chosen to serve. At heart he remained an expatriate Rhinelander, to whom much in the Empire was still essentially alien. Significantly it was from Johannisberg in the summer of 1824 that he wrote to the Duke of Wellington, 'Europe has for a long time held for me the essence of a fatherland'.[14] Yet sentiments which seemed convincing as he looked across the vineyards to the great river of his youth rang hollow in Vienna, where he had always found Asian influences brushing the city's eastern suburbs. Within the Chancellery it was wise not to over-tax the mind in a quest for political ingenuity and comforting to assume that what was good for Austria was good also for Europe: a multi-national Empire and a multi-national continent both needed to preserve diversity hallowed by tradition; and society in every land was bound together by a common desire for stability and discipline. The Habsburg presence discouraged broader loyalties or original thought in govern-ment.

Metternich did not himself introduce a repressive administration into Austria, and at times he chafed at its clumsy imperfections, but he accepted it as a convenient vehicle for his method of government and even extended his range of operations.[15] Within the Austrian Empire all responsibility for internal security rested with Count Josef von Sedlnitzky, who was Chief of Police from May 1817 to March 1848; and he it was who assigned imprisoned Italian patriots to the Spielberg. But it was Metternich's name which liberals everywhere linked with the system of police spies, censors and prosecutors, binding the Promethean spirit of Romanticism to a rock in Moravia; and ultimately they were right, for it was the Chancellor who gave to the system he had inherited its demoralizing aspect of permanence.

While the system was at its zenith, in the mid-1820's, foreign diplomats began to dub Metternich 'the Grand Inquisitor of Europe'. The nick-name was not unmerited. The Chancellor had at his disposal an external spy-service which fed him with reports from the major European capitals and from academic circles in Germany and Italy, supplement-ing the dossiers of Sedlnitzky's agents inside the Empire. From all this information Metternich could build up his case against individuals or against institutions, pursuing his search for the grand international conspiracy with the vigilance of the old Holy Office. Gentz thought this persistent heresy-hunting the Prince's most obsessive self-delusion, but Metternich refused to see any absurdity in it.[16] War against secret societies was to him essentially a continuation of diplomacy by other means, an extension of his responsibilities as Foreign Minister. He was so convinced of the menace of revolution to the social order that he was prepared to intervene personally in the harassment of the *Carbonari*. This he made clear in the famous meeting which he had with Count Federico Confalonieri in the cells of police headquarters at Vienna.[17]

Confalonieri, whom Metternich had known in Paris at the time of Marie Louise's marriage celebrations, was arrested in Milan as a liberal revolutionary in December 1821, after hints from Bubna and other prominent Austrian officials that good sense dictated for him a long visit to Switzerland. The Count was charged with treason and condemned to death but, after a slow process of appeal, the Emperor eventually commuted the sentence to imprisonment in the Spielberg. Metternich insisted the Count should be brought to Vienna on his way to Moravia; and on 2 March 1824 the Austrian Chancellor went down to the cells in order to plead with an Italian aristocrat, who had already spent twenty-seven months in close confinement, to give details of the 'European conspiracy' of which he was convinced that the Count had been a member. It is difficult to understand what Metternich hoped to discover after so long a lapse of time. He was certainly worried about Italian affairs, especially as the Emperor Francis was planning another visit to Milan, but it is probable he wished to see Confalonieri merely because he could not comprehend the mental processes of an arisocrat turned patriot. If this was the case then Metternich was disappointed. His own report of the strange encounter shows he fared worse than the unfortunate Count; for, as at his first meeting with Talleyrand eighteen years before, Metternich said too much and his companion revealed nothing. They parted, with an exchange of civil courtesies, after two hours of talk: the Chancellor went to a ball, the Count to a dungeon. Never again did Metternich step forward as interrogator; it had been easier to face Napoleon at Dresden.

He was content to remain a more distant figure over German affairs. In 1824 the Carlsbad Decrees, which had originally been introduced as five-year emergency legislation, were due to expire: but Metternich had no intention of giving the liberals the pleasure of seeing the Decrees fade into oblivion. That summer he supervised, from Johannisberg, arrangements for renewing the Decrees and for curbing even further the independence of the Diet in Frankfurt.[18] Member states of the Confederation were to ensure that the censorship of books and periodicals continued with unrelaxed vigilance. Powers of surveillance over universities were renewed and the Mainz Commission formally reconstituted as a permanent body. Conversely it was agreed by representatives of the German states that henceforth the proceedings of the Federal Diet should not be made public; newspapers might inform their readers of its rulings, but not of the discussions which preceded their enactment. He was well pleased with his work in Germany that year. As in 1818, he prided himself on coming as a political Messiah to the German princes. Old quarrels seemed forgotten. The Bavarians, alarmed by the discovery of a republican cell among students at Erlangen, were almost obsequious; and in Württemberg and

Prussia the last sympathizers with liberalism were removed from the administration. It is true some of the puny German duchies were already alarmed at the way in which Prussia was building up her economic strength by imposing tariff treaties on smaller neighbours; but as yet Metternich saw no evil in the spread of a *Zollverein*. Better Free Trade than free debate. He still thought exclusively in political terms; and, as Germany entered the second quarter of the nineteenth century, there seemed little to challenge Austrian predominance.

At times, indeed, Metternich claimed an even greater primacy. He had long become accustomed to offering the Russians the benefit of his experience in combating liberalism. Now he did not hesitate to tender unsolicited advice to other rulers as well as the Tsar. The death of Louis xviii enabled him to patronize Charles x, whom he was shrewd enough to perceive would never have kept the throne in the uncertain loyalties of the Restoration. He watched with interest the rivalry which developed in France between Villèle (who was Prime Minister from December 1821 to January 1828) and Chateaubriand, whom Villèle dismissed from the Foreign Ministry in June 1824; and he hoped the new King would bolster up a soundly conservative-minded ministry, undisturbed by such rebellious spirits as Chateaubriand.[19] Increasingly Metternich was coming to distrust the influence of intellectuals in politics: 'I wish for the good of humanity there could be learning but no learned men,' he once wrote to Dorothea Lieven.[20] His assumption that universities bred revolt led him to react with dismay to the news that, across the Channel, the Benthamites were planning to establish a college in London. 'It is my absolute conviction', he told Gentz, 'that England could not exist five years beside this University'; and he was so alarmed that in September 1825 he asked the Austrian ambassador, Esterhazy, to inform George iv that 'I am certain in my own mind I am right in saying that should the project be ever approved, it would be all up for England'.[21] Despite Metternich's entreaties a college was duly established in Gower Street in 1828. England survived.

The death of Eleonore Metternich; and strained relations with Russia (1825)

Yet he had little opportunity in 1825 to reflect on the Benthamites or the prospect of rebel students in London. For him it was a year of personal sorrow, frustration in foreign affairs, and political dangers nearer home which he could not always comprehend. Early in January he 'began to have serious fears' about his wife's health.[22] It was clear that, like her daughters five years previously, Eleonore was suffering from a tubercular infection. By the end of the month there was no doubt that she was dying and, as soon as his work permitted, the

Chancellor set out westwards for Paris to be with her. He was at her sickbed for several days before she died on 19 March.

Though there was always in their relationship a dignified reserve, he grieved sincerely for the woman who had partnered his fortunes and tolerated his weaknesses for thirty years. But in Paris it was impossible for him to confine himself to private mourning. The opportunity for political intrigue was too great. He dined with Charles x, with Villèle and with Louis Philippe, Duke of Orleans (for in French politics Metternich still had a shrewd eye to the future). He dined, too, with Talleyrand, met Pozzo di Borgo again and scored so easy a social triumph in the salons that malicious tongues commented on the speed with which he was reconciled to Eleonore's death and her thoughtfulness in parting from this world in the French capital. Still in Paris on 11 April, Metternich could write to the Emperor Francis: 'I have every reason, so far, to be satisfied with my stay here. It will certainly have good results.'[23] The sentiment was not in the best of taste. Nor, strangely enough, was it even accurate; for reports of patronizing asides about the Tsar, which Metternich had thrown carelessly into his conversation, soon reached St Petersburg from Pozzo and fanned a cold fire of resentment in Alexander's heart. His French journey brought the Chancellor little credit: the possibility that sorrow and inner uncertainty led him to overact the social lion did not commend itself to those who flattered him and envied his success.

He remained in Paris for more than four weeks after Eleonore's death. At one time he thought of crossing to England, where George iv had indicated he would be welcome. Anglo-Austrian relations were strained over the Eastern Question and over Canning's support for Latin-American independence; and theoretically a series of meetings between the British Foreign Secretary and the Austrian Chancellor might have led to a new understanding. But Canning thought otherwise. He had some grounds for suspecting that, over the last twelve months, there had been plots between the King, Wellington, the Lievens and Metternich to oust him from office; and he made it clear to the British ambassador in Paris that Metternich could not expect a sympathetic reception in London.[24] Wellington ingeniously proposed to Dorothea Lieven that Metternich might cross from Dieppe to Brighton, where the Duke and Dorothea would await him and escort him to Windsor. After a meeting with the King he could then return to France without going to London and thus avoid Canning. Subsequently George iv even suggested he might himself go to Brighton and entertain the Chancellor there. Yet Metternich held back: it was not clear to him what he could gain by serving as the King's trophy in a quarrel with a minister of undoubted popularity. It is also probable that, at this moment, he preferred to avoid the embraces of Dorothea Lieven (who wrote to him from Brighton on 8 April with the remarkable information she had 'been here for a week gazing at the French coast').[25]

Eventually Metternich left Paris on 21 April; he never visited the city again. He travelled in a leisurely style by way of Lyons, Nîmes, Marseilles, Nice and Alessandria to Milan, where he arrived on 7 May. It was a pleasant spring journey and he enjoyed the scenery of Provence and the Corniche as his son's open carriage rumbled down the long roads to Lombardy.[26] In Milan he was joined by his Emperor and all the familiar problems of administering provinces where national sentiment still wilfully obscured the manifold virtues of alien rule. Most of the diplomatic corps had followed Francis south to Milan that summer. Among them was Cardinal Giuseppe Albani, long a friend of Metternich and a supporter of Austrian policy in Papal counsels. While in Milan Albani handed Metternich a letter from Leo XII in which the Pope recorded his pleasure at hearing that the Chancellor wished 'to be admitted into the College of Cardinals'. If he really desired to become a Cardinal, the Pope was prepared to put his name forward at the next consistory. Since Metternich had never thought of following the example of Richelieu or Mazarin he was perplexed at the Pope's offer; for Cardinal von Metternich, though no doubt a worthy dignitary in the bigoted eyes of Charles X, would have carried little authority in Berlin or London or St Petersburg. He asked Albani for an explanation and found it disturbingly simple: he had, in an earlier conversation, mentioned to the Cardinal his predilection for the colour red; and it was assumed that this remark clearly indicated he hankered for the red hat of a Prince of the Church.[27] The honour was courteously declined.

From Milan Metternich accompanied Francis on a short visit to Genoa. There was an amiable meeting with the King of Sardinia-Piedmont and his heir presumptive, Charles Albert, who seemed abjectly penitent for the patriotic impulses which had so disturbed Metternich in the troubled months of 1821. The court returned to Milan and, early in July, dispersed as the hot weather hit the city. Metternich travelled in his great six-horse carriage to Como and through the Valtelline to spend a month with his daughters Leontine (who was now fourteen) and Hermine (not yet ten) at Bad Ischl in the Salzkammergut. Ischl, although a spa, was not then as highly developed as Carlsbad or Teplitz and he was able to enjoy the peace of the mountains in privacy.[28] But reports and despatches continued to arrive for him from Vienna. Outside Austria the diplomatic turmoil over the Eastern Question was by now worse than ever. It had disturbed him in Paris and Milan; and at times it even ruffled his seclusion in the mountains.

Although the Tsar never succeeded in summoning to St Petersburg a full congress of sovereigns and plenipotentiaries, he was determined to use the series of ambassadorial meetings as authorization for vigorous action against the Turks. In February 1825 it seemed as if some dramatic move by Russia over the Eastern Question was inevitable, for in that month Ibrahim (the son of Mehemet Ali of Egypt) landed in the Peloponnese with a new and efficient army and made such rapid progress against the Greek insurgents that disaster threatened the whole national revolt. Alexander, however, still wished to be certain of moral support from his Austrian, French and Prussian allies; and while the Tsar clung with pathetic obstinacy to the outward form of the Alliance, no assistance for the Greeks came from St Petersburg. The skill of the Greek seamen saved the islands from Ibrahim's ruthless troops; but the slow pace of negotiation in Russia was a terrible contrast to the agonies of vengeance on the Greek mainland.[29]

The conferences in St Petersburg dragged wearily on through the first quarter of 1825 and into the spring. In order to embarrass the Russians and counter their plan for three dependent principalities, Metternich instructed Lebzeltern to propose that the Great Powers should recognize an independent Greek state. Although he had in mind only a comparatively small area this was far too drastic a solution for the Russians, not least because there were so many sectional groups among the Greek insurgents that it was by no means clear whose authority could be recognized. The Tsar and Nesselrode accordingly declined to accept the Austrian proposal, as Metternich had always assumed that they would, and Lebzeltern at once made it clear Austria could never sanction forcible intervention against the Turks. The whole of March and April was spent in fruitless wrangling around the conference table until, by the middle of May, everyone accepted stalemate.[30] Meetings of the conference were suspended and it was no longer possible to disguise Russian resentment at Metternich's persistent temporizing. Alexander lost all patience with him, for he seemed to treat Russian concerns with casual neglect and his vaporous boasting in Paris rankled. At last the Tsar resolved on a change of policy. It was seven years since he and Metternich had 'found one another again' at Aix, and in that period his Austrian partner had never once favoured specifically Russian interests. Henceforth, Alexander insisted, Nesselrode and his diplomats should exclusively pursue the traditional objectives of the Russian State.[31] The Alliance, if not dead, was certainly buried.

Nor was this the only enchantment of the Aix Congress to evaporate that summer. On 24 June, while Metternich was still in Milan, Dorothea Lieven set out from London and, crossing Germany and Poland, arrived in St Petersburg a fortnight later. It was her first visit home to

Russia for thirteen years and she was determined to cut a figure worthy of her talents and reputation. At Verona in 1822 she had been cold-shouldered by her fellow countrymen and petted by Metternich and Wellington. Things were different now. The Austrian Chancellor, although still a regular correspondent, had become less fascinating and (unpardonably) less fascinated. She had wintered in Italy in 1823–24 and he had failed to cross the Alps to her; and this spring he had remained deaf to her siren call from the stones of Brighton beach. Mr Canning, on the other hand, who had for so long been a burden shared by both of them, was 'beginning to make me pretty speeches'.[32] There was, indeed, much that Dorothea Lieven could tell her Imperial master at Tsarskoe Selo.

At first, however, she doubted if she could penetrate the haze of mysticism into which his mind had once more retreated. Alexander received her with some reserve; the gloomier passages of the Old Testament, which formed his lighter reading these days, were a cold preparation for such an encounter. Yet, since she was clearly neither the wife of Ahab nor of Potiphar, he gradually found what she had to say interesting. She argued, as he himself believed, that the time had come to abandon the Austrian connection: she added – and this was to him a fresh impression – that Canning was no Jacobin and that, as the personal enemy of Metternich, his friendship was not to be rejected out of hand.[33] For over a month Alexander showed no reaction to her advice and she was forced to remain a silent observer of the diplomatic scene in the capital. On 29 July she dined with Nesselrode and Lebzeltern and listened to long talks over Austro-Russian relations without contributing any remarks which the ambassador thought worthy of comment.[34] Then, on the night before she was to leave for England, he authorized Nesselrode to visit her and propose, in a remarkably devious manner, she should let Canning know that if Britain approached Russia for a settlement of the Eastern Question he would not find his initiative rejected.[35]

Countess Lieven was delighted at being made the bearer of an important message. She hastened back across the continent with such eagerness she collapsed at Calais, took to her bed and lost most of the time she had saved by her exertions. Yet she did not entirely forget her old attachments. From Reval, five days after her conversations with Nesselrode, she dropped a breathless note to Metternich:[36] 'I come back rich, very rich in precious knowledge . . . I have no time to tell you all . . . I will tell you what is most urgent; there is a certain coldness towards you. I beg you to give the matter serious thought . . . Trust in my tact and my zeal. Do not reply that I am wrong, and that it is you who are right. Even if you are, be quick, waste no time in arguing; but try to make your peace.'

Metternich already knew from Lebzeltern's reports he was unpopular in St Petersburg, and he was not unduly disturbed by Russian hostility.[37] It was, he thought, a passing phase which would end once Alexander discovered diplomatic isolation involved a loss of influence within the continent as a whole. Hence Metternich replied to Dorothea Lieven's letter with almost insufferable disdain: 'It is quite natural that they should seem much offended with me at St Petersburg,' he wrote on 1 October. 'But what is there for me to fear? The noise? What signifies noise in our day, when all types of voice can be heard in every direction? . . . Thick mists lie over the Neva, but soon they will be blown away; for there they are beginning to see once more that the road which they have taken is not the right one.'[38] He was incorrigibly complacent. Certainly he did not suspect that Dorothea Lieven, whom a few months previously he had greeted as 'my dearest friend of the last seven years and of all the future,'[39] should be the instrument of nemesis. Yet by the end of that same month she and her husband had visited Canning at Seaford and prepared the diplomatic revolution which, by the following summer, was to leave Austria almost isolated in Europe.

Metternich, Széchenyi and the Hungarian Diet of 1825–7

When he received Dorothea Lieven's letter from Reval Metternich was already engrossed in the intricacies of an unfamiliar question. The Hungarian Diet had not been convoked since 1811 and the administration was eager to obtain legal sanction for the financial reforms which had been imposed on Hungary, as on other parts of the Empire, in the preceding decade. Metternich, who was friendly with many of the great Magyar families but knew little of the country, advised Francis to summon a Diet in 1825: there would, he predicted to Gentz, be 'much empty talk, never rising to anything higher than mere personal and local interest'; but by 'returning to the constitution', Francis would, he thought, be sure of inspiring the members of the Diet with 'a good spirit' and 'great enthusiasm'.[40] This was a complete miscalculation on Metternich's part. When the Diet was opened on 11 September it immediately embarked on a series of criticisms of royal encroachments on the traditional rights of the Hungarian ruling class; and it continued to defend its interests for almost three hundred sessions, until it dispersed in July 1827.

Metternich himself was no more than an observer of the Diet's affairs, although as Court Chancellor he had honorific duties to undertake while Francis was officially resident in Hungary for its sessions. Privately Metternich despised the whole affair. He described the Diet to Gentz as 'one of the most tiresome constitutional *divertis-*

sements in the world' and complained that 'it not only interferes with my time, my customs and daily life but actually forces me to change my language and my robes. I have to speak Latin and dress like a Hussar, and the only liberty which I take on this occasion is a refusal to wear moustaches'.[41]* The Diet met in the city which he knew as Pressburg (Pozsony to the Hungarians and Bratislava to the modern Czechs and Slovaks). It is only forty miles down the Danube from Vienna and he tried, as much as possible, to keep in touch with foreign affairs by frequent journeys back to the Chancellery. He told Dorothea Lieven on 1 October that 'Today I am travelling back and forth between the two capitals, happily no farther from each other than two London suburbs; in one I am a German and in the other a Hungarian; a strange fate.'[42] At first he refused to take the Diet seriously but, as the sessions continued, Sedlnitzky's agents disturbed his complacency with tales of fiery opposition from the younger Magyars. Probably the police exaggerated the unrest and almost certainly he read more into their reports than the situation warranted. Moreover it seems to have looked blacker to him after he finally left Pressburg for Vienna in the middle of November. He was at all events sufficiently alarmed to lament, early in December, that in Hungary he had encountered 'all those things' against which he had fought throughout his public life.[43]

Such round condemnation is surprising. The Hungarian Diet was a bi-cameral institution of considerable antiquity in which the Upper Table of magnates dominated a Lower Table of spokesmen from the counties and boroughs. It was no more democratic than an Elizabethan Parliament although every bit as jealously tenacious of its privileges. Over social reform its members were, with a few exceptions, more conservatively minded than Metternich and far less sympathetic towards the peasantry. The danger, in Metternich's eyes, came from national pride rather than from the 'Jacobinism' which he had found in Italy and in the German universities. He was particularly worried by the activities of Colonel Count Stefan (István) Széchenyi, a thirty-four-year-old aristocrat who had distinguished himself at the battle of Leipzig and who was related by marriage to some of the Chancellor's closest friends. It seemed inexplicable to Metternich that this elegant butterfly, whom everyone in Viennese society knew by the familiar diminutive 'Stefferl', should emerge as leader of the Hungarian Opposition. His behaviour was unpredictable. On 3 November Széchenyi, a great landowner, suddenly offered the Diet a year's income from his estates to establish a National Academy for promoting the Magyar language and literature. This impromptu gesture of munificence made

* Metternich had become a titular Hungarian magnate by a decree issued by Francis in Paris on 25 May 1814. He received the gift of the seigneurie of Daruvár in Croatia-Slavonia (*Mémoires*, vol. vii, pp. 649–51).

him at once a popular and respected figure in Pressburg; and it is small wonder that, exactly a week later, Metternich sent a private invitation to the 'Magyar Maecenas' to call on him and discuss the political situation in the Hungarian Kingdom.[44]

Metternich had two conversations with Széchenyi before the end of the year 1825: the first was at Pressburg on 12 November and the second in Vienna on 8 December.[45] On each occasion the Chancellor, with his long experience of political debate, was convinced he had the best of the discussion; and he was probably right. He appears to have confused and depressed the young Hungarian, although it is significant that in his diary for 12 November Széchenyi noted that Metternich seemed only to enjoy listening to himself. Nevertheless, after each meeting, Széchenyi reiterated his arguments in memoranda where he could state his principles without being side-tracked into current topics by a wily old diplomat; and, though Metternich told Francis the errant 'Stefferl's' views were well-meaning but misguided, he was himself impressed by Széchenyi's understanding of the nature of constitutional opposition. Széchenyi had travelled in England and his creed brought strange echoes of Holland House into the Chancellery. He believed in 'the highest possible degree of civilization and enlighten-ment', in equality before the law, in religious toleration, and in loyalty to one's country and to its King as an embodiment of patriotic service. He abhorred violence and revolution as deeply as any Tory; and yet he had plans for ending the economic stagnation of Hungary; and he 'confessed' to Metternich – a little naïvely perhaps – that some of his thoughts were 'very liberal'. Metternich remained puzzled. He had known hostility from reactionaries, from democrats and from radicals; but now he was faced by a new type of adversary, a Whig. He warned Széchenyi his political career would have a tragic ending and police spies continued to observe his public and social activities, but he never lost contact with Széchenyi and was prepared to court him as an ally against the extremism of less capacious minds. Although the Pressburg Diet showed that, in many ways, Metternich had been too super-ficially clever over Hungary, he was right to single out Széchenyi as the one personality who mattered among all the noisy hotheads of Pressburg.

The accession of Tsar Nicholas I

In the last week of December the British ambassador in Vienna sent Canning a long account of events at the Diet in the course of which he maintained that 'Metternich's attention for the last month has been wholly devoted to the affairs of Hungary'.[46] This was not strictly true: though Hungary had never been far from his thoughts, its political problems were not directly his responsibility. Most of his working days were occupied with the routine activities of diplomacy while, in his leisure hours in the second half of 1825, he read memoirs of the Napoleonic period and discussed with Gentz his own record of what had happened in those febrile years, for he had begun to draft autobiographical fragments while at Ischl in August and – as so often – he relied on Gentz 'to read and polish' what he had written. Then, in the middle of the month, an unforeseen event brought past and present sharply together and threw the future into doubt. At midnight on 13 December Metternich heard from his consul in Warsaw that Tsar Alexander had died suddenly twelve days previously at Taganrog, where he had contracted a fever while travelling to the Crimea. Metternich received the news with mixed feelings. He was uncomfortably aware that Alexander was four years his junior in age and it was clear the fatal illness resembled his own collapse at Lemberg during the autumn journey of 1823. 'This unexpected catastrophe has touched me very deeply,' he wrote, perhaps with sincerity. But he admitted that the Tsar had of late been disinclined to follow his advice and, by the start of the New Year, he had well recovered his sense of oracular infallibility: 'If from the heights of Paradise events below can occupy one, then Alexander now understands me better than ever he did on earth and his soul should come to meet and support mine,' he declared. A young Tsar, he thought, would be less inclined to listen to the 'honeyed words' of those who were, in reality, his enemies; and Metternich hoped the Russians might once again seek a negotiated settlement of the Eastern Question through the mediation of Austria, rather than resort to force or to Canning.[47]

At first, however, there was a technical difficulty: was Russia ruled by Tsar Constantine I or Tsar Nicholas I? Constantine, effective governor of Poland since 1814, was the elder brother but he had married a Polish Countess (who was a Roman Catholic) and had no wish to exchange his residence in Warsaw for the Russian throne. Nicholas had been secretly nominated heir-apparent by Alexander, but he too was reluctant to accept the Imperial Crown and actually took an oath of allegiance to Constantine. During the uncertainty over the succession, groups of army officers in St Petersburg and the Ukraine threatened a political revolt; and in order to forestall the conspiracy, Nicholas agreed on 26 December he should himself be proclaimed Tsar. He at once authorized stern measures against the dissident officers. By the end of the year the new Tsar's position was secure and in January there was a flurry of activity in the European chancelleries as the governments searched for fitting envoys to convey congratulations to Nicholas on his accession. In London Canning, who was by now collaborating closely with the Lievens, proposed that the Duke of Wellington should represent George IV on this special mission. In Vienna Metternich was in a quandary: in earlier years he would probably have made the journey to St Petersburg himself; but the prospect of a Russian winter does not appear to have attracted him, and he looked elsewhere for an envoy.

He was by no means displeased to find all his old warnings to Alexander of plots and conspiracies justified by the recklessness of the 'Decembrist' officers. 'It is nothing more nor less than a precise copy of (the revolts) in Madrid, Naples and Turin', he wrote to his son Victor in Paris,[48] and he added a marginal comment to Lebzeltern's report indicating that he personally had never doubted the officers were 'convinced liberals'. But the form of the revolt posed embarrassing problems. Some of the conspirators were eminent members of the Russian aristocracy: one was a friend of the Schwarzenberg family; and another had taken refuge in the Austrian Embassy, for Lebzeltern was his brother-in-law. In these circumstances it was particularly difficult to find an Austrian emissary to equal Wellington in stature. Eventually it was decided to send the Archduke Ferdinand to St Petersburg, amply fortified with memoranda from Metternich; but at the same time the Chancellor hit on the ingenious plan of currying favour with Wellington himself. Their relations were cordial: they had often exchanged letters and compliments; and they had consoled each other with reservations about Mr Canning's policy and the prospects for his political survival. Moreover the Duke's younger brother, Sir Henry Wellesley, was now ambassador in Vienna, and Metternich went out of his way to flatter the Wellesley family in conversation with Sir Henry. A private letter was despatched from brother to brother: 'Metternich is quite prepared to enlist under your banners,' Henry wrote to Arthur, 'and to leave the interests of Europe in your hands, satisfied that they cannot be placed in better'.[49] It was almost a gesture of abdication: the 'coachman of Europe', as Metternich liked to imagine himself, had become a mere postilion.

But Wellington's expedition to Russia brought little comfort to Metternich. The Duke – often exhausted, sometimes confused, and always perplexed – found it difficult enough to fulfil Canning's instructions, let alone reconcile them with vague sentiments from his adversary in Vienna. On 4 April Wellington, fearing the Russians were about to march on Turkey, concluded a protocol with Nesselrode which provided for British mediation between Turks and Greeks in order to create an autonomous Greek state within the Ottoman Empire; and it was also agreed that Britain and Russia might 'jointly or separately' intervene in the conflict should mediation fail.[50] This agreement, as Metternich soon perceived, represented a diplomatic reversal for Austria; for, though the British were as anxious as he was to avoid war in the East, their conditions of peace differed markedly from his own. Canning was pledged to Greek autonomy while he remained convinced that any re-drawing of the map in Eastern Europe, however small in the first instance, would disturb the whole balance of the continent. 'We look on the Ottoman Empire,' he was to write later to Paul Esterhazy, 'as the best of our neighbours ... the last bastion standing in the way of another Power.'[51] Nothing could induce him to accept coercion of the Sultan.

The news of the Anglo-Russian Protocol reached Metternich at the end of April and filled him with despondency. It was, however, no more than the first of a series of disappointments over policy which he was to receive in the course of the next eighteen months, nearly all of them stemming from the hostility of Tsar Nicholas. Throughout the summer and autumn of 1826 negotiations between the Russians and Turks were held in the little town of Akkerman at the mouth of the Dniester: and in October a convention was signed there which gave considerable powers of autonomy to the princes of Serbia, Moldavia and Wallachia. This agreement vitally influenced the lower Danube and yet the Austrians were virtually ignored in the diplomatic deliberations.*[52] A more blatant affront to Metternich's susceptibilities came in August 1826 when, on the instructions of Nicholas, Nesselrode rejected a proposal from Metternich that the Great Powers should meet in Congress to discuss the affairs of Portugal, where the British were supporting the 'constitutionalists' against clericalist reactionaries.[53] But, while his brother may have once been interested in the fate of Madrid, Nicholas was not going to be distracted from the East by political squabbles on the Tagus. By the autumn of 1826 Metternich could no longer doubt he was dealing with a new Russia and with an autocrat who, unlike Alexander, combined stubborn resolution with limited sympathies. 'It appears to be obvious', the Chancellor wrote sadly in November, 'that the young Tsar ... feels a certain dislike towards me.'[54]

At times it seemed over the Greek Question almost as if all his enemies were coming together to scorn Metternich. Capodistrias, from Swiss exile, was active once more, championing the Greek moderates and preparing to return to his homeland once the power of Ibrahim's army was contained. Pozzo di Borgo, who in the past had shown no more love for the English than for the Austrians, was in October seen walking through Paris in genial conversation with Canning; and Metternich was rightly convinced that between them they were steering the French away from the Alliance and towards intervention in

* Reaction to news of the Convention of Akkerman varied in Vienna. Gentz, who was a specialist on the affairs of Moldavia-Wallachia, was relieved that Russo-Turkish disputes in such a vulnerable area should be settled without war, but others saw it as a diplomatic rebuff.

Greece.[55] By the summer of 1827 the British and French had even agreed with the Russians that, if the Sultan declined an armistice, a naval blockade should be imposed by the three Mediterranean squadrons on the Turks. Such behaviour appeared to Metternich fraught with danger and he refused to associate himself with these measures, certain they would sooner or later lead to disaster. Nothing now remained of the diplomatic web on which he had prided himself a few years before. Only Frederick William III of Prussia continued to stand loyally by the Alliance, as Metternich understood it; and outside the German Confederation, Prussia still counted for little.

Antoinette von Leykam

Metternich accepted his eclipse in 1826-7 with surprising resilience and equanimity. Gentz did not hesitate to blame the Lievens (husband and wife) for the diplomatic revolution which had favoured Canning at Metternich's expense;[56] and it seemed significant that, as the first of the Coronation Honours, Tsar Nicholas should have bestowed on his ambassador in London the title of Prince. But Metternich himself was slow to break off all correspondence with Her Serene Highness Princess Lieven and she continued to feed him morsels of gossip. Even at the end of April, while inwardly fuming at the Anglo-Russian Protocol, Metternich wrote to her and jokingly asked if she knew 'a young heiress who was wealthy, beautiful, virtuous, witty and endowed with a great name', one who could bring happiness to his family; for he had confidence in the Princess as a matchmaker.[57]

And yet was Metternich's question really so light-hearted? His private affairs had often in the past sharpened her pen and it is tempting to see in his words a provocative sting of irony. They served, moreover, as a prelude to the storm which was to end their long romance by letter. For by now Metternich was seriously considering marrying for a second time and his choice had fallen on a girl in her twentieth year, whom Dorothea Lieven had already sought to claw in the winter of 1823-4. The news that Metternich was paying daily visits to Antoinette von Leykam in the spring of 1826 roused Dorothea to cold fury, and on 16 May she sent the haughtiest of all her letters to Vienna.[58] Was 'Mademoiselle Leykam' his future wife or his present mistress? For, while it was clear neither the father nor the mother deserved the honour of visits from the Chancellor, it was said that the daughter was very pretty. But he need not fear: she would not seek revenge for his inconstancy. 'What a strange man you are! Taking notice of a little girl! I should look funny, if I were to bother myself with a little boy!' He was unmoved by her censure and his letters continued to come intermittently until the end of October. Regretting perhaps her impetuosity, she wrote once a fortnight throughout that summer and autumn, sending him *vignettes* of the English court: of Wellington and Canning in the Cottage at Windsor; of George IV awkwardly dandling on his knees 'the little future Queen', the seven-year-old Victoria; of drives in phaetons and picnics beside the Thames. But she could not re-capture the spirit of their earlier exchanges. On 2 November she wrote: 'Let us start again from the beginning. We should be hard put to it, you and I, to find in the whole world people of our own calibre'.[59] From Vienna there was no reply.

It must be admitted that Princess Lieven was not the only critic of Metternich's infatuation with Antoinette von Leykam. She was a petite blonde with a small mouth set in a heart-shaped face, sweet-natured and artistic. But she came from a family of far less standing than the Metternichs and she was thirty-three years younger than the man she was to marry. On the day she was born Metternich had attended, for the first time, a reception of the diplomatic corps by Napoleon at St Cloud; and she was even younger than his son, Victor, who had himself been much attracted to her. Viennese gossip made her social background humbler than it was and insisted that the Prince had forbidden Victor to make her his wife because she did not come from one of the great families. Some of Metternich's oldest friends were genuinely shocked and absented themselves from the capital.[60] All these snobbish prejudices were without foundation: Antoinette's mother was an Italian, Antonia Pedrella, who had sung in opera at Naples; but the Leykams themselves had, for several generations, held minor posts in the diplomatic service. By a curious coincidence Antoinette's grand-father had been one of the intermediaries between Prince Kaunitz and Countess Beatrice at the time of Clement's betrothal to Eleonore. Now Beatrice, still mentally alert and active, strongly disapproved of her son's decision:[61] if Clement wished to marry a young girl, she failed to understand why he had not chosen Melanie, the daughter of Molly Zichy-Ferraris, a family with whom the Metternichs had been on close terms for many years; had not Melanie been among the first to send Clement a letter of condolence when poor Eleonore died? There were others who shared Beatrice's surprise; Countess Molly and the twenty-two-year-old Melanie thought it tactful to winter in Hungary.

Metternich himself took no notice of these criticims and innuendoes. He was angry that society should question the decisions of his private life; and he believed (rightly) that Antoinette's grace and charm would soon melt all opposition in Vienna. Moreover, the Emperor Francis warmly supported the Prince, for he sympathized keenly with a widower's loneliness.[62] On 8 October, the day upon which the forth-coming marriage was publicly announced, Francis created Antoinette Countess of Beilstein; and on 5 November she became the second

Princess Clement von Metternich-Winneburg. They were married, very quietly, at Hetzendorf on the outskirts of Vienna.

When the news reached England Princess Lieven sought to spite her former lover with a phrase that would echo through the drawing-rooms: 'The knight of the Holy Alliance has finished up by making a misalliance,' she scoffed.[63] But, in his brief fourteen months of marriage to Antoinette, it was the knight who found happiness and the Dulcinea in London who searched for new adventures.

CHALLENGE RESISTED

Crisis in the East (1827–9)

On 5 November 1827, the same day as the wedding ceremony at
Hetzendorf, news of the Battle of Navarino reached Vienna, and
Metternich spent the first weeks of his second marriage deep in study
of the Eastern Question. The destruction of the Turkish and Egyptian
Fleets by the combined naval squadrons of Britain, Russia and France
seemed to him 'an appalling catastrophe', although he had anticipated
a serious incident since September when he heard the Allies were
resolved on blockading southern Greece.[1] He feared that Russia, with
British and French naval and diplomatic support, would march on
Constantinople and the three powers might then proceed to partition
the Ottoman Empire with scant regard for Austrian interests. Emperor
Francis was alarmed by these gloomy prospects and wished to mobilize
a hundred thousand men in southern Hungary so as to assist the Turks
to check a Russian thrust into the Balkans. But, although Tatischev
(now ambassador in Vienna) reported to Nesselrode the Austrians were
contemplating the occupation of Serbia and the Danubian principalities,
there was always a peace party in the capital which insisted that the
Empire's economy could not afford a military expedition; and at heart
Metternich knew the peace party was right. Moreover it was inconceivable to him that Italy and Germany should remain quiet once the
Austrian Army was engaged in the East. If war would thus spread chaos
across Europe, it must at all costs be avoided.

Navarino may, as many believe, have saved the Greeks from the
wrath of Ibrahim, but it hardened the attitude of the Sultan towards
the Russians. The Turks refused to fulfil the conditions agreed at
Akkerman over the Danubian principalities and in April 1828 the
Russians at last went to war with the Sultan. But, to Metternich's relief,
they fought alone; for Navarino had in one sense eased the situation. It
induced the British to draw back. Canning had died suddenly in August,
two months before the battle, and throughout that winter British
foreign policy lacked direction or purpose. In January 1828 Wellington
became Prime Minister and did not attempt to hide his disapproval of

the 'untoward event' which had robbed 'an ancient ally' of its fleet. Metternich was pleased at what, in a letter to his son, he termed 'England's public spirit'.² He had always found it easy to work with Wellington and he was further encouraged in June when Lord Aberdeen became Foreign Secretary, for there remained in his mind happy memories of the 'dear simpleton' who had negotiated the Anglo-Austrian understanding of 1813. Thus in the summer of 1828 it became possible for the first time in six years for the Austrians and British to co-operate over European problems. At the end of December Metternich tentatively suggested there was much in favour of summoning another congress over Eastern affairs, to meet perhaps in Vienna. But this kite was flown far too high and it was not difficult for Wellington and Aberdeen to ignore it. The Duke had never liked congresses, and his chief wish at the moment was 'to get out of the Greek affair without loss of honour'.³ He was not alone in this sentiment.

From 1828 onwards Metternich deliberately stood aside from the Eastern Question for as long as he could. Sure that there would be no lasting combination between Britain and Russia, he preferred to observe what was happening and avoid specific commitments. Much remained uncertain. The Russians were burning their fingers in the campaign against Turkey. Six months of hard fighting had brought their troops no farther south than the port of Varna as winter closed around them. Not until the following spring were they able to make real progress, and even so it took the whole summer to thrust across the Balkan mountains. By then Nicholas and his advisers were doubting the wisdom of seeking to break up the Ottoman Empire, and at Adrianople in September 1829 the Turks were offered and accepted remarkably generous terms. The peace treaty left the settlement of Greece to a ministerial conference and imposed upon the Turks hardly more restraints than they had already acknowledged at Akkerman. It was only in Asia that Russia made substantial gains from the war; and this did not particularly disturb her Austrian neighbour.

Metternich condemned the Adrianople Treaty as a severe blow to Turkish power but his complaints were more a matter of form than of substance. Privately he was well satisfied with the turn of events.⁴ He did not participate in the conferences at Poros or London over the form and boundaries of the new Greek state, although he made it clear to Aberdeen he was prepared to accept an independent Greece rather than an autonomous principality as a surer guarantee against Russian influence. His views appear to have carried weight with Wellington. Metternich was well served by his ambassadors in London and St Petersburg and watched with interest the growing suspicion between the two signatories of the 1826 Protocol. Occasionally he fed their mutal animosity with subtle observations faithfully transmitted to Wellington or to Nesselrode by his representatives.[5] Thus he transformed the isolation he had earlier feared into a source of strength rather than weakness.

By the close of 1829 Metternich could report to Francis – a little optimistically, perhaps – that the Turkish Crisis was over and that it had led to the collapse of that menacing partnership of Russia, England and France. The Peace of Adrianople seemed to him to mark a divide in Europe's affairs and he therefore used the occasion to explain his policy to the Emperor in a memorandum which he wrote in the pompous 'Chancellery style' of which he was a master exponent. He did not, he told the Emperor, wish to resurrect the old Quintuple Alliance, 'to which Austria alone has been faithful'; but he planned to resume good relations with all the former Allies rather than seek any new paper agreement. His approach would therefore be essentially pragmatic, for he was convinced any country wishing to return to the spirit of the old Alliance – 'the exclusive aim of which was the triumph of the con- servative system' – must 'sooner or later range itself alongside Austria'. The Empire would thus inevitably emerge once more as the centre of European order. If, however, the Monarchy was to discharge this function adequately it was essential to improve the economy, to reform the administration of the Army and to attend to faults in the internal structure (particularly 'the condition of Hungary'). It was a lengthy document; and at the end of it Francis wrote the one word, *'Placet'*.[6]

Personal sorrows and public frustration

The Chancellor was relieved his policy and system had escaped so lightly from the Eastern conflict which he had long dreaded. Yet the burden of work and worry had been considerable through the winter of 1828 and the first half of 1829 and, during all this period, he had not been able to get away from Vienna and seek rest in Bohemia or the Rhineland, although he did travel occasionally out to Baden. Nor was it only his professional duties that wearied him. For these months brought personal tragedies as hard to bear as the sorrows of 1820. His mother's death in November 1828 was not unexpected, for she was old and frail, but he felt the loss keenly. Six weeks later, on 7 January 1829, Antoinette gave birth to a son, Richard, who was to win distinction as ambassador in Paris under the Second Empire. But within five days of Richard's birth Antoinette contracted a post-natal fever and less than a week later she was dead, still only in her twenty-third year. Once more it seemed to Metternich as if he had suffered a wound which would never heal: 'I have lost all that remains of my happiness,' he wrote to an old friend at the end of the month.[7] The Emperor, for whom the loss of a young wife created a new bond of sympathy with his Chancellor, offered Metternich a temporary home in the Hofburg to spare him association with the recent past, but he declined the offer and buried himself in official duties.

The tragedy of Antoinette darkened a grey shadow already hanging over his private life. He had suspected for many months that his son Victor was suffering from a tubercular weakness similar to the disease which had carried off his sisters Marie and Clementine and their mother. Victor, who was serving as a junior diplomat in Paris, did not come to Vienna during the fourteen months of his father's second marriage. By the autumn of 1828, however, the symptoms of consumption were so alarming that he left Paris and spent the winter in Italy, seeking the sun and pure air of the Mediterranean. His health improved but, wanting a permanent cure, he returned to Vienna in July 1829 for medical advice and treatment. His father was greatly shocked by his condition at first and spent hours at his bedside that summer. Nursed by his young sisters, Victor seemed gradually to recover his strength and the Chancellor even took a brief holiday in Bohemia during the autumn. But with the approach of a Viennese winter, Victor rapidly declined and, on the last day of November, he died. By now Metternich was sadly accustomed to bereavement; and yet the letters which he wrote after Victor's death are heavy with melancholy held in restraint.[8] They are calmer and more resigned than on earlier occasions, but they reflect a loneliness of the soul. Few people were left in whom he could confide: his brother, Joseph, who held a minor governmental post, had not been close to him since their student days (and was himself to die a year later); his sister Pauline had never even begun to understand him; Gentz was unpredictable and irascible; and Dorothea Lieven an error of the past. There remained the womenfolk of the Zichy-Ferraris family; and inevitably he turned to them for consolation and inner serenity, for it was not in his nature to be a totally independent personality.

Yet he kept Christmas of 1829 and the New Year festivities wretchedly alone and deep in reminiscence. He was entering now his third decade as Foreign Minister and the European scene, though familiar, was hardly cheering. Even his natural allies, the champions of conservative causes, at times alarmed him by their excesses.[9] Francis i of Naples, who succeeded King Ferdinand in 1825, had encouraged the suppression of unrest in the Salerno district with mediaeval barbarity. Charles x of France had appointed the Prince de Polignac as Prime Minister in August 1829 and embarked on a provocative policy of reaction which converted the royalist press into hostile critics. Nor were Polignac's excursions into foreign affairs any more comforting, for he seemed to hanker after a Franco-Russian alliance and showed little regard for Austrian interests. Elsewhere liberalism crept forward. Metternich was uneasy at educational experiments in Prussia, at young King Ludwig of Bavaria's enthusiasm for artistic and cultural novelty, at reports that the *Burschenshaften* were meeting once more in secret within the German universities, and at the new political romanticism spreading eastwards through France and Germany to Poland and finding its heroes in the Napoleonic revolution, not in some distant age. Moreover the Tory Government of Wellington filled him with dismay by its indecision: 'The administration', he wrote to Paul Esterhazy early in 1830, 'is like the Duke . . . a singular composition of noble and essential qualities, eccentricities and veritable deficiencies'; and he complained that Canning's malignant influence still haunted the political world.[10]

Early in May he took the holiday which he urgently needed. He travelled to the Rhineland and remained at Johannisberg for over a month, but he continued to be worried by news which reached him from across the French frontier, where Polignac was defying the wishes of the elected Chamber in home affairs and embarking on an expedition to seize Algiers as a means of courting glory and popularity for Charles x. Metternich was almost beside himself with indignation at such folly: 'The fate of the monarchy in France and the peace of Europe are at this moment being played out like cards in a game of *écarté*', he wrote to Apponyi, the Austrian ambassador in Paris, on 5 June; and, casting another baleful glance at the parliamentary confusion across the Channel, he added 'What chaos in Paris and in London! Viewed from a distance one would say they were a couple of madhouses'; he could see nothing for 'Europe' except 'the dangerous rôle of waiting upon events'.[11] He sensed that the challenge of revolution was nearer than at any time since he had come to identify himself with Europe. In 1820 he had known what response to make and the sovereigns had listened to him. Ten years later no one was interested in what he had to say: they had heard it all before. He even proposed a conference over Algeria, in the hope of bringing the governments together; but, as he himself admitted, 'the assembling of a conference . . . remains very problematical'.[12] He returned, empty of ideas, to Vienna.

There was, however, still Nesselrode. The two statesmen had not met since the autumn of 1823 when Nesselrode had come to Metternich's sickbed in Lemberg, and in those seven years the Eastern Question had separated them in all its complexity. But when Metternich heard, on his return from the Rhineland, that Nesselrode intended to take the waters at Carlsbad, he determined to travel to Königswart and seek a meeting with the man whom he had known for over a quarter of a century. He accordingly set out for Bohemia in the fourth week of July and he took with him Friedrich Jäger (the eye specialist who had accompanied him to Italy in 1817) and Gentz who knew Nesselrode even better than he did himself.[13] It must be admitted that

Gentz came only with reluctance. His thoughts, as he declared at the time, remained with Fanny Elssler, the twenty-two-year-old ballerina with whom he had fallen in love earlier in the year; and neither kindly words from Metternich nor an exchange of sentimental letters could reconcile him to absence from Vienna that summer. He had never hidden his preference for the spas of the Austrian heartland rather than those of Bohemia and, on this occasion, he cannot have been the easiest or most useful of companions for Metternich. Significantly their relations remained cool for several months after the trip to Bohemia and not entirely, it would appear, through differences in policy.

Metternich travelled directly to Carlsbad rather than to Königswart and met Nesselrode on 27 July. He subsequently informed the Emperor that he had found the Russian 'shy' and therefore received him 'with complete absence of restraint'. This meant, in effect, that the unfortunate Nesselrode had to sustain a verbal buffeting of reproaches which would, with almost any other statesman, have led to a complete rift between their two countries. But Nesselrode possessed an equable temper and had no wish to perpetuate a quarrel at a time when, as both men believed, Europe approached a crisis in its affairs. They parted amicably after two conversations and agreed to meet again in August when Nesselrode went to Franzensbad, near Königswart, for further treatment at its thermal springs.[14]

The July Revolution in Paris (1830) and its effects on the Habsburg Monarchy

But late on the evening of 4 August Metternich received a message from the Rothschilds' courier service in Frankfurt that, on 27–8 July, Paris had risen against the inept administration of Polignac and Revolution had 'won the day'. The news shocked Metternich. When he read it he collapsed at his desk and, as Dr Jäger dashed forward to revive him, he was heard to moan 'My whole life's work is destroyed'.[15] He rallied, however, rapidly and by midnight had decided on his immediate course of action. He would seek out Nesselrode and ensure that Austria and Russia faced the new menace in common accord. Perhaps there might even be a broader conference; for, technically, the Quadruple Alliance of 1815 was still valid and the Austrian, British, Prussian and Russian governments were bound to consult together over any revolutionary change of administration in France. But when the two statesmen met in Carlsbad on 6 August Nesselrode refused to consider a formal conference. He favoured an emergency decision and, without much difficulty, reached a basis of understanding with Metternich. There would be no intervention in the internal affairs of France provided the new government did not seek to extend its interests beyond the existing frontiers or threaten to foster revolution in other states. This statement of principles was jotted down by Metternich on a scrap of paper and was therefore subsequently known by diplomats as the *chiffon de Carlsbad*. Although he would have liked a full reunion of the three Eastern autocracies, Metternich was satisfied with the *chiffon*. He cut short his visit to Bohemia and, to Gentz's evident satisfaction, returned at once to Vienna, where he arrived on 10 August.[16]

Metternich feared the example of Paris would be speedily emulated elsewhere in Europe. 'We must turn our attention without delay to Italy,' he had written to Francis from Königswart. 'It is there that the revolutionary impulse will indubitably spread.'[17] He was, of course, ultimately correct in his diagnosis of the fever of revolt but there was a delay of several months before the barricades went up in the cities of the peninsula, for the Italian conspirators were not prepared to risk savage repression by a premature uprising. Meanwhile paroxysms of public impatience shook other regions of the continent. In the autumn the people of Brussels carried to the streets their demand to be governed by themselves rather than by the Netherlands; and in Brunswick, Saxony and Hesse-Cassel there was a sudden rush of liberal constitutionalism to the head. More surprising news still reached Metternich in November. The Polish garrison in Warsaw rose against Russian domination and found itself, against all the odds, in control of the central Vistula. And in London Wellington, bowing to the agitation for parliamentary reform, resigned in the middle of the month and the Whigs came into office for the first time in twenty-three years. Early in December Metternich heard that Aberdeen had been succeeded as Foreign Secretary by Lord Palmerston: it was, as yet, a name that meant nothing to him.

These dramatic changes provoked surprisingly little reaction in Vienna. Metternich had for so long expected the conservative order to be challenged that he watched all that was happening with a curious detachment. 'Old Europe is at the beginning of the end,' he wrote to Nesselrode on 1 September, 'and, since I am determined to perish with it, I shall know how to do my duty . . . New Europe, however, has not as yet even begun its existence, and between the end and the beginning there will be chaos.'[18] At times he seems to have anticipated his political Doomsday with an almost morbid relish.

Yet perhaps the European scene was not as sombre as he painted it. Gentz, for example, insisted events in France were for the general good, although he had harsh words to say about the Belgians. Metternich, too, was prepared to reserve his judgement over the French. The July Revolution had led, not to a republic, but to the establishment on the throne of the Orleanist dynasty; and Louis Philippe sent General Belliard to Vienna at the end of August on a special mission of reassurance. The General took some pains to explain to a mildly incredulous Chancellor how Louis Philippe had successfully won over the Republican movement in France by embracing Lafayette on the balcony of the Hotel de Ville on 31 July. 'A kiss is, indeed, little price to ask for the destruction of a republic,' Metternich remarked sardonically. 'Do you really think it is possible to bestow such power on all kisses in future?'[19]

At heart Metternich, who had known the new 'King of the French' for twenty years, had little confidence in his ability to survive, but so long as he kept the radicals under control Austria was willing to recognize his claim. There was, at all events, no danger now of a Franco-Russian alliance, since Tsar Nicholas could never bring himself to accept a dynasty which owed its Crown to 'the will of the people'. Even the Belgian Question had, at first, one merit in Metternich's eyes: for it led the King of the Netherlands to propose a conference of the signatories of the 1815 Treaty in order to settle his dispute with the Belgians. Although Metternich regretted that the conference should meet in London, it was at least a means of bringing together the old Allies.[20] He did not foresee the partnership of Talleyrand and Palmerston becoming such a formidable combination that the rift between the Eastern autocracies and the West was broadened rather than healed by the London Conference. His obsession in 1830 was still Italy and, with ominous reports reaching him in November from Rome and Modena, he was glad for the French and British to be distracted by the problems of Belgium and for the Russian Army to be tied up in Poland; for, above all, he demanded a free hand to keep order in the peninsula. German aberrations might wait for later chastisement jointly by Austria and Prussia; and, after a fresh display of revolutionary patriotism at Hambach in the spring of 1832, new repressive legislation was duly rushed through the Federal Diet.[21]

Metternich rightly discounted the spread of this particular virus of revolution to any of the Habsburg lands, apart from Lombardy and Venetia; and even in these provinces he did not anticipate the disturbances unless they were fomented from beyond the frontier. All remained peaceful in Galicia, where Prince August Lobkowitz had served as Governor since 1826 and successfully won Polish support by conciliatory gestures. None of the Slav peoples in the Empire as yet thought in dangerously nationalistic terms: the Austrian authorities patronized Czech and Slovene cultural studies with little fear of political consequences; and although a small section of the Croatian landowners voiced grievances, it was concerned solely with preservation of class privileges, mainly at the expense of the Magyar gentry. Within the heartland of Austria itself Sedlnitzky's police could find few signs of unrest, apart from the almost traditional complaints at heavy taxation.[22] The Emperor was as popular as ever with his German-speaking subjects, especially in Vienna, and Metternich was by now accepted as part of the natural order of existence, a landmark like the spire of the *Stefansdom* and hardly less immutable.

There remained, as always, the Hungarian Problem. The Magyar magnates were potentially an aristocratic Fronde and liable to embarrass the Monarchy with petty demands, but they were no less afraid of social revolution than Metternich or Sedlnitzky and the general political uncertainties of 1830 led them to act with restraint. Francis was himself anxious to have his son, Archduke Ferdinand, crowned as King of Hungary: the unfortunate young man, an epileptic, was so mentally retarded that his succession to the Imperial titles seemed in doubt; and a Hungarian coronation was a recognized method of ensuring the sovereign rights of an heir to the throne during his father's lifetime. At the same time the government in Vienna hoped it would be possible to secure additional army recruits from the Hungarian counties. Francis accordingly summoned the Hungarian Diet once more to Pressburg in the autumn of 1830. All prospered well: the Archduke was solemnly crowned on 28 September; and the Diet dutifully voted the recruits in exchange for the promise of procedural concessions and, in particular, for freedom to use the Magyar language rather than Latin in its official communications.[23] Metternich was well pleased with the work of the Diet and especially with the moderation shown by István Széchenyi. So long as Széchenyi remained the idol of the younger magnates the Diet was a convenient safety valve which emitted much hot air to avoid an explosion. Metternich continued to distrust many of the Hungarian's projects, suspecting that even his efforts at improving commerce and navigation on the Danube were in some way a cloak for anti-governmental activity, but he never doubted the Count's loyalty to the dynasty and he was prepared to protect his reputation against allegations of dangerous radicalism. A cool friendship between the two men, based on a respectful incomprehension of one another, lingered on from the Coronation Diet to the 'Long Diet' of 1832–6.

Marriage to Melanie Zichy-Ferraris (January 1831)

While the Coronation Diet was in session Metternich made a decision over his private life which inevitably associated him more closely with the Hungarian magnates. On 16 October 1830, he held a conversation with Melanie Zichy-Ferraris at Pressburg which, as she recalled in a diary entry a year later, 'settled my fate'; and by the second week in November their betrothal was an open secret.[24] The news produced none of the consternation which had followed the announcement of his second marriage three years before. Melanie was twenty-five and her bridegroom fifty-seven but the two families had been friendly for so long that no one was surprised by an alliance between them. A few years earlier it had seemed as if Melanie might become the wife of István Széchenyi: she had arranged the first political discussion between Metternich and Széchenyi in 1825; and her sister had, indeed, married one of his elder brothers. More recently Baron von Hügel had thought himself engaged to her. Melanie, however, was a woman of such pride and ambition that she could be satisfied only by a husband of Metternich's prestige and stature. Her journal suggests the office of Chancellor fascinated her more than 'my poor Clement', for whom she felt sympathetic affection rather than a deep attachment. It is also probable that at first he, for his part, looked upon this third marriage primarily as a social convenience: Melanie differed in appearance and character from the women who had stirred his passion: she had jet black hair, proud eyes (one green, one blue), a strong mouth and chin, and a plump figure; and by temperament she was – in contrast to Eleonore and Antoinette – impetuous, haughty, tactless and masterful.[25] Yet, whatever the considerations which induced the marriage, there is no doubt their relationship kindled a fire of love which lasted for almost a quarter of a century. They were married on 30 January 1831, by the Papal Nuncio in Vienna. Two days later Princess Melanie was received in audience by the Emperor. 'Make him happy, for he deserves it,' Francis said: it was a command she willingly obeyed.[26]

Problems of Italy and the fate of the Duke of Reichstadt

He certainly needed domestic consolation in those early weeks of 1831. The 'revolutionary impulse' had at last reached Italy. Encouraged by declarations from Paris that France would protect 'the liberty and independence' of other peoples, Italian patriots organized conspiracies in Parma and Modena and in the Papal States. Metternich was not surprised: he had already received reports of activity by 'French agents' and 'Bonapartists' in the central regions of the peninsula; and the possibility of a successful insurrection in the Papal States was increased by confusion in Rome itself, for Pius VIII (who had succeeded Leo XII in 1829) lived for only twenty months after his election and in the first weeks of 1831 the Cardinals were again in conclave to choose a new pontiff. On 2 February they elected Cardinal Capellari, who took the name of Gregory XVI; and on the following day Bologna, the second largest city in the Papal States, rose in a revolt which soon spread to Ravenna, Ferrara, Ancona and other towns. Within three weeks Papal authority in central Italy was limited to Rome and Orvieto. The rulers of Parma and Modena had sought refuge in Austrian Lombardy; and in Bologna a National Congress proclaimed 'the United Provinces of Italy', hoisted the red, white and green tricolour flag over the city, and appealed to Louis Philippe for recognition and material aid.[27]

Metternich learnt of the rising on 12 February. That day Princess Melanie noted in her diary: 'Clement was woken by some half a dozen couriers who brought bad news from Italy: already Ferrara and Bologna are in open revolt.'[28] Marie Louise of Parma and the Duke of Modena appealed for Austrian assistance and received it readily. But Metternich acted with caution over the Papal States, refusing to move any troops southwards until an official request for intervention from Pope Gregory arrived in Vienna. The Chancellor was confident the Italian insurgents could be easily dispersed. He was far more concerned over the attitude of the French and, for a few weeks that spring, it looked as if there would be a clash between the new Orleanist Monarchy and the Empire. Metternich himself appears to have been willing to risk a preventive war, but he was opposed by influential advisers at court and in the administration, even by Gentz.[29] It was a familiar argument: the financial structure of the Monarchy would never stand the strain of military expenditure; and the Archduke Charles, with a distant echo of past controversies, doubted the efficiency of the Army in a major campaign and the wisdom of wasting lives and material in what was essentially an ideological conflict. Fortunately the French were equally disinclined to fight and Metternich contented himself with sending Austrian troops southwards into Parma and Modena and eventually into the Papal States as well. By 21 March the Austrians had re-occupied Bologna and most of the troubled region. A week later the revolutionary government surrendered Ancona, the key fortress on the Adriatic, and all seemed over. Order was thus restored in the peninsula at far less cost than in 1821 and without French intervention. Melanie, full of admiration for her 'wise and honest husband', was able to record in her journal on 18 April that the Emperor had bestowed on him 'the Grand Cross of the Order of St Stephen set in diamonds, to mark the successful conclusion of the business in Italy.'[30]

The honour, as Metternich feared at the time, came a little prematurely. French prestige had emerged from the first nine months of the Orleanist Monarchy battered and scarred. Although Louis Philippe's actions could never attain the rhetorical heights scaled so smoothly by his ministers in the Chamber, some gesture was needed to remind the voters of France they were subjects of a revolutionary dynasty. With belated daring the French accordingly sent two frigates to anchor off Civitavecchia and took the lead in assembling a conference of ambassadors which submitted a programme of 'indispensable' reforms to Pope Gregory. Metternich was puzzled by French policy, not least because Casimir Perier, the French Prime Minister, coupled his display of vigour in Italy with proposals for a general conference on multi-lateral disarmament and pious regrets at the increasing size of

Austria's military establishment. Metternich responded well: he suggested discussions on disarmament might begin at Aix-la-Chapelle; and in early July approved the evacuation of Austrian units from Papal territory.[31] The consequences were predictable: the conference on disarmament never met at Aix or anywhere else, for the suggestion aroused as much distrust as a threat to mobilize; and, with the departure of the Austrians, a second insurrection broke out in Bologna. By the end of January 1832 Austrian troops were back in the Papal States. The French, nerving themselves at last for action, sent a small naval force into Ancona and announced they would occupy the town until the Austrians withdrew north of the Po. Metternich did not take the French retort very seriously: it was 'a mere bagatelle', he told the ambassador in Paris;[32] but the aftermath of these insurrections continued to plague Austro-French relations until 1838 when the twin trophies of Bologna and Ancona were at last restored to Papal keeping.

The July Revolution in Paris and the unrest in Italy made acute another problem which, for many years, Metternich had deliberately thrust to the back of his mind. Napoleon's son, once infant King of Rome and since 1818 titular Duke of Reichstadt, was brought up at the Austrian court as a Habsburg Prince. Although his mental training was always carefully supervised and his contacts with the outside world restricted, he had been educated by competent tutors and was treated by his grandfather, Emperor Francis, with gruff kindness. And yet the two people in the Habsburg circle who had known him when he was the hope of France persistently neglected him: his mother, Marie Louise, because his existence perforated the butterfly world she had created for herself; and Metternich because, in an ordered Europe, there was no future for the talisman of a lost adventure. Not until the summer of 1830 did Metternich hold a serious political conversation with the young man and the meeting was hardly a success, for the Chancellor's conscience put him ill at ease, while the nineteen-year-old Duke was shrewd enough to be on guard against verbal indiscretion. Count Anton Prokesch von Osten, a diplomat and friend of both Gentz and Reichstadt himself, noted that whenever Metternich was forced to think of the Duke 'the expression on his face was like that of a man swallowing a bitter pill'.[33] Prokesch was too young to remember the banquet at the Tuileries when Austria's new Foreign Minister had proposed a toast to a King of Rome who was not yet born.

Momentarily during the Italian crisis Metternich, mastering his scruples, was prepared to use the pathetic Duke as a political weapon. Bonapartism was in the air. The leaders of the Bolognese were veterans of Napoleon and Murat: Hortense and her two sons were in the Papal States during the rising, the elder dying at Forli from measles and pneumonia and the younger escaping from Ancona to become (eventually) Napoleon III; and throughout France a phantom Grand Army was riding from oblivion into folk-lore. From Vienna in January and February 1831 the warning went out to the French government in letters from Metternich to the ambassador which, he felt confident, would be intercepted: 'Has no-one in Paris ever thought of showing gratitude to us for our extreme tact in the matter of Napoleon II? We really deserve some praise in this matter . . . ,' he wrote on 18 January. And a month later, he said, 'The ties of relationship existing between the Imperial family and the late Napoleon have won us the confidences of those who adhere to the former French Empire. The son of Napoleon lives in Vienna; his father's followers, in turning their eyes to him, must naturally look also towards his grandfather.'[34] And, lest there should be doubt of his meaning, Metternich enclosed letters he had received at the end of 1830 from Joseph Bonaparte offering to lead Napoleon II back to France and save Europe from 'republican agitation'. 'Needless to say,' Metternich added, 'no reply whatsoever was made to these approaches.'[35]

It is probable that Metternich was no more sincere than Louis Philippe, who that April sought to appropriate the Napoleonic Legend by restoring the Emperor's statue to the column in the Place Vendôme. Both were playing with names, dropping symbols into a well of mediocrity to thrill at their echo. For Reichstadt the game was cruelly unreal. He had been ill for more than two years: he was six feet tall, very slender, and his face had a dangerous pallor. The diagnoses of the medical experts were far from consistent but Dr Staudenheim had noted as early as 1828 'a tendency to scrofula' and it seems impossible that Metternich, with the experience of his son so vivid in his mind, should have failed to recognize the symptoms of tuberculosis. Was this, one wonders, a reason why his meeting with the young Prince in the summer of 1830 achieved so little? Victor Metternich had prolonged his life by seeking the sunshine of Italy, but that was a region where no son of Napoleon could be permitted to reside so long as the peninsula rang with patriotic sentiment. And so he was left to waste away in Vienna. People saw him in 1830 and 1831 at plays and the opera and the ballet, filled with admiration for Fanny Elssler (whom, in private life, he never once met). In February 1832 his health broke completely. They took him to Schönbrunn where, on 22 July, he died in the room in which his father had dictated peace to his grandfather's envoys twenty-three years before. Marie Louise was with him at the end and it was she who distributed the pathetic treasures of his filial devotion. To Metternich was thus bequeathed a wash-stand used by Napoleon on Elba.[36] The Chancellor accepted the gift 'as a token of gratitude'. Was it, perhaps, a final irony from beyond two graves?

The third Princess Metternich

Such a disloyal thought never troubled Melanie, who noted the arrival of the wash-stand with customary pride in her journal. His wife's admiration for Metternich soared higher with every despatch he handed her to read, and there were many. They talked politics at breakfast – 'I am amazed at the extent of my ignorance,' she confessed three weeks after her marriage – and now and again she would follow him into the study of the Chancellery to watch over his shoulder as his pen moved effortlessly across the drafts of endless memoranda.[37] Sometimes she would listen as Clement and Gentz argued. The old man was tiresomely critical of current policies and she often bristled with indignation, particularly as he seemed reluctant to spend his last years writing her husband's *Memoirs*. But on other days their talk would slip amiably enough into reminiscence and she did not doubt that Clement enjoyed Gentz's company: there was even one morning in the summer of 1831 when she had found them blowing soap bubbles together for the benefit of Richard; and when, in the following June, she heard that Gentz had died she grieved for him and for her husband.[38]

In those early years of marriage Melanie was inordinately possessive of Metternich. She graced his receptions, proud of mirroring what was already history, and she enjoyed the social round of the Vienna season – balls 'too lovely for a mere mortal', banquets where she wore diamonds in her hair and Paris gowns embroidered with gold, gala occasions at the Opera where people bowed to her, dropping careful phrases in the intervals and watchfully studying her response. Yet she was not content to remain a decorative escort or hostess. In the Chancellery she would establish herself in an antechamber to Clement's study, interposed between her husband and those who sought to disturb him. At times she would speak imperiously to diplomats and petitioners and she showed to the full that rigid concern for rank and precedence which so often stiffened Habsburg society with petty jealousy. Even her husband seems, at least once, to have been vexed by her arrogance. At the New Year's ball of 1834 the French ambassador had observed to her that her tiara shone like a crown on her head and she had replied, 'And why not? At least it is my own property'. Representatives of the July Monarchy were sensitive over such matters and her remark strained the relations of France and Austria for two months until Metternich, in exasperation, said to the ambassador: 'You must accept my apologies, Monsieur, but it was not I who brought up my wife!'[39]

Such friction within the partnership was rare, although Melanie never acquired Eleonore's instinctive good sense. If her journal is to be trusted, Melanie found greatest delight, not in the public festivities, but in those evenings when Clement was alone with her and would talk of the past: of how his wisdom had stood between the Crown and anarchy; of Napoleon at St Cloud and Fontainebleau and Dresden; and of all – or, in the case of Laura Junot, almost all – that discretion had omitted in the latest volumes of recollections from Paris. 'Everything Clement has to say was of the highest interest and I wish I could write down every one of his words,' she confided to her diary.[40] In her enthusiasm she even began to copy and edit what he had already written about other times, diligently applying herself – though not for long – to the secretarial task which Gentz had declined to undertake. She thus gradually came to identify herself with the legend which her husband was creating of his own progress through the early years of the century. It seems never to have bothered her that most of what he had to say stopped short at 1815, for to both of them the politics of the last decade and a half were as formless as a pattern in limbo. They might almost have been acting out their public lives in an endless epilogue.

Occasionally at Melanie's receptions young diplomats felt time to be standing still and looked on the Chancellor as a man old before his years. After his bout of fever at Lemberg in 1823 he had become a little deaf, although not sufficiently seriously to spoil his 'exquisite delight' in listening to music. His eyes were strained and his face drawn and sunken. He was still elegant and moved with dignity, but the waves of his hair were grey by now and he affected a weariness of voice which, at times, he may well have felt in spirit if not in body. Yet, to outside observers, his private life in the 1830's seemed rejuvenated by what he used to call 'romantic love', a dangerous condition which, though gratifying to Melanie, caused his medical advisers concern. His third family continued to grow.[41] At the end of February 1832 a daughter was born and named after her mother: she was to survive both parents by more than sixty years, outlasting even the Habsburg Monarchy. A boy was born in the spring of 1833, in time for Clement's sixtieth birthday, but he died within two months. A second son, Paul, arrived in October 1834 to be followed by a third son, Lothar, three years later. Throughout the thirty-nine years Metternich held office he always had sons and daughters under fourteen in his family circle. Without the hours spent in the nursery or at parties and picnics the Metternichs' life would have been an intolerable succession of parade occasions, as artificial as a minuet. His contact with the children, together with the scientific curiosity which he had never abandoned, prevented the Chancellor's mind from becoming totally closed to reality.

It must be admitted that, in this respect, Melanie was of little help to him. Her interests were limited, far more so than those of Eleonore or Antoinette. She was deeply religious, although in her spiritual experience it would seem that faith prevailed over charity, and she had an almost terrifying sense of vocation. Unfortunately her consciousness of mission isolated her from most sections of society and thereby created a higher barrier between her husband and the people than he appreciated at the time. A young woman so resolute in her prejudices inevitably aroused resentment in Vienna, particularly among the bourgeoisie whose social pretensions filled her with such ineffable contempt. Who but Princess Melanie von Metternich would have insisted on taking with her when she dined at the home of a prominent banker her own golden set of knives, forks and spoons? And who else would have kept white gloves available on a silver platter for gentlemen who had forgotten such essentials of dress at a reception of learned scholars?[42] Her habits were not always endearing. Critics maintained that her will shaped Clement's policy, but there is no evidence this was the case. She listened to him, she sympathized, she flashed anger with her lightning eyes; but, if at times she ventured to give advice, it was generally so extravagant in form that no person of Metternich's experience attended to it. With her furious temperament and uncompromising tongue she undoubtedly attracted to herself much of the vexation felt towards him and the system he personified. In her journal entries she saw herself often enough as an avenging sword, indignant on his behalf; but her greatest service to him was as a shield, deadening the blows of adversaries at home and beyond the frontiers.

Conflicts with Palmerston; and accord with Tsar Nicholas at Münchengrätz (September 1833)

By the end of 1832 a new name was recorded high on the list of these foreign opponents of her husband. Lord Palmerston was no less exasperating than Canning and far more ubiquitous. In his first two years at the Foreign Office he had clashed with Austrian interests in the Netherlands, Italy and Germany and had sounded discordant notes of liberalism in Greece, Portugal and Spain. Some of his actions seemed to Metternich totally indefensible. It was hard for Austrian pride to accept advice from London on the occupation of Bologna or to recognize the English had any right to excite themselves over reform of the Pope's temporal possessions.[43] But it was intolerable that Palmerston should protest at the six resolutions which the Diet of Frankfurt passed in the summer of 1832 to ban all revolutionary meetings and tighten, yet again, academic discipline within the Confederation. Palmerston's action was rendered even less acceptable by the fact that he justified intervention in German affairs with a reference to Britain's responsibility, as a signatory of the Treaty of Vienna, for saving Germany from the perils of revolution; and Metternich was forced to write a stern answer to the protest demonstrating to his own satisfaction, if not to Palmerston's, that England had no right whatsoever to concern herself with the internal affairs of the Confederation. Drafting such a rebuke was, wrote Melanie, 'a labour of love' for him: but it had little effect on British policy.[44] When, to counter a radical conspiracy, Austrian and Prussian troops occupied Frankfurt in the spring of 1833 Palmerston did, indeed, content himself with informal hints of disapproval; but by the following summer he was claiming a right to protest at their presence in the city and citing the Treaty of Vienna once more, totally unrepentant. It was inconceivable to Metternich how he could persist in so many errors and misconceptions. To attempt collaboration with such a man was constantly vexing. 'In short, Lord Palmerston is wrong about everything,' Metternich wrote at the foot of a despatch to London in February 1833[45]; and in his eyes this fallibility did not lessen with the passage of time.

Yet there was, in reality, a closer affinity of outlook between the two men than either would admit. Both desired peace among the European nations; both thought it could best be preserved through an orderly system of international relations; both treated with respect what Palmerston called 'the principles of the Grand Alliance created at Chaumont'[46]; and both believed in the merits of diplomacy by conference. Each, however, knew the convener of any assembly of ministers or ambassadors had enormous prestige and influence and each wished his own capital city to serve as the centre of the diplomatic system. Palmerston's success in championing Belgian independence around a conference table in London rankled more with Metternich than the actual breach made by the Belgians in the Vienna Settlement. Just as the events of 1830 had challenged Metternich's concepts of order, so Palmerston was challenging his mastery of the diplomatic skills. The new threat, no less than the old, had to be resisted.

It mattered most over the Eastern Question. In the spring of 1832 the powers agreed – significantly in conference in London – on the establishment of a Greek Kingdom; and a dispute which had troubled Europe for over a decade seemed at last to have been settled. But by the end of the year another crisis in the East was already threatening the stability of the continent.[47] Mehemet Ali, Pasha of Egypt, was dissatisfied with his treatment by the Sultan after intervening in Greece; and in the summer of 1832 his son, Ibrahim, began an advance across Syria and through the Taurus Mountains towards Constantinople. He defeated the main Turkish army in December at Konya and five weeks later his Egyptian army had reached the Anatolian town of Kutayha, barely 150 miles from Constantinople itself. The power of the Ottoman Sultans, already weak in Europe, was now crumbling in Asia Minor as well. The possible disintegration of Turkey posed questions for the Foreign Ministers of all the major European states and there seemed little likelihood of their agreeing on a common answer.

It was with reluctance that Metternich turned once more to the Eastern Question. There was nothing in it for Austria to gain, only the prospect of new entanglements. He had always looked unfavourably on suggestions for partitioning the Ottoman lands; and, in the spring of 1833, he told the British ambassador firmly 'that he should consider the day when this system (partition) should be entered upon as the last of the Austrian Empire'.[48] Nor was this the only reason why he disliked the Eastern Question. It was a problem he could not control, slipping from his hands when he thought he was its master. He therefore responded to the new emergency in the East with a double proposal to the French and British: a multi-lateral guarantee, with which he was sure the Russians would associate themselves, safeguarding the Sultan against his rebellious Egyptian vassal; and the acceptance of Vienna as a centre for joint negotiations over the Eastern Question. The French, who had a certain sympathy with Mehemet Ali, were evasive; and the British uncooperative. For Palmerston, too, favoured a conference: it should, he felt, meet in London; but if, for some incomprehensible reason, London was not acceptable to other governments then he recommended a convention which might be signed in Constantinople itself. Vienna was clearly over the edge of Palmerston's map. Inwardly he remained convinced Metternich was conjuring up some ingenious piece of trickery, probably in collaboration with the Tsar, and when he discovered that Talleyrand (now French ambassador in London) also thought highly of a possible meeting in Vienna, Palmerston retreated behind his insular shell and declined a conference anywhere outside England. Metternich was exasperated with such manoeuvres and by the midsummer of 1833 all attempts to bring Austria and Britain together in a common policy had deteriorated into charges and counter-charges of bad faith.[49]

These exchanges between Vienna and London were time absorbing but essentially peripheral. What really mattered to Metternich was the attitude of Tsar Nicholas I in St Petersburg. The *chiffon de Carlsbad* had marked the beginning of better relations between Austria and Russia. The Austrians had shown caution throughout the Polish Revolt of 1830–1: they had not encouraged the Polish rebels, although some volunteers had slipped across the frontier from Galicia and enlisted in the Polish Army; and when refugees had fled into Galicia as the revolt collapsed, the Austrians had given them sanctuary but, very properly, returned their arms to Russia.[50] Metternich believed he had thus placed himself in Russia's debt, and as a further gesture he encouraged the Emperor to remove Prince Lobkowitz from his post as Governor and entrust effective control of the Poles in Galicia to an ominously named bureaucrat of stern inclination, Baron Krieg. Nicholas was certainly anxious to co-operate with the Austrians (and, for that matter, with the Prussians) over Polish affairs but he was not conscious of any sense of gratitude over events in Galicia. There is no reason why he should have been, for it was never to Metternich's own interest to show sympathy with the Polish firebrands.

Yet Metternich seems to have convinced himself, when the Eastern Crisis flared up once more at the end of 1832, that he was in the Tsar's confidence. He always spoke with genuine conviction of Russian moderation in his conversations with the British ambassador.[51] But apart from letting the Austrians know that Russian policy was now based on preservation of the Ottoman Empire rather than on partition, Nicholas kept his intentions well hidden from Austrian eyes. When Constantinople seemed threatened by Ibrahim's army in Anatolia the Sultan appealed to Nicholas for military assistance, and Russian warships and transports entered the Bosphorus. The presence of a Russian force encouraged Ibrahim to accept a compromise settlement which extended Mehemet Ali's dominions to the Euphrates and the foothills of the Taurus range. The Sultan's throne was thus saved; but the Russians sought a price for their intervention and until they obtained it fourteen thousand Russian soldiers were encamped on the Asiatic shores of the Bosphorus. On 9 July 1833 Sultan Mahmud II accepted the Treaty of Unkiar-Skelessi, a defensive alliance between Russia and Turkey valid for eight years and secretly pledging the Turks to close the Dardanelles to foreign warships if Russia were at war. The terms of the Treaty were not especially remarkable; what staggered Europe was the consciousness that Russia now wielded more authority and influence in the Turkish capital than ever before.

Metternich was surprised by Unkiar-Skelessi and, as the first reports to reach Vienna came from a French source, he refused to credit them.[52] He had already planned to leave the capital for Bohemia in the middle of July, taking Melanie on her first visit to Königswart and subsequently crossing Bohemia to Teplitz, where a meeting had been arranged between the Austrian and Prussian rulers for the second week in August. Since he saw no reason to change his plans, he set out from Vienna on 17 July. He was therefore absent from the capital, and comparatively inaccessible to foreign diplomats, when the existence of the Treaty was confirmed and its secret clauses revealed early in August. The ambassadors hurried to Teplitz, only to find the Chancellor wrapt in mystery. For on 18 August he had received news from St Petersburg that the Tsar was himself prepared to come to Bohemia and meet his brother sovereigns.[53] Metternich had been pressing for such a conference since the summer of 1831, but coming as it did so soon after Unkiar-Skelessi and his departure from Vienna, the meeting with the Tsar and his ministers inevitably aroused mistrust in Paris and in London.[54]

For the moment, however, Metternich cared little what they thought of him in the Western capitals. He was elated by the prospect of another Troppau, with Russians and Prussians once more in attendance on his word. There had been no meeting between an Emperor of Austria and a Tsar of Russia for ten years, and it was six years since Metternich and Frederick William of Prussia had had the opportunity to discuss German affairs. Now the Chancellor hoped 'the three Continental courts' would re-capture the spirit of that sacred abstraction which he always termed 'the Alliance'. He was even prepared on this occasion to welcome a formal agreement on paper, to complement the understanding reached by Nicholas with the Sultan.

All went well at Teplitz.[55] Frederick William III agreed with Metternich's remarks on the need to combat revolution in Germany, much as he had done in their talks at the same spa fourteen years before. But Metternich had two disappointments. He found Ancillon, the Prussian Foreign Minister, less accommodating than his King; and he learnt that Frederick William would be unable to meet the Tsar in Bohemia since the Russian visit coincided with military reviews in Berlin and Magdeburg and it was inconceivable that the head of the House of Hohenzollern should miss a couple of grand parades for a mere conference. He was, however, prepared to send the Crown Prince to the meeting and his absence did not greatly trouble Metternich, who was inclined too readily to assume a political superiority over the Prussian government which economic realities were fast denying. For though he could spot revolutionary conspiracies with the eyes of a lynx, Metternich remained strangely myopic towards customs unions. Prussia in 1833 was still for him the old Junker state of Blucher and Hardenberg: but not for much longer.

Emperor and Tsar met at last on 10 September at Münchengrätz (Mnichovo Hradiště), some forty-five miles north-east of Prague. It was, thought poor Melanie, 'a small and filthy town' and there was little to do. The two monarchs and the Crown Prince of Prussia hunted stags while Metternich held long discussions with Nesselrode and with the Russian police chief, General Benckendorff.* There were troops to be inspected and Nicholas was allowed to put a regiment of Hungarian Hussars through its paces. They played billiards and whist, attended innumerable banquets, and watched an indifferent company of actors perform *The Servant of Two Masters* (an interesting choice of play, pre-

---

* General Benckendorff (1783–1844) was a kindly, amiable and absent-minded man totally different in character from the traditional Chief of Police in an autocratic state. He had known Metternich in 1807–8 when he was attached to the Russian embassy in Paris. He was Dorothea Lieven's brother and appears to have sent to his sister an account of the Metternichs at Münchengrätz which amused her but, although there was an intermittent exchange of letters between the Austrian Chancellor and Benckendorff from 1833 until 1842, no mention was made of Princess Lieven or her activities. (See the articles by J. S. Squire on Metternich and Benckendorff in the *Slavonic Review* for 1967, cited in the bibliography.)

sumably fortuitous). All this dragged on for ten days and in the interludes between these pursuits the Tsar and Metternich talked.[56]

The Chancellor was well content. Nicholas, who had never met him before, had been primed by Nesselrode and appears to have oiled his vanity with ironic flattery, which he accepted at its face value. Clement informed Melanie that the Tsar's first words to him had been: 'I am come to place myself under the command of my chief.'[57] This remark is so out of character it is tempting to assume either Metternich's hearing was playing tricks on him or he was lying; but it is possible the Tsar's heavily sardonic sense of humour prompted him to make some such salutation. He certainly had no intention of accepting Metternich's advice, as his brother had done at Aix and Troppau. A Russian source records a different exchange of words. Metternich said, 'Sire, I beg you not to think that I will finesse with you'; and the Tsar answered, 'Prince, I know you'. Significantly Nicholas wrote back to the Tsarina, 'Every time I come near to him, I pray God to preserve me from the Devil.'[58] Their discussions did, however, make a little progress; but, since Münchengrätz was not a conference with a prepared agenda, they retained a superficial informality. 'Prince Metternich, what do you think of the Turk?', asked Nicholas at one moment. 'Is he not a sick man?' And the Chancellor, too fly to give an answer to a leading question, retorted, 'Is Your Majesty addressing the doctor or the heir?'[59] By the end of the week Nicholas, who had none of the extravagant moods of Alexander, was beginning to thaw. Metternich, he conceded in a letter to his wife, 'is a chatterer, but he can be amusing'.[60]

Yet there was far more to the Münchengrätz meeting than the mere bantering of diplomatic repartee. From the conference emerged three agreements which together formed the basis of a conservative league and bound the courts of Vienna, St Petersburg and Berlin for another twenty years. A convention signed at Münchengrätz on 18 September pledged the Austrians and Russians to support the existing structure of the Ottoman Empire and to act in common if partition of Turkey appeared imminent. On the following day a second convention included mutual guarantees of their Polish possessions and a promise of assistance to each other if there should be another rebellion in Poland. And finally agreement was reached on a Triple Declaration (signed a month later in Berlin) by which the governments of Austria, Prussia and Russia asserted their willingness to aid any sovereign who appealed for help in combating insurgent liberalism. At the same time Tsar Nicholas gave a verbal assurance he would support Archduke Ferdinand should difficulties arise within the Habsburg Monarchy over his succession; and arrangements were made for an exchange of intelligence reports on terrorism between Metternich and Benckendorff.[61]

It is likely the two conventions on Turkey and Poland were originally

drafted by the Russians and only the Triple Declaration, with its echoes
of the Troppau Protocol, was the work of Metternich. But he returned
to Vienna at the end of September satisfied with the outcome of the
meeting. The sole concession he had made was over the Poles and, since
radicals in London and Paris were now vigorously championing Polish
independence, Metternich was prepared to take a far firmer line against
them than in earlier years. He was confident he had re-established
monarchical solidarity in Central and Eastern Europe after the challenge of 1830–1 and the divergencies which marred the end of Tsar
Alexander's reign. Metternich, however, genuinely regretted that
Nicholas insisted on keeping secret the precise nature of the agreements: he was prevented from explaining to Palmerston why he was
convinced Russia had no immediate designs on Turkish territory.[62]
The secrecy shrouding Münchengrätz threw shadows of suspicion
among the British and French and the continent was divided more
sharply than ever before into a conservative and a liberal camp. In
April 1834 this division was emphasized still further by the conclusion of
a Quadruple Alliance between Britain, France, Spain and Portugal.
Although its specific purpose was to safeguard constitutional rule
in the Iberian peninsula, the Alliance was intended by its creator,
Palmerston, to serve as 'a powerful counter-poise' to the Münchengrätz combination.[63]

'I should like to see Metternich's face when he reads our treaty,'
wrote Palmerston to his brother with impish irreverence on the day
before the Alliance was formally concluded.[64] Unfortunately no diarist
was at hand to record the Chancellor's visual response to the news, but
his written comments are evocative in themselves: Palmerston, he
complained, had allied himself not merely with the Orleanists in Paris
but with 'revolution incarnate in its most dangerous form' (alias the
Spanish liberal movement); and he consoled himself with the prediction that the Quadruple Alliance would bring 'bitter fruit' to its
creator.[65] His indignation was not a simple jealous reaction to Palmerston's initiative, as the British thought. He was genuinely afraid that,
under French influence, Naples might be drawn into the new combination and the Italian Question would thus once more be raised in an
acute form. Nor was this his only fear. The English press and the
House of Commons seemed to have abandoned all restraint in attacking
the policies of the Tsar; and he read, with considerable misgiving,
reports of exercises by British warships off the entrance to the Dardanelles. With Palmerston apparently showing greater irresponsibility than
even Canning, it looked to Metternich as if Europe was drifting into
war.

There were two ways of meeting the crisis: he might seek an understanding with the Quadruple Alliance; or he could intrigue against

Rioting at the western entrance to
Vienna, March 1848

Emperor Francis Joseph as a
young man

Metternich in old age (from a contemporary photograph)

A caricature of 1848: 'A hand of whist' – Metternich (right); Crown Prince of Prussia (centre); Louis Philippe of France (left) while away their time in exile in London

A caricature of 1849.
Metternich, isolate in exile, surveys the chaos following his downfall

Rudolf von Alt's water-colour of Metternich's family in his new palace
on the Rennweg, Vienna in 1852 (see p. 333)

View of Vienna in the late 1850s showing (on extreme left) the Chancellery (in centre)
the Hofburg and (on extreme right) the Karlskirche

Palmerston in England and force him out of office. Metternich tried both methods. On 17 July he sent a long despatch to Hummelauer, the Austrian *chargé d'affaires* in London, authorizing him to propose a Four-Power Pact by which Britain and France would join Russia and Austria in saving the peace of Europe with a series of territorial guarantees.[66] The English showed little interest. Hummelauer spent two hours with Palmerston on 29 July vainly seeking to convince him of Metternich's sincerity. Three days later he was received by the new Prime Minister, Lord Melbourne, who heard Hummelauer with customary sympathy and bland incomprehension. By the middle of August Hummelauer had to admit defeat to Metternich who, not unreasonably, felt grieved with Palmerston for having received his overture in such a cavalier fashion. He made further approaches in the autumn but was again rebuffed.[67] The alternative was to use Hummelauer to convince Melbourne it was only Palmerston who prevented Austria and Britain from jointly restraining Russia in a close understanding. Hummelauer duly saw Melbourne again at the end of September and the Prime Minister listened politely to the Austrian complaints.[68] He did not always agree with Palmerston's manners or methods, but the internal strains within his cabinet were far too tense for him to risk a conflict with a minister so popular in the country.

Palmerston knew of Metternich's manoeuvres and was confident of overcoming them. The contest, however, never began in earnest. On 15 November 1834, King William IV, believing the Whig Government was falling apart, dismissed Melbourne and invited Wellington and Peel to form an administration, pending an election. There is no evidence the King was aware of continental intrigues against Palmerston, nor would he – unlike his brother, George IV – have participated in a plot of this kind. But by his sudden action King William succeeded in achieving more than Metternich had hoped. Palmerston was in eclipse and in Vienna pious hopes were held out for a new Tory ministry.

The incident had a curious epilogue. On 16 November Palmerston sent a cheerful valedictory to Fox-Strangeways, in the embassy at Vienna: 'We are out', he wrote, 'Tell this immediately to Metternich, it will gladden his heart and be the most agreeable thing he has ever heard from me.' But when the message was given to him, Metternich was not amused. He treated Fox-Strangeways to a sententious lecture on the dignity of diplomatic exchanges, and he wrote an account of the whole affair to Hummelauer with the comment that 'it was a new manifestation of all that was odious and inexplicable in the mind and character of the late first Secretary of State.'[69]

In the following spring the Whigs returned to office; and Palmerston was back once more at the Foreign Office. By then the war clouds in the East had dispersed and the Quadruple Alliance was beginning to disintegrate; but it is small wonder that Metternich found the English parliamentary system unattractive. A political calendar which alternated five months of Tory rule with four years of Palmerston stood in clear need of revision.

MONARCHY WITHOUT A MONARCH

Death of the Emperor Francis (March 1835)

In the autumn of 1834 Metternich completed a quarter of a century as principal minister to the Emperor Francis. It was a partnership of rare cordiality and understanding. As early as 1818 the Prince had boasted confidently to Dorothea Lieven, 'Whatever I want is always what he wishes to do: he is convinced of this,'[1] and throughout the following decade their mutual trust remained unimpaired. The two men worked together week after week and the Chancellor often spent an hour or more a day discussing with his sovereign affairs of state or matters of lesser moment, for both men enjoyed trivialities. Francis retained Metternich in the Ballhausplatz because he could not believe there was anyone else in the Empire so gifted with diplomatic perspicacity; and Metternich consolidated his position by not pressing the Emperor hard over topics on which he held strong opinions, such as Hungary or reform in the Italian states. For, like most of the later Habsburgs, Francis was conscientious but lacking in imagination. He could not stretch his mind sufficiently to envisage the consequences of any reform, even the modest improvements in central government of the Empire which Metternich tentatively suggested from time to time. As Francis grew older, his hostility to innovation was intensified. 'I want no change', he told one of the court officials in June 1831. 'This is no time for reforms.'[2] And when, five months later, there was talk of improving the conditions of peasant tenure in Bohemia, he dismissed the subject almost querulously: 'No! No! Leave it well alone!' he declared.[3] It might almost have been an epitaph on his reign.

Yet Francis was sensible enough to realize he could no longer keep every decision over policy in his own hands. In 1826 his health had given way and, though he recovered by the end of the year, he seemed frail and prematurely old. He was sixty-two in 1830 and he began, at last, to share some of his responsibilities, although he could never imagine a government in Vienna in which the Emperor did not have the final word. In foreign affairs he relied, as for so long, on Metternich; but over financial matters and over domestic policy in general he tended to turn increasingly to a great Bohemian landowner, Count Francis Kolowrat-Liebsteinsky, who had first come from Prague to Vienna as a State Councillor at the time of the Emperor's illness. Kolowrat's rise was rapid; for within a year he was acting as supreme administrative controller of finance and by the summer of 1830 he had joined Metternich and the head of the Treasury (Count Nadasdy) in the newly-established 'Permanent Inner Conference', under the presidency of the Emperor. This four-man committee was the nearest Austria came to cabinet government in the reign of Francis, but it did not in any way curtail the monarch's prerogative.

Francis had considerable respect for Kolowrat's abilities, especially when in 1831 his budget provided for a small surplus of revenue instead of the customary deficit. Metternich, on the other hand, disliked Kolowrat personally, railed at the economies he imposed upon military expenditure, and distrusted his ambition.[4] He seemed to be another Wallis, who had indeed been his predecessor as principal administrative official in Prague; but Kolowrat had a ruthless quality which Wallis never possessed and he had a wider following, for he did not mind posing as a liberal to thwart Metternich or as a champion of Slav consciousness in order to curb Magyar patriotism. Kolowrat is not a sympathetic figure: he was fractious and temperamental, retiring in dudgeon to his estates when he could not get his own way and constantly threatening to resign – a gesture which never failed to influence Francis, who hated the thought of having to find a successor. Yet Kolowrat despised the court and the administration; he confessed as much to Karl von Kübeck, one of the chief civil servants in the Department of Finance, on 11 January 1833. 'Believe me,' Kübeck reports Kolowrat as having said,[5] 'anyone who is forced to serve in the immediate circle of the Emperor must become either a philosopher or an intriguer or a grazing beast (*ein Vieh*) in order to endure it.' Francis, perhaps fortunately, does not seem to have known what Kolowrat thought of life at the centre of affairs. At the time when he made this remark all the machinery of government passed through his hands, except for the control of foreign policy and strategic decisions.

The ascendancy of such an influential figure would have been a matter of concern to Metternich at any point in his career; but it had particular significance in the early 1830's because of uncertainty over the future character of the Monarchy itself. Francis and Metternich had long been agreed that respect should be paid to the principle of legitimacy. For this reason they had emphasized the rights of Archduke Ferdinand both at his coronation as King of Hungary in 1830 and in the conversations with Tsar Nicholas at Münchengrätz three years later. But everyone at court dreaded the prospect of an Emperor who was a simpleton. Who would be the real ruler in Vienna? Would Ferdinand's uncles, the Archdukes who had lost the fight with Metternich in his early years in the Ballhausplatz, at last revenge themselves on the Chancellor? It was reasonable to suppose that he would not long survive his patron and protector, especially now there was a minister whom the dissidents might follow. Kübeck, who had to work closely with Kolowrat from day to day, had few illusions about the future: the pages of his journal for 1834 acknowledge each anniversary in the life of Francis with valedictory foreboding; and on 6 October he predicted anarchy when the Emperor died.[6] Though Metternich might respect the natural order of succession, Kübeck and many of his colleagues had doubts over the wisdom of such a course. And yet, if Ferdinand's claims were ignored, who would take his place? His younger brother, Archduke Francis Charles, was hardly any more intelligent than Ferdinand and there was widespread distrust of his ambitious wife, Sophie of Bavaria. Ferdinand had in 1831 married Princess Maria Anna of Savoy but it was soon generally known at court that he was incapable of becoming a father. The next in line of succession after Francis Charles was therefore the child whom Archduchess Sophie had borne in August 1830, Francis Joseph; but were he to follow his grandfather on the throne there would have to be a long period of regency, and such a solution was hardly more attractive than the accession of Ferdinand himself. Not surprisingly Melanie Metternich's journal, like Kübeck's, contains fervent entreaties for preservation of the Emperor's good health.[7]

The year 1835 opened with several weeks of bitterly cold weather in Vienna.[8] A cutting north wind swept down on the city from the Marchfield. Francis remained in the Hofburg deep in work: there was trouble with the Transylvanian Diet and long discussions over proposed reductions in the size of the standing army, an economy dear to Kolowrat's heart. On the evening of Monday, 23 February, the Emperor went to the *Burgtheater*. Next day he developed a feverish chill and cancelled his engagements. By Wednesday morning his illness was diagnosed as pneumonia and his faithful Viennese were gripped with anxiety. Metternich, Kolowrat, Nadasdy and Sedlnitzky were in almost continuous conference by the end of the week. Crowds waited silently outside the Hofburg or flocked to the cathedral to pray for his recovery. Austrian securities fell on the foreign market but were bolstered up by the Rothschilds, whom Metternich had assured that there would be no drastic changes in government or policy. On Saturday people began to take heart: reports said the Emperor was rallying; and it was noticed that the lucky number in the State Lottery that weekend combined the digits twelve with forty-three and sixty-

seven with eighteen.[9] Francis had been born on the 12th of the month
and was in his forty-third year on the throne: he had just celebrated his
sixty-seventh birthday, and the battle of Leipzig, the outstanding
victory of his reign, had been won on 18 October. These were slender
portents on which to rest hopes, but the superstitious were encouraged
and on Monday morning the good news was even conveyed to the
ailing Emperor, for one of the cooks in the palace had won a substantial sum of money in the draw. Yet death could not be mocked by
such devices, even in a city which traditionally refused to take despair
seriously. He became feverish again on Monday evening; and in the
small hours of Tuesday, 2 March 1835, the reign of Francis came at last
silently to its close.

Emperor Ferdinand

Metternich was deeply moved by the Emperor's death, even though it
had been anticipated for so many months. He had lost, so he told Marie
Louise, someone who was to him 'as a father, a master and a friend'.[10]
But he was too active to mourn for long. Ten days after the change of
Emperors, he sent a circular letter of reassurance to the ambassadors
in the various European capitals: 'Never, at any time or in any country,
was the transition from one reign to the next accomplished with less
commotion,' he asserted. 'Austria is today still the same as yesterday
and the same as she will always be.'[11] Such confidence was, however,
far too emphatic to be true. As soon as Francis was dead, there was a
momentary fit of confusion, much as Kübeck had predicted, and the
court appears even to have hesitated over the succession. But not for
long. Metternich had prepared for the crisis with all the thoroughness
with which he used to await the opening of an international conference.
As long ago as 1832 he had induced Gentz to draft a final political
testament which the Emperor would bequeath to his heir. When
Francis lay dying, the original document was revised and presented for
signature on Saturday, 28 February, not by the Chancellor – on whom
Kolowrat kept a suspicious eye – but by the Emperor's confessor,
Bishop Wagner. Within a few hours of Francis's death, Metternich
saw to it that this document was made known to the surviving
members of the Permanent Inner Conference, together with a second
testament on ecclesiastical matters which was drafted by the Bishop
himself.[12]

The dead Emperor's political guidance to his son and heir left
nothing to doubt. Ferdinand was enjoined 'not to alter the basic
structure of the State', to keep concord within the Imperial family and
to seek advice 'from my brother, the Archduke Ludwig'. The final
paragraph was even more explicit: 'Bestow on Prince Metternich, my

most faithful servant and friend, the confidence which I have shown him over so many years. Do not take any decision concerning public affairs or people without hearing him. In return I beg him to render to you the sincere and faithful devotion which he has always displayed towards me.' There was no mention of Kolowrat or any other minister, nor indeed of Francis's three ablest brothers, Archduke Charles, Archduke John and Archduke Palatine Joseph. It was difficult for any committee to challenge such testimony: Metternich's ingenuity had prepared a death-bed palace counter-revolution in order to ensure that everything would 'go on as before'.

At first his intrigue appeared entirely successful. Poor Ferdinand was accepted as Emperor; the Viennese crowds even managed to show a warm affection for 'dotty Ferdy' ('*Nandl der Trottel*'). The court officials remained gloomy: 'We now have an absolute Monarchy without a monarch,' sighed Kübeck after Ferdinand's first ceremonial audience on 14 March.[13] Archduke Ludwig, whom Francis had tended to consult from time to time over the preceding five years, was happy to remain a spectator of political affairs, contentedly repeating at the conference table his sole maxim of government, 'To let it rest is the best way of dealing with it'. Metternich was left with a free hand in foreign affairs while Kolowrat continued to head the financial administration. The struggle for power was by no means over, but for the moment Kolowrat preferred to build up his reputation among those who despaired of Metternich's immutability rather than challenge the Chancellor openly.

Meanwhile Metternich did all he could to keep the machinery of government running down well-worn grooves. In September he set off for another Imperial and royal frolic at Teplitz.[14] Tsar Nicholas and King Frederick William III were there with a numerous retinue, but it was a sad occasion. General Benckendorff noted, at the time, that Ferdinand seemed 'a poor weak creature, feeble in body and mind, a ghost of a monarch'; and Nicholas was not impressed by the man whom he had pledged himself at Münchengrätz to support. Metternich did his best to stage-manage the monarchical reunion. There was a monument to unveil at Külm, to remind the old Allies of the bonds of 1813; there were parades and celebrations; there was even a grand entry into Prague. The Chancellor was gracious to the Tsarina, whom he had known as a child of seven in Berlin, for she was the daughter of Frederick William and Queen Louise; and he did his best to please the Russians by spoiling the representative of the next generation, the Grand Duchess Olga, aged thirteen. But Emperor Ferdinand was overwhelmed by it all. He could not remember who all his guests were: life would have been far simpler had his brother, Archduke Francis Charles, or Metternich been the host. Ferdinand was content for the Archduke to represent him at the next Teplitz reunion.

Politically the meeting of 1835 emphasized Metternich's dependence on the Tsar. In earlier years the Chancellor had excited Tsar Alexander's mind with bogeys from conspiratorial Paris: now Alexander's brother re-paid Metternich in kind, with tales of Polish plots, not merely in Paris where the Polish Democratic Society had its headquarters, but in Cracow, the Free City created by the Treaty of Vienna in 1815 and serving as a nerve centre for Austrian Galicia and for the Russian puppet 'Congress Kingdom' of Poland.[15] It was agreed that external pressure should be applied to Cracow by the Russians and Austrians so as to curb the radical agitation and if the authorities in the city proved unable to restrain the radicals, token military forces from Russia, Prussia and Austria would enter Cracow to maintain order. Nicholas would willingly have erased the Free City from the political map entirely, and he had little patience with Metternich's diplomatic subtleties, but the Austrian remained cautious. He was reluctant to destroy any creation of the 1815 settlement for fear of its effects on liberal revisionist sentiment in France and Britain. In 1836 troops from the Three Powers did, indeed, enter Cracow and remained in occupation for five years, but technically there was as yet no infringement of the city's independent status. Throughout that period the Russian and Austrian intelligence services worked closely together and a representative of Benckendorff's police department was seconded to Vienna in order to co-ordinate counter-revolutionary activity. The Austrians were convinced that Cracow and Galicia were danger spots, and they were taking no chances with the Poles. Radical Polish unrest always facilitated Austro-Russian collaboration.

From Prague in October 1835 Metternich informed the Austrian ambassador in Paris that the understanding reached during the Teplitz meetings was more comprehensive and amicable than at any such previous encounters.[16] This may well have been the case, for there was nothing at the moment in Europe which divided the three autocratic powers. They shared a common dislike of Palmerston – 'that perfidious pig of a man', as Nicholas was to call him – and a common suspicion that Louis Philippe's bourgeois monarchy might soon give way to something far more dangerous to the stability of Europe. They were willing to lend verbal support to the Carlists in Spain, just as Palmerston was willing to champion 'constitutionalism' and the rights of the Poles in his speeches in the House of Commons. The continent remained ideologically partitioned, but not dangerously so. With the Eastern Question quiescent, Europe was outwardly calmer than for several generations. There was a minor storm early in 1836 when an English radical journalist published secret despatches written by Pozzo di Borgo seven years previously in which he roundly criticized

Metternich and Wellington,* but the Chancellor's irascible response was intended to discredit his old enemy, Pozzo, rather than to ruffle the waters of diplomacy; and in this he succeeded.[17]

Similar flashes of indignation lit the European scene from time to time over the following three years. Palmerston could always be counted on to resent Metternich's unsolicited advice over Spain, while the Austrians and Russians objected to British protests at the military occupation of Cracow. There was a longer angry exchange between Britain and Russia in the winter of 1836–7 concerning the freedom of movement for merchant vessels in the Black Sea, a question over which Metternich stepped forward as mediator only to be rebuffed by the Tsar and Nesselrode and scorned by Palmerston and Melbourne.[18] Yet, despite such moments of excitement, these years provided an interlude of comparative calm in Great Power politics. Much of the heat went out of international relations; and when in 1839 trouble again arose between the Sultan and Mehemet Ali, there was markedly less tension and mistrust between the Eastern and Western 'camps' than in the crisis of 1833–4.

Italy, Germany and Hungary in the late 1830s

It was a quiet period, too, for other problems. Metternich remained well-informed on Italy: but he considered conditions in the peninsula better than a few years earlier. The *Carbonari* and its offshoots were discredited by the events of 1830–1; they had been replaced by the 'Young Italy' movement of Giuseppe Mazzini, a secret society which sought to educate the youth of the peninsula into a high sense of moral and political duty rather than permit them to undertake isolated acts of terrorism. In 1834 the government of Charles Albert, who despite his earlier backsliding had come to the Piedmontese throne in 1831, struck at Mazzini's movement and dealt it a severe blow. Many people believed that Young Italy would never recover: but not Metternich. He was convinced that Mazzini, whose character he well understood, would reorganize the movement and make it a dangerous force again; but he was well pleased with Charles Albert's vigilance and he saw no immediate threat to Austrian control of the peninsula, apart from French flag-waving in Ancona and the persistent failure of the Papacy to improve administration in the states of the Church or to ensure that its

* Pozzo di Borgo was transferred from the Paris Embassy to London early in 1835. The documents came from Polish circles in Paris, and Wellington suspected that in the first place they were provided by 'a certain lady, not fat but fair and more than forty, who had a good deal of influence in the Russian Embassy'. This would appear to be a thinly veiled description of Dorothea Lieven, but it is only fair to point out that the Princess's reputation frequently led her to be blamed for any mischief-making activity involving her former admirers. (For the whole incident, see Webster, *Foreign Policy of Palmerston*, vol. II, p. 559.)

officials fulfilled reforms already announced in Rome. Milan was prosperous, the trade of Venice improving; and in 1838 the coronation of Ferdinand with the Iron Crown of Lombardy provided an opportunity to grant some of the patriot conspirators an amnesty. In twenty years, Metternich commented smugly, he had seen Italian sentiment towards the Habsburgs turn from black to grey and now to white.[19]

Metternich also believed he had succeeded in re-asserting the sovereignty of the princes within the German Confederation and in curbing the liberal enthusiasm of 1830–1. In June 1832 a new series of Six Articles was enacted by the Federal Diet in Frankfurt which re-affirmed the Carlsbad Decrees and established the principle that state laws should not run counter to the spirit of federal legislation. A ministerial conference in Vienna, which dragged on through the first half of 1834, confirmed supremacy of the princes over parliamentary institutions and provided for the establishment of a Federal Court to adjudicate between harassed governments within the Confederation and any popular assembly which sought to defy the traditional system.[20] For several years after the Vienna Conference, the political machinery seemed to work well and gave Metternich little trouble. Yet even before the ministers came to Vienna, he had at last become aware of the *Zollverein*, and had drawn up a memorandum for Emperor Francis on the dangers for Austria of a Prussian-dominated Customs Union. On several occasions between 1834 and 1841 Metternich sought to moderate Austrian tariffs in the hope of gaining admission the the *Zollverein* and thereby counter-acting the power of Prussia. Economic matters were, however, technically outside his sphere of responsibility and he was not inclined to press for acceptance of a policy which he did not entirely understand.[21] It is hard to escape the conclusion that he was only conscious of the new forces in Germany when he was actually travelling within the northern states of the Confederation. Reports reaching his desk in the Vienna Chancellery were still concerned with university unrest and censorship, not with the intangibles of economic change.

Inevitably, the affairs of Hungary took up much of his time. He was always willing to listen to the Hungarian aristocrats among Melanie's family and friends. Many of them were prejudiced in favour of the old order but there were others who had caught the enthusiasm of Széchenyi, and 'Stefferl' himself was still received socially in circles which had little sympathy with his ideals. To Metternich, Széchenyi remained an enigma. When in March 1835 Széchenyi brought a dredging machine from England to clear the bed of the Danube east of Vienna, Metternich and his wife, most members of the court in residence, and Kolowrat (who had ministerial responsibility for importing such equipment) all took a Sunday afternoon promenade in the Prater to witness a demonstration of 'the ingenious instrument', and Melanie thought the social event worthy of record in her journal.[22] The Chancellor realized that Széchenyi's schemes for improved navigation on the Danube would bring commercial benefit to the whole Empire and he was not unsympathetic to Széchenyi's principal campaign in these years, a proposal for a permanent toll-bridge to link Buda (Ofen) and Pest, joined as yet only by a pontoon dismantled each winter.[23] But Metternich was suspicious of the political undertones which accompanied each of Széchenyi's ideas; for was not even the bridge intended as a weapon against feudalism, since it declined to provide exemption for the nobility from paying a toll on crossing from one bank of the Danube to the other? This was a revolutionary notion: exemption from taxation was a cherished privilege, almost as sacrosanct as the Hungarian Constitution itself. Already the Diet of 1832 was showing a more radical spirit than its predecessors, and sentiments were expressed in Pressburg which would never have been tolerated at Frankfurt. Where would it end?

Széchenyi knew that the younger generation of Magyars lacked political caution and, as early as 1835, he feared disaster. Eight weeks after the death of Emperor Francis he offered Metternich to act as 'mediator between the Austrian Government and Hungary . . . playing the role of a go-between . . . in an extremely independent position'.[24] Neither Metternich nor the Archduke Palatine Joseph saw any need to accept his services: they ascribed his offer to vanity and ambition. There was a further exchange of views between the Chancellor and Széchenyi at the end of January 1836; they talked, not only of the bridge project and other commercial enterprises, but about the political clubs in Hungary, now beginning to swing towards the radical nationalism of a new popular idol, Lajos Kossuth. Once again Széchenyi undertook to seek formation of a centre group, more progressive than the conservative supporters of the Crown but capable of holding in check the radical opposition. All he asked from Metternich was the administration's support for his paternalistic reforms. Yet still Metternich remained unresponsive. He sensed a growing risk of unrest in the Kingdom, and he preferred reinsurance from outside to collaboration with a man who still had considerable following in the country. In May 1837 Metternich obtained from Tsar Nicholas a written pledge that 'at all costs Austria could count on Russia' to intervene should the social order be menaced by a Hungarian revolt.[25] The Chancellor's hesitant attitude to the Hungarian Problem in the early years of Ferdinand's reign is a sad commentary on his declining powers of political prescience.

Yet did he still possess the influence over Hungary which he had enjoyed while Francis was alive? Kolowrat's following was growing rapidly since his control of administrative appointments within the frontiers of the Empire gave him extensive rights of patronage. For several years Kolowrat had wished to oust the head of the Hungarian

Chancery, but he was an old friend of Emperor Francis and it was not until May 1836 that Kolowrat at last secured his dismissal.[26] In his place, Kolowrat nominated Count Fidel Palffy: he did not speak the Magyar language; he did not understand the depth of Hungarian national sentiment; but he had the inestimable good fortune to be married to Kolowrat's daughter. From 1836 until the end of 1838 Palffy sought to enforce in Hungary a clumsy policy of repression. He opposed every mercantile and commercial project initiated by Széchenyi, and he raised the prestige of Kossuth by casting him into prison. Even the Hungarian aristocrats in Melanie Metternich's circle were critical of Palffy, and by implication of Kolowrat as well. And since Kolowrat was a patron of the Czechs and Croats, his standing among most Hungarians fell steadily throughout the fifty-five months of Palffy's tenure of office. By 1839 Metternich seems to have assumed responsibility for the internal affairs of Hungary once again; but by then time was running out.

Elsewhere Kolowrat held his ground against Metternich. Disputes over the size of the standing army, which had begun in the last years of Francis, continued around the conference table. The Chancellor was able to rely on support from the Adjutant-General, Count Karl Clam-Martinitz, and from his old colleague of the 1813 campaign, General Radetzky, now Commander-in-Chief in northern Italy; but he offended the most influential and respected member of the military circle, Archduke Charles, by rejecting a proposal from the Archduke that, because of the incapacities of his nephew Ferdinand, he should himself be made generalissimo of the armed forces. Year after year Metternich was defeated by Kolowrat on the size of the army budget. The strength and equipment of the troops remained below standard at the very time when the Prussian General, Radowitz, was increasing his country's control of federal fortresses within Germany. Kolowrat also successfully blocked attempts by Metternich to improve relations with the Papacy through a Concordat, although concessions were granted to the Jesuits, whom Metternich – and, even more, the pious Melanie – regarded as valuable intellectual allies against presumptuous doctrines of subversion.[27]

Metternich's conflict with Kolowrat and Archduke John (1836)

There was a brief period, in the autumn of 1836, when it seemed as if Metternich might eliminate Kolowrat and secure control of every activity of government. Metternich was anxious to cut tariffs as a step towards reconciling the Austrian commercial policy with the *Zollverein* and, as a first gesture, he proposed a reduction in the duty levied on sugar. This, however, would have proved a severe blow to the sugar-beet interests, one of the most profitable undertakings in Bohemia; and it immediately aroused Kolowrat's wrath, for he still considered himself a spokesman in Vienna for the Czech lands. He may also have felt piqued at Metternich's supervision of arrangements for Ferdinand's coronation with the insignia of St Wenceslas in Prague on 7 September; and he certainly did not hesitate to let the Chancellor know he thought the scale of festivities a waste of Bohemia's funds. For whichever reason – and probably for both – Kolowrat threw one of his fits of temperament and threatened to resign.[28] Before anyone could have the good sense to take him at his word, he withdrew to his Bohemian estates, with six months leave of absence for reasons of health. Metternich's relief at his departure from Vienna was qualified only by fear that he would have difficult scenes with Kolowrat during the visit to Prague; but, although there were long talks between the two men behind closed doors, the public spectacle of the coronation went well enough. Poor Ferdinand was duly hailed as King of Bohemia: he was rather good at such occasions; the rôle called neither for dramatic talent nor exercise of the mind; and he was always happy acknowledging cheers in the street.

Kolowrat's self-imposed retreat gave Metternich the opportunity of drawing up a plan for comprehensive reforms in the system of government.[29] He appears to have discussed them with his one reliable political ally, General Clam-Martinitz, while they were in Bohemia for the coronation; and the two men subsequently developed the project after the Chancellor's return to the capital in the last week of September. Metternich wished to create two new consultative bodies: a Conference of State, which would in effect be an executive cabinet under the presidency of the Chancellor; and a nominated council of ministers and departmental heads (*Reichsrat*), which would have a purely advisory function, but would also meet under the chairmanship of the Chancellor. Had these institutions been set up in the form he envisaged, Metternich would have become effective head of state, so long as the Emperor remained a nonentity. It was a bold plan, the most determined attempt which Metternich ever made to assert a right to govern Austria as well as Europe. The project thrust almost all other matters from his mind that autumn. Melanie, who does not seem to have been in her husband's complete confidence over these proposals, was worried at the state of his health. She blamed his weariness on Kolowrat and the disputes which had caused the minister to go off to his estates. It was, she thought, still troubling her husband: 'That business often prevents him from sleeping,' she noted in her journal on 28 September.[30]

Yet Metternich was less concerned with past bickering than with the immediate future. He had proposed constitutional changes in the previous reign without success: would this latest plan of 1836 have any more chance of acceptance than its predecessors? From Archduke

Ludwig there was little to fear, for the new councils would relieve him of duties he found tedious. But his brothers were unlikely to be so compliant: Charles was always hostile to Metternich, Joseph unreliable, and Rainer a cipher. And now it was also necessary to reckon with Archduke John, who at the end of August had emerged from retirement and come to Vienna. He was an intelligent and mildly unconventional man of fifty-four who for twenty years had lived under a cloud of Imperial displeasure in Styria, where he encouraged Slovene culture and lived happily in morganatic union with a postmaster's daughter (whom he married in 1827). His memory kept fresh old resentments of Metternich, slights going back to 1813 and even earlier; and he had taken the opportunity of his journey to the capital to warn Ludwig of the Chancellor and his methods. Nor was this all. From Vienna Archduke John had gone on to Prague for the Bohemian coronation and had there met, not only his other brothers, but Kolowrat as well. The two men found they had much in common, and Kolowrat seems to have let the Archduke know of his grievances against the Chancellor. John was convinced Metternich was a tool of the Jesuits, a foreigner who could never understand the unique character of the Habsburg realm, 'a person who sought salvation in antiquated ideas'.[31] The Archduke had genuinely liberal sympathies and was not going to see the old system of government perpetuated by such a man. When aroused, John was a formidable opponent.

By the last days of October the details of constitutional reform were available for Archduke Ludwig's consideration. He accepted the plan readily enough and it was made public on 31 October; but when reports of Metternich's design penetrated to the backwoods of Bohemia, the news had a remarkably therapeutic effect on Kolowrat. Although he had only enjoyed two months of his sick leave, he hastened to let Archduke John know what was happening, and the Archduke was alarmed at this latest evidence of Metternich's unscrupulous ambition. Kolowrat re-appeared in Vienna at the end of the second week in November and the Archduke John came up from Gräz a fortnight later, bounding with political energy. The two men formed an alliance which remained in being until the revolutions of 1848. Ludwig, considerably shaken by the reaction to Metternich's proposals, had second thoughts and decided it would be safer to leave the whole matter to be thrashed out around a conference table.[32]

Archduke John saw to it that Metternich was isolated. On 30 November he visited all the important members of the court, including the Dowager Empress and the Archduchess Sophie, and he then sounded out the leading departmental ministers. Only Clam-Martinitz gave Metternich unequivocal support. Finally John went to the Ballhausplatz for an interview with the Chancellor himself. It was, the

Archduke declared, 'a stupid oversight that he should wish to become president' of the two councils. They talked for three and a half hours and, by the end of their exchange, it was clear to Metternich he had little following in the capital and had lost the battle. On 5 December Ludwig presided over a conference attended by Archduke Francis Charles, Metternich and Kolowrat, and a week later the final amended form of the constitutional project was promulgated in the Emperor's name. There were, indeed, to be two new institutions, but Metternich's proposed *Reichsrat* was trimmed out of recognition and nothing more was said of the presidential status of the Chancellorship. The idea of a Conference of State was retained: its permanent members were the Archdukes Ludwig and Francis Charles, Metternich and Kolowrat, with consultants summoned for particular problems. Nominally the Conference was under the chairmanship of the Emperor, but in practice it was intended that the Archduke Ludwig should preside at its sessions. The Conference was advised by a larger Council (*Staats-und Konferenzrat*) of seventeen specialists from the government departments. This system survived until the revolutionary disturbances of 1848. Effectively imperial authority was shared by a triumvirate of Ludwig, Metternich and Kolowrat, with Francis Charles helping to nod or shake the Habsburg head when Ludwig was too confused to take a decision. Metternich and Kolowrat were on even worse personal terms than before and did all they could to restrain each other. It was a cumbersome arrangement, a divided commission of sovereignty. Upon the Monarchy without a monarch was imposed a Regency without a regent.

Old problems unresolved and the question of a railway policy

It seemed as if Metternich had reached the end of his career. Archduke John had organized a massive vote of no confidence among those who counted in Vienna. Even before John's intervention, Palmerston had heard enough in London to comment, 'Metternich is not immortal and will pass away in time'; and when news of the final settlement reached him, Palmerston wrote cheerfully, 'This seems a prelude to the decline of Metternich's power, and a great blessing for Europe it would be that his orb should set in the night of private life.'[33] Undoubtedly in a constitutional monarchy Metternich would have resigned in December 1836. He does, indeed, seem momentarily to have contemplated resignation, but the prospect was not attractive. Unlike Kolowrat, whose landed wealth enabled him to decline any stipend, Metternich was far from rich. He entertained luxuriously and spent considerable sums on renovating Königswart and Johannisberg, as well as purchasing a second Bohemian castle at Plass in 1826, another drain on his resources over the years. Moreover, by the end of 1836 he still had four children

living in the family circle, with appropriate style. Leontine had married
Count Moritz Sandor, a reckless Hungarian horseman of much wealth
in 1835, and Metternich had no wish to be eclipsed by the splendour of
his son-in-law. Melanie, who was once more pregnant, had expensive
tastes and came from a family so hard pressed that Kübeck (and many
others in Vienna) believed she had received a substantial monetary gift
from the Russians at the time of her marriage. Metternich owed much
to the generosity of the Rothschilds and other benefactors, but there was
no guarantee he could count on financial assistance once he ceased to be
a power in the land. All in all, it was not difficult for him to put aside
thoughts of resignation; and it is true that in his own sphere of foreign
affairs, no one as yet challenged his competence or authority.

The problems were tediously familiar. He read reports of repression
in Naples, of endless feuding in Spain, of the fleeting passage of conspirators between Paris and Poland. His intelligence service provided
him with intercepted correspondence of most leading governments. He
thought himself as omniscient as ever, although much of the information
he gained was of little value, for the reputation of his secret agents and
cipher specialists was well known abroad and many states took precautions to protect their couriers from harassment.[34] The solutions
Metternich put forward were all well tried and worn: the suspension of
those who taught dangerous doctrines, stricter censorship of plays and
pamphlets, the need for the three Münchengrätz Allies to subsidize a
respectable journal to be published in Cologne and calm the nationalistic enthusiasm of the Rhinelanders. He reacted predictably to any
matter brought before him. Yet was he, perhaps, becoming bored by
the fixity of his existence? In the summer of 1838 there was, once again,
a reunion at Teplitz and soon after his arrival he reported first impressions in a letter to Melanie: 'The King (of Prussia) regularly takes the
same number of pinches of snuff,' he said, 'Wittgenstein utters the same
idiocies; everything is changing except these personages and myself
who retain my position within this framework of immobility.'[35] He was
becoming as fossilized as his old master, Francis, had been.

There were, of course, some new topics to stir interest at meetings of
the Conference of State. Steam-power posed problems for even the
oldest institutions. The 1830's saw the spread of railways to the continent, particularly to Bavaria and Saxony, and inevitably there was
much railway talk in Vienna and Prague. Emperor Francis had looked
at the development with predictable suspicion: he thought rail tracks
would speed, not commerce, but revolution. Metternich, with his perpetual technological curiosity, was less rooted in prejudice and he was
encouraged to think favourably of railways by Solomon von Rothschild.[36] Kolowrat, too, supported the idea of better communications,
and so did Kübeck and most other senior ministers in the administration.

Inevitably disagreements arose over the regions which might profitably be served by railways and the routes they were to follow: Kolowrat thought primarily of the Czech provinces, Metternich hankered after links with Lombardy and Venetia, and there was a vocal Hungarian lobby. But, in 1837, work began on a *Nordbahn* from Vienna to Brünn (Brno) in Moravia and by the following spring sufficient progress had been made in the plains around the capital for high dignitaries of state to undertake their first railway journey. Melanie duly recorded the event in her journal on 8 May 1838: 'Went with the children and mother to look at the locomotive. Clement had been on a trip by train along with the Dowager Empress, Archduchess Sophie, the Archdukes – among whom we found even the little Archduke Francis Joseph – and Count Kolowrat. The excursion by this new device was eminently successful and everyone was well pleased with it. Moreover the weather could not have been better.'[37]

Another year passed before the line was formally opened, and even then trains remained a novelty. In mid-June 1840 the Chancellor and his wife were induced to take their carriage out to the Prater at nine in the morning in order to see the arrival of a train of forty-eight wagons bringing pigs and bullocks to market.[38] By 1841, three hundred miles of track had been constructed within the Empire and, by the time of the Chancellor's fall from power, the figure was three times as high. Metternich, who had always been a markedly itinerant minister, warmly approved of speedier communications and travelled by train wherever possible, especially on his journeys to the Rhineland. He also favoured the building of steamships and the harnessing of steam power for river traffic. In such matters he was certainly no reactionary.[39]

Disappointments over the Eastern Crisis (1839–40)

Over essentials of world policy Metternich's viewpoint changed little with the passage of time. He had always believed the geographical position of Vienna made the city a natural centre for settling disputes between the powers and, although he had not succeeded in drawing together all his fellow statesmen since the autumn of 1822, he never abandoned the hope of being once more host to an international conference. He accepted that full Congresses were no longer appropriate, least of all in the Austria of poor Ferdinand, but he thought there was still much to commend a calm discussion of distant problems by diplomats gathered around a table, preferably his own table in the Ballhausplatz Chancellery.

Suddenly in the summer of 1839 it seemed momentarily as if he might well have his wish satisfied. The Eastern Question was once more posed, and in a dramatic fashion.[40] In May Turkish troops crossed the

K

Euphrates and advanced on Ibrahim's positions in north-eastern Syria, determined to avenge the humiliations imposed on Sultan Mahmud by his Egyptian vassal in 1833. But not even the advice of Captain Helmuth von Moltke could bring victory to the Turkish commanders (if only because they ignored it); and on 24 June the Turks were routed at Nisib, and Ibrahim's Egyptians stood ready yet again to advance to the Taurus. Before news of the disaster could reach Constantinople, Sultan Mahmud had drunk himself to death, and his fleet, which had sailed from the Dardanelles to search out the Egyptians, found them at Alexandria and promptly changed allegiance to Mehemet Ali. The Turkish problem was back in the hands of the Great Powers, more intractable than ever.

Metternich had anticipated a major crisis for several months and was better prepared to meet its challenge than he had been for many years. Even before Nisib, he had taken the initiative in seeking to bring his colleagues together. Using the French as intermediaries, he proposed that representatives of the five powers should meet in Vienna and work out a common policy towards Turkey.[41] He knew he could count on Prussia and France, even though he was uneasy at the extent of French sympathy for Mehemet Ali; and he thought his understanding with Nicholas and Nesselrode would ensure Russian consent. But, as usual, it was Palmerston who worried him. There had been an improvement in Anglo-Austrian relations over the previous two years but he had no illusions about the British Foreign Secretary. Early in July he heard that Palmerston had accepted the proposal, though with a bad grace and with reservations over the form of any conference. The two men still did not trust each other: Palmerston privately made it clear he thought Metternich was treading one of the 'crooked paths' to which he was 'so prone'; and Metternich told Paul Esterhazy that Palmerston was like someone who had recovered at the point of death, a rare occurrence among the greater sinners.[42] But, despite his shaft of irony, Metternich was delighted with the turn of events. Without awaiting a reply from St Petersburg, the representatives of the five powers in Vienna sent a collective note to Constantinople on 27 July assuring the Grand Vizier they were united in seeking to safeguard stability in the East. It was a document which lacked precision, for there were differences in attitude between the various governments, but Metternich was confident he could bring order out of the conflicting interests. He remained in Vienna, despite the summer heat, preparing for the next meetings and determined to be master of any discussions. Melanie complained that one day he had worked for fifteen hours without a break. And yet to be accepted once again as prime arbiter between the nations was worth hours of labour. Even Palmerston admitted (though not to Metternich) that to settle the Turkish business would be a greater contribution to

European peace than any man had achieved since Waterloo.[43] But it was disturbing that July should end with still no word from St Petersburg.

It came at last on 7 August. Count Karl Ficquelmont, the Austrian ambassador to the Tsar, travelled back in person to explain to the Chancellor that Nicholas would not recognize Vienna as a centre for discussion of the Eastern Question. The Tsar even maintained that Austria had associated herself with the Anglo-French combination against Russia's interests.[44] Metternich was bitterly disappointed by this fresh revelation of Nicholas's lack of confidence in his Austrian partner, especially since it coincided with evidence of a deepening rift between the British and French. For three days Metternich worked with Ficquelmont to try and salvage the conference. On Sunday, 11 August, Melanie found him in a state of near collapse. He worked at his papers for another three hours on the Monday morning, went to the Kunsthistorische to inspect (and reject) models for a monument to Emperor Francis, and returned exhausted to the Chancellery. Melanie was seriously alarmed: by Wednesday he was so ill that she thought he had suffered a stroke. There could be no question of his remaining in Vienna, with all the diplomatic activity around him. Ficquelmont was left in charge of foreign affairs and, as soon as he was well enough to stand the journey, Metternich travelled slowly to Johannisberg where he spent five weeks recuperating in the Rhineland.[45]

His illness lost Austria the initiative over the Eastern negotiations, although throughout the crisis Turkey relied upon 'his' collective note of 27 July as proof that the powers were agreed on protecting the Sultan's interests. When Metternich resumed work at his desk in the Chancellery at the end of October he found, as he had anticipated, a changed situation. Nicholas, like his brother in 1825, turned directly to England, despatched a special emissary to London in September, and reached agreement on a common policy with Palmerston. Metternich was forced to recognize that London, rather than Vienna, was the diplomatic centre for decisions over the Eastern Question, and he sent Neumann to England as a personal envoy.[46] By the first weeks of 1840 Palmerston and the Austrian, Prussian and Russian representatives had accepted a common programme to preserve the Ottoman Empire and limit the dominions of Mehemet Ali. It took another six months for these conditions to be settled in detail and even longer for Mehemet Ali to be induced to withdraw from the Levant, but the discussion showed a common determination on the part of the Four Powers not to allow the Eastern Question to stampede Europe into war. It was the French who, in this respect, were out of step, especially when in March 1840 Adolphe Thiers became head of the government in Paris, for he was an ambitious politician with intensive national pride and an obsessive respect for the ruler of Egypt.

Metternich had scant regard for Thiers' quality of statesmanship: he was a frock-coated Bonaparte, seeking to re-enact events which had thrilled his imagination as a child and were to inspire him as a historian. There was no doubt in Metternich's mind that Thiers would try and assert himself in the Eastern Crisis, since he was that unusual combination, an opportunist with little sense of reality: 'Travelling light and being distinctly agile, he is one of those men who, like a cold draught, penetrates through every crack,' he wrote picturesquely to the Austrian ambassador in Paris.[47] Thiers had clashed once already with Metternich when, as transient premier in 1836, he sought a Habsburg bride for Louis Philippe's second son only to find the Austrian Chancellor disenchanted with French marriage politics.[48] Now four years later he tried to combine the enterprise of 1798 with the initiative of 1805, seeking to retain Syria for Mehemet Ali by making warlike gestures towards the Rhine. Metternich, who had known the genuine article of Bonapartism, was unimpressed by this synthetic substitute; but there was sufficient alarm in the German states for the Austrian Chancellor to take advantage of the crisis Thiers had created. In the last days of August he proposed the establishment of a permanent European League of Great Powers to prevent future wars by enforcing existing treaties and renouncing the use of force, but this was too nebulous a scheme for Palmerston and too generalized for the Russians and within three weeks it became a mere curiosity.[49]

By the beginning of October, however, Metternich was himself uneasy. He feared that Thiers, while not wishing to pit French arms against the fortresses of the Rhineland, might fancy an Italian campaign and set the whole peninsula aflame; and he had some awkward exchanges with Kolowrat, who persisted in complaining that Austrian policy was too dependent upon what happened in London. To Palmerston's contempt, he wavered: it might, perhaps, be wiser not to provoke the French by ejecting Ibrahim from the whole of Syria; a partition plan could keep the diplomats talking until even Thiers wearied of heroic attitudes. Hence on 7 October – the day a French frigate moored off St Helena to bring back Napoleon's body to Paris – Metternich proposed the summoning of a congress to one of the smaller German cities, possibly Wiesbaden, so as 'to prevent the conflict from degenerating into war in Europe'.[50] But Palmerston was impatient and nerveless: 'We must not look to words at this time, only to facts,' he told Nathan Rothschild.[51] His resolution was speedily justified. Within a fortnight Thiers was forced out of office and within a month the Egyptians were withdrawing from Syria. There was no longer any sense of imminent crisis in the European capitals; and nothing more was heard of the Wiesbaden Congress.

The following spring Metternich made a final effort to gain acceptance as mediator over the Eastern Question.[52] He suggested that the five ambassadors in Vienna should permanently watch events in Turkey and tender collective advice to the Sultan. Once again Palmerston was unhelpful: he indicated, with frank comments on Austrian inconsistency, that he failed to see any value in such a system.[53] Nor was Tsar Nicholas interested in the proposal: Metternich, he testily complained to the British ambassador, always thought that from his study in Vienna he could 'direct and instruct all the world'.[54] For a third time in a year Metternich's initiative was repulsed. His orb had set, not 'in the night of private life', but in the full day of public office; and he spent the remaining years of his Chancellorship half in shadow.

A SENSE OF CONFLICT

Metternich and the internal problems of the Habsburg Monarchy (1841–4)

The people of Vienna entered the fifth decade of the century socially at ease and undisturbed by murmurings of political controversy from distant regions of the Monarchy. A few years earlier there had been some rioting in the capital over food prices, and Sedlnitzky's agents still kept an anxious eye on what was taught in the university. But in 1840 nothing seemed to challenge the existing order. For many sections of the population it was a time of comfortable prosperity; and in these early years of Ferdinand's reign, several foreign travellers commented on the rather smug contentment of the Viennese and attributed their lack of interest in political matters to the official encouragement of music and other forms of light amusement. Mrs Frances Trollope, for example, wrote that 'this singularly strong national *besoin* of amusement and music and the manner in which it is not only unchecked, but cherished by the authorities, furnishes, in my belief, one of the principal keys to the mystery of the superior tranquillity and contentment of the populace of this country over that of every other.'[1]

Although Mrs Trollope's observations were never profound, there was some justification for the impression she had obtained in her seven-month visit. This was the age of Franz Liszt and Clara Wieck (and of her less esteemed husband, Schumann); and popular taste was shaped by the waltzes of the elder Strauss and of Joseph Lanner. The three-month season of Italian opera at the Karntertortheater was packed with enthusiasts and so were Nicolai's concerts with the Vienna Philharmonic. Nor were these entertainments a mere appendage to aristocratic existence. 'There is music everywhere,' complained Franz Schuselka.[2] 'To any serious observer the people of Vienna seem to revel in an endless state of intoxication ... For them it is always Sunday, always Carnival time.' Such incorrigible frivolity filled a man of Schuselka's rebellious spirit with despair; and he added contemptuously, 'The only point of anything for the Viennese, of even the most important event in the World, is that they should be able to make a joke about it.' They seemed unlikely ever to be inspired by the earnest idealism of revolutionaries.

Vienna was, however, changing in character more than Mrs Trollope suspected or Schuselka perceived. The heart of the city looked little different from the days of the Congress but tenements had begun to spring up in the area beyond the demilitarized glacis of inner fortifications, and outside the city gates new blocks of houses were going up in suburbs which had been pleasant villages in 1815. Throughout the late 'thirties peasant families were flocking into town, becoming manual labourers in new industries or finding employment in railway construction. The population statistics jumped remarkably: 248,000 in 1820; 384,000 in 1840; and over 400,000 in 1848. Vienna still had less than a fifth as many inhabitants as London and only a third as many as metropolitan Paris, but it had more than Manchester or Birmingham or Lyons and, in the central belt of Europe, it was equalled only by Berlin and the sprawling hive of Naples.[3] Each of these cities was troubled by unrest in the early 1840's, but during these years the poorer wage-earners of Vienna hardly asserted their presence; and it is not surprising that Metternich and other members of the administration totally ignored the growing social problem at the heart of the Monarchy. If there were slums on the fringe of the city, most members of the aristocracy and bourgeoisie and many of the skilled craftsmen remained unaware of them. Only once in Metternich's printed *Memoirs* is there a reference to these poorer districts of Vienna: on 13 March 1843 Melanie recorded in her journal that she had just taken 'quite an original walk with Clement through Josefstadt and Schottenfeld', an area hardly more than a mile from the Chancellor's official residence in the Ballhausplatz. She was, it appears, amused by what she saw, and, on her return, confessed almost breathlessly in her diary, 'It is a world of which I knew nothing at all'.[4] Five years later to the very day it trespassed into her own existence.

She was far more conscious of discontent in Hungary, and so was her husband. No one, indeed, could fail to notice the clamour from Pest and Pressburg. Kossuth, released from prison under an amnesty in 1840, became in the first days of 1841 editor of a newly founded newspaper, *Pesti Hirlap*, which he soon made into a powerful organ by the brilliance of his invective against everything emanating from Vienna. By February 1841 Széchenyi, too, was alarmed by Kossuth's narrowly Magyar appeal, fearing that he would perpetuate strife by inciting other nationalities to hatred of the Hungarians. Széchenyi even urged the authorities to enforce stricter censorship of *Pesti Hirlap* and in his own speeches and writings he preached tolerance and moderation. Belatedly Metternich tried to organize an Austro-Hungarian Committee of politically reliable magnates who would counter Kossuth's alleged radicalism, but no centralist spokesman could gain a fraction of Kossuth's following and, though Széchenyi was heard with respect, he seemed out of touch with the mood of his compatriots. In March 1843 Metternich prepared two long memoranda on the whole problem of national sentiment within the Monarchy, in which he roundly condemned the Hungarians for making patriotic feelings a divisive force, dangerous to stability.[5] He was too old and tired to suggest a remedy.

Two months later the Metternichs travelled to Pressburg for the opening of another Diet. This time, accompanied by most of the court, they made the trip down the Danube from Vienna in two and a half hours by one of the new river steamers. They stayed for only the first four days of the Diet and Melanie, at any rate, was relieved and surprised that the inauguration had gone smoothly. Yet, as the Chancellor feared, disputes soon broke out between the radical groups and the centralist magnates and this time they were made worse by the enmity of many Hungarian deputies towards the representatives from Croatia. Before the Diet dispersed in 1844 Metternich had begun to seek an alternative to Kossuth's headstrong nationalism.[6] With the help of a group of 'progressive conservatives' he proposed a comprehensive public works programme as a distraction from narrowly political objectives. This initiative came at least nine years too late. With Széchenyi's backing in 1835, he might have secured the interest of the Hungarians before they were captivated by Kossuth's gold tongue; but in 1844 Széchenyi was a man of the past, even though the Diet was still seeking sanction for many of his earlier proposals. To Kossuth it appeared as if Metternich wished to sweep Hungary, with its traditional tariff barriers, into a Vienna-dominated *Zollverein* and he answered this newest challenge by proclaiming the virtues of 'national economics'. It was an idea that made sense to a people proud of having at last achieved recognition of their language in government, law and education. Progressive conservatism foundered on national passion almost before it was launched.

During these years Metternich gave more attention to the problems of national identity than at any other moment in his public career, and many of his judgements showed acute perception. At heart he was still a good Rhinelander, despising Magyars and Slavs and many of the Latin peoples as well: he used to insist that his summer residence to the east of Vienna's inner city was the ultimate frontier of civilized Europe.* But he always recognized that concern with linguistics and the character

---

* This appears to have been a slightly tedious joke, figuring several times in Metternich's small-talk. His summer villa was in the Rennweg, within a district of Vienna which then took its name from the principal route to the east, the Landstrasse. Having declared in 1820 that 'Asia begins at the Landstrasse', he varied his wit nine years later and maintained that 'my house on the Rennweg marks the frontier of civilization'. But in 1836 he described one of the Schwarzenberg estates on the Austro-Hungarian border as 'the place where Europe ends and Asia begins'. (Cf. Barany, *Stephen Széchenyi*, p. 381.) Apart from his journey to Galicia in 1823, Metternich never travelled farther east than Komaron, little over a hundred miles downstream from Vienna.

of regional culture was a natural consequence of the eighteenth-century Enlightenment. Hence he consciously accepted nationality while invariably rejecting nationalism; and in this respect he was a sounder analyst of the Monarchy's ills than any public servant within its frontiers. It is, however, clear from the two memoranda of March 1843 that this distinction imposed an artificial barrier on his actions.[7] He distrusted Magyar nationalism as exemplified by Kossuth and he also regarded three of the Slav movements as dangerous, 'Polonism', 'Czechism' and 'Illyrianism', which he had earlier patronized. The Poles were too easily duped by conspirators in Paris and too anxious to involve the three partitioning powers in quarrels between each other: he had turned finally against Polish national sentiment at München-grätz in 1833, and he remained convinced of the rightness of his decision. Czech sentiment he had discounted so long as it was largely cultural but he had now become alarmed at the extent to which Palacký, the scholar-patriot of Bohemia, was reflecting in his literary studies what Metternich regarded as Germanic notions of liberalism. 'Illyrianism' was too pan-Slavonic to be any longer acceptable in the Chancellery, for Metternich had no wish to see Slovenes, Croats, Serbs and perhaps even the Bulgars united under the Tsar's patronage, especially when he found that during the Eastern Crisis of 1840 Ljudevit Gaj, the Illyrian messiah, was fomenting trouble in Turkish Bosnia and taking money from Russian agents. Yet, while frowning on these three 'advanced' forms of Slav national-consciousness, Metternich was still ready to encourage in 1843 the specifically Croatian national revival (even under Gaj) and he also found much to commend in the virtues of the Slovaks, among whom national sentiment was as yet hardly vocal. The fact that both the Croats and the Slovaks were bitterly opposed to Kossuth's frenzied Magyarization contributed to their acceptability at court, though Metternich was reluctant to sanction any deliberate policy of setting off one nationality against the other. It was difficult to predict the consequences of any such explosion.

Some of Metternich's policy towards the national minorities reflected tensions within the Conference of State. Kolowrat was a warm champion of both Palacký and Gaj, and Archduke John had shown a sympathetic interest in Illyrianism. After his illness in 1839 Metternich still found it difficult to collaborate with Kolowrat. Early in 1840 the Chancellor lost his principal political ally, Clam-Martinitz, and although the effect of Clam's death was partially offset by the discrediting of one of Kolowrat's chief supporters, Metternich was left time and again on his own at the sessions of the Conference. He could generally rely on Kübeck to counter Kolowrat's intrigues, but Kübeck was by no means an uncritical admirer of the Chancellor; he seems to have found Metternich's tendency to 'speak in images' at the Conference particularly wearisome. Kolowrat, to give him his due, respected Metternich's intelligence and good intentions. He once explained his difficulties to Kübeck. Metternich, he complained, 'always adopts a patronizing tone towards me, informing me that five plus three only makes eight but that five times three makes fifteen.' For him 'all events are connected and the Anglo-Chinese opium dispute must have an effect on our finances, and so on; and he says all this when I merely ask if he approves of the Northern Railway constructing an extension to Pressburg. And then there is the intolerable vanity of the man, who in all his life has never been wrong, who has always foreseen everything – and still foresees everything – that has happened and that did not happen. To put it briefly, I just cannot get on with him!'[8]

Kübeck, chronicling these observations in his journal, added the wry comment, 'Equal poles always repel one another.' Such constant personal animosity could not, unfortunately, be dismissed with a sardonic aside; its consequences were serious for the Monarchy, perhaps even for Europe. Metternich complained that Kolowrat did not forward to him important documents concerning internal affairs, and Kolowrat appears to have resented Metternich's attempts to improve communications between Vienna and northern Italy. No administrative decisions of importance were taken by the Conference of State, and the Monarchy drifted gradually towards chaos. 'Clement plays the part of Jeremiah, and no-one listens to him,' wrote Melanie in her journal on 10 August, 1843.[9] The Conference needed inspiration, not lamentation; and this was a quality which none of its members possessed.

By now the feeble character of central administration had begun to alarm members of the aristocracy who were not by nature inclined to toy with liberal notions.[10] In 1842 Viktor von Andrian, a member of the titled nobility from the Tyrol and himself a government official, published a pamphlet on *Austria and her Future* in Germany and copies were smuggled back across the frontier of the Monarchy. It was by no means a revolutionary tract, but primarily a reasoned appeal for wide-spread governmental reforms through provincial assemblies. These institutions were traditionally dominated by the feudal aristocracy and were concerned with purely local and regional issues; but Andrian's ideas fired enthusiasm in some of the predominantly German-speaking areas of the Monarchy such as Styria and Lower Austria. The Estates of Lower Austria, a body in which there were spokesmen for commerce as well as for the landed interest, took the lead in pressing for reforms; and they found they could rely for protection upon Kolowrat. Since the Lower Austrian Estates met actually in Vienna, their activities were of considerable importance; and in the very year in which Andrian's pamphlet was published, several members of the Estates formed a 'Juridical and Political Reading Union' (*Juridisch-*

Politischer Leseverein) in Vienna, with which some professors from the university, high civil servants and army officers of field rank associated themselves. Similar bodies were set up in Prague and in Gräz, where the *Leseverein* was benevolently tolerated by Archduke John. Sedlnitzky and Metternich regarded these innocent-sounding associations as spearheads of dangerous liberalism: the fact that they flourished in comparative freedom is sure proof of the Chancellor's slackening grasp on public affairs. Inevitably the *Leseverein* looked towards Kolowrat as the man of the future and thus helped to spread the legend of his liberalism.

Frederick William IV of Prussia; Queen Victoria; and Tsar Nicholas

Fortunately for Metternich there was little tension in foreign affairs during the first half of the 1840's. With Thiers out of favour in Paris the pseudo-Bonapartist effervescence subsided, and Guizot established a bourgeois conservative government in France which, from time to time, won qualified approval from the Austrian Chancellor. Relations between Austria and Sardinia-Piedmont were unusually cordial: and in 1842 Metternich was gratified by Charles Albert's decision to negotiate a marriage for his son, Victor Emmanuel, with Archduchess Maria Adelaide, daughter of the Viceroy of Lombardy-Venetia, Archduke Rainer.[11] Field-Marshal Radetzky, in command of Austrian troops in northern Italy, was also delighted by this latest marriage alliance. It would, he felt, considerably ease his strategic problems, and he even committed himself to the optimistic prediction that henceforth the Piedmontese Army would serve 'as the advance guard of the Imperial forces' in protecting the peninsula from the hidden menaces of the French. For the moment, the atmosphere over the Lombard Plains was pleasantly friendly and there was a healthy sense of prosperity.

The situation was less agreeable on the Rhine. In June 1840 King Frederick William III of Prussia had died, after forty-three years of varying fortunes on the throne. His son and successor, Frederick William IV, combined in his muddled mind a romantic nostalgia for a non-historical past with a conviction of his own creative genius. Had Metternich been younger, he might perhaps have ridden the new King's prejudices as once he had Tsar Alexander's. He made the mistake of lecturing Frederick William IV in much the same terms as he had been accustomed to use to his father. They met at Stolzenfels, near Coblenz, in August 1845: Frederick William listened politely to Metternich's views and embraced him when they parted; but he does not appear to have absorbed any of the Chancellor's good advice. It was not a happy encounter.[12] Queen Victoria and King Leopold of Belgium were guests of Frederick William in the Rhineland that summer. The

Queen did not make a favourable impression on Metternich when they met at Stolzenfels: he thought her childish and too much influenced by her uncle Leopold and by her husband; and he found her 'not so much English as plain Coburg'. Victoria, for her part, had reservations about the Austrian Chancellor, whom she complained was didactic in manner and inclined to speak slowly, but whose general attitude she admitted was friendly. The truth seems to have been that the Queen found him boring and was not good at disguising her feelings.[13]

Although Victoria's failure to find his company entertaining no doubt vexed Metternich, it was not of major importance to him in determining policy. Far more serious was the odd behaviour of Tsar Nicholas in the closing months of 1845.[14] Six years earlier there had been talk of marrying the Archduke Albrecht, son of Archduke Charles, to the Tsar's elder daughter, the Grand Duchess Olga (whose good looks had so impressed Metternich when he met the Imperial family at Teplitz in 1835). When, however, Albrecht went to St Petersburg, Olga thought poorly of him and nothing more was heard of the project. In 1845 Olga was twenty-three and eminently marriageable; and so, at the age of twenty-eight, was Archduke Stephen, son of the Palatine of Hungary. A Habsburg-Romanov marriage alliance seemed good sense to many in Vienna and St Petersburg. The Tsar approved; Olga approved; Stephen approved; but not the Austrian Empress or the Dowager Empress. Nor, above all, did that veteran of marriage diplomacy, Metternich. For Stephen was heir-designate to his father and he was popular in Hungary. The Chancellor therefore feared an intrigue by which eventually Stephen and Olga would become King and Queen in an independent Hungary, backed by the full strength of the Tsar's army; and Metternich accordingly supported and encouraged a demand by the two Empresses and the Catholic faction at court that Olga should first be received into the Roman Church.

Nicholas was deeply offended: he was a good father, proud of Olga; and at that very moment he was in conflict with the Catholics in Poland. In October he suddenly left Russia for a tour of Italy. To Metternich's surprise he avoided Vienna and passed through Prague – where he met Stephen – before travelling south to Milan to be fêted by the Viceroy and Radetzky's army. He then proceeded to Sicily, causing consternation especially in Rome by his unpredictable movements. Eventually early in December he had an audience with the Pope, set off northwards and arrived unexpectedly in Vienna on 30 December in a thoroughly bad temper. It was his first meeting with Metternich for seven years, and the last they were to have until after the Chancellor's retirement.

Socially the Tsar's visit was a minor disaster. It is probable that once he found the Habsburg court adamant over the religious issue, he resolved to play the rôle of an awkward guest. Melanie Metternich retained from the Münchengrätz meetings a sentimental tenderness towards him and he had frequently exerted himself to send her flattering messages (although after an earlier meeting he had confessed to his wife that he could not stand the sound of Princess Melanie's voice). On this occasion he made little effort to please. Melanie noted in her journal on New Year's Eve, 'I went towards him and found him much changed. The expression on his face has hardened even more and there is nothing about his mouth to relieve the intense severity of his glance.' And when Metternich embarked on one of his interminable surveys of world affairs, Nicholas cut him short with the injunction, 'Not a word about politics! I have come only to talk to your wife.' Personalities were, indeed, putting a severe strain on the Münchengrätz partnership.[15]

Nicholas spent merely three days in Vienna and avoided discussion of awkward questions. He gave assurances of Russia's peaceful intentions toward Turkey and of his willingness to stand by the Münchengrätz undertakings. At one moment he turned abruptly to Metternich and declared, 'This realm will survive as long as you. What is to follow it?' Yet the question was essentially rhetorical: he cared little about the answer. Resorting to his one overworked metaphor he let his family know that Austria was 'sick, very sick', and he added that everything about the visit had been 'odious'. He told the Tsarina that Archduke Ludwig was irresolute and Archduke Francis Charles so spineless he even asked the Tsar to intercede with Metternich so as to secure his own succession. To Nicholas the Habsburgs were now a pathetic dynasty; before a military review, he had watched as the unfortunate Emperor Ferdinand 'was helped into the saddle with all the precautions normally taken to safeguard a frightened woman'. Nor was he impressed by Metternich, whom he described as a mere shadow of himself, talking more than ever but thinking and moving with the weariness of age and long service. It was, the Tsar implied in his letters, as well for his family to avoid close association with a Monarchy which was heading so assuredly to disaster.[16] Later in the year Grand Duchess Olga married the heir to the throne of Württemberg, her first cousin. To her father's experienced eye Stuttgart looked a more secure home than Vienna or Pest; and at least it did not harbour at court a 'party of Piety' intent on robbing his daughter of her Orthodox faith.

No doubt many of the Tsar's strictures sprang from personal pique; his poor impression of the Habsburg court in the mid-forties may well have been exaggerated. But there were others who perceived that the mainspring of the Chancellor's vitality had snapped during his illness in 1839 and that he was dragging himself through the routine of administration because it never occurred to him there was a tolerable existence outside public life. Melanie protected him so far as possible from awareness of his own decline: she was proud of her husband; and from genuinely tender sentiment she was anxious to sustain the confidence he needed always to feel in himself. Moreover she honestly believed no one else in Vienna could shoulder the weight of affairs which the septuagenarian Chancellor still bore. Nor was she the only shrewd woman in the capital to regard him as the fount of political wisdom. Archduchess Sophie still treated his judgements with awed respect, and she insisted on sending her son, Francis Joseph, to Metternich for weekly instruction in the art of government as soon as he reached his seventeenth birthday.[17] The Chancellor's own son, Richard, accompanied the Archduke during these tutorial sessions. He was a year and a half older than Francis Joseph.

Melanie, however, was more of a realist than Archduchess Sophie. She could see the gradual falling away of Clement's powers of thought and action. 'He no longer has the strength to fight as he has done in the past,' she noted at the start of 1840.[18] Two years later he had another illness, though not so serious as in the summer of 1839. Possibly it was a slight stroke for it certainly left him tired and ponderous. In the winter of 1845–6 it was primarily on Melanie's insistence that Metternich at last resolved to transform his summer villa on the Rennweg into a residence where the family might live throughout the year. The villa was little more than a mile and a half from the centre of Vienna. Melanie wanted a palace in the capital where she could move if Clement died in office. She does not seem to have discussed with him the possibility of retirement; but the new house on the Rennweg, which was not completed until the spring of 1847, would also be convenient should illness or intrigue force him to vacate the Chancellery. It was an impressive building with three main floors, fifty windows along the front façade, and a balcony bearing the Metternich-Winneburg coat-of-arms over the main entrance. Beneath the balcony was carved the least appropriate inscription in Vienna, *Parva domus, magna quies*; for even in this final architectural venture, Metternich's character remained true to form.[19]

The Polish Question and the annexation of Cracow (1846)

Yet during these last two years of Metternich's public career, there was no prospect of 'great calm' reigning within any residence, small or otherwise, which the Chancellor might occupy. Less than two months after Tsar Nicholas's ill-tempered visit to Vienna, new dangers in Poland once more drew the three Eastern autocracies together. Reports from secret agents throughout the winter had indicated that the exiled Poles in Paris were planning an insurrection in Galicia and the Prussian territories around Poznan. The Prussians acted vigorously and at once arrested the co-ordinator sent from France, Mieroslawski. In Vienna Metternich tended to discount the significance of these reports: he had known of the pipe-dreams of the Parisian Poles for many years, and in recent months there had been a crop of hysterical rumours from Galicia of brigand outrages. On 17 February, however, the local commander at Tarnow in western Galicia was told by a group of Polish peasants that they had been urged to rise up and massacre all Germans and Jews and sack their shops in the towns. Although at first as disinclined to believe them as his superiors in Vienna, he became convinced of the truth of this tale when the peasants returned to him on the following day. He found it relatively simple to show them it was their duty to uphold the existing order, advice which many interpreted as an invitation to butcher any members of the Polish landowning class suspected of disloyalty to the Monarchy. There were scenes of bloodshed and destruction around Tarnow – and farther east, around Lemberg – for two or three days; and it is probable that some 1,500 to 2,000 Polish landowners perished at the hands of the peasants. At the same time, in neighbouring Cracow, Polish patriots proclaimed an independent republic and hoisted the old Polish flag over the city-hall.[20]

News of the disorders reached Vienna speedily. The Government was surprised and there were recriminations around the conference table. Kolowrat thereupon withdrew from all activity with one of his neurasthenic indispositions, and it was left to Metternich to meet the challenge in Galicia. For the moment there was little enough for him to do: the armed forces quickly restored order in Galicia; and in the first week of March detachments of the Russian, Prussian, and Austrian Armies once again occupied the Free City of Cracow and accepted the surrender of the Polish rebels. Eleven days later Metternich raised, at the Conference of State, the problem of Cracow's future, for he was conscious that the time had come to make a break in the Vienna Settlement. Cracow was too dangerous a nest of revolutionaries to be permitted the half-real independence of the 1815 compromise.[21]

The Galician disorders had repercussions throughout the Empire during the course of the following two years. When Count Hartig, one of Metternich's close associates, later came to write the earliest narrative account of the 1848 Revolution, he saw events in Galicia as the first danger signal for the Monarchy.[22] He maintained, however, that the authorities misunderstood the significance of what had taken place: they were so gratified by the loyal assistance 'received from the people' in the Polish districts that they failed to perceive the extent of revolutionary nationalistic feeling and concentrated unduly on the social problem in the countryside. There is much truth in this judgement, even if it is essentially the product of hindsight. The immediate problem for Metternich and his colleagues in the Conference of State was how far they could go in rewarding the peasants by abolition of feudal dues without appearing to condone massacre of the gentry class and without setting a precedent for other areas in both the Austrian lands and Hungary. A series of compromise measures, which removed superficial grievances while leaving the basic feudal obligations untouched, made the peasants restless while angering the gentry by cutting off sources of income. Despite the pressing problems which lurked in the towns and cities, Metternich could never entirely trust the peasantry for the remainder of his period in office; and troops remained on the alert in Galicia, the Czech rural areas and the specifically Austrian provinces for fear of a new wave of arson and murder.

The main consequences of the Polish troubles were diplomatic. After seven months of hard diplomatic negotiations with the Russians and Prussians, the formal annexation of Cracow to the Austrian Empire was proclaimed in November 1846. Metternich regarded this event as a personal victory:[23] he considered that he had saved a city which was of considerable strategic importance to the defence of Austria from falling into Russian hands, for Tsar Nicholas would never have permitted Cracow to return to its treaty status. The wisdom of Metternich's action is questionable: the Monarchy acquired some six hundred square miles of territory populated by a vocal and intelligent national minority of dissident Slavs; and for this gain he alienated the British and French, although it must be admitted that Guizot's protests lacked sincerity. The Chancellor also ensured that the collective venom of the Polish Committee in Paris, a body of considerable prestige among liberals throughout the continent, would be henceforth unleashed on the 'Metternich System' and its eponym. The Poles made masterly propaganda out of the alleged encouragement given in 1846 by the Galician authorities to peasants with a grievance against landowners; and, although the diplomatic envoys in Vienna knew how horrified Metternich had been by reports of the excesses, public opinion abroad hardened once more against the Chancellor and what was held to be his diabolical policy.

The English press thundered righteously against this breach in the Treaty of Vienna and Palmerston denounced the seizure of Cracow in the traditional speech at the Lord Mayor's banquet in London's Guildhall.[24] In France the comments were even more hostile and went beyond the Polish Question to tackle the whole basis of Metternich's philosophy of government. The tone of the satirical Paris magazine *Charivari* was solemnly discussed by the Austrian Conference of State in April 1846 and again seven months later.[25] But it was the far more sober *Revue des Deux Mondes* (a periodical which the Chancellor received regularly) which caught the general mood of the whole continent and warned him of imminent change. In an open letter Professor Alexandre

Thomas bade farewell to the age of Metternich: 'A sense of conflict is pervading the world,' he began, 'and not all the wiles of the politicians can suppress it: for, Prince, it is you yourself who has failed. May God grant peace to you, then; for men want it no more.'[26]

As a valedictory, Thomas's article showed an almost Rousseau-esque flourish of style: but it left the person to whom it was addressed unmoved; for, fatalist that he was, it told him nothing he did not know. A meek surrender of authority had no appeal for him, least of all when notice to quit was served by a French academic. Convinced as ever of his duty to preserve the Monarchy, he had no time to consider what Europe thought of him. In two years he would have held office longer than Kaunitz: in two years Archduke Francis Joseph would be eighteen years old and able to succeed, without a regency, if Ferdinand abdicated: in two years, if he were spared that long, perhaps Prince Metternich might begin to consider retirement; but not yet.

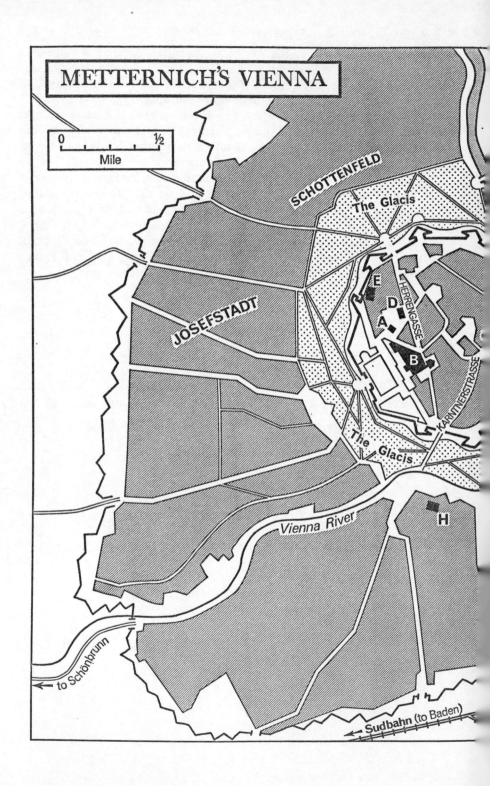

METTERNICH'S VIENNA

0 ———————— ½
Mile

SCHOTTENFELD

The Glacis

JOSEFSTADT

E

D

A

B

HERRENGASSE

KARNTNERSTRASSE

The Glacis

Vienna River

H

to Schönbrunn →

← Sudbahn (to Baden)

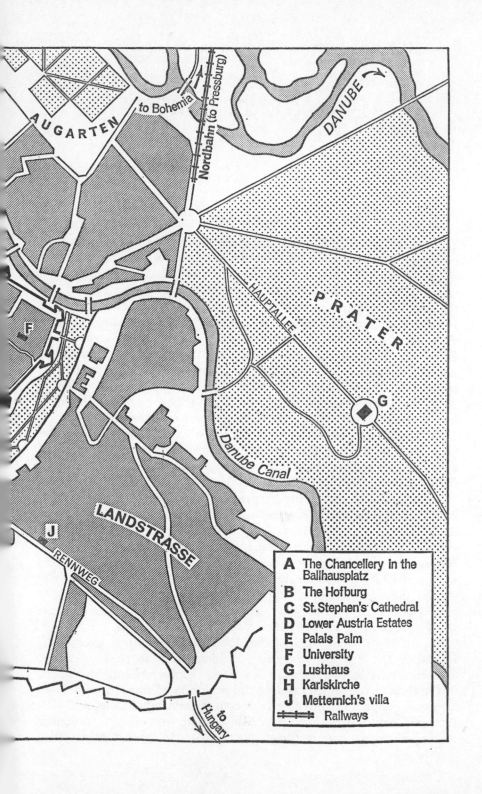

AUGARTEN

to Bohemia

Nordbahn (to Pressburg)

DANUBE

DANUBE

PRATER

HAUPTALLEE

F

E

G

Danube Canal

J

LANDSTRASSE

RENNWEG

to Hungary

A The Chancellery in the Ballhausplatz
B The Hofburg
C St. Stephen's Cathedral
D Lower Austria Estates
E Palais Palm
F University
G Lusthaus
H Karlskirche
J Metternich's villa
╫╫╫ Railways

CHALLENGE TRIUMPHANT

A 'liberal' Pope and a civil war in Switzerland

The pace of events in Europe, politically slow for a decade and a half, quickened perceptibly in midsummer 1846. While Polish indignation smouldered in centres of exile, crisis came to the Italian peninsula and was swiftly followed by the threat of civil war in Switzerland. At the same time Central Europe felt the bleak hand of what in Britain and Ireland was long after known as 'the hungry 'forties': three years of poor harvests and potato blight in the richest farming areas of the Habsburg Monarchy, disease among the cattle on the Danubian Plain, and everywhere in the Empire the threat of rising prices and unemployment. Not all these social questions were directly a responsibility of Metternich, but he seems in these years to have been reluctant to leave any matters of importance to other members of the Conference of State. He was able to take seven weeks away from Vienna in the hottest part of the summer of 1846 but, after his return from Königswart that autumn, he remained constantly working in the Chancellery until his fall from power eighteen months later.

Foreign diplomats, hardly surprisingly, believed him a sick man. The Piedmontese envoy even went so far as to inform Turin he was dying. But he was not. Though often despondent and tiring himself with work which in earlier times he would have delegated, he somehow survived; and day after day interminable despatches and memoranda poured forth from his study over the Ballhausplatz. Sound advice echoed the warnings of almost forty years in words which came so readily to his pen that they had lost all actuality; and, in the end, the prophet of disaster was caught unready for the inevitable.

Until the spring of 1846 Metternich remained content over affairs in Italy.[1] There was a disturbing incident in June 1844 when two Italian officers in the Austrian Navy, the brothers Bandiera, landed in Calabria in the hope of setting the peninsula aflame with rebellion: they speedily paid the price for their courage and convictions, and Italy remained mournfully silent. A year later there were demonstrations at Rimini in the Romagna: once more no sparks ignited other cities.

Relations with Charles Albert of Sardinia-Piedmont were less happy than at the time of his son's marriage, because of tiresome disputes over trade problems and railway policy; but it was only in May 1846 when a medallion was found to be on sale in Lombardy-Venetia with the head of Charles Albert on one side and a patriotic quartet of Dante, Raphael, Columbus and Galileo on the other that Metternich began to suspect the King of Piedmont's political ambitions to be as devious as his commercial ethics. And at that point, in midsummer 1846, Pope Gregory xvi died and Cardinal Mastai-Ferretti was elected pontiff by a conclave which was inspired so swiftly by the Holy Spirit that the Cardinal-Archbishop of Milan, a good Austrian, arrived too late for the deliberations.

The new Pope, who took the title Pius ix, was not a 'liberal', as many people (including Metternich) soon came to believe.[2] He was, however, a member of a different generation from his predecessor, for he had been born in 1792, spent his youth in Napoleon's Italy, and was not ordained a priest until 1819 (the year in which Metternich paid his only visit to Rome). As Bishop of Imola, Pius ix had seen for himself the weaknesses of government in the Papal States and he wished to reform the administration. Metternich had every sympathy with such a policy: he had vainly pressed the need for enlightened change on Gregory xvi for fifteen years. Yet he was alarmed by the extent of the Pope's reforms – amnesties, relaxation of censorship, establishment of a council of state, a prospect of ministerial government. He was still more worried by the way in which Italians, inside and outside the Papal States, came to regard Pius ix as their God-given liberator, the man who would lead them to unity and independence. It was not surprising to read of the streets of Rome echoing with shouts of '*Viva Pio Nono*' as the new pontiff drove from palace to basilica; but it was disturbing there should also have been cries of '*A basso Metternich*'; and ominous that no one took action against those who uttered such scandalous imprecations. In Genoa and Naples the clergy at least honoured past and present by praying for the Pope's conversion, beseeching the Almighty to save him from the serpent of national pride: but in Turin, Palermo, Florence – even in Rome – there were priests who invoked God's blessing on the name of Italy; and in February 1848 the Pope himself became one of their number.

Seven months before that momentous pronouncement the Italian Crisis was transformed into an affair of Europe. The Austrians had long enjoyed treaty rights to garrison the citadel of Ferrara, south of the Po in the Papal Romagna. In the summer of 1847 they stretched these privileges. Hostile demonstrations led the local commander to send for reinforcements and, with Metternich's approval, to occupy the whole of the city. This action produced as noisy a diplomatic storm as the annexation of Cracow: the Pope protested, Charles Albert protested, Palmerston protested. British warships were sighted in the Adriatic and in the Ligurian Sea; and in the autumn Palmerston induced the Prime Minister, Lord John Russell, to send the Earl of Minto – a member of his cabinet who was, as it happened, also his father-in-law – to Turin, Florence and Rome in order to assure the Italians of British sympathy. Metternich was surprised at the vigour of foreign reaction to the Ferrara incident[3]: he denied all intention of interfering in the internal affairs of the Italian states and, early in December, the Austrian garrison was once more withdrawn to the shelter of the citadel. But what most puzzled Metternich were the thunderous expostulations of Palmerston and the despatch of Minto on a roving mission through the Italian trouble spots. It was reasonable to suppose that Palmerston, whom he could never begin to understand, had for some extraordinary whim of policy determined to foment disorder in the peninsula. To this challenge Metternich responded predictably with an attempt to undermine Palmerston's position: he wrote to the Duke of Wellington, and he tried an indirect approach to Prince Albert.[4] This, however, was a clumsy move. A technique which had failed against Canning in 1824 and misfired ten years later against Palmerston was far too rusty to succeed in 1847. Neither the Duke nor the Prince had any means of ousting a Foreign Secretary. On the other hand if Metternich merely sought support in restraining Palmerston's apparent hostility towards Austria, his initiative was not entirely wasted, as events in 1848–9 were to show; but by then he was no longer in office.

Possibly Metternich overrated the importance of external interference in Italy during 1847: it would have been sensible to concentrate on problems nearer the centre of the Empire. In retrospect, he seems to have given excessive attention to the achievement of narrowly diplomatic objectives, and in particular to the establishment of an Austro-French understanding. He had sought collaboration with the July Monarchy as soon as the Anglo-French entente finally collapsed with Palmerston's accusations of double-dealing by Guizot over the marriages of the Queen of Spain and her sister in October 1846. Now the Austrian Chancellor and the austere Protestant, who had invited the French bourgeoisie to 'enrich themselves' over the past seven years, came together. Neither man wished to see a united Germany – especially one backed by Prussian might – nor a united Italy; and both feared the spread of revolution. Guizot was prepared to assure Metternich of French collaboration in Italy: no more flag waving at Ancona; no encouragement of Charles Albert in his fickle policy; no hesitation about intervening alongside Austria if Papal rashness threatened upheaval 'in one or other of the Italian States'. It was many years since the Chancellor had received such fair words and promises from the French capital. Perhaps in time this new-found friend would strike at the Polish Committee in Paris and curb the enthusiasm of Mazzini's agents in southern France. Meanwhile he would at least align the French with Austria and the Russo-Prussian combination in support of the Swiss Catholic cantons against the Federalist liberals of Berne. For a constitutionalist parliamentarian Guizot had, indeed, travelled far. Almost he had made the Orleanist Monarchy respectable in the eyes of Melanie Metternich; and, like her husband, he was following an ambitious foreign policy which took scant notice of his country's immediate interests or resources.[5]

It was therefore in partnership with Guizot that Metternich entered his final winter of foreign discontent. The two men had never met, but they had much in common: a belief in conservative order; a sense of historical purpose; a dryly academic contempt for current opinion. And now both statesmen, against the wishes of their colleagues, bound themselves loosely to the *Sonderbund*, a group of seven cantons defying the legitimate government of Switzerland. It was a mistake in policy for both Metternich and Guizot. In Vienna the Chancellor was faced with opposition from Kolowrat and from Kübeck. They maintained around the conference table that the Swiss secessionists were concerned only with safeguarding Jesuit influence; they could not see why Austria should give financial aid, let alone military support, to such a cause. Patiently Metternich argued that the dispute epitomized the greater contest in Europe, that the *Sonderbund* stood for traditional values of society endangered by radical democrats, and that if the seven cantons were defeated, liberals throughout the continent would take heart and precipitate revolution. Reluctantly the Conference of State authorized concentration of ten thousand Austrian troops on the Swiss frontier and offered the *Sonderbund* an interest-free loan. Guizot, too, held out the prospect of sympathy and aid. Palmerston, on the other hand, encouraged the government in Berne, though he urged the Swiss authorities to avoid a civil war.[6]

Metternich would have been wiser to leave Switzerland to her own affairs; and it could be argued that it was his own folly which converted a domestic squabble into a major ideological confrontation. He showed none of the skill with which he had met the potentially greater threats of 1820 and 1830. Fearing the effect of intervention on the Monarchy and the German Confederation, he willingly accepted Guizot's proposal for an international conference to settle the dispute. But on 4 November 1847, the Swiss Federal Army struck. There was a brief civil war, with only 128 casualties on the two sides. By the end of the month the *Sonderbund* had collapsed and Lucerne, its centre of resistance, was in federal hands. Neither the Swiss nor their British friends now wanted any conference; and Metternich had suffered a major loss of prestige. 'The Powers are faced today with radicalism in control', he wrote: what had happened in Switzerland was 'a harbinger of revolution in Germany'.[7] In the last days of 1847 he gained the consent of the Prussians and of Guizot to a joint invasion of Switzerland should the federal government maintain its objections to a conference. Nothing more was heard of this project. The New Year brought its own problems; and beside them Switzerland seemed of minor concern.

Growing unrest in Italy (1848)

His inept handling of the *Sonderbund* question gave the Chancellor's enemies in Vienna the proof they required that he was no longer competent, even in his own specialized department of foreign affairs. It was clear by the end of the year that his weeks of office were numbered. Perhaps he sensed it himself. 'Clement is admirable', wrote Melanie in her journal at the beginning of 1848, 'Fear never holds him, but sometimes he is much agitated'; and on 2 January he drew up what he termed a political horoscope for the year in which he saw radical forces, long veiled by less militant forms of liberalism, about to emerge and confound society.[8] It must be admitted that, in the late 1840's, this was a fairly safe prediction for anyone's almanack. Nevertheless Metternich went farther than mere generalization. He was not so apprehensive over the immediate prospects for France as in the early summer of 1830, and he ignored the changing moods of people in Vienna. He was, however, sure he could indicate where the danger would come: not Germany or Hungary; not Switzerland, despite the tragic fiasco at Lucerne; but in Italy, and more particularly Rome.

He had, on the face of it, a good chance of being right; for the peninsula was daily news in Vienna at the end of 1847. Over several weeks couriers brought him dramatic reports from the Italian cities: reforms promised in Turin; demands made in Florence; the Pope acclaimed anew in Rome; Austrians ostracized in Venice and Milan. It did not matter greatly if Lombards refused tickets for the State Lottery, or Venetians walked out of Austrian-sponsored festivities in the Piazza San Marco; but it certainly did matter when the Milanese resolved not to smoke tobacco from the Imperial factories. For such admirable self-denial cut Austrian revenue from a lucrative monopoly, and also led to frayed tempers.[9] There were riots in Milan for the first time in a quarter of a century, and they subsequently followed the patriot embargo on tobacco to Pavia and Padua. Nor did the situation improve with the turn of the year. By mid-January revolution had come to the towns and villages of Sicily and sent tremors throughout the South; and within another seven weeks the threat of disorder induced the rulers of Naples, Tuscany and Sardinia-Piedmont to promulgate liberal constitutions. Soon the rights of man would be sealed in the states of the Church.

The Chancellor responded to this fresh challenge from Italy in three ways,[10] none of them original. He sent Ficquelmont, whom he regarded as his present understudy in foreign affairs, to Milan in the hope of shocking the Viceregal bureaucracy into efficient administration. He extracted from the archives the proposals he had outlined in 1817 for creating an Italian Chancery, and cast an affectionate eye over them. And, lest the troubles continue, he resumed negotiations with Guizot for joint intervention in the peninsula in order to save the Italians from their own revolution. Little was achieved by any of these methods: the civic authorities in Milan were unaccustomed to decision making; and Guizot was less inclined to burn his fingers than a year before. Metternich, for his part, seemed unable to concentrate his thoughts on the present. Thus, on 7 February 1848, the Austrian ambassador in Paris found himself reading to Guizot a letter in which Metternich gave a detailed account of what Napoleon told him, nearly forty years before, were the reasons why Italians could not be trusted with liberal institutions.[11] No doubt Guizot, as a connoisseur of historical anecdote, appreciated such revelations; given the urgency of the hour, he chose to base policy on facts less hallowed by time. He accepted an obligation to march beside the Austrians should Revolution come to Rome itself; and he firmly but politely advised Charles Albert not to let the Piedmontese stampede him into a war to liberate Lombardy. But it was difficult for a minister of Louis Philippe to partner Metternich closely at such a time. He could hardly object to constitutions which followed so faithfully the Parisian model of 1830, especially when at home he was straining every nerve to defend it.

Metternich did not begin to appreciate Guizot's difficulties until well into February. Life at court in Vienna continued to be introspective, as suspicion had made it ever since Ferdinand's accession. Its brittle gaiety was briefly dimmed at Christmas 1847 by news of the death of Marie Louise, at fifty-six prematurely old and bloated with dropsy. For Metternich her death meant, not so much a break with the past, as an additional complication in Italy, a vacancy in the Duchy of Parma at an awkward moment. Although the unfortunate woman had been despised for years in Vienna, she was the Emperor's sister and convention cast the court into mourning.'[12] But by 9 February all the candles were once more blazing in the Hofburg for a private performance of Kotzebue's five-act comedy, *Wirrwarr* ('Disorder'), with the principal part played by the Archduke Francis Joseph and with Richard Metternich and four members of the Széchenyi family in supporting rôles. Melanie, Richard's step-mother, commended the

performance in her journal, although she regretted the choice of title
at that particular moment.[13] And a certain coldness was creeping into
Melanie's mind towards the Archduchess Sophie, Francis Joseph's
mother; for in January an anonymous pamphlet had appeared entitled
'*The Sybilline Books out of Austria*' and its author (who was, in fact, tutor
to the Archduke Rainer's children) dedicated his work to the Archduchess Sophie. Such a gesture might have been forgiven, even if the
pamphlet was published abroad so as to avoid censorship: what
seemed inexcusable was its ornate and involved apostrophe by which
Austria was made to call on Metternich 'to give her back her lost
thirty years'. Bitterly Melanie noted that 'everyone today looks to poor
Clement for help' and yet 'they wish to make him responsible for the
errors of others in previous years.' While it is clear from Archduchess
Sophie's papers she was not involved in any plot against Metternich,
many people in Vienna – including, it would appear, Melanie Metternich herself – firmly believed Sophie was working for the Chancellor's
fall. Throughout February and early March there must have been
within the palace an almost stifling atmosphere of intrigue and
suspicion.[14]

Meanwhile the situation in Italy continued to look ominous: troop
movements reported from across the Piedmontese frontier; fresh
violence in the streets of Milan; further concessions by timid rulers in
the smaller states. At the start of the last week in February Radetzky
placed the whole of Lombardy-Venetia under martial law, and it
seemed as if events were, indeed, fulfilling Metternich's prediction. By
now, however, there was an even more serious revolutionary spirit
active in France; and on 27 February, when Vienna received news of
Radetzky's proclamation, rumours were already circulating in the
Austrian capital of unrest in Paris. Hence when the stock market re-
opened after the weekend on Monday, 28 February, there was a rush of
panic selling.[15] 'If Guizot falls, we are all of us lost,' exclaimed Melanie
Metternich that evening, much to the surprise of a young diplomat who
was with her, for few outside the governing circle appreciated how close
the links between Paris and Vienna had become in the previous two
years.[16]

The February Revolution in Paris and its effects on the Habsburg Monarchy (*1848*)

At five o'clock on the Tuesday afternoon a telegram from the Rothschild
information service let Metternich know that Guizot was out and that
on the previous Thursday Louis Philippe had abdicated. In a letter
which he wrote a few hours later the Chancellor admitted events in
France had surprised him, 'at least in part'; but he did not realize

their full extent until the following morning when news arrived of the proclamation of a Republic. In St Petersburg the information almost unhinged Tsar Nicholas, who silenced a ball at the palace with the stentorian pronouncement, 'Gentlemen, saddle your horses! France is a Republic!' Metternich's reaction was more restrained, though equally characteristic: 'Europe finds herself today faced with a second 1793, and Europe was less prone then to catch the disease which was laying France low.' He would co-ordinate arrangements with Prussia and Russia and stop the British from playing with Italian radicalism by conjuring up once more the old Jacobin bogey, for he was sure even Palmerston had no desire to unleash revolutionary war. Observers commented on Metternich's serene calm: it is probable that, while he foresaw fresh difficulties in Italy and mentioned the Rhineland and Poland as areas to be watched, he still had no fear for the heart of the Monarchy. His own position was not in doubt. 'My dismissal would mean revolution,' he declared after lunch on 1 March, though in his conversation he kept harking back to Emperor Francis's failure to implement his proposals for internal reform in 1817 and 1826.[17] Yet it seemed clear to him that in a foreign crisis of such magnitude Austria needed his experience: for who else was there left to recall Brunswick's invasion, or Coburg at Valenciennes, or the treason of Dumouriez?

The Monarchy as a whole received the news from Paris with far less assurance than its Chancellor. In Vienna and most of the large cities there was a run on the banks, with everyone anxious to change notes for silver, since it was assumed foreign crisis involved expenditure on the army which, in its turn, would mean additional taxes, heavy inflation and the depreciation of paper money. Yet the students in Vienna were slow to respond to the intensity of excitement in France. The reason for this was primarily social rather than political. In 1848 the solemnities of Lent began unusually late – Ash Wednesday fell on 8 March – and the week in which Vienna learnt of the French revolution coincided with the annual *Fasching*, the Austrian equivalent of a *Mardi Gras* carnival, which was celebrated this year with exuberance in exceptionally mild weather. Student enthusiasm in Catholic Vienna that week thrilled, not to the thought of distant barricades, but to the voice of Jenny Lind triumphant in the Karntertortheater. It is significant that the earliest meeting of student societies to discuss what had happened in Paris is reported to have been held on 9 March: no general gathering of students in Vienna was convened until 12 March, the first Sunday in Lent.[18]

With Vienna concerned over other matters, the political initiative was seized by the Hungarian liberals in Pressburg. In the autumn of 1847 it had become necessary to summon a new Diet in order to elect Archduke Stephen as Palatine in succession to his father, Joseph, who had died earlier in the year. The lower House in the Diet was dominated by the representative of Pest, Lajos Kossuth, at the peak of his influence as an orator and with a formidable programme of reforms to urge on his fellow members. On 3 March Kossuth delivered an impressive speech in which he called for the establishment of a responsible government in Hungary and for similar institutions for the nationalities outside the Hungarian Kingdom; only by control of finance would Hungary and the other lands of the Empire check the extravagant policies of the Establishment in Vienna. His words were scrupulously loyal to the dynasty and his proposals embodied in an Address to the Crown, which was carried by acclamation; but the speech was virtually a declaration of war on the old system, and on the Austrian Chancellor as its representative. By devious exercises in procedural filibustering Metternich and the other members of the Conference of State prevented the Address from being officially received in Vienna; but reports of Kossuth's speech were circulating in the capital by the next weekend and they were soon followed by the full text.[19]

Metternich himself does not appear to have been troubled by events in Vienna until Friday, 10 March, and even then he discounted the more alarmist rumours. Throughout the week he held talks with General von Radowitz, who had come from Berlin with offers of Prussian support in case of a French attack on Austrian territory in return for concessions by Austria to Prussia over the form of the German Confederation. These negotiations proceeded against a background of mild discontent in the capital, the principal grievance being the chronic financial instability of the Empire and the failure of the authorities to publish detailed budgetary figures. The Lower Austrian Estates were due to meet on 13 March and, as usual, resolutions had begun to circulate among the members of the Estates and of the *Leseverein* in the preceding week; but they contained nothing more outspoken than a complaint that the Emperor's present councillors tended to separate the sovereign and his subjects. A meeting of the regional Manufacturers' Association (*Gewerbeverein*) on 9 March was attended by Archduke Francis Charles and by Kolowrat: it produced some healthy and constructive criticisms, though with none of the fiery rhetoric of Pressburg. Both Metternich and Archduke Ludwig had sought the opinion of Sedlnitzky on the situation in the capital: and he had given them reassurances. Since he had never been inclined to minimize any danger, they took him at his word. The Conference of State met on the Friday morning and issued a statement which denied any Austrian intention of attacking the new French Republic while reminding all subjects of Emperor Ferdinand that the government had the strength to put down any insurrection and would not hesitate to use force to save the Empire from anarchy. It was not so much a growl as a warning bark from a faithful housedog. And yet on that same morning a highly placed civil servant advised Melanie to have her jewels put in safe custody; and her step-daughter Leontine had found a notice fastened to the outer door of her town residence, 'Down with Metternich! No alliance with Russia! Only concessions!' It promised to be a worrying weekend; but on Saturday Sedlnitzky came round once more to the Chancellery, full of confidence. 'Nothing of importance will happen,' he declared.[20]

As if to justify Sedlnitzky's complacency Saturday, 11 March, passed without incident. That morning a petition organized by Alexander Bach, a brilliant young lawyer with political ambitions, was handed to the secretarial committee of the Lower Austrian Estates for consideration at Monday's meeting. It went far beyond the customary subjects discussed by the Estates: a wide range of proposals included the public inspection of state accounts, guarantees for basic liberties, and the summoning of representative institutions for the whole Monarchy. Bach's petition was supported by several hundred signatures, mostly from members of the professional class conscious of having investments to protect and doubtful if the administration could safeguard them. In the evening a group of students, many of them from the medical faculty of the university, prepared a second petition: it sought greater freedom in teaching, called for abolition of censorship, made the traditional reference to liberty of worship, and added – in very general terms – a plea for some system of representative government. The students agreed the petition should be presented to the Emperor himself, after they had submitted it to a general gathering in the central hall of the university on Sunday morning. At this point, Sedlnitzky's police became uneasy and suggested to the Rector of the university that he might like special precautions to be taken. But the Rector felt the sight of police might inflame tempers: he assured the authorities his professors would guide and restrain the student body.

Metternich spent Sunday morning quietly in the Chancellery: he wrote to the envoys in Brussels and Rome, although what he had to say was of little importance. Half a mile away, in the university, life was suddenly more thrilling, for the professorial staff proved less compliant than their Rector suggested. Dr Anton Füster, a member of the Theological Faculty, was moved to eloquence at early Mass: Lent, it seemed, was a season of hope and courage, and out of travail Truth would triumph. It was a good start to the day; and throughout the morning, a contemporary account declares, 'the heads of the young people' were 'too much excited by some of the professors to attend to the dictates of prudence and reason'.[21] The students hurriedly signed their petition and agreed that two university teachers of liberal reputation should convey it to the palace. Professor Hye – who had shocked the authorities in 1846 by raising doubts on the legality of Cracow's annexation in a doctoral dissertation – and Professor Endlicher were duly received by Archduke Ludwig, and in the afternoon were summoned to an audience with Ferdinand himself. The petition was accepted and the students informed it would receive 'due consideration'. This, however, was an anti-climax and the students resolved to meet again next morning and to go in procession across the inner city to the *Landhaus* in the Herrengasse, where at nine o'clock the Lower Austrian Estates would begin their session. The two dissident movements would thus come together at the *Landhaus*, which stood almost directly behind the Chancellery, its entrance portico only three hundred yards from Metternich's study window.

Here was the point at which authority should have acted, if order were to be maintained. The president of the Lower Austrian Estates raised his doubts with the police, but was given the customary assurance. And Archduke Ludwig was troubled, though for some days his brother John had been with him in the Hofburg to strengthen his resolve and he does not appear to have pressed for any particular precautions to be taken. Archduke John himself later explained the inactivity as a consequence of Metternich's own self-confidence: 'The Prince,' he wrote, 'was the only person to whom you could talk, and he was firmly convinced he could handle the situation with written memoranda and speeches. Everyone else was impossible.'[22] At Kübeck's suggestion the Conference of State decided to make a concession, which the Chancellor had long favoured, and invite representatives from all the provincial Estates to Vienna for discussions. No publicity was, however, given to this decision – which was, perhaps, just as well, for it fell far short of the petitioners' hopes.

That evening there was an odd thrill of apprehension in the city and its suburbs, no deep hatred and very little fervour, merely an acceptance of the fact that on Monday political life was going to change, probably for the better. Foreign diplomats and members of high society flocked to Melanie's reception in the Chancellery, curious to see how the Metternichs were taking the buffeting of fortune. The general impression was that they took it well: his nonchalance was, perhaps, a little over played; and conceivably her glow of social eminence a trifle rouged. But Melanie was never a patient woman and Princess Felicie Esterhazy was there to try her. 'Is it really true you are going tomorrow?' asked Felicie. 'Why?' replied her hostess; and with studied silliness Felicie explained, 'They've told us to buy up candles for an illumination tomorrow, because something big is going to happen.'[23]

The resignation of Metternich (13 March 1848)

Monday, 13 March, was an overcast day although the temperature was mild. The students marched to the Herrengasse and were outside the *Landhaus* at nine in the morning. So were many spectators, 'intruders of the better classes', as one witness called them. But having reached the *Landhaus*, the students were unsure of their next move, for the Lower Austrian Estates had no intention of permitting outsiders to burst in from the courtyard and disrupt their own deliberations. It began to look as if Austria was, after all, in the throes of a 'No Revolution'. Metternich carried on working his way through normal engagements: that morning he was to receive General von Radowitz for the latest exchange of ideas about the German Confederation. Princess Melanie, watching the crowd from the upper windows, bristled with contempt: 'Now we can see how the Viennese run a pocket revolution. All they need is a stand selling sausages to make themselves happy.'[24]

Yet, though the students might lack a Camille Desmoulins or a Danton to inspire them, they soon found amateur orators of their own. Dr Adolf Fischhof, a young physician from the General Hospital, called for freedom of the press, trial by jury, a parliamentary assembly and for unity among all the peoples of the Monarchy. And a Tyrolean student, with the powerful lungs of a mountaineer, had the inspired notion of reading Kossuth's speech in German translation, while printed copies were hawked among the onlookers. There were loud cheers at every mention of a constitution and, for the first time, a clear vocal demand for the dismissal of the Chancellor. The shouting penetrated to Metternich's study although the Prince, being deaf, could not distinguish all that was said: a secretary made notes, for future reference.

The general commotion made it impossible for the members of the Lower Austrian Estates to continue their meeting, especially as some of the students were seeking to force their way into the *Landhaus*. Shortly before noon, the president of the Estates gave up all pretence of keeping order. A deputation was sent to the Hofburg to inform Archduke Ludwig of the people's demands. The crowd slowly moved away from the Herrengasse to the Ballhausplatz, between the Chancellery and the Hofburg itself. They saw the Archduchess Sophie and Archduke Francis Charles in the Imperial gardens and cheered. For good measure, they cheered when someone mentioned the Emperor's name as well. By now they were willing to cheer anyone – except Metternich, for general notions of revolutionary change were rapidly giving way to a particular objective, the dropping of Europe's aged coachman.

Soon after midday Archduke Ludwig sent for the Chancellor. He came across the Ballhausplatz, guarded by troops and with Melanie watching anxiously from behind the curtains. No one molested him.

People noticed he was as immaculately dressed as ever: trousers of light grey, a dark green frock coat, black silk cravat; and he carried his gold-embossed cane as though it were a staff of office. He had no hesitation in telling Archduke Ludwig what was to be done. There were fourteen thousand troops in and around the city. They should clear the streets and restore order. At the same time he personally would see the spokesmen of 'the rabble' and inform them of the Conference of State's decision to seek advice from the various regional Estates. Ludwig authorized his thirty-year-old nephew, Archduke Albrecht, to fetch guard detachments into the city from the barracks in the suburbs and to close the city gates, for by now there were reports of shop-wrecking and rumours of a general attack upon property by the labourers who squatted in wretched poverty beyond the walls.

The events of the afternoon are confused. Metternich appears to have returned to the Chancellery, having recommended that Field Marshal Prince Windischgraetz (who was in Vienna on a private visit from Prague, and who was to dine with the Chancellor) should be given plenipotentiary authority to restore order, since it was too difficult a task for an inexperienced commander like Archduke Albrecht. But while there was hesitation in the Hofburg, the mood of the people turned uglier. Someone threw a missile at Albrecht; and shortly before two o'clock, a patrol of Italian soldiery was caught in the narrow streets by a hostile crowd and opened fire, killing five civilians. Immediately what had been a demonstration became a riot, with reports of arson and serious looting arriving at the War Ministry and the Hofburg during the afternoon. At one point there was an attack on Metternich's new house on the Rennweg, although it was saved from destruction.

There were now, in effect, two revolutionary forces at work in the capital: the political liberals from the *Landhaus* and the university, supported in general by the bourgeoisie and the craftsmen among the workers; and a socially destructive mob of underprivileged, exploiting the breakdown in government. The groups were mutually hostile but linked by resentment of the Army. In the middle of the afternoon the Burgomaster of Vienna proposed to Archduke Ludwig that the Army should be withdrawn from the city and that its safety should be entrusted to the Civic Guard, an auxiliary force under the Burgomaster's command; and there was also a proposal that students should be enrolled in an 'Academic Legion', which would help to protect property. There was, not surprisingly, hesitation in the Hofburg; but by five o'clock the Civic Guard had already begun to collaborate in restoring order and there was an unofficial truce in the inner city. A deputation from the Guard, together with some members of the Lower Austrian Estates, went once more to the Hofburg; and delivered a virtual ultimatum. If by nine o'clock in the evening the students were armed, the soldiery withdrawn and Metternich dismissed from office, they would ensure the safety of the city: otherwise they would go over to the side of the revolution.

Metternich and Windischgraetz were summoned to the Hofburg at six o'clock; and at first found the court outwardly firm. Windisch-graetz, who was in civilian clothes, returned home to change into his uniform on the understanding he would assume sole command in Vienna. But once he was gone, the factions at court hostile to Metter-nich began to voice their complaints; and by seven o'clock Ludwig had authorized the establishment of an Academic Legion and had ordered the troops back to their barracks. Finally he told Metternich bluntly that he must tender his resignation. But the Chancellor was not prepared to surrender so meekly. He began to explain the difficulties any successor would find: he looked beyond Vienna to the troubles of Hungary, Italy and Germany; and, getting into his stride, cast an experienced eye over the unstable map of Europe. After an hour and a half of listening to Metternich, Archduke John became restless. He took out his watch: 'Prince, we have only another half an hour', he said, 'And we are still not yet resolved on the answer we shall give to the people.' And Kolowrat contributed his comment: 'Your Imperial Highness, I have sat in conference with Prince Metternich for twenty-five years and I have always heard him go on in this way, never coming to the point.'[25]

The sands were running out for Metternich. He demanded that each member of the Imperial family who was present – and they included young Francis Joseph – should personally absolve him from the oath he had taken to Emperor Francis to stand by Ferdinand. Finally Emperor Ferdinand himself asserted his authority: 'Tell the people I agree to everything,' he said, and retired to bed.

At nine o'clock Metternich announced his resignation to the latest deputation from the people. Uneasy at their blatant display of ingrati-tude, some members of the court congratulated him on his self-sacrifice. Windischgraetz, arriving fully accoutred after one of the slowest changes of dress on record, was aghast at the news and tried to make Metternich and the Archdukes reverse their decision: 'This must not be!' he declared, doing nothing with magnificent resolution. And the ex-Chancellor returned wearily across the Ballhausplatz to the palace which had been his home for more than a third of a century. Melanie awaited him in the antechamber, hardly doubting the news he would bring. 'Well, are we quite dead?' she asked gallantly. 'Yes, my dear', he answered, 'We are dead.'[26]

L

EXILE

Flight to England

Metternich spent Monday night in the Chancellery on the Ballhaus-platz, his official residence for the past thirty-nine years. He enjoyed, says his wife, 'the sleep of a righteous man after an act nobly done'.[1] Elsewhere in Vienna things were less peaceful. Windows blazed with lamps and candles to celebrate the Chancellor's fall; and in some districts households slow to welcome liberty with illuminations found the glass of their homes shattered by champions of freedom. Beyond the gates there was, for much of the night, a ring of fire: flames shot up from fractured pipes of the new gas lamp-standards; toll-houses pillaged earlier in the afternoon were still smouldering; and at one point cheap alcohol from a looted warehouse overspilt into the embers and was itself ignited. Soon after dawn on Tuesday students began to parade down the streets of the inner town. They wore white ribbons as a symbol of emancipated purity, and they brought news that Sedlnitzky, too, was dismissed and the press declared free from censorship. The city was in a dangerous mood, its surface jubilation tense with menace. A recruiting office was opened to register names for the National Guard while in the University quarter, between St Stephen's Cathedral and the Danube Canal, the Academic Legion organized its first patrols. It was doubtful if, on this third day of unrest, the more turbulent spirits could be restrained from striking Jacobin attitudes.[2]

Throughout the morning Metternich remained in the Chancellery and members of the administration came to consult him, partly from habit and partly from fright at having to take decisions of their own in a crisis. 'I am no longer anybody,' he told them, 'I have nothing more to do, nothing to discuss with anyone.' Some of his visitors urged him to withdraw his resignation and others to leave Vienna before the revolutionaries took control of the city gates. There were rumours of an attack planned on the Chancellery building and a message reached the Prince from the Hofburg indicating that Archduke Ludwig would not guarantee his safety so long as he remained in the capital. In the early afternoon the Metternichs slipped away through the garden gate and found temporary refuge in the town house of Count Taaffe on the Löwestrasse, only a few hundred yards away.

Fortunately the fallen Minister still had friends loyal to him. Foremost among them was Baron Charles von Hügel, whose father had served Count Francis George and whose brother had once been in love with Melanie. 'I found I could not foresake the very old man with a broken frame and a broken heart,' Hügel wrote in a letter a few days later.[3] In the weeks which followed Metternich's dismissal, the Baron took charge of his affairs and guided the family to safety. Metternich himself had only the equivalent of £50 in ready cash and, until money reached him from the Rothschilds, Hügel had to finance Clement and Melanie, the four youngest children, a maid and a valet. And at first it was Hügel who decided where they should go.

Sensing that Taaffe's home was too near the centre of trouble, he arranged for the Metternichs to travel to the family seat of the Liechtensteins at Feldsberg, on the borders of Moravia. The children were sent on to Nikolsburg by rail, escorted by another loyal friend, Count Rechberg. Hügel, the Prince and Melanie dined on Tuesday evening at Taaffe's and set out after dark in a common fiacre as far as the Prater, where they changed into one of the Liechtenstein carriages. They journeyed painfully slowly along old roads which, at that time of year, were in bad repair; they dared not risk interception on the new road, for there was a rumour that Kolowrat had ordered the Prince to be detained in the city. Feldsberg is barely forty miles from Vienna but they did not reach the castle until two o'clock, a six-hour journey. Although Rechberg and the children had already arrived, the castle was bitterly cold and nothing was ready for them. It took a couple of hours to get a fire going in a corner of one of the great rooms. At four in the morning the seventy-four-year-old ex-Chancellor sank exhausted on to a sofa. His family covered him with rugs, too weary themselves to look far into the future. It was 15 March and, in the city from which they had fled, the liberals were waiting to welcome Kossuth, who was coming from Pressburg to give Hungary's salutation to Austria's revolt.

The Metternichs remained for a week in Feldsberg, for the Prince was in a state of nervous collapse after the shock of dismissal and flight. They might have stayed longer but the local burgomaster was alarmed at the mood of the townsfolk in neighbouring Nikolsburg and feared for their lives. Leontine joined them on 21 March and urged her step-mother to go to England, for by now unrest had spread across the continent from the Adriatic to the Baltic.[4] Hügel had already advised the Prince to think of an English sanctuary, and the family at last agreed that Clement and Melanie should set out for the Dutch coast, with Rechberg, Hügel and Richard Metternich (now nineteen) as escorts, leaving the younger children in Leontine's care until the crisis passed.

There followed nine days of discomfort and anxiety as the Metternichs travelled for five hundred miles across states erupting in revolution. So far as possible they avoided the towns. They went through Moravia and into Bohemia, skirted Prague and entered Saxony with a brief stop in Dresden, full of memories for the Prince. Then on to Brunswick, Hanover and a quiet corner of Prussia until eventually they reached the Rhine in the Dutch city of Arnhem on 31 March. Sometimes they journeyed by coach and sometimes by train, their passports bearing the name 'Mayern' on one day and 'Matteux' on another.[5] They had disappointments: the Archbishop of Olmütz and the local military commander refused to permit them to stay in the Moravian capital. Often, as Hügel writes, they were 'in expectation of some frightful catastrophe'. Melanie was alarmed by the sight of anyone who might be a student, and unhappy at having to travel from Olmütz to Prague in an ordinary railway carriage, with a mother and howling child as neighbours. (The train guard hurriedly moved the Metternichs to another coach). At times they were recognized, notably in Teplitz where the Prince had made so many visits; but discovery of their identity always seems to have evoked respect rather than abuse. Probably they were never in such danger as Melanie and Hügel feared, but the newspaper reports of what was happening in Berlin, Milan and in Hungary filled them with alarm and despair; and it was as well they did not have to pass through any of the revolutionary centres. The uncensored press carried gleeful accounts of their flight, though with no pretence of accuracy: it was an irresistible gift to the satirical cartoonists of France and the German lands.

For most of the journey Metternich remained in cheerful spirits, despite the 'frightful news from our Italy'.[6] He seems to have been comforted by the thought that his own fall had released all these passions in the continent. But at Arnhem his health gave way again and he had to rest for another week before travelling to Amsterdam on 5 April, and going on to The Hague on the following day. Here they were worried by news from England, for the government was taking precautions to counter the massive Chartist demonstration planned for the following Monday (10 April). The Metternichs decided to remain on the outskirts of The Hague until it became clear whether or not London would succumb to the revolutionary virus. Life in Holland was expensive but peaceful, and both Charles von Hügel and Metternich himself enjoyed the spring flowers in the Dutch gardens. It was not until the afternoon of 19 April that the fugitives embarked on a steam packet-boat at Rotterdam and, as the Prince wrote in a humorous note to his daughter Leontine, crossed the North Sea in the company of

'twenty oxen, sixty to eighty calves, and half a hundred sheep'.[7] In
the Thames estuary a brig ran into the steamer and damaged its
rudder, but the vessel continued safely up river and landed the Metternichs at Blackwall, only five miles from the centre of London, at mid-
morning on 20 April (Maundy Thursday). After a short journey by
train and cab, they arrived at the Brunswick Hotel in Hanover Square,
where they stayed for a fortnight until they found a house to rent for the
summer months.

Although Melanie thought London oppressively large and unsympathetic, her husband enjoyed his first weeks in England. Most of the
great names called at the hotel on courtesy visits: he met, for the first
time, his old adversary Palmerston and his former ally, Guizot, now
like the Prince forced into exile. Before the end of April Metternich had
formed a new friendship with Disraeli, who easily succumbed to his
charm and was fascinated by his ceaseless flow of reminiscence. And
there were old friendships to renew as well. Wellington, now nearly
eighty and like Metternich a relic from a legendary past, was generous
with his hospitality and visited the exiles almost every day, either in the
morning or evening. He was constantly thinking of unusual diversions
for the Prince's entertainment: a visit to a Chinese junk which had
sailed around the Cape of Good Hope and was moored in the East
India Docks; a guided tour of Apsley House to inspect his trophies on
the eve of the Waterloo Banquet; and a proposal that, as a senior
Doctor of Civil Law in the university of which the Duke was Chancellor,
Metternich should serve on an Oxford deputation to present an address
to the Queen.[8] But the Prince politely declined this honour: he had
seen enough of students and academics in recent months; and there is
no doubt that he expected a more formal acknowledgement of his
presence in London by the English court. As a young man of twenty-
one he had been received by George III: now, at seventy-five, the old
King's grand-daughter ignored him. The Metternichs did, indeed,
exchange visits with William IV's widow, but Victoria remained silent.
It was an affront which continued to rankle with Melanie, who did not
share her husband's enthusiasm for English society.

The young children of the family were brought over from Germany
later in the summer and the Metternichs leased a house in Belgravia
(44, Eaton Square) for four months. The Prince was surprised by the
growth of London, with its maze of endless streets bustling with
activity. He noted details at great length in his letters to Leontine.
Water omnibuses on the Thames were a sound idea, he thought, and he
commended one-horse cabs as an economic means of urban transport
which Vienna might copy.[9] One morning he went to the Barclay Perkins
brewery in Southwark and spent four hundred words describing its
amenities:[10] it is interesting that he should have been received there

with great respect, for when another Austrian visitor, General Haynau, toured the brewery two years later he was attacked by the draymen and nearly lynched; but, whatever the workers might think of the Metternich System, they bore no ill-will in 1848 towards its fallen master.

Each day of his sojourn in London he read through the French and English newspapers, carefully noting every peak on the revolutionary fever chart: the hurried departure of the Imperial family from Vienna to Innsbruck in May; the establishment by members of the Academic Legion of a Committee of Public Safety in the Habsburg capital; the Piedmontese advance in Lombardy; and the heady nationalism of Kossuth in Budapest. By midsummer Metternich sensed the fever was abating. In Paris Cavaignac had quelled the workers and in Germany the Frankfurt Assembly invited a Habsburg, the Archduke John, to serve as head of a provisional executive for all the territories of the old German Confederation. Liberals in Italy no longer looked on Pius IX as their prophet, while on 24 July the guns of Marshal Radetzky, who had once gone forward with Metternich along the roads to Paris, routed the Piedmontese at Custozza and brought an armistice to northern Italy. Some events touched Metternich deeply: he was especially saddened by news that Windischgraetz's wife had been killed when Prague rose in revolt on 12 June. Her death evoked poignant memories in a man who was living more and more in the past that summer, for she had been one of the Schwarzenberg girls rescued from the fire at the Paris embassy in 1810, in which her mother had perished, and she was a childhood friend of his beloved daughter, Marie. Without any hesitation, he approved Windischgraetz's subsequent bombardment of Prague, even though it was a city whose beauty he admired. He believed Windischgraetz's action ensured that the revolution would be contained, and he was right. But he did not foresee the horrors awaiting Vienna in October before order was restored, nor the long agony of Hungary.[11]

It was strange to be a distant spectator of momentous events and, despite his ready acceptance by the English, the hours seem at times to have moved slowly for him in London. He read as much as his tired eyes permitted, following the English parliamentary reports. Occasionally he sent his son Richard to listen to a debate at Westminster and catch for him the mood of the parties. He would write letters to friends and former colleagues: a note to Archduke John, who had long distrusted him, produced no response; but Radetzky replied to his message of congratulation with a warmth and sympathy which heartened him.[12] From time to time an item of news or an echo of conversation led him to reflect on his own past policies, though never too deeply for comfort. He had few regrets, apart from a conviction that he should have been permitted a freer hand in the Monarchy's internal administration. What was happening on the continent merely proved to him the accuracy of his own predictions: had he not always insisted that liberty must be protected from the presumptuous thinker if it were not to lapse into licence?

Nor was he the only refugee to examine his political conscience in these troubled months. One morning he met Guizot by chance on the steps of the British Museum and the two men dropped easily into a conversation about the present and the recent past. Suddenly Metternich came out with his daily aphorism: 'Error', he declared, with a smile of contentment, 'has never come into my mind'. Perhaps he was laughing at himself, but it is unlikely. Guizot claims to have answered this preposterous assertion by admitting that he personally had been more fortunate, for he had on several occasions discovered his mistakes. Yet, if so, the irony of his reply was almost certainly lost on Metternich. Self-esteem had become for him the bread of existence. If once he doubted his political righteousness, he would sense that nobody now need respect his opinions. Infallibility of judgement was the ultimate illusion making exile tolerable.[13]

He took no active part in public affairs. Briefly he played with the idea of establishing a conservative journal, of collaborating with Guizot in challenging the assumptions of the revolutionary manifestos; but no one was interested. His voice did not, however, go unheard. Disraeli profited from his knowledge of European politics; and there were odd traces of Metternich's philosophy in two speeches made by the member for Buckinghamshire in the House of Commons that summer. On 5 June Disraeli condemned the Liberal tendency to treat foreign affairs as a matter of sentiment rather than of common sense; and on 15 August he delivered a devastating attack on Palmerston's persistent obsession with 'the modern and new-fangled' doctrine of nationality. So impressed was Metternich with his pupil's performance in the House of Commons that he wrote to Baron Wessenberg, by now the Austrian Foreign Minister, and drew his attention to Disraeli's remarks. But his letter seems to have gone unnoticed by Wessenberg who was, at the time, fully occupied with the threat of French intervention in Italy.*[14]

* It is interesting to note that Wessenberg was an exact contemporary of Metternich, who had made considerable use of his abilities in 1813-16. Subsequently his liberal sympathies had kept him out of Austrian service and he was considerably surprised to be summoned from retirement in May 1848 and given the portfolio of Foreign Affairs. After serving as virtual Prime Minister of Austria from July to November 1848, he resigned in favour of Schwarzenberg and returned to his estates in the Breisgau. He died in 1858.

The Austrians investigate Metternich's administration while the ex-Chancellor remains exiled in Brighton and Brussels

The ex-Chancellor's persistent letter-writing must frequently have been an embarrassment for his former colleagues in Vienna. It was difficult to know how to deal with his advice: should his opinions be heard with deference – for no present member of the foreign service had such experience of France and Italy – or should they be ignored, as the counsels of one who had lost touch with reality? The mood of public opinion in the Austrian capital was still resolutely hostile to Metternich. On 23 June the *Wiener Abendzeitung*, one of the many newspapers which had sprung up once the censorship was abolished, published an article accusing Metternich of having received fifty thousand ducats a year from Tsar Alexander between 1815 and 1825 and seventy-five thousand ducats a year from Tsar Nicholas after his accession. The article went on to charge Metternich with massive peculation of public money and with having surrendered Austria's interests for Russian gold. It blamed him for the chronic weakness of Austrian finances and concluded with a rhetorical flourish by denouncing his 'indiscriminate squandering of State funds' and his 'provident charity for absolutism in every quarter of the globe'.[15] The authorities dared not ignore such an attack. They ordered an official investigation into Metternich's handling of the Foreign Ministry accounts during his term of office and, until the inquiry was concluded, all the Prince's property in Austria was sequestered so that any arrears might be charged against it in the first instance.

An investigation which sought to probe the Austrian financial bureaucracy over a period of thirty-nine years would, at any time, have been a long and formidable proceeding; and, during months of passion and revolutionary change, it was almost impossible. Interim reports in September 1849, December 1849 and May 1850 gradually cleared Metternich of the more flamboyant charges listed in the article, but a new committee dragged its way through another six months of study before abandoning the task, for lack of formal proof. There is no doubt that Metternich had accepted gifts from foreign sources, though these were normally tokens of esteem rather than outright monetary payments, and it is clear that he had benefited from his patronage of the Rothschild banking house, especially at the Congress of Verona; but he had never taken bribes, nor was he ever dependent on foreign funds as a regular source of income. His expense claims during the period of the early congresses had, indeed, been remarkably high, as members of the investigating committee soon perceived when they studied the accounts; but this extravagance was an inevitable consequence of a diplomatic system which placed emphasis upon personal contact and display. In the years of the Restoration any statesman who claimed primacy in public affairs had to waste time and money on showmanship if he were to be accepted at the value he set upon himself; and ultimately the Austrian authorities recognized it was unjust to penalize Metternich for a financial burden incurred 'in a glorious epoch of service to the Imperial House' (as Felix Schwarzenberg was to put it).[16] Such matters could not, however, be settled speedily and, so long as uncertainty persisted, Metternich preferred to remain outside the frontiers of the Empire. Ironically, during the two and a half years of the investigation, he had to rely for financial survival on loans from the Rothschilds and from the Tsar, for he could not draw on any resources within the Austrian lands. Moreover, until the autumn of 1850, bureaucratic jealousy and pettiness denied him the pension to which, as an ex-minister, he was legitimately entitled. Both husband and wife sought to economize during their English visit, not always successfully. They found London, in particular, expensive.

In the autumn society moved out of town. So far as their circumstances permitted, the Metternichs wished to follow the fashion and establish themselves at the seaside. But the Prince had no intention of burying himself a long way from the centre of affairs. In a letter to his daughter, Leontine, he explained that he was thinking of settling somewhere whence London was accessible, just as Vienna had been from Baden. He considered Hastings and Torquay, but dismissed them as too remote.[17] There remained Brighton, a town of which he had heard so much in earlier days from Paul Esterhazy and Dorothea Lieven and to which George IV had vainly urged him to come more than twenty years before. Now, at last, in mid-September 1848 Clement and Melanie moved down to the Sussex coast. They leased number 42, Brunswick Terrace and stayed there until the last week of April 1849.

Life in Brighton was less hectic than in London. They read and exchanged civilities with other worthies and played whist; they walked slowly along the esplanades, up the Steine and past the fading flamboyance of the Pavilion to the Assembly Rooms, and back to the bow-windowed serenity of Hove. They seem always to have been alert, noting fleeting details of everyday events, she in her journal and he in those endless letters. Both of them were saddened by the news from Vienna: the tragedy of István Széchenyi's mental collapse; the lynching of Latour, the Minister of War, on 6 October; and the week-long siege of the Imperial city by the armies of Windischgraetz and Jellacić. Melanie was relieved to hear that the Metternich home on the Rennweg had been spared from destruction, though Kolowrat's town house was burned to the ground. But it all seemed oddly distant from Sussex, where Melanie was sustained by the comforting tranquillity of the sea. 'I found God once more in that boundless horizon', she wrote in her diary, 'and with it came faith and hope, which has restored my courage for the future.'[18]

Her husband, too, gained satisfaction from watching the changing patterns of the waves and the passage of vessels up and down the Channel, that 'maritime Corso' as he called it in a letter to Leontine. He particularly enjoyed following, with his fading eyes, the packet-boat plying between Brighton and Dieppe.[19] As he explained to Leontine, it pleased him to think he was no more than eleven hours from Paris. For, though he had no liking for a French Republic, he remained at heart a European and he felt less isolated in Brighton, where a steamer could bring him the French newspapers only a day after their publication.

Was he bored? Perhaps so; but London was only fifty miles away, less than two hours by rail, and visitors continued to call on the Metternichs, especially during the parliamentary recess. Not all of them could be sure of a welcome from Melanie, who was brusque not only to Palmerston but to Disraeli as well. Clement, however, interested himself particularly in the contest for leadership of the English Conservatives and continued to give Disraeli advice, which was received with warm and open gratitude. In a letter to his wife on 7 January 1849, Disraeli described a trip he had made to Brighton to consult 'Professor Metternich'[20]: 'I never heard such divine talk: he gave me the most masterly exposition of the present state of European affairs, and said a greater number of wise and witty things than I ever recollected hearing from him on the same day. He was indeed quite brilliant, and his eyes sometimes laughed with sunny sympathy with his shining thoughts.' Disraeli hoped later in the year the Metternichs would come and stay with him at Hughenden, the manor in the Chilterns which he had recently purchased; but they never took the opportunity of travelling to Buckinghamshire and their experience of English country life was limited to five days in December at Stratfieldsaye, Wellington's estate on the borders of Hampshire and Berkshire. While most visitors complained that Stratfield Saye was overheated, Metternich was delighted by its standard of comfort; and he was fascinated by the orderly division of the Duke's day, with bells which rang an hour before dinner and valets who would light candles at eleven o'clock so that the ladies would know when to retire to bed. Melanie (whose journal entries become less enthusiastic as the winter drags on) says nothing of the customs and pursuits of Stratfieldsaye, but she is prepared to concede that their host gave them a friendly welcome.[21]

From November to February life in Brighton was enlivened by the presence of that lost enchantress from Regency days, Princess Dorothea Lieven. Metternich had not seen her since 1822 and, after the breach in their friendship, they exchanged only formal letters of condolence at times of family bereavement. For a decade and a half fortune was far from kind to Princess Lieven.²² In 1834 her intrigues in English politics had induced Palmerston to secure the recall of her husband and herself from the Russian embassy in London. Once back in St Petersburg she found the repressive atmosphere of Nicholas I's court tedious and her revulsion at everything Russian was completed by a tragedy in 1835, when within the same month she lost two sons in an epidemic of scarlet fever. That autumn she quarrelled finally with her husband, left St Petersburg in despair and settled in Paris where she built up a new reputation for herself as a political hostess and, from 1840 onwards, as the devoted companion of Guizot. She might well have become his wife, for her husband had died in 1838, but she could never accept the social diminution of ceasing to be a Serene Highness – 'Imagine *me* being announced as Madame Guizot!' she exclaimed to a friend – and she chose to pass her later years beside the chief statesman of France in respectable (if irregular) domesticity. With Guizot she suffered the inconvenience of exile, which brought her back to London and Brighton, to Palmerston and Metternich. She had left a note for her former lover at the Brunswick Hotel within a few days of his arrival in London, but he was in no hurry to renew their friendship; and at Brighton it was Melanie who took the lead in securing a reconciliation between them.²³

Melanie called on Princess Lieven early in November and spent two hours gossiping with her; before the end of the month she had made a second visit, this time with her husband, and Guizot was also present. By December Melanie and Dorothea were outwardly such good friends that they could discuss whether or not Palmerston had changed for the better: Princess Metternich could see no improvement; but Princess Lieven, always fickle in her sympathies, thought his manner distinctly less arrogant. In January Melanie wrote simply in her journal: 'We are seeing much of Princess Lieven. She keeps us in touch with what is going on in Paris. She is in the process of winning herself over to (Louis) Napoleon.' Dorothea Lieven even established a small salon in Brighton and it was there, at the end of January, that Melanie Metternich had a long conversation with Lord Macaulay, whose views on the historical origins for the spiritual claims of the French Crown were, she thought, positively unsound. The great man was weak on King Clovis, and she returned to their temporary home to check it all up in a reference book, though apparently with little success. Like her husband, she missed the library they had accumulated in Vienna.²⁴

Metternich himself found Dorothea much changed, an impression which is hardly surprising after the passage of more than a quarter of a century, but his comments on her seem guarded. She, of course, could not long remain silent, nor had the years taken the sting from her tongue. Early in January 1849 she wrote to the French diplomat, Barante: 'I see M. and Mme. de Metternich every day. She is stout, vulgar, open, kind and well-mannered. He is full of serenity, self-satisfied, endlessly chattering, very tedious and slow and awkward, very metaphysical, boring when he talks of himself and of his infallibility, charming when he talks of the past and especially of Emperor Napoleon.'[25] It is a recognizable pen-portrait of Clement, though not perhaps of Melanie. She fortunately remained unaware of what her friend thought of her but Dorothea could not always hide her feelings these days. Once in that same month Lord Aberdeen's son was present when Metternich was reading extracts from his memoirs to a small group in Brighton, including Dorothea Lieven who suddenly threw herself wearily back in her chair and exclaimed: 'Oh God! How boring all that is!'[26] The incident did not help endear the Princess to her former lover.

In the spring of 1849 the Metternichs came back to London, partly because they needed more accommodation since Leontine was expected on a visit from Germany and was bringing the Prince's only grandchild, Pauline Sandor (then aged thirteen). Melanie succeeded in securing a lease of a suite of rooms in the Old Palace at Richmond, where Elizabeth 1 had died; and the family duly moved to Surrey on 23 April. Once again there was an endless stream of visitors: Wellington brought a specially-cut short coat to protect the Prince's health from the chilly spring breezes off the Thames; and Johann Strauss called, only to be told by Melanie that the people of Vienna were an ungrateful mob, who had treated her husband badly.[27] A few weeks later Princess Lieven was at Richmond, staying at the Royal Hotel. She made a vivid impression on young Pauline Sandor who, seventy years afterwards, recalled a woman looking 'as if she had stepped out of some ancestral portrait': 'Dressed in black and wearing an enormous hat with a green shade over her eyes and carrying a large fan, she paraded before us, stately and imposing, never deigning to glance at us miserable earthworms.' And in this curious autumn of Metternich's life, his grand-daughter saw two other figures from the past at Richmond: one, Dorothea de Dino, the last of the Sagan women, she remembered as well dressed and distinguished, speaking beautiful German in a rich melodious voice*; the other, Katharina Bagration, was frail and withered and still wrapt in the daring veil-like chemises she had affected during the great Congress, gazing earnestly through watery blue eyes at the man who had made love to her in Dresden nearly half a century before. Pauline Sandor came from too protected a society to feel pity: 'It was all we

---

* In her Memoirs (*Geschehenes, Gesehenes, Erlebtes*, p. 18) Pauline Metternich-Sandor maintains that the distinguished woman she saw at Richmond was Wilhelmine of Sagan, Dorothea de Dino's sister. This, however, cannot have been the case for Wilhelmine died at the end of November 1839. On this point Srbik accepted, without question, Pauline's testimony (cf his *Metternich*, Vol. II, p. 305) and several biographers have followed Srbik's lead.

could do to prevent ourselves from laughing outright,' she writes in her reminiscences.[28]

In June Dorothea Lieven commented to a friend on Metternich's thin appearance and lack of gaiety, and a month later he was seriously ill. 'Prince Metternich has a fainting fit every day,' she wrote to Lady Holland on 2 July. 'People around him are worried and these are certainly bad symptoms at seventy-six.'[29] The Duke sent him one of the best doctors in London, but Melanie and Leontine continued to be disturbed by his anaemic condition. He was extremely depressed at the failure of the new rulers of Austria to acknowledge their debt to him: by now the chief minister was Felix Schwarzenberg, whom he had long regarded as a friend; and on 2 December 1848, poor Ferdinand had handed over his Imperial responsibilities to Francis Joseph. Metternich had written to both Emperor and Minister; and although he received a formal reply from Schwarzenberg in February, there was no word from Francis Joseph. During her father's illness, Leontine confidentially sent a message to Archduchess Sophie and sought some gesture of sympathy from the Habsburg court. At last, on 2 August, Metternich received a letter written by Francis Joseph at Schönbrunn in the previous week: the young Emperor regretted rumours of his illness, expressed his 'unalterable regard' for his former mentor, and looked forward to welcoming him 'in a not too distant time' in the country to which he had devoted such 'glorious activity'. There is little doubt that these sentiments, whether sincere or not, did much to restore Metternich's health.[30] By the beginning of September, Dorothea Lieven could note – with some surprise – that he was once more visiting his friends in Richmond and Bushy and Kew.[31]

But Melanie had begun to tire of England. Her own health was poor – she had suffered from chronic abdominal pains since the birth of her youngest son, Lothar, in 1837 – and she did not look forward to autumnal mists beside the Thames at Richmond, for she was complaining of the cold and damp even in the first week of September. There were other matters, too: she was worried over the provision of good Catholic tutors for her children; and she was constantly clashing with Lady John Russell (the wife of the Prime Minister) and with Lady Palmerston over their sympathies for Kossuth and the Hungarian national movement. From the comments in Melanie's journal it seems at times as if Princess Lieven encouraged the feud:[32] her taste for self-advertisement naturally inclined her towards intrigue; and Melanie, who was normally so sharp at perceiving mischief and treachery, never learnt what a tiresome friend Dorothea could be. Metternich himself wished to move back to Brighton for the winter: but from mid-August onwards Melanie began to urge him, gently but persistently, to cross the Channel and settle in Brussels. It would, she insisted, be cheaper there and he would be more in touch with the affairs of the continent. At last Metternich yielded; he wrote to King Leopold and sent Richard ahead to look for accommodation. They left Richmond on 7 October and spent three nights in Mirvat's Hotel (which was, soon after, re-named Claridge's). Wellington and Disraeli and all their English friends came to bid them farewell; and on 10 October they were seen off from Charing Cross Station as if they were royalty. After a calm crossing from Dover to Ostend they arrived in Brussels on the following afternoon and moved temporarily into the Hotel Bellevue.[33]

They remained in Brussels for more than a year and a half, far longer than Metternich anticipated. He had been encouraged by news from Austria: the last centres of resistance, eastern Hungary and Venice, had capitulated; and he believed friends at court would welcome his return although he had long made it clear that, after 'fifty years of plaguery', he did not wish to become politically active again. He could, almost certainly, have slipped back to Bohemia and lived quietly on his estates: but personal pride ruled this out. Never, he said, would he return 'secretly like a thief'; and there was still the tiresome investi-gation into the Foreign Ministry accounts to be wound up. So the family settled in a small house on the Boulevard de l'Observatoire which they leased from the distinguished violinist, Bériot. It was cramped, but economical: the Prince calculated that the cost of living was less than half as high in Belgium as in England.[34]

Outwardly Metternich was content with life in Brussels. The Belgian court treated the whole family with kindness, even though as Chancellor Metternich had never been well-disposed towards the dynasty, nor indeed to the Belgian nation. People visited the Metternichs in Brussels just as they had in London and Brighton: the King of Bavaria; the Duchess of Cambridge; the socialist Louis Blanc; the notorious General Haynau; Adolphe Thiers searching for material to write his study of the Consulate and Empire; Princess Lieven without Guizot; Princess Lieven with Guizot; writers and scientists and musicians. Some called out of curiosity, some from courtesy, some for gossip; others needed information or advice which was readily given but rarely taken. Letters from the German states and from within the Empire asked for the Prince's opinion on a host of topics and sometimes he had to try and remember what he had thought about Tuscany in the mid-'thirties or Hungary in the early 'forties. Metternich proudly claimed he was 'consultant specialist to the great world-hospital'; and he still possessed enough influence in London for the occasional 'inspired' paragraph in *The Times* or one of the quarterlies.[35]

These activities did not always assist his personal cause. He was scrupulously careful to avoid openly criticizing the new government in Vienna and he had no intention of offending Schwarzenberg or of embarrassing the young Emperor. But he could not entirely hide his disapproval of much that was being done: excessive centralism rather than the introduction of a federal system, his old panacea; the folly of an insincere experiment with constitutional machinery of foreign patent; the blind hostility towards everything Magyar which precluded exploiting the old conservatives at a time when radicalism was broken and discredited. He did not appreciate the bitterness which the revolutions had caused within the governing circle, a mood which naturally ruled out the subtlety he commended. Schwarzenberg once told Metternich's daughter he treated the memoranda reaching him from Brussels with the respect he reserved for the gospels,[36] but there is no doubt that at times the old man's dogmatism was unpalatable. So long as he was in Belgium he was too susceptible to Prussian influence for Schwarzenberg's comfort. It would have been far more convenient if he had come back unobtrusively to Königswart or Plass and busied himself with improving his Bohemian estates. But at all costs Schwarzenberg was determined to keep him away from Vienna until he had moulded Francis Joseph to his own image.

Back to the Rhineland; a meeting with Bismarck; and return to Vienna (1851)

By the spring of 1850 Metternich was homesick for his garden on the Rennweg. 'Blossom time will soon be here again,' he wrote to Leontine. 'Go to the villa when the lilac is in flower and give it my greetings.'[37] Two years of exile had begun to break his spirits and the tedium increased through the following months, although the family did their best to keep him supplied with books and pamphlets, for his mind remained active and he enjoyed sharpening it on political polemics. In the autumn the Metternichs were forced to leave the Boulevard de l'Observatoire and find yet another home in the Sablons area of the city. To the Prince a move seemed now hardly worthy of comment if it were still within the Belgian capital. Richard had left them to enter the Austrian diplomatic service, Paul was now sixteen and would soon become a military cadet, even Princess Melanie had gone to Ems for a week with her daughter (also named Melanie) and had spent a couple of nights in Coblenz: only Clement remained rooted in Brussels. That winter he had another bout of fainting fits, a sign of physical weakness and despair; and at last on 27 March 1851 Melanie induced him to write directly to Schwarzenberg and ask if he might return to Vienna provided he gave an undertaking not to participate in public life. The answer arrived on 10 April: Francis Joseph authorized Schwarzenberg to say that he personally would be glad to tender to Metternich in Vienna sentiments of gratitude for his past services. It was a cumbersome but tactful way of inviting the ex-Chancellor to accept the empty honours of an elder statesman.[38]

But now that he had the opportunity of returning home, he was in no hurry to make the journey. All should be done with dignity; and there was no sense in arriving back in Vienna in time for the midsummer heat. The Metternichs decided to spend the warmest months on the Rhine at Johannisberg, which they had not visited for six years. They arrived there on 11 June and stayed until the middle of September, with the local German newspapers commenting politely but curiously on everything they did.[39] Not all of Metternich's activities in that summer of 1851 pleased Schwarzenberg. Relations between Austria and Prussia had been tense for over a year, for the government in Berlin accepted the revival of Habsburg authority in the German lands with reluctance. And despite his avowed intention of remaining above political controversy, Metternich could hardly refuse an exchange of courtesies with the Prussians so long as he was in residence on his Rhineland estate.

On 6 August the Prussian delegate to the resurrected German Diet in Frankfurt visited the Metternichs at Johannisberg. He was, thought Melanie, an intelligent man, with 'the best political principles': she found Herr Otto von Bismarck pleasant and witty, and Clement enjoyed a long conversation with him.[40] At thirty-six the future Chancellor of the German Empire had reached a turning-point in his career, moving away from a narrow Junker Toryism to a more realistic and accommodating policy of diplomatic compromise. Neither Bismarck nor his host had any regard for the unified and democratic Germany of liberal dreams; and they found close identity in both their theories of government and their concepts of statecraft. At Frankfurt Bismarck, who had earlier praised the Austrian approach to German affairs, was already in conflict with Schwarzenberg's representatives; but the shadow of these disputes did not fall across the sunlight of Johannisberg. Bismarck recalled, in later years, the mellow flavour of his host's wine and the long survey of half a century of Europe's affairs to which he was also treated. Although he found Metternich extremely deaf, he was able to pose questions which caught the old statesman's interest; and he claimed that, at one point, Metternich advised him to ensure that Prussia became a 'satiated State', for only thus could she share with Austria the maintenance of orderly government across the continent. Metternich certainly found Bismarck a stimulating conversationalist and a good listener: they met again a year later in Vienna.

Twelve days later Metternich had a visit at short notice from King Frederick William IV of Prussia, who was travelling down the Rhine from Coblenz to Mainz and could not allow himself to pass Johannisberg 'without honouring the hero of the day'. But Metternich had long distrusted the King's vacillating mind and he regarded the reformist activity which he had followed between 1842 and 1848 as one of the principal causes of the German Revolution. He accordingly accepted the King's flattery with reservations, especially when Frederick William's remarks thinly veiled an attack upon Schwarzenberg and his policy. For though Metternich sincerely believed in Austro-Prussian collaboration, he had no intention of being pushed forward as Frederick William's nominee in any contest with Schwarzenberg. If the King undertook his visit as a political manoeuvre, it was a failure and much that he said merely irritated Metternich; but it was gratifying once more to be the centre of activity, especially when discussion carried no responsibility for action. Frederick William remained at Johannisberg for two hours: 'The King's visit pleased Clement,' noted Melanie in her journal.[41]

The Metternichs left Johannisberg for Vienna on 16 September. The rulers of the German states would not allow them to pass quietly through their lands, especially now that the ex-Chancellor had been singled out for Prussian attention. The Grand-Duchess of Baden entertained them at Mannheim, the King of Württemberg in Stuttgart. For much of the journey as far as Ulm, they travelled in royal trains, put especially at their service. They then jogged along as of old in a four-horse carriage for forty-five miles over the Bavarian roads to Donauworth, where they embarked on a river-steamer which carried them slowly down the Danube by way of Regensburg and Linz and through the Wachau, until the steep wooded slope of the Leopoldsberg loomed up on the right bank of the river and they were at last on the outskirts of Vienna. At half-past four in the afternoon of 24 September they landed at Nussdorf to be met by a crowd of friends, with a sprinkling of servants and retainers. A three-carriage cavalcade, with the Prince and Leontine in the first coach, Princess Melanie and her brother following, and young Melanie and Pauline Sandor behind, conveyed the family in style over the last four miles to their house on the Rennweg. Afterwards poor Melanie, deeply moved, described the homecoming in detail in her journal: 'We found the villa just as we had left it,' she wrote contentedly and added, with happy licence, 'The flowers seemed to greet our return.'[42]

ELDEST STATESMAN

Emperor Francis Joseph and Schwarzenberg

When Metternich arrived back in Vienna Emperor Francis Joseph was in Lombardy and it was not until the end of the following week that he returned to his capital. He visited the ex-Chancellor in his home on the Rennweg during the morning of Sunday, 3 October, while Melanie was still at Mass. She tells us in her journal how she hastened back from church, received a friendly greeting from her monarch, and listened on the threshold of her husband's study as the two men talked for a couple of hours, 'the Emperor asking Clement's advice on a great many topics'.[1] Already it was clear that, even had he wished to do so, Metternich would never be permitted to pass these last years musing quietly in the mists of reminiscence. Indeed, by a perverse trick of fortune, in the final phase of his personal history he was to spend less time looking back than during the interlude of exile or the frustrating decade which preceded it. It is as if the triumph of resurgent Bonapartism in France had dispelled his strange nostalgia for the First Empire; and he began to live once more for the present, even occasionally smiling on the future, as his grand-daughter was to note.

Had it been otherwise, he could never have survived so long. When he disembarked at Nussdorf, Kübeck, seeing him for the first time since the March Days, commented on the old man's frailty, on the weariness of his body and spirit;[2] and yet he was to outlive Kübeck by four years, and the wife who had cosseted him in exile by three. Once back in Vienna he adapted himself with surprising ease to the tempo of the new reign. He soon became convinced of a personal obligation to advise the grandson of his old master. It was, of course, impossible to temper his own innate conservatism with any fresh notions of government; but that did not matter. At twenty-one Francis Joseph was as rigid a Tory as any autocrat three times his age, and Austria moved into the half-century of Marx and Darwin with a lingering attachment to divine right and universal monarchy.

At first Metternich was aided by the indomitable resilience of his wife. 'It did not take me eight days to see what was happening in the life of Vienna and to discover all sorts of intrigues', Melanie noted in her journal with happy belligerence.[3] She found the political scene confused but exciting. Before his abdication Ferdinand had conceded a constitution to the liberals and held out promise of a parliament. But as the soldiery restored order in the city streets, all prospect of lasting reforms faded away. The new Emperor's subjects were assured of a single elected assembly for the Empire and a responsible government under a Prime Minister; but these institutions, they were told in the spring of 1849, must await the end of 'the provisional emergency'. Hence when the Metternichs arrived back in Austria, the country was governed by a nominated Prime Minister (Prince Felix Schwarzenberg) and by a cabinet which issued 'provisional' decrees of ominously permanent character. An advisory council had been meeting intermittently for more than a year under the chairmanship of Kübeck in order to determine the structure of a constitution which none of its members really desired. Even in governing circles there was no agreement over future lines of action, and by the autumn of 1851 a clear breach was opening between the Schwarzenberg ministry and an ultraconservative opposition, which was led by Kübeck and supported by Windischgraetz and the Army. It was important for both groups to secure Metternich, with his prestige and experience, as an ally.[4]

The ex-Chancellor was too shrewd to identify himself closely with either faction. He did not entirely approve of Schwarzenberg's foreign policy and he had considerable reservations about the activities of the Minister of the Interior, Alexander Bach, who had once been an outspoken member of the Lower Austrian Estates but who was now imposing a uniform system of administration throughout the Habsburg lands. Both Schwarzenberg and Kübeck made a point of cultivating the Metternichs; and even Bach, so long a critic of the Prince's policy, visited him within a few days of his return and sought to atone for the rash rhetoric of earlier years. The general tone of Metternich's letters from Brussels and Johannesburg had encouraged the Kubeck faction to hope for his support. But, for the moment, he chose to remain in the background, content for people to seek him out in the house on the Rennweg and determined to size up Francis Joseph's opinions before voicing his own. For when the Emperor moved among his generals, as he had done during the visit to Lombardy, he naturally inclined towards the Kübeck-Windischgraetz combination and they had every hope he would soon publicly announce the abandonment of the projected parliamentary constitution; but the young man admired Schwarzenberg and respected Bach, and in the capital no one could be certain which way he would turn.

While Metternich rarely emerged from his study and his gardens, Melanie could not reconcile herself to such discreet anonymity and she was able to keep him well informed of what she thought was going on. There were old affronts she found hard to forget or forgive and past kindnesses which warmed her sympathy; and she was not the most unprejudiced of observers. Unfortunately she retained from the early months of 1848 suspicion of the Archduchess Sophie's treachery and she exchanged some barbed remarks with the Emperor's mother before prudence induced both ladies to abandon their private contest from public duty. Melanie had little regard for Bach and had always preferred Windischgraetz to Schwarzenberg. But in the first days of January 1852 she could not resist accompanying her daughter as chaperon to the Schwarzenberg Ball in the Chancellery on the Ballhausplatz, where she had reigned as hostess for seventeen years. Although Francis Joseph was present and the Archduchess, Melanie was well content with all she saw: 'They had invited everyone from what we call the second rank of Society,' she wrote imperturbably in her journal that night.[5]

If Melanie's inclinations were towards the ultra-conservative faction, so, too, by the end of the year were her husband's. Kübeck had insisted on seeking his opinion over the next stage of constitutional development and had taken note of his views. Clearly Francis Joseph agreed with Kübeck, for in the week before Christmas Metternich received an informal note from the Emperor – it was signed 'Your faithful pupil and friend' – which invited his comments on the latest proposals for government, a patent drafted by Kübeck which would ensure that Austria should be ruled directly by the monarch with the assistance of a nominated advisory council (*Reichsrat*).[6] Metternich was gratified by Francis Joseph's sign of confidence in him and he proceeded to draft a two-thousand-word memorandum, in which he once more pressed for the establishment of a system of consultative provincial diets who would send their own representatives to the *Reichsrat*. Unfortunately, more than a fortnight elapsed between the Emperor's request for Metternich's advice and the completion of his memorandum. The new system was therefore announced in a decree on New Year's Eve 1851, two days before Metternich put the final touches to his draft.[7] But it made little difference. Kübeck's nominated *Reichsrat* had scarcely more influence than similar councils in earlier reigns and for the last four years of Metternich's life it never even met. The truth was that, until defeat and middle age made him cautious, Francis Joseph was too headstrong to welcome collective advice. He would listen to Metternich and other veteran counsellors individually and, when they confirmed his views, he would act on what they had said; but councils, nominated or elected, might too easily clip his prerogatives and he wanted none of them.

By February 1852 Schwarzenberg, who was in his early fifties, had begun to feel the strain of office so severely that he was advised to rest. He could not, however, relax his grip on affairs, for he was determined to consolidate the strong position in Germany which his policy had won for Austria at Prussia's expense in the previous two years. The burden was too great: on 5 April he had a heart attack and dropped dead to the floor. Though Metternich was not entirely in sympathy with all Schwarzenberg had sought to achieve, he mourned a man whom he liked and respected. For Francis Joseph the blow came as almost a national tragedy and he wept as he stood beside the bier of the dead Prime Minister. It was by no means clear who could succeed him. The army officers and the aristocracy would never support Bach, the Emperor's first choice. Kübeck, in his seventy-second year, shrank from such responsibilities. No one thought of Kolowrat who, discredited by his failure to check the spread of revolution, had retired to his Bohemian estates in 1848 and was rarely in Vienna. And, for that matter, nobody thought seriously of Metternich: he had pledged himself to keep out of public life; he was slow, infirm and impossibly deaf; and, in the last resort, his name reminded too many people of a bankrupt system. There remained a sad shortage of talent in the Austrian administration.

Advice from the Rennweg (1852–5)

Upon reflection, and with Kübeck's prompting, Francis Joseph took charge of policy himself, a natural corollary to the New Year's Eve Patent of government.[8] Austria would have no Chancellor and no Prime Minister; but she required a Foreign Minister, and to this post the Emperor appointed Count Ferdinand von Buol-Schauenstein, a career diplomat of whom Schwarzenberg had spoken well earlier in the year. Metternich, who had at one time befriended Buol's father, held no high opinion of the son: he had been Austrian envoy in Turin in 1848 when Charles Albert embraced the Italian national cause; and subsequently, as ambassador in St Petersburg, he succeeded in offending the Tsar. Buol, Metternich remarked, was 'sharp but neither broad nor deep'; and yet he was prepared to support his former subordinate's claim for office in 1852. It was a strange decision. The poor man was so manifestly incompetent that he could not possibly control the external policy of a great empire – unless, of course, he turned for guidance and support to its former Chancellor. There is little doubt that by now hidden power, without tedious restraints of daily administration, was sweeter to Metternich than the mere trappings of authority. Once he had almost been Richelieu: might he now, in old age, become a lay Father Joseph?

Buol officially assumed his duties in the Foreign Ministry exactly a week after Schwarzenberg's death and, as Melanie duly noted, 'He

came at once to visit Clement, showing a proper respect to him'.[9]
Three days later a messenger was taking Metternich's detailed comments on despatches from London back to Buol's study in the Chancellery building: on 16 April there was a brief analysis of Austro-Saxon
relations, amplified by second thoughts a week later; and by the
following month a regular flow of background information on English
politics was being sent from the Rennweg to the Ballhausplatz. So it
continued throughout the year, with Buol forwarding interesting
despatches for Metternich's annotation, especially if they came from
Paris. Sometimes the old man rambled excessively over matters of
lesser moment: the relative status of Austrian and Prussian representation at the Duke of Wellington's funeral troubled him in October; and
in December he affected to believe that the new Emperor of the
French should have styled himself 'Napoleon v'.[10] But, as in his
communications to Francis Joseph, much that the Prince said was of
value. If an analysis of the case against a Papal coronation for Napoleon
III rested on confusion of rumour and precedent, his views on linking
recognition of the French Imperial title with guarantees of European
peace were moderate and statesmanlike.[11] At times that winter his
phrases rang with the wisdom of long experience: 'Revolts originate
within the lower orders of society, revolutions always arise from
failings of government,' he commented on reports from Paris in
January 1853.[12] And when, soon afterwards, the Russians and French
began to dispute the privilege of protecting the Palestinian Holy
Places, he was alive to the danger: 'To look at changing ideas in
philosophy and literature so as to convince oneself of the impossibility
of new wars of religion is pure folly,' he wrote gloomily and added,
'As a device for disrupting political peace, fanaticism is as old as the
world.'[13]

Yet did Metternich really possess influence over the shaping of
Austrian policy during these months? Foreigners were convinced at the
time that he did, and their visits to him were no mere acts of courtesy.
The British ambassador sought his intervention when a surfeit of
Palmerstonian bluster had weakened good relations between the two
governments. Bismarck, determined to keep Austria out of the *Zollverein*, came to Vienna and called on Metternich in order to gauge the
strength of his opponents; and when Tsar Nicholas arrived on a state
visit to Francis Joseph in 1852 he slipped away quietly to Metternich's
study within twenty-four hours of reaching the capital, and he returned
for a further long conversation on the eve of departure.

So far as the Viennese were concerned Metternich was a symbol from
the past. They recognized him only on rare occasions, in his carriage
trotting down the Hauptallee of the Prater, visiting Kübeck perhaps or
the Esterhazys, and on church festivals accompanying Melanie to

Mass, very thin and a little unsteady in his walk but proudly erect, still fastidious over the cut of his coat and the folds of a cravat. Once, in February 1853, he surprised everyone – and possibly himself – by calling on Buol in the Ballhausplatz, entering the Chancellery for the first time since his flight through the garden gate five years previously.[14] It was hard to think of him as a power behind the throne, the eldest statesman of the Empire; and not many people made the effort to do so. He looked like a retired banker, contentedly seeking lost enchantments in stuffy domesticity.

This, indeed, was the scene which Rudolf Alt caught that winter in water-colour:[15] a family group of seven frozen in immobility at the far end of a high-ceilinged salon, portraits and windswept landscapes on the walls, the trinkets and trophies of half a century positioned meticulously on pedestals and tables. The Prince himself bends low over a newspaper, dim eyes disdaining a reading-glass. His widowed sister, Pauline, is huddled facing him in a chair, dark shawls veiling the passage of her years. Two daughters sit beside their father, listening perhaps as he reads aloud; his grand-daughter sews in a distant corner; and his youngest son, Lothar, stands by the door in tight-fitting tunic, dwarfed by the heavy drapes, a bored fifteen-year-old with hand in pocket. Dominating the picture as of right is Melanie, full flowing dress sweeping to the carpet, and leaning forward so that she seems the only person capable of decisive movement. Alt's painting faithfully mirrors that sense of security regained which permeates the writings of both the Prince and his wife in these years. Perhaps, too, it reflects a little more than met the artist's eye; for this is a room of cluttered comfort, so bourgeois in its insensibilities that it could never spring to life with the bustle and effort of high politics. It remained what it was meant to be when the new palace on the Rennweg was first designed: a withdrawing-room for a man 'plagued by fifty years of public service'.

But in his study, farther along the first floor, the Prince was still ready to spend the morning hours writing endlessly at his desk. By the spring of 1853, when he celebrated his eightieth birthday with a splendid dinner and could not quite decide whether to approve of the marriage of young Melanie to a distant Zichy cousin, his pen was once more explaining the intricacies of the Eastern Question, of how Austria must keep her freedom of action and yet somehow restrain Russia without offending the Tsar.[16] Buol knew little enough of the background and appears to have attended to Metternich's strictures on the general trend of world policy with interest, if not enthusiasm. Francis Joseph, already showing that conscientious regard for kingship which he was to carry into the twentieth century, insisted on conducting personally all direct negotiations with Nicholas, even though he confessed to his mother that he found the whole question perplexing. Buol duly handed over to Francis Joseph the advice he had received from Metternich. At times it was, indeed, far from comforting: 'The Russian Court is completely in error,' Metternich wrote in mid-July 1853, as the Tsar's armies prepared to move southwards across the Danube estuary; and he added, later in the same letter, 'The present mood (in St Petersburg) worries me like a bad dream'.[17] Yet he was willing to give a decisive lead to his ex-pupil at Schönbrunn: 'There is only one attitude which Austria can assume in this situation and that is the line taken during the Graeco-Egyptian affair.'[18] The man who had so often burnt his fingers over Greece and Mehemet Ali had now no doubt of the absolute need for Austria to remain neutral in any conflict over the future of Turkey.

Francis Joseph was genuinely grateful for Metternich's comments and let him know how much he respected his judgements. The Prince was pleased by the Emperor's message although he wrote, rather complacently, that it was 'proof that his mind is moving in step with mine ... towards universal peace'.[19] Throughout the summer of 1853 Buol continued to receive detailed advice from Metternich, including a sound historical survey of the successive crises in the 1820's, for the ex-Chancellor always believed in the continuity of other statesmen's policies no less than of his own, and as Nesselrode was still at the Russian Foreign Ministry he may well have been right. When in the autumn Buol sought a compromise which would save both Turkish independence and Russian prestige, he was following the Metternich tradition and, for some months, there were dark allusions in London and Paris to the spectre of a new Holy Alliance.

But Buol was not content to sit indefinitely on the diplomatic stage as Metternich's dummy. As war loomed nearer in the East, so Buol became ambitious: he was tempted to interpose Austrian forces between the Russian and Turkish armies on the lower Danube, thereby ensuring Habsburg control of the great river from Linz to the Black Sea; and he believed he might safeguard the Austrian position in the Italian peninsula by diplomatic co-operation with France and Britain rather than with Russia. But, though Francis Joseph was attracted by Buol's change of policy, few of the great names in Vienna welcomed it or understood its over-subtlety. Most of the military circle sympathized with the Russians and, while Metternich would not associate himself with the sabre-rattlers, he became increasingly alarmed by the general trend of Buol's policy. On 3 June 1854 he tried for the last time to spell out his doctrine of neutrality: Austria, as the central power on the continent, could never risk appearing 'either as the advance guard of the East against the West, or of the West against the East'.[20] It was a simple principle of action: perhaps it held Buol back from entering what people would soon be calling the Crimean War. But ultimately it was too lacking in enterprise for a young Emperor or for a Foreign Minister in search of reputation. At the beginning of December 1855 the Austrians concluded an alliance with the Western powers. Though still stopping short of war and seeking acceptance as mediator, Buol thus severed the bonds which linked the courts of Vienna and St Petersburg. In doing so he broke finally with the Metternichian past.

The death of Princess Melanie; the marriage of Metternich's son to his grand-daughter

By now, in those stifling rooms on the Rennweg, the years were growing shorter and the days longer. In June 1853 Melanie's health, long a matter of concern, began to fail rapidly. By the following month she was so weary that she was forced to dictate the journal she had kept diligently through so many changes of fortune. Soon there was little to record in it and a sad winter darkened the Metternich Palace. For one evening – it was a Sunday in late November – the lights shone out again as young Melanie became Countess Zichy and the social cream of Vienna fêted the Princess's only daughter. But then the gloom returned over Christmas and the New Year until on 3 March Clement, for a third time, found himself a lonely widower. It comforted him that, as he wrote, Melanie had 'set forth quietly to her eternal home': but with her departed the life force of his own existence. His unmarried daughter, Hermine, kept house for him in his last years and he turned far more than in earlier times to religion. Each Sunday he went to Mass and in the afternoon he would study St Paul; did he, one wonders, find consolation in the epistles because they were nearest in form to his habitual reading matter?[21]

He spent the two years which followed Melanie's death very quietly, though he would still receive visitors to Vienna and take his carriage to call on old friends in the city or its outskirts, and he enjoyed walking in his gardens or in the park at Königswart, for he went each July to Bohemia and remained there throughout the hottest weeks of the year. He wrote and read for several hours each day, following the war in the Crimea with interest and still sending occasional scraps of information to Buol; but there was little doubt that he had at last accepted his exclusion from the centre of affairs. When Kübeck succumbed to an epidemic of cholera in September 1855, there were few of his old colleagues left alive and none from his own generation. It seemed improbable that his own constitution could survive any more winters.

And then suddenly, on the eve of his eighty-third birthday, the Prince began to show almost sprightly energy. It began, character-istically, with a firm statement to Buol in the opening paragraph of a letter in May 1856: 'I am dead, but I belong to that category of corpses in which the nerves go on vibrating and in which moral questions are revived by influences which, for want of something better, I will describe by the word "galvanic".'[22] It was, he claimed, the hostile attitude of the court of Turin towards Austria which had produced this effect on him; and he proceeded to treat Buol to some astringent comments on Piedmontese policy in general and the intrigues of Cavour in particular. But, though the fate of Italy continued to excite him for the remainder of his life, the real reason for tish new enthusiasm may be found in his domestic affairs. That winter his son Richard, serving as Secretary in the Paris Embassy, had returned to Vienna on two months leave. Not only had he aroused his father's interest in Napoleon III's policy towards Italy, but he had also caused a social sensation by becoming engaged to Pauline Sandor, his step-sister's daughter. Since in 1850 Pauline's father had lost his reason, the child spent her most formative years in the Metternich household and was a particular favourite of her grandfather, who was also closely attached to Richard. While Leontine, Pauline's mother, found the idea of such a marriage 'startling' – as well she might – Metternich himself was 'overjoyed' and busied himself with arrangements for the wedding, which was celebrated in Vienna on the last day of June.[23] He seems also to have been flattered that summer by a visit from Katharina Bagration, who was still so eccentrically dressed that he thought it advisable to mention her strange appearance in a note to the Foreign Minister before she made her way to the Ballhausplatz.[24]

This mood of euphoric serenity, which made his mental faculties alert and gave him new physical vitality, led him to undertake fresh travels. From Königswart, which he complained was being invaded by tourists from nearby Marienbad, he travelled to Dresden where Richard was now envoy, as his father had been fifty-five years before. In the following autumn the Prince went, for the first time in many years, to the Rhineland and stayed for several months at Johannisberg, a journey repeated in the summer of 1858. He was surprised at the ease with which improved communications enabled him to visit Coblenz, Mainz and the other cities of his childhood and youth and by the extent of river traffic. During his last years he seems to have gained greater satisfaction from these weeks in the Rhineland than from his visits to either Königswart or Plass, perhaps because Johannisberg held for him happier memories, perhaps because it was so firmly placed in the mainstream of European life. Still the visitors came to pay their respects to him: the King of the Belgians; Bismarck for a third time; Thiers to discuss the final volumes of the *Consulate and Empire*. On 16 August 1857 he entertained at Johannisberg the fifteen-year-old Prince of Wales, for whom he produced vintage wine from his cellars and vintage anecdotes from the First Empire and Regency. Prince Albert, who had made no gestures towards the Metternichs in 1848, was now delighted that his son should have the benefit of a conversation with the ex-Chancellor. One suspects, however, that the future Edward VII found the visit tedious: for in his personal diary he merely commented that his host was 'a very nice old gentleman and very like the late Duke of Wellington'.[25]

Metternich, Francis Joseph and the war with France and Piedmont (1859)

By the summer of 1858 Metternich was seriously disturbed by the trend of Buol's policy towards both France and Piedmont. He had no desire for the Austrians to appease Cavour but he suspected that the Piedmontese were seeking to goad Francis Joseph and his generals into an act which would place the Habsburg Empire in the wrong. Without waiting to be asked, Metternich sent warnings to Buol and, at the same time, used his contacts with the English Tories to counter British sympathy for the Italian cause.[26] Buol, however, had become increasingly resentful of advice and appears to have distrusted the close friendship between Metternich and the Austrian ambassador to France, Count Joseph von Hübner. It was no doubt galling for Buol to have Metternich writing of Napoleon 'the uncle' and Napoleon 'the nephew' as if he comprehended the pattern of the century's history; and at times Metternich lacked tact in wondering if Buol had received information which had happened to reach him by express communication. From Buol's point of view the ex-Chancellor was even more tiresome over Italy than he had been over the Eastern Question: had he not himself served at Turin? He was disinclined to treat the messages which reached him from Metternich with the respect of earlier days; and Francis Joseph for his part seems to have wished to consult Metternich only when he had already taken decisions which he had come to regret.

It was on 20 April 1859 that Francis Joseph came to the Rennweg to seek the old Prince's advice on the Italian Question.[27] For more than a week the Emperor had been badgered by his soldiers and by Buol to take firm action and end the provocative pinpricks of the Piedmontese along the Lombard frontier; and on the previous day there had been a decisive war council in the Hofburg. Now at last he had determined to ask for Metternich's opinion. According to Pauline Metternich-Sandor, her grandfather expressed it vehemently: 'For heaven's sake, send no ultimatum to Italy!' he begged the Emperor, who was forced to reply 'It went out yesterday'.[28] There is no reason to doubt the veracity of this anecdote. Certainly Francis Joseph was alarmed by the uncompromising character of Metternich's advice. He

felt that the war machine was running away with him: within a
fortnight, first Piedmont and then France had accepted the challenge
so casually thrown down on 19 April; and Francis Joseph knew he had
blundered. As five badly equipped army corps stumbled slowly
across the Ticino, the Austrians sensed they had lost a pointless war
even before the slaughter had begun. Almost pathetically in the first
days of May 1859, Francis Joseph begged Metternich for guidance;
and as a sign of good intent, he dismissed Buol from the Foreign
Ministry.

Hence on the eve of his eighty-sixth birthday Metternich found himself called upon to give critical advice at a moment when his country
found itself fighting a foreign war for the first time in two generations.
And the task was beyond his resources. He secured the appointment of
Rechberg, loyal friend from 1848, as Buol's successor; but his other
projects – a mission to Berlin and St Petersburg to arouse the Eastern
courts in defence of the sanctity of the international order, a plea to
England to arm against neo-Bonapartism – were couched in the
language of the 1830's, if not earlier.[29] They belonged to the system
which Buol had finally cast aside in December 1855. It was left to
Rechberg, to Hübner and to Richard Metternich to improvise a policy
which would save Austria from total disaster; but nothing could
protect the army in Lombardy from humiliation.

Metternich followed the reports of the campaign with keen attention, feeling its reversals deeply. He had a personal interest – his son
Paul was serving as a junior officer – and he also felt that it was a final
commentary on the settlement of 1815. On 21 May Francis Joseph came
to the Rennweg for the last time: he was about to leave for the Italian
Front, hoping to bring order and precision into what was clearly
chaos; and before he went, he wished to give to Metternich a vital
task. He was to prepare secret documents arranging a regency for
Crown Prince Rudolph (a boy of two) in case of his father's death,
and he was also to draw up a testament for Francis Joseph as he had
done for his grand-father nearly thirty years before. Metternich was,
however, by now very weak. He had to receive the Emperor in bed and
their conversation made slow progress, partly because of his deafness.
It was three hours before Francis Joseph could take his leave; and on
the very next day Metternich had to write to him seeking clarification
of his intentions.[30]

Three days later Hübner, forced to leave Paris by the coming of war
just as Metternich had been fifty years previously, came to visit him.
They spent the morning together, the Prince leaning on the ambassador's arm as they walked in the garden in the spring sunlight.
Although much of his conversation was lively, he appears to have
wandered dreamily at the end. ' "I was a Rock of Order" he said to me

again and again as we parted,' Hübner wrote later.[31] Metternich
retired to his study, but he could not draft the papers for which Francis
Joseph had asked. Each day he became weaker: 'bad news from the
battle front brought him an evergrowing feeling of pain and sorrow,'
wrote his grand-daughter Pauline who had moved temporarily into the
Rennweg mansion as her husband, Richard, had gone as diplomatic
attaché with the Emperor to Lombardy.[32] On 5 June, as Rechberg was
with him, the first reports arrived in Vienna of the defeat of Magenta;
and Metternich fell to the floor in a fainting fit. He never fully recovered, although he insisted on getting up each morning that week, and
on 10 June was even carried on a chair into his garden. The weather
was hot and oppressive; and he was short of breath. The end came next
morning, shortly before noon.[33]

His body lay in state for three days beneath the awe-inspiring
Baroque dome of the Karlskirche. Despite the absence from the capital
of many dignitaries because of the war, almost everyone of rank and
distinction in Vienna came to pay respect to a man who had served the
dynasty for almost seventy years and given his name to the age in which
most of his mourners had been born. On 15 June his funeral cortège
moved slowly away from the Karlskirche and he began the last journey
to Bohemia. In 1920 he had converted an old chapel on his estate at Plass
into a family mausoleum, dedicated to St Wenceslas and St Clement;
and it was under their patronage that his remains were finally interred,
in quiet woodland beside the river Strela, twenty miles from the town of
Pilsen (Plzen).[34]

The death of Metternich excited little interest in the foreign press,
and in Austria it was soon forgotten in the bad news which continued to
come from the battle zone of Italy. In later years both Bismarck and
Disraeli remembered him with respect. But, by the close of 1859, his
son Richard had become ambassador in Paris and the statesmen were
beginning to think of him as 'Metternich' rather than his father. At
first it seemed, indeed, as if Richard's shrewd understanding of power
politics would eventually bring him to the Chancellery in the Ballhausplatz; but he developed an intensive dislike of the Prussians and,
after 1866 and 1870, his hostility to the Bismarckian *Reich* excluded him
from preferment. His wife, Pauline, having conquered Paris in the
early 'sixties by her artistic gifts and personality, became for the last
quarter of the century the idol of the Viennese, who cheered her
carriage through the streets and sang doubtfully flattering verses in her
honour. Richard lived on in retirement only until 1895, but Pauline
outlasted the Habsburg Monarchy itself, dying at the age of eighty-
five in the autumn of 1921, a revered relic of patrician society.[35]

Nor was Pauline the only member of the Metternich family circle
to see Austria become a Republic. On 11 November 1918, as the last

Habsburg Emperor prepared finally to withdraw from Schönbrunn,
Melanie Zichy-Metternich – nearly eighty-seven but still vividly
remembering the turbulence of 1848 – arrived at the palace with a
message of comfort for the Empress Zita. 'Revolutions', she said in an
echo of her father's style, 'are like floods. They pass over the land and
cover it. But they do not last for ever. And when the flood-tide falls, the
land comes up again.'[36]

So no doubt political life seemed to all of Metternich's children. But
this time Melanie was over-optimistic. The events of 1918 were more
than a revolution. They did not swamp the old Empire the Chancellor
had served: they swept it away. By the time Melanie died twelve
months later, a line of frontier posts separated Vienna from Bohemia,
and her father's mausoleum at Plass lay within the Republic of Czechoslovakia, a political structure which he had certainly never envisaged.
Today there is little in Vienna associated specifically with Metternich:
no statue, but a road which cuts through the gardens he had so admired
along the Rennweg honours his name; and the Metternich Palace in
which he died still looks out towards the Karlskirche. Yet for more than
sixty years it has been, not a private residence, but an embassy: for,
with a pleasing touch of historical irony, the house of the man who had
thought Italy no more than a geographical expression became in 1908
the home of the Italian ambassador; and so, with two interludes of
war, it has since remained.

METTERNICH – WINNEBURG

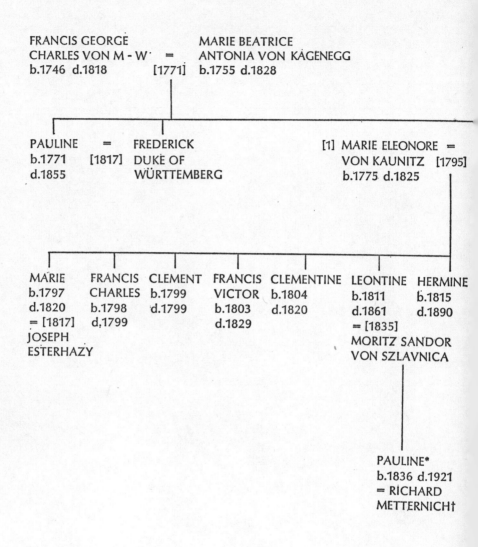

FRANCIS GEORGE
CHARLES VON M - W   =   MARIE BEATRICE
b.1746 d.1818   [1771]   ANTONIA VON KÁGENEGG
                            b.1755 d.1828

PAULINE   =   FREDERICK   [1] MARIE ELEONORE =
b.1771   [1817]   DUKE OF   VON KAUNITZ   [1795]
d.1855   WÜRTTEMBERG   b.1775 d.1825

MARIE   FRANCIS   CLEMENT   FRANCIS   CLEMENTINE   LEONTINE   HERMINE
b.1797   CHARLES   b.1799   VICTOR   b.1804   b.1811   b.1815
d.1820   b.1798   d.1799   b.1803   d.1820   d.1861   d.1890
= [1817]   d,1799   d.1829   = [1835]
JOSEPH   MORITZ SANDOR
ESTERHAZY   VON SZLAVNICA

PAULINE*
b.1836 d.1921
= RICHARD
METTERNICH†

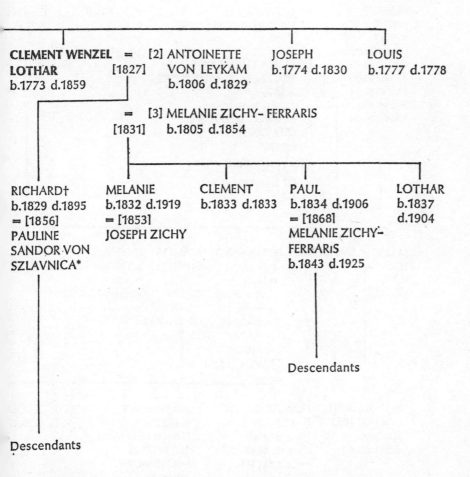

CLEMENT WENZEL = [2] ANTOINETTE   JOSEPH   LOUIS
LOTHAR   [1827] VON LEYKAM   b.1774 d.1830   b.1777 d.1778
b.1773 d.1859   b.1806 d.1829

                = [3] MELANIE ZICHY- FERRARIS
            [1831]   b.1805 d.1854

RICHARD†   MELANIE   CLEMENT   PAUL   LOTHAR
b.1829 d.1895   b.1832 d.1919   b.1833 d.1833   b.1834 d.1906   b.1837
= [1856]   = [1853]   = [1868]   d.1904
PAULINE   JOSEPH ZICHY   MELANIE ZICHY-
SANDOR VON   FERRARIS
SZLAVNICA*   b.1843 d.1925

                                                 Descendants

Descendants

M

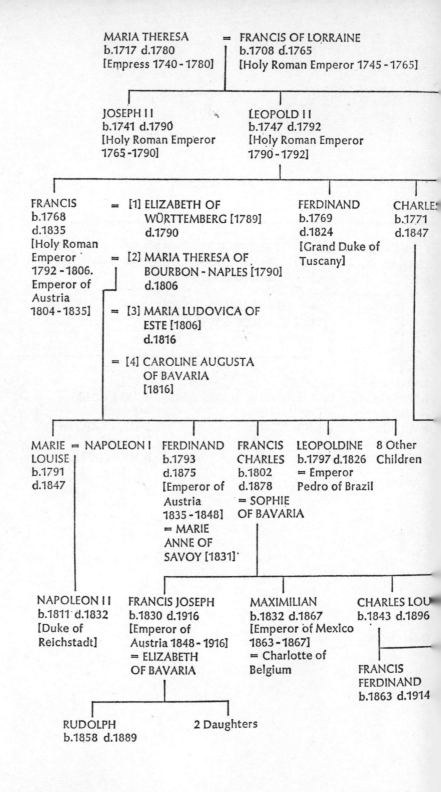

MARIA THERESA = FRANCIS OF LORRAINE
b.1717 d.1780   b.1708 d.1765
[Empress 1740 - 1780]   [Holy Roman Emperor 1745 - 1765]

JOSEPH II   LEOPOLD II
b.1741 d.1790   b.1747 d.1792
[Holy Roman Emperor   [Holy Roman Emperor
1765 -1790]   1790 - 1792]

FRANCIS   = [1] ELIZABETH OF   FERDINAND   CHARLE
b.1768   WÜRTTEMBERG [1789]   b.1769   b.1771
d.1835   d.1790   d.1824   d.1847
[Holy Roman   [Grand Duke of
Emperor   = [2] MARIA THERESA OF   Tuscany]
1792 - 1806.   BOURBON - NAPLES [1790]
Emperor of   d.1806
Austria
1804 - 1835] = [3] MARIA LUDOVICA OF
                 ESTE [1806]
                 d.1816

             = [4] CAROLINE AUGUSTA
                 OF BAVARIA
                 [1816]

MARIE = NAPOLEON I   FERDINAND   FRANCIS   LEOPOLDINE   8 Other
LOUISE   b.1793   CHARLES   b.1797 d.1826 Children
b.1791   d.1875   b.1802   = Emperor
d.1847   [Emperor of   d.1878   Pedro of Brazil
                     Austria   = SOPHIE
                     1835 - 1848]   OF BAVARIA
                     = MARIE
                     ANNE OF
                     SAVOY [1831]

NAPOLEON II   FRANCIS JOSEPH   MAXIMILIAN   CHARLES LOU
b.1811 d.1832   b.1830 d.1916   b.1832 d.1867   b.1843 d.1896
[Duke of   [Emperor of   [Emperor of Mexico
Reichstadt]   Austria 1848 - 1916] 1863 - 1867]
                 = ELIZABETH   = Charlotte of
                 OF BAVARIA   Belgium   FRANCIS
                                                          FERDINAND
                                                          b.1863 d.1914

RUDOLPH   2 Daughters
b.1858 d.1889

SIMPLIFIED GENEALOGY OF
THE HABSBURG DYNASTY

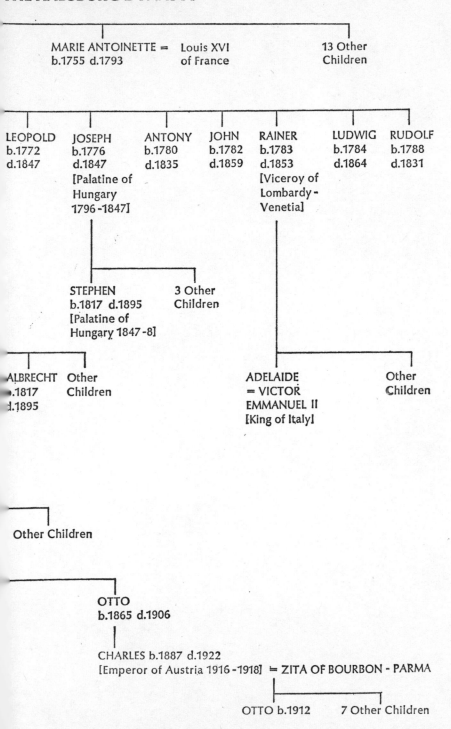

MARIE ANTOINETTE = Louis XVI   13 Other
b.1755 d.1793   of France   Children

LEOPOLD	JOSEPH	ANTONY	JOHN	RAINER	LUDWIG	RUDOLF
b.1772	b.1776	b.1780	b.1782	b.1783	b.1784	b.1788
d.1847	d.1847	d.1835	d.1859	d.1853	d.1864	d.1831
	[Palatine of			[Viceroy of		
	Hungary			Lombardy -		
	1796 -1847]			Venetia]		

STEPHEN   3 Other
b.1817 d.1895   Children
[Palatine of
Hungary 1847 -8]

ALBRECHT Other   ADELAIDE   Other
b.1817   Children   = VICTOR   Children
d.1895   EMMANUEL II
                          [King of Italy]

Other Children

OTTO
b.1865 d.1906

CHARLES b.1887 d.1922
[Emperor of Austria 1916 -1918] = ZITA OF BOURBON - PARMA

OTTO b.1912   7 Other Children

REFERENCE NOTES

Full details of the books and articles cited in this reference section will be found in the Bibliography. The reference *Mémoires* refers to the French edition of the *Mémoires, Documents et Ecrits* of Prince Metternich: Volume I is mainly a collection of autobiographical fragments; Volumes II to VIII are principally documents.

Other abbreviations used are as follows:

AHY: *Austrian History Yearbook*
Burckhardt, *Buol:* Carl J. Burckhardt, *Briefe des Staatskanzlers Fürsten Metternich-Winneburg an Grafen Buol-Schauenstein*
Corti, *Frauen:* E. C. Corti, *Metternich und die Frauen*
Corti, *Mensch:* E. C. Corti, *Mensch und Herrscher*
EHR: *English Historical Review*
Grunwald, *Vie:* C. de Grunwald, *Vie de Metternich*
Hanoteau, *Lettres:* Jean Hanoteau (ed.), *Lettres de Prince Metternich a la Comtesse Lieven*
HHSA: Documents in the *Haus-, Hof- und Staatsarchiv* in Vienna
JCEA: *Journal of Central European Affairs*
JMH: *Journal of Modern History*
Oncken, *O und P:* Wilhelm Oncken, *Öesterreich und Preussen im Befreiungskriege 1813*
Sbornik: Sbornik Imperatorskago Russkago Istoriceskago Obscestva (Collected Papers of the Imperial Russian Historical Society)
Srbik: Heinrich Ritter von Srbik, *Metternich, Der Staatsmann und der Mensch*
Ullrichova: *Mett-Sagan:* Maria Ullrichova, *Metternich, Sagan – Ein Briefwechsel*
Webster, *Castlereagh:* C. K. Webster, *The Foreign Policy of Castlereagh*
Webster, *Palmerston:* C. K. Webster, *The Foreign Policy of Palmerston*
Weil: M. H. Weil, *Les Dessous de Congrès de Vienne*

Chapter 1: Rococo

1 Srbik, I, pp. 54–5; Mathy, *Franz Georg von Metternich*, pp. 19–24.
2 Srbik, I, p. 56; Grunwald, *Vie*, p. 19.
3 See Metternich's letter to his mother when he revisited Coblenz in September 1818, *Mémoires*, III, pp. 116–17; cf. his letter to Dorothea Lieven of 1 December 1818, Hanoteau, *Lettres*, pp. 39–40.
4 Riesbeck, *Travels in Germany*, III, p. 259.
5 Letters of Francis George Metternich to Clement Metternich, April 1785 and December 1790, *Mémoires*, I, pp. 217–18.
6 *Ibid.*, I, p. 9.

7   Srbik, I, pp. 62–66: *Mémoires*, I, p. 6; Bruford, *Germany in the Eighteenth Century*, p. 233.
8   *Mémoires*, I, p. 8.
9   Srbik, I, pp. 63–64.
10 Metternich to his son, Victor, 16 April 1829, *Mémoires*, IV, p. 552.
11 Ford, *Strasbourg in Transition*, p. 169.
12 *Mémoires*, I, p. 7; Srbik, I, p. 67.
13 *Ibid.*; Missoffe, *Metternich*, p. 16; Grunwald, *Vie*, p. 21.
14 Ford, *op. cit.*, pp. 168–74; *Mémoires*, I, p. 11.
15 Srbik, I, pp. 65–66 and pp. 88–91, and III, p. 41.
16 Countess Beatrice to Clement Metternich, 8 July 1789, quoted from the family archives by Srbik, I, p. 67.
17 Arthur Young, *Travels in France*, p. 180. (Cf. Ford, *op. cit.*, pp. 242–47 and p. 252).
18 *Mémoires*, I, p. 10.
19 Countess Beatrice to Clement Metternich, 28 July 1789, Srbik, I, p. 68.
20 *Mémoires*, I, pp. 8–9; Srbik, I, p. 70; Grunwald, *Vie*, p. 19; Missoffe, *op. cit.*, p. 22; Mathy, *op. cit.*, pp. 108–10.

Chapter 2: World in Ferment

1   *Mémoires*, I, pp. 12–13 and VIII, pp. 573–74; Srbik, I, pp. 91–94; Bibl, *Metternich*, pp. 31–32.
2   Mathy, *Franz Georg von Metternich*, pp. 137–47; *Mémoires*, I, p. 11.
3   Missoffe, *Metternich*, p. 36 (citing Carlo Bronne, *Esquisses au Crayon Tendre*).
4   For the Marie Constance de Caumont incident, see the article by the Duc de la Force in *Revue des Mondes*, 1936, and Metternich's account in Hanoteau, *Lettres*, p. 41. (Cf. Corti, *Frauen*, I, pp. 23–28.)
5   Thompson, *French Revolution*, pp. 259–61; Lefèbvre, *French Revolution*, pp. 220–27.
6   Mathy, op. cit., pp. 164–65; Grunwald, *Vie*, pp. 23–24; *Mémoires*, I, p. 13.
7   Lefèbvre, op. cit., pp. 252–56.
8   *Mémoires*, I, p. 15.
9   *Ibid.*, I, p. 16.
10 *Ibid.*, pp. 16–17. On the Desandrouin Mission, see Helleiner, *The Imperial Loans*, pp. 4–16.
11 *Mémoires*, I, p. 17.
12 *Ibid.*, I, p. 18.
13 *Ibid.*, I, p. 19. For Howe's movements, see Bryant, *Years of Endurance*, pp. 111–13.
14 *Mémoires*, I, p. 20; Srbik, I, p. 79.
15 Thompson, op. cit., p. 244.
16 Mathy, op. cit., pp. 195–208; Srbik, I, pp. 73–77.
17 Metternich's pamphlet is printed in *Mémoires*, I, pp. 336–42.
18 Corti, *Frauen*, I, pp. 31–42; *Mémoires*, I, p. 21; Hanoteau, *Lettres*, p. 42.
19 Corti, *Frauen*, I, pp. 43–44.

20 *Mémoires*, I, p. 22.
21 Corti, *Frauen*, I, pp. 45–46.
22 For the military history of the French armies during this period, see Chandler, *The Campaigns of Napoleon*.
23 Mathy, op. cit., pp. 214–15; *Mémoires*, I, p. 23.
24 *Ibid.*, I, pp. 351–69.
25 Metternich to his wife, Eleonore, 8 December 1797, *Mémoires*, I, p. 347.
26 The same to the same, 22 December 1797, *Ibid.*, I, p. 354.
27 Extract from *Le Publiciste*, quoted by Missoffe, *Metternich*, pp. 56–57.
28 Macartney, *The Habsburg Empire*, p. 172.
29 *Mémoires*, I, pp. 28–29.
30 Corti, *Frauen*, I, p. 68.

Chapter 3: Dresden and Berlin

 1 *Mémoires*, II, pp. 1–16; Srbik, III, p. 44.
 2 Bonnefons, *Un Allié de Napoléon*, pp. 22–23.
 3 *Mémoires*, I, p. 33.
 4 Corti, *Frauen*, I, p. 85.
 5 Grunwald, *Vie*, p. 33 (citing *Mémoires de Madame de Boigne*).
 6 Sweet, *Friedrich von Gentz*, p. 63 and p. 69.
 7 Bonnefons, op. cit., pp. 105–109; Missoffe, *Metternich*, p. 68. See the article on La Rochefoucauld by Marchand in *Revue d'Histoire Diplomatique*, 1934.
 8 Kraehe, *Metternich's German Policy*, pp. 31–37; Ramm, *Germany 1789–1919*, pp. 54–55.
 9 Colloredo to Thugut, July 1803, quoted from the archives by Corti, *Frauen*, I, p. 79.
10 *Mémoires*, I, pp. 36–37 and II, pp. 17–30.
11 Cf. Gentz, *Tagebucher*, I, p. 45, with Prokesch-Osten (ed.), *Depeches Inédites . . .*, I, p. 149.
12 Corti, *Frauen*, I, p. 81; *Mémoires*, I, p. 37.
13 Srbik, I, pp. 105–107; Sweet, op. cit., pp. 97–99; Krache, op. cit., pp. 36–37.
14 Mann, *Secretary of Europe*, p. 103.
15 Sweet, op. cit., p. 98.
16 Deutsch, *Genesis of Napoleonic Imperialism*, pp. 218–28.
17 *Mémoires*, I, pp. 41–43.
18 Kraehe, *op. cit.*, pp. 37–39.
19 Srbik, I, pp. 107–108; *Mémoires*, II, pp. 45–66.
20 For Metternich's contemporary account of the Tsar's visit, see *Memoires*, II, pp. 66–71. For his considered verdict on Alexander, see *Mémoires*, I, pp. 315–22.
21 Cobenzl to Metternich, 19 November 1805, *Mémoires*, II, pp. 79–80.
22 Kraehe, op. cit., p. 41.
23 Napoleon to Joseph Bonaparte, 3 December 1805, *Correspondance de Napoleon I*, XI, No. 9538, p. 445.
24 Macartney, *Habsburg Empire*, pp. 156–57.

25   Metternich to Gentz, 21 January 1806; Wittichen and Salzer, *Briefe* . . . *von Gentz*, III, p. 44.

26   *Mémoires*, II, pp. 99–102. (Cf. Botzenhart, *Metternichs Pariser Botschafterzeit*, p. 2 and pp. 5–6).

27   Macartney, op. cit., pp. 181–82.

28   *Mémoires*, I, p. 50 and II, p. 70.

29   See the quotation from a St Petersburg journal of March 1806 printed in *Mémoires*, I, p. 221.

30   Nesselrode, *Lettres et Papiers*, III, p. 132.

31   Napoleon to Talleyrand, 26 March 1806, *Correspondance de Napoléon I*, XII, No. 10023, pp. 220–21.

32   Floret to Stadion, 28 March 1806, printed by Botzenhart, op. cit., p. 8.

33   Corti, *Frauen*, I, p. 91.

34   *Mémoires*, I, p. 51.

35   Gentz to Metternich, 23 September 1806, Wittichen and Salzer, op. cit., III, pp. 58–59.

36   Metternich to his wife, Eleonore, 28 June 1806, Corti, *Frauen*, I, p. 91.

37   *Ibid.*, pp. 90–92.

Chapter 4: Ambassador to Napoleon

1   Mann, *Secretary of Europe*, pp. 123–24.

2   *Ibid.*, p. 127.

3   Metternich to his wife, Eleonore, 2 July 1806, Corti, *Frauen* I, p. 92.

4   For Metternich's journey, see Botzenhart, *Metternichs Pariser Botschafterzeit*, pp. 22–26, and the article by Grunwald in *Revue de Paris* for August 1936, pp. 494–95.

5   Metternich to Stadion, 11 August 1806, Grunwald article cited above, pp. 497–98.

6   *Ibid.*, pp. 500–03.

7   Metternich to Stadion, 11 August 1806, *Ibid.*, pp. 503–04. Material on Floret's assistance to Metternich at this time and on the links with Lord Yarmouth may be found in HHSA, Frankreich Varia, 58.

8   Hauterive, *La Police Secrète du Premier Empire*, III, No. 96, p. 42.

9   Botzenhart, op. cit., p. 74; Corti, *Frauen*, I, pp. 94–95.

10   Metternich to his wife, Eleonore, 20 August 1806, *Ibid.*, I, p. 95.

11   Metternich to Marie Constance de Caumont, 22 October 1806; Duc de la Force, *Revue des deux Mondes*, October 1936, p. 654.

12   *Ibid.*

13   Metternich to Stadion, 8 February 1807, HHSA, Dipl. Korr. Frankreich, Karton 200, Fascicle 2.

14   Abrantès, *Souvenirs*, VIII, p. 408.

15   Hauterive, op. cit., IV, No. 295, p. 139.

16   *Ibid.*, IV, No. 39, p. 18 and No. 42, p. 20.

17   *Mémoires*, I, p. 311.

18   Grunwald article, loc. cit., p. 519.

19   *Ibid.*, p. 527.

20   Hauterive, op. cit., IV, No. 186, p. 87.

21 Missoffe, *Metternich*, p. 114; Grunwald, *Vie*, p. 48.

22 Botzenhart, op. cit., p. 120.

23 Metternich to Stadion, 26 July 1807, HHSA, Dipl. Korr. Frankreich. Karton 200, Fascicle 7. An abridged version of this despatch is printed in *Mémoires*, II, pp. 118–20; and see also the Grunwald article cited above, pp. 526–8.

24 Metternich to Stadion, 19 August 1807, HHSA, Dipl. Korr. Frankreich, Karton 200, Fascicle 8.

25 The same to the same. 12 November 1807, HHSA, Dipl. Korr. Frankreich, Karton 200, Fascicle 11. (Cf. Grunwald, loc. cit., p. 534).

26 The same to the same. 11 October 1807, HHSA, Dipl. Korr. Frankreich, Karton 200, Fascicle 10.

27 Starhemberg to Metternich, 5 January and 10 January 1808; Metternich to Starhemberg, 15 January 1808, HHSA, Frankreich Varia, 58, Fascicle 72.

28 Metternich to Stadion, 12 November 1807, Grunwald article, loc. cit., pp. 536–37.

29 The same to the same, 24 September 1808, *Mémoires*, II, p. 237.

30 The same to the same, 18 January 1808, *Ibid.*, II, p. 144.

31 The same to the same, 26 January 1808, *Ibid.*, II, p. 155.

32 The same to the same, 18 January 1808, *Ibid.*, II, p. 149; and 26 January 1808, cited in Botzenhart, op. cit., p. 198.

33 *Ibid.*, p. 195.

34 Metternich to Stadion, 27 April 1808, *Mémoires*, II, p. 170.

35 The same to the same, 23 June 1808, *Ibid.*, p. 187. The quotation beginning 'In moments of crisis . . .' is taken from a letter of Metternich to Stadion on 1 July 1808, cited by Grunwald in his article 'La fin d'une ambassade' in *Revue de Paris* for October 1937, p. 510.

36 Botzenhart, op. cit., p. 234.

37 Metternich to Stadion, 27 April 1808, *Mémoires*, II, pp. 167–73.

38 Metternich's contemporary report of this famous incident is printed in *Mémoires*, II, pp. 194–9. A later version is given in the autobiographical section of *Mémoires*, I, pp. 63–4, and does not agree with the earlier record. He also refers briefly to the incident in a letter of 1823, printed in *Mémoires*, IV, p. 13. For the version of the Russian ambassador, Count Tolstoy, see *Sbornik*, vol. 89, pp. 644–46 (in French). Other reports are cited by Botzenhart, op. cit., pp. 239–41.

39 Tolstoy to Kurakin, 18 August 1808, *Sbornik*, vol. 89, p. 644.

40 Grunwald article, 'Fin d'une ambassade', loc. cit., p. 824.

41 Metternich to Stadion, 26 August 1808, *Mémoires*, II, p. 212.

42 Garros, *Quel Roman que ma vie! Itinéraire de Napoléon Bonaparte*, p. 299.

43 Grunwald article, 'Fin d'une ambassade', loc. cit., pp. 828–9: *Mémoires*, II, pp. 216–27.

44 Grunwald article, 'Fin d'une ambassade', loc. cit., p. 830.

45 Vandal, *Napoléon et Alexandre I*, I, pp. 442–60: Garros, op. cit., pp. 301–03.

46 Botzenhart, op. cit., pp. 268–9; Hauterive, op. cit., IV, No. 870, p. 432.

47 Botzenhart, op. cit., pp. 270–84.

48 The first and the third memoranda are printed in *Mémoires*, II, pp. 240–57. For the second memorandum, see Beer, *Zehn Jahre Osterreischer Politik*, pp. 525–28.

49 Hauterive, op. cit., IV, No. 996, p. 499.

50 *Ibid.*, IV, No. 1020, pp. 513–14.

51 *Ibid.*, IV, No. 1097, p. 554.

52 *Ibid.*, IV, Nos. 1115 & 1116, p. 564.

53 *Ibid.*, IV, No. 1157, p. 591.

54 Metternich to Stadion, 31 January 1809, HHSA, Dipl. Korr. Frankreich, Karton 205, Fascicle 1; Duff Cooper, *Talleyrand*, pp. 186–8; Hauterive, op. cit., IV, No. 1034, p. 521.

55 Metternich to Stadion, 25 January, 2 February, 17 February, 7 March 1809, HHSA, Dipl. Korr. Frankreich, Karton 205, Fascicles 1–3. The despatches of 25 January, 2 February and 17 February are printed in part in *Mémoires*, II, pp. 263–74.

56 Garros, op. cit., p. 314.

57 *Ibid.*

58 Metternich to Schwarzenberg, 9 April 1809, and Metternich to Stadion, 11 April 1809, HHSA, Dipl. Korr. Frankreich, Karton 205, Fascicle 4. These letters are printed in part in the Grunwald article (already cited), but there is a minor error in the dating.

59 *Mémoires*, I, pp. 66–67.

60 There is a detailed description of Metternich's departure from Paris in Floret's Journal, 26 May to 29 May 1809. HHSA, Frankreich Varia, 58, Fascicle 72 (19). Floret's Journal is an interesting manuscript document of fifty-seven pages, covering the period from the last week in May until the third week in October 1809. An earlier Journal by Floret, preserved in the same box, covers the period from 30 April to 28 October 1806. (See reference 7, above.)

Chapter 5: Collaboration

1 Floret's Journal, 29 May to 6 June 1809, HHSA (as cited above); *Mémoires*, I, pp. 73–74.

2 Metternich to Stadion, 4 July 1809, HHSA Dipl. Korr. Frankreich, Karton 205, Fascicle 9; *Mémoires*, I, pp. 74–81.

3 Corti, *Frauen*, I, p. 164 (citing Gentz's papers); *Mémoires*, I, p. 81: Floret's Journal, loc. cit., 5–6 July 1809.

4 *Mémoires*, I, pp. 82–3; and see also Metternich's letter to his mother on 25 July 1809, *Mémoires*, I, pp. 228–29.

5 *Ibid.*, I, p. 85.

6 Metternich to his mother, 17 August 1809, *Mémoires*, I, p. 230; see also *Mémoires*, I, pp. 86–87.

7 Metternich to Emperor Francis, 10 August 1809, *Mémoires*, I, pp. 304–08.

8 Kraehe, *Metternich's German Policy*, p. 110.

9 *Ibid.*, pp. 114–16: *Mémoires*, I, pp. 90–92.

10 Metternich to his wife, Eleonore. *Ibid.*, I, p. 233.

11 Floret's Journal, loc. cit. early October: Floret to Metternich, 21
    November, HHSA, Dipl. Korr. Frankreich, Karton 205, Fascicle 12.
    See also, Grunwald, *Vie*, pp. 81–82.
12 Schwarzenberg to Metternich, 4 December and 21 December 1809:
    Floret to Metternich, 21 December 1809. All three documents are
    in HHSA, Dipl. Korr. Frankreich, Karton 205, Fascicles 11 and 12.
    The most important of these three communications is Schwarzenberg's
    despatch of 21 December, a postscript to which reports a conversation
    with Laborde on the previous day in which the possibility of a proposal
    of marriage from Napoleon to Marie Louise is mentioned. For the
    whole topic of the marriage negotiations, see Corti, *Frauen*, I, pp. 199–
    204; and Grunwald, *Vie*, pp. 81–91. Both Corti and Grunwald make
    use of the material in the Vienna archives, although without detailed
    references.
13 *Mémoires*, I, pp. 94–98.
14 Garros, *Quel Roman . . .* , p. 339.
15 See the report from the Prussian archives, quoted by Grunwald, *Vie*,
    pp. 85–86.
16 Eleonore Metternich to her husband, 3 January 1810, *Mémoires*, II,
    pp. 314–16.
17 Corti, *Frauen*, I, pp. 225–26.
18 See the material from the Chantemesse papers cited by Missoffe,
    Metternich, pp. 121–25; Grunwald, *Vie*, pp. 91–92; Corti, *Frauen*, I,
    pp. 215–22 and II, 148–49.
19 *Ibid.*, I, p. 232.
20 *Mémoires*, I, p. 100; Corti, *Frauen*, I, pp. 248–51 and p. 258.
21 Srbik, I, pp. 129–31; Kraehe, op. cit., p. 124.
22 Buckland, *Gentz' Relations with the British Government*, pp. 31–33; Buck-
    land, *Metternich and the British Government*, p. 182, 211–12.
23 *Mémoires*, I, pp. 109–12; Srbik, I, p. 132.
24 *Memoires*, I, p. 292 (footnote added in 1853 to the character study of
    Napoleon originally written in 1820).
25 *Ibid.*, I, p. 279.
26 Metternich's summary of a conversation with Napoleon, 8 September
    1810, *Mémoires*, II, p. 391.
27 Report on the fire at Prince Schwarzenberg's Ball written by Metternich
    for Emperor Francis, July 1810, *Mémoires*, I, pp. 301–07; Corti, *Frauen*, I,
    p. 271.
28 *Mémoires*, I, p. 112.
29 On Wallis, see Macartney, *Habsburg Empire*, p. 195; Buckland, *Mett.
    and Br. Govt.*, p. 193; *Mémoires*, I, p. 116.
30 For Metternich's views on Francis, see *Mémoires*, I, p. 138 and IV, p. 109,
    and his more critical comments in 1848 in Hubner, *Année de ma Vie*,
    pp. 18–19. See also, Macartney, op. cit., pp. 147–49.
31 Corti, *Frauen*, I, pp. 279–80; Kraehe, op. cit., p. 120 and p. 135.
32 Correspondence between Metternich and Emperor Francis, 16 January
    to 16 February 1812, HHSA, Familienakten, Kaiser Franz, Karton 24;
    cf. Srbik, I, p. 143.

33   *Ibid.*, I, p. 135.
34   Buckland, op. cit., p. 186.
35   Macartney, op. cit., pp. 193–94.
36   *Mémoires*, I, p. 118 and II, pp. 442–51.
37   Srbik, I, p. 143: *Mémoires*, I, pp. 116–17; Macartney, op. cit., p. 195.
38   *Mémoires*, II, pp. 399–415.
39   Craig, *Politics of the Prussian Army*, p. 58.
40   Srbik, I, p. 141; cf. Metternich to Emperor Francis, 15 January 1812, *Mémoires*, II, pp. 435–39.
41   Buckland, op. cit., pp. 324–31.
42   On the Dresden conferences, see Vandal, *Napoléon et Alexandre I*, III, pp. 402–25: Palmer, *Napoleon in Russia*, pp. 17–23.
43   *Mémoires*, I, p. 123 and II, pp. 461–63.
44   Caulaincourt, *Memoirs*, I, pp. 108–09.

Chapter 6: Peace and War

 1   These intercepted documents, together with a covering letter from Metternich to Emperor Francis (dated 13 August 1812), are now enclosed in a folder in HHSA, Familienakten, Kaiser Franz, Karton 24. (Re-classification of archives has, in this instance, invalidated the reference to 'Karton 128' in Dr J. K. Mayr's first-rate aid to research, *Metternichs Geheimer Briefdienst*, p. 30.) The folder was used by Corti, cf. *Frauen*, I, pp. 351–55.
 2   Grunwald, *Vie*, p. 99; Corti, *Frauen*, I, pp. 358–59.
 3   Buckland, *Metternich and the British Government*, pp. 360–72.
 4   Palmer, *Napoleon in Russia*, p. 52 and p. 82.
 5   Buckland, op. cit., p. 384.
 6   Kissinger, *World Restored*, pp. 24–26.
 7   Oncken, *O und P*, I, pp. 36–7.
 8   Kissinger, op. cit., pp. 43–4.
 9   Oncken, *O und P*, I, pp. 80–82.
10   Grunwald, *Vie*, p. 106.
11   Francis to Napoleon, 24 January 1813, Oncken, *O und P*, I, pp. 407–08.
12   Kraehe, *Metternich's German Policy*, pp. 154–56; Kissinger, op. cit., pp. 50–52.
13   Webster, *Castlereagh*, I, p. 111. For the Wessenberg mission in general, *Ibid.*, pp. 122–26.
14   Buckland, op. cit., p. 486.
15   Grunwald, *Vie*, p. 108.
16   Kissinger, op. cit., pp. 57–64; Palmer, op. cit., p. 262; Markham, *Napoleon*, pp. 200–10.
17   Oncken, *O und P*, II, pp. 336–43.
18   Kissinger, op. cit., pp. 70–75.
19   Metternich to his daughter, Marie, 8 June 1813, quoted in Corti, *Frauen*, I, pp. 375–76.
20   Ullrichova, *Mett-Sagan*, pp. 21–26.

21 *Ibid.*, pp. 26–27.
22 Kissinger, op. cit., pp. 75–76; Kraehe, op. cit., p. 179. See also, *Mémoires*, I, pp. 250–53.
23 Metternich to Stadion, 23 June 1813, Oncken, *O und P*, II, p. 362; Corti, *Frauen*, I, p. 378.
24 Metternich's contemporary reports to Emperor Francis, dated 26 June 1813, are in *Mémoires*, II, pp. 461–63. A more dramatic version is given in his autobiographical fragment, *Mémoires*, I, pp. 147–54; and see also, *ibid.*, I, pp. 253–56.
25 For the French version of the interview, see Caulaincourt's record (edited by Hanoteau) in *Revue d'histoire diplomatique* for 1933, pp. 430–8; and Fain, *Manuscrit de 1813*, II, pp. 36–38. See also Grunwald, *Vie*, p. 118; and the bibliographical analyses by Srbik, I, pp. 715–16 and III, p. 56.
26 Gentz, *Tagebücher*, I, p. 265.
27 Srbik, I, pp. 160–61; Kraehe, op. cit., p. 180.
28 Kissinger, op. cit., pp. 81–82.

Chapter 7: Negotiating Valiantly

1   Srbik, I, p. 161 and p. 164; *Mémoires*, I, pp. 165–66.
2   Grunwald, *Vie*, p. 126.
3   Chandler, *Campaigns of Napoleon*, pp. 903–12.
4   Cathcart to Castlereagh, 7 September 1813, Webster, *Castlereagh*, I, p. 155.
5   See, for examples, *Mémoires*, III, pp. 224–25 and VI, p. 69.
6   Metternich to Hudelist, 6 October 1813, HHSA, Int. Korr. 76.
7   Kissinger, *World Restored*, p. 99; Webster, *Castlereagh*, I, pp. 150–53; Srbik, I, p. 166.
8   Nicolson, *Congress of Vienna*, p. 58.
9   Aberdeen to Castlereagh, 12 November 1813, Webster, *Castlereagh*, I, p. 174.
10 Fournier, *Congress von Chatillon*, p. 91.
11 Chandler, op. cit., pp. 912–36; Metternich to Duchess of Sagan, 20 October 1813, Ullrichova, *Mett-Sagan*, pp. 81–82.
12 *Mémoires*, VII, p. 648.
13 Bonnefons, *Un Allié de Napoléon*, pp. 460–62.
14 Metternich-Sandor, *Geschehenes, Gesehenes, Erlebtes*, p. 24.
15 Metternich to Duchess of Sagan, 6(?) November 1813, Ullrichova, *Mett-Sagan*, pp. 98–99.
16 Kissinger, op. cit., pp. 100–01; Srbik, I, p. 166.
17 Webster, *Castlereagh*, I, pp. 169–78.
18 Sorel, *L'Europe et la Révolution Française*, VIII, pp. 209–10; Webster, *Castlereagh*, I, pp. 174–75; Nicolson, op. cit., pp. 61–62.
19 Kissinger, op. cit., p. 103.
20 Webster, *Castlereagh*, I, p. 202.
21 Sorel, op. cit., VIII, p. 213; Kraehe, *Metternich's German Policy*, pp. 257–58; Srbik, I, p. 168.

22   Nesselrode to his wife, Maria, 16 January 1814, quoted in Grimsted, *Foreign Ministers of Alexander I*, p. 208.
23   Metternich to Gentz, 13 January 1814, Wittichen and Salzer, *Briefe . . . Gentz*, III, pt. 1, p. 204.
24   Metternich to Hudelist, 23 January 1814, HHSA, Int. Korr. 77; Metternich to Duchess of Sagan, 21 January 1814, Ullrichova, *Mett-Sagan*, p. 183.
25   Castlereagh to Liverpool, 26 February 1814, Webster, *Castlereagh*, I, p. 218.
26   *Ibid.*, p. 201.
27   For the Langres Conference, see the following: Srbik, I, p. 171–72; Kraehe, op. cit., pp. 288–90; Webster, *Castlereagh*, I, p. 204.
28   On Chatillon, see Kissinger, op. cit., pp. 119–27 and Fournier, op. cit., *passim*.
29   Stadion to Metternich, February 1814, Fournier, op. cit., p. 93.
30   *Ibid.*, p. 342.
31   *Ibid.*, pp. 93–94.
32   Napoleon to Emperor Francis, 21 February 1814, *Correspondance de Napoléon I*, XXVII, No. 21344, 224–27.
33   Fournier, op. cit., p. 194.
34   Fournier, op. cit., p. 226.
35   Webster, *Castlereagh*, I, pp. 213–26.
36   Metternich to Hudelist, 13 March 1814, HHSA, Int. Korr. 77: Krache, op. cit., p. 311.
37   Metternich to Stadion, 13 March 1814, Srbik, I, pp. 174–75.
38   Metternich to Hudelist, 14 March 1814, HHSA, Int. Korr. 77.
39   Metternich to Hudelist, 29 March 1814, HHSA, Int. Korr. 77; Webster, *Castlereagh*, I, p. 243.
40   *Ibid.*, pp. 244–45.
41   Metternich to Hudelist, 7 April 1814, HHSA, Int. Korr. 78.

Chapter 8: The Business of Victory

1   Metternich to Duchess of Sagan, 13 April 1814, Ullrichova, *Mett-Sagan*, p. 243.
2   *Mémoires*, I, p. 194; Metternich to Hudelist, 15 April 1814, HHSA, Int. Korr. 78.
3   *Mémoires*, I, pp. 194–95; Corti, *Frauen*, I, p. 438.
4   Stacton, *The Bonapartes*, p. 79; Corti, *Frauen*, I, pp. 449–51.
5   *Ibid.*, I, p. 442.
6   Haas, *Metternich, Reorganization and Nationality 1813–18*, pp. 17–20 and pp. 32–33.
7   On Bentinck, see Webster, *Castlereagh*, I, pp. 253–60 and Nicolson, *Congress of Vienna*, pp. 185–92.
8   Haas, op. cit., p. 27.
9   *Ibid.*, p. 28.
10   *Ibid.*

11 Metternich to Bellegarde, 15 May 1814, *Ibid.*, pp. 34–35. (Partly reproduced in facsimile, *ibid.*, facing p. 166.)
12 Webster, *Castlereagh*, I, pp. 280–81.
13 *Mémoires*, I, p. 200.
14 *Ibid.*, p. 201; Metternich to Hudelist, 25 May 1814, HHSA, Int. Korr. 78.
15 Castlereagh to Liverpool, 5 May 1814, Webster, *Castlereagh*, I, p. 265.
16 *Ibid.*, p. 283.
17 Metternich to Hudelist, 24 May 1814, HHSA, Int. Korr. 78.
18 Metternich to Duchess of Sagan, 8 June 1814, Ullrichova, *Mett-Sagan*, p. 257.
19 Webster, *Castlereagh*, I, p. 278 and pp. 288–92.
20 *Ibid.*, p. 292.
21 Anonymous pamphlet in the Bodleian Library, Oxford, *Correct Account of the Visit . . . to the University and City of Oxford*, p. 23.
22 There is a full account of the Guildhall dinner, including details of the seating plan, in *The Annual Register* for 1814, pp. 552–67.
23 Nicolson, op. cit., p. 116.
24 Webster, *Castlereagh*, I, pp. 293–95.
25 Metternich to Hudelist, 25 June and 26 June 1814, HHSA, Int. Korr. 78; Webster, *Castlereagh*, I, p. 295.
26 Metternich to Emperor Francis, 5 July 1814, quoted in Corti, *Frauen*, I, p. 462. A copy of a letter from Francis to Louis XVIII seeking his approval for Marie Louise's journey is enclosed in HHSA, Int. Korr. 78. It appears to have been sent from Vienna as early as 18 June.
27 *Mémoires*, I, p. 205 and pp. 264–65.

Chapter 9: Vienna

1 Metternich to his wife, Eleonore, 19 September 1814, Corti, *Frauen*, I, p. 471.
2 There is a valuable selection of contemporary accounts of the Congress in Spiel, *Der Wiener Kongress in Augenzeugenberichten*. See also, Nicolson, *Congress of Vienna*, pp. 160–63.
3 Grunwald, *Vie*, p. 141.
4 Srbik, I, p. 720 (cf *ibid.*, I, p. 187).
5 Humboldt to his wife, 15 October 1814, Sydow (ed.), *Humboldt Briefe*, V, p. 105; Webster, *Castlereagh*, I, p. 334.
6 Gentz, *Tagebücher*, I, pp. 309–10; Sweet, *F. von Gentz*, p. 193.
7 Duff Cooper, *Talleyrand*, pp. 249–52; Gentz, *Tagebücher*, I, p. 312.
8 Grimsted, *Foreign Ministers of Alexander I*, ch. 2 passim, and pp. 202–14 and 226–31.
9 Weil, nos. 502 and 503, p. 368.
10 Webster, *Castlereagh*, I, p. 346.
11 Haas, *Metternich, Reorganization and Nationality*, p. 53.
12 Webster, *Castlereagh*, I, p. 341; Nicolson, op. cit., p. 194.
13 Metternich to Emperor Francis, 24 October 1814, Corti, *Frauen*, I, pp. 477–78; Srbik, I, p. 189; Du Coudray, *Metternich*, p. 139; Webster, *Castlereagh*, I, p. 348.

14 Weil, I, No. 661, pp. 460–62.
15 Grunwald, *Vie*, p. 152.
16 Du Coudray, op. cit., p. 139 (citing Talleyrand's *Correspondance Inedité*); for the Poles, see Weil, I, No. 529, p. 383.
17 Chambonas, *Anecdotal Recollections*, p. 97; Weil, I, No. 292, p. 233.
18 *Ibid.*, I, No. 599, p. 424 and No. 636, p. 445.
19 Metternich to the Duchess of Sagan, 31 October 1814, Ullrichova, *Mett-Sagan*, p. 269.
20 Weil, I, No. 661, pp. 460–62.
21 Gentz, *Tagebücher*, I, p. 324.
22 Grunwald, *Vie*, p. 146.
23 Weil, I, No. 636, p. 445.
24 Spiel, op. cit., pp. 147–48 and p. 173; Nicolson, op. cit., p. 163; Webster, *Castlereagh*, I, p. 332.
25 *Ibid.*, I, pp. 349–50; Kissinger, *World Restored*, p. 161.
26 *Ibid.*, p. 162.
27 Nicolson, op. cit., pp. 146–47.
28 Webster, *Castlereagh*, I, pp. 367–68.
29 Nicolson, op. cit., pp. 192–93; Srbik, I, pp. 214–16.
30 Weil, I, No. 1036, p. 669 and No. 1066, pp. 686–87.
31 Kissinger, op. cit., pp. 167–70.
32 Gentz, *Tagebücher*, I, p. 344.
33 *Ibid.*, I, pp. 348–49.
34 Corti, *Frauen*, I, p. 485 (cf. Missoffe, *Metternich*, pp. 216–17 and p. 223).
35 Nicolson, op. cit., p. 132; Weil, I, No. 270, p. 238.
36 *Ibid.*, pp. 130–300 *passim*.
37 *Mémoires*, I, pp. 204–6.
38 Srbik, I, pp. 200–3.
39 Webster, *Congress of Vienna*, p. 139.
40 Gentz, *Tagebücher*, I, p. 365.
41 Webster, *Castlereagh*, I, pp. 441–2; Kissinger, op. cit., p. 177.
42 *Ibid.*, p. 176.
43 *Mémoires*, I, p. 328; cf. Stein's version, quoted by Grunwald, *Vie*, p. 152.
44 Du Coudray, op. cit., pp. 156–57.
45 Webster, *Congress of Vienna*, pp. 142–46; Haas, op. cit., pp. 58–61.
46 Webster, op. cit., pp. 134–41 and pp. 147–53.
47 Weil, II, No. 2518, p. 616.
48 Chambonas, op. cit., p. 241.
49 Corti, *Frauen*, I, p. 482.
50 Gentz, *Tagebücher*, I, p. 386.
51 Metternich to his daughter, Marie, 24 June 1815, *Mémoires*, II, p. 518; Gentz, *Tagebücher*, I, p. 387.

Chapter 10: Dabbling in the Shifting Sand

1 Guedalla, *The Duke*, p. 274; Metternich to Talleyrand, 25 June 1815, *Mémoires*, II, pp. 519–20.

2 Marie Metternich to her father, 15 June 1815, quoted in Corti, *Frauen*, I, pp. 516–17.
3 Metternich to his daughter, Marie, 13 July 1815, *Mémoires*, II, pp. 523–5.
4 Gentz, *Tagebücher*, I, pp. 400–30.
5 Bartlett, *Castlereagh*, p. 156; Kissinger, *World Restored*, pp. 179–80; Webster, *Castlereagh*, I, p. 462 and pp. 471–72.
6 Guedalla, op. cit., pp. 284–85.
7 Castlereagh to Liverpool, 20 September 1815, Webster, *British Diplomacy*, p. 381.
8 Schenk, *The Aftermath of the Napoleonic Wars*, pp. 37–41; Schwarz, *Die Heilige Allianz*, pp. 50–57; *Mémoires*, I, p. 211.
9 Kissinger, op. cit., pp. 184–5 and p. 227; Webster, *Castlereagh*, I, pp. 482–84 and II, pp. 54–55.
10 Webster, *British Diplomacy*, p. 381.
11 Quoted by May, *The Age of Metternich*, p. 14.
12 Metternich to his mother, 6 December 1815, *Mémoires*, II, p. 528.
13 *Ibid.*, p. 529. Metternich to Hudelist, 8 December 1815, quoted in Haas, *Metternich, Reorganization and Nationality*, p. 81.
14 *Ibid.*, p. 84.
15 Metternich to Emperor Francis, 29 December 1815, *Ibid.*, pp. 82–85 (quotation from p. 85).
16 *Ibid.*, p. 82.
17 Mann, *Secretary of Europe*, p. 269.
18 Haas, op. cit., pp. 92–94.
19 *Ibid.*, pp. 97–111.
20 *Ibid.*, p. 101.
21 Gentz, *Tagebücher*, II, pp. 75–76.
22 Emperor Francis to Metternich, 1 July 1816, *Mémoires*, VII, p. 653.
23 Metternich to Dorothea Lieven, 1 December 1818, Hanoteau, *Lettres*, p. 45.
24 *Ibid.*, p. 46.
25 Gentz, *Tagebücher*, II, p. 89.
26 Metternich to Nesselrode, 20 August 1817, *Mémories*, III, p. 57.
27 Stewart to Castlereagh, 24 January 1820, Webster, *Castlereagh*, II, p. 196.
28 On Saurau, see Emerson, *Metternich and the Political Police*, pp. 63–66; and Haas, op. cit., p. 216.
29 Corti, *Frauen*, II, pp. 52–63.
30 Metternich to his wife, Eleonore, 10 June and 4 June 1817, *Memoires*, III, p. 23 and p. 26.
31 Metternich to his wife, Eleonore, 17 July 1817, *Mémoires*, III, p. 37.
32 Haas, op. cit., p. 113.
33 *Ibid.*, p. 114.
34 Metternich to Emperor Francis, 29 August 1817, *Mémoires*, III, p. 47.
35 Gentz, *Tagebücher*, II, pp. 164–5.
36 Haas, op. cit., pp. 116–17.
37 *Ibid.*, p. 116, p. 179 and p. 215; Metternich to Emperor Francis, 27 October 1817, *Mémoires*, III, pp. 63–75.
38 Haas, op. cit., pp. 132–35 and pp. 180–81.

39   *Mémoires*, I, pp. 117–18; III, pp. 75–7; VIII, pp. 527–30; cf. Srbik, I, p. 462.
40   Metternich to Francesco Guicciardi, 24 December 1817, quoted by Haas, op. cit., p. 136 (cf. *Ibid.*, p. 216).
41   *Ibid.*, p. 156. Macartney, *The Habsburg Empire*, p. 208.

Chapter 11 : Aix and Carlsbad

 1   Bombelles to Metternich, 27 October 1817, quoted in De Sauvigny, *Metternich and his Times*, pp. 177–8; Ramm, *Germany*, p. 148.
 2   Pollard, *Cambridge Modern History*, x, p. 364.
 3   De Sauvigny, op. cit., p. 177; Sweet, *F. von Gentz*, p. 214.
 4   Srbik, I, pp. 585–88.
 5   Webster, *Castlereagh*, II, pp. 122–23.
 6   *Ibid.*, II, pp. 93–4.
 7   *Ibid.*, II, p. 130.
 8   *Ibid.*, II, pp. 122–3.
 9   Metternich to Esterhazy, 5 April 1818, quoted by Webster, *Ibid.*, II, p. 123.
10   Metternich to his wife, Eleonore, 13 July 1818, *Mémoires*, III, p. 105.
11   Metternich to Emperor Francis, 18 April 1818, *Mémoires*, III, pp. 144–45.
12   Metternich to his wife, Eleonore, 30 July 1818, *Mémoires*, III, pp. 105–6; Corti, *Frauen*, II, pp. 71–2.
13   Metternich to his mother, 13 August 1818, *Mémoires*, III, p. 108.
14   Webster, *Castlereagh*, II, pp. 127–30.
15   Metternich to his wife, Eleonore, 11 September 1818, *Mémoires*, III, p. 113.
16   The same to the same, 12 September 1818, *Mémoires*, III, pp. 114–15.
17   The same to the same, 1 October 1818, *Mémoires*, III, p. 124.
18   Kissinger, *World Restored*, p. 215 and p. 220.
19   Metternich to his wife, Eleonore, October 1818, *Mémoires*, III, p. 127.
20   Webster, *Castlereagh*, II, p. 164.
21   Metternich to Wittgenstein, 14 November 1818, *Mémoires*, III, pp. 177–88.
22   Sweet, op. cit., pp. 217–18.
23   Corti, *The Rise of the House of Rothschild*, p. 226.
24   Memorandum by Gentz, November 1818, *Mémoires*, III, pp. 170–76.
25   Marie Esterhazy-Metternich to her mother, 16 November 1818, quoted by Corti, *Frauen*, II, p. 82; Metternich to his wife, Eleonore, 1 October 1818, *Mémoires*, III, p. 126.
26   For the early life of Dorothea Lieven, see the biographies by Montgomery Hyde and Priscilla Zamoyska cited in the bibliography. See also, Temperley (ed.), *Lieven Diary*, pp. 17–55; Quennell (ed.), *Private Letters of Princess Lieven*, pp. ix–xxii; and the sketches by Sir Lewis Namier in *Vanished Supremacies* and by Lytton Strachey in *Portraits in Miniature*.
27   Count Corti was responsible for identifying Dorothea Lieven as the recipient of many of the private letters printed, generally in an abridged form, in the *Mémoires*. For Corti's comments on the extent of the correspondence, see his *Frauen*, II, p. 86.

28 Metternich to Dorothea Lieven, 1 December 1818, Hanoteau, *Lettres*, p. 45.
29 The same to the same, 20 November and 1 December 1818, and 15 March 1819, Hanoteau, *Lettres*, p. 18, p. 43 and p. 245.
30 The same to the same, 6 December 1818, *Ibid.*, p. 56.
31 The same to the same, 7 December 1818, *Ibid.*, p. 56.
32 The same to the same, 14 December 1818, *Ibid.*, p. 59; Metternich to his daughter, Marie, 17 December 1818, *Mémoires*, III, p. 134.
33 Metternich to his wife, Eleonore, 2 April 1819, *Ibid.*, III, p. 194.
34 The same to the same, 10 April 1819, *Ibid.*, III, p. 201.
35 Metternich to Gentz, 23 April 1819, *Ibid.*, III, p. 245.
36 The same to the same, 7 May 1819, *Ibid.*, III, p. 255.
37 Metternich to his wife, Eleonore, 19 June 1819, *Ibid.*, III, p. 220.
38 Srbik, I, p. 588; Annexe 336, 23 March 1819, *Mémoires*, III, p. 232; Kissinger, op. cit., p. 238.
39 Gentz to Metternich, 1 April and 23 April 1819, *Mémoires*, III, p. 227 and p. 243.
40 Metternich to his wife, Eleonore, 10 April 1819, *Ibid.*, p. 200.
41 Metternich to Gentz, 23 April 1819, *Ibid.*, p. 246.
42 Gentz to Adam Müller, 3 June 1819, Wittichen and Salzer, *Briefe von und an Friedrich von Gentz*, III, pt. 2, p. 460.
43 Metternich to Gentz, 17 June 1819, *Mémoires*, III, p. 262.
44 Metternich to his wife, Eleonore, 27 July 1819, *Ibid.*, III, pp. 224–25.
45 Metternich to Emperor Francis, 30 July 1819, *Ibid.*, III, pp. 269–73. (Quotation from p. 272.)
46 Summary of Diet's proceedings printed in *Mémoires*, III, pp. 284–97.
47 Neumann to Metternich, 19 October 1819, quoted by Webster, *Castlereagh*, II, p. 192.
48 Bernstorff and others to Metternich, 30 August 1819, *Mémoires*, III, p. 298.
49 Metternich to his wife, Eleonore, 1 September 1819, *Ibid.*, pp. 226–27.

Chapter 12: 'My Friends the Spiders'

1 Private letter of Metternich, 3 September 1819, *Mémoires*, III, p. 307.
2 Metternich to Neumann, 16 November 1820, *Ibid.*, III, p. 317.
3 Kissinger, *World Restored*, pp. 244–45; Grimsted, *Foreign Ministers of Alexander I*, pp. 246–47.
4 Ramm, *Germany*, p. 149; Metternich to Emperor Francis, 31 March 1820, *Mémoires*, III, p. 390.
5 Metternich to Emperor Francis, 14 May 1820, *Ibid.*, III, p. 402.
6 Private letter of Metternich (probably to Dorothea Lieven), 17 February 1820, *Ibid.*, III, p. 334.
7 Private letter of Metternich, 25 February 1820, *Ibid.*, III, p. 335.
8 Metternich to Dorothea Lieven, 17 December 1819, *Ibid.*, III, p. 315.
9 Private letter of Metternich, probably to Dorothea Lieven, 19 January 1819, *Ibid.*, III, p. 330.
10 The same, 11 April 1820, *Ibid.*, p. 340.

11   For the illness of Clementine Metternich, see *Mémoires*, III, pp. 335–47.
12   For the illness of Marie Esterhazy-Metternich, see Corti, *Frauen*, II, p. 135 and *Mémoires*, III, pp. 359–62.
13   Private letters of Metternich, 28 July and 25 September 1820, *Ibid.*, III, pp. 362–63 and pp. 368–69; Corti, *Frauen*, II, pp. 136–37.
14   Private letter of Metternich, 25 July 1820, *Mémoires*, III, p. 361.
15   Webster, *Castlereagh*, II, p. 243; Schroeder, *Metternich's Diplomacy*, p. 27.
16   Webster, *Castlereagh*, II, p. 235.
17   Metternich to Esterhazy, 9 July 1819, quoted by Schroeder, op. cit., p. 24.
18   Haas, *Metternich, Reorganization and Nationality*, pp. 159–60.
19   Webster, *Castlereagh*, II, pp. 262–63 and, for this section in general, Schroeder, op. cit., pp. 47–59. See also, his article on 'Austrian Policy' in JCEA, XXII, No. 2 (1962), p. 142. (Cf. Kissinger, op. cit., p. 253).
20   Schroeder, op. cit., pp. 55–58.
21   Quoted by Kissinger, op. cit., p. 257; see also, Schroeder, op. cit., pp. 60–61.
22   Private letter of Metternich, 15 August 1820, *Mémoires*, III, p. 366.
23   Metternich to Dorothea Lieven, 6 October 1820, *Ibid.*, III, p. 369.
24   Private letter of Metternich, 21 October 1820, *Ibid.*, III, p. 374.
25   *Ibid.*, III, p. 373.
26   Quennell, *Private Letters of Princess Lieven*, p. 19, p. 23 and p. 158; private letter of Metternich, 21 October 1820, *Mémoires*, III, p. 373.
27   Schroeder, op. cit., p. 69.
28   Stewart to Castlereagh, 3 November 1820, Webster, *Castlereagh*, II, p. 525.
29   Kissinger, op. cit., pp. 264–65.
30   Castlereagh to Stewart, 16 December 1820, Webster, *Castlereagh*, II, p. 304.
31   Esterhazy to Metternich, 21 February 1821, *Ibid.*, II, p. 326.
32   Private letter of Metternich, 1 December 1820, *Mémoires*, II, p. 380.
33   Private letter of Metternich, 15 December 1820, *Ibid.*, III, pp. 382–83.
34   Metternich to Tsar Alexander, 15 December 1820, *Ibid.*, III, pp. 425–55. For an English translation, see Mack Walker, *Metternich's Europe*, pp. 111–27; and for comments on the document, see also, Woodward, *Three Studies in European Conservatism*, pp. 45–56.
35   Metternich to Dorothea Lieven, 4 January 1821, *Mémoires*, III, pp. 446–47; cf. Corti, *Frauen*, II, p. 153.
36   *Mémoires*, III, p. 464, p. 67 and p. 468.
37   Schroeder, op. cit., pp. 104–06. For the description of Capodistrias 'writhing like a devil', see Metternich's letter of 8 January 1821, *Mémoires*, III, p. 449.
38   Schroeder, op. cit., p. 108.
39   *Ibid.*, pp. 97–98; Kissinger, op. cit., p. 278.
40   Private letter of Metternich, 15 March 1821, *Mémoires*, III, p. 460; Kissinger, op. cit., p. 279.
41   Gentz, *Tagebücher*, II, p. 396.
42   Stadion to Metternich, 8 April 1821, quoted by Schroeder, op. cit., p. 120.
43   Metternich to Stadion, 21 and 22 April 1821, *Mémoires*, III, pp. 496–502.

44 Private letter of Metternich, 18 May 1821, *Ibid.*, III, p. 468.
45 Emperor Francis to Metternich, 25 May 1821, *Ibid.*, VII, pp. 656–57; private letter of Metternich, 28 May 1821, *Ibid.*, III, p. 469.
46 Private letter of Metternich, 23 July 1821, *Ibid.*, III, p. 473.

Chapter 13: Power's Foremost Parasite

1   Anderson, *The Eastern Question*, pp. 49–54.
2   Taylor, *Habsburg Monarchy*, p. 36.
3   Chambonas, *Anecdotal Recollections*, p. 193.
4   Metternich to Stadion, 26 March 1821, *Mémoires*, III, p. 492; private letters of Metternich, 20 April and 6 May 1821, *Ibid.*, III, p. 465.
5   Kissinger, *World Restored*, pp. 290–91. See the retrospective survey by Capodistrias written in Geneva on 24 December 1826 and printed (in French and Russian versions) in *Sbornik*, III, pp. 163–292. Especially relevant to this section, pp. 259–64.
6   Tsar Alexander to Metternich, 17 July 1821, *Mémoires*, III, p. 472.
7   Kissinger, op. cit., pp. 294–96; Capodistrias survey, *Sbornik*, III, p. 269.
8   Metternich to Lebzeltern, 8 October 1821, quoted by Webster, *Castlereagh*, II, p. 366.
9   *Ibid.*, II, pp. 374–75. For Metternich's account of his rhapsodic reception by George IV, see his letter of 25 October 1821, *Mémoires*, III, p. 481.
10 Helleiner, *Imperial Loans*, p. 157.
11 Metternich to Emperor Francis, 29 October 1821, *Mémoires*, III, p. 523; Webster, *Castlereagh*, II, p. 381.
12 Private letter of Metternich, 9 November 1821, *Mémoires*, III, p. 483; Metternich to Lebzeltern, 3 December 1821, quoted in Schroeder, *Metternich's Diplomacy*, p. 177.
13 Helleiner, op. cit., pp. 157–58; private letter of Metternich, 21 December 1821, *Mémoires*, III, pp. 483–84.
14 Private letter of Metternich, 6 March 1822, *Ibid.*, III, p. 537.
15 Kissinger, op. cit., pp. 303–04; Schroeder, op. cit., p. 191.
16 Private letter of Metternich, 25 July 1822, *Mémoires*, III, p. 552; cf. Grimsted, *Foreign Ministers of Alexander I*, pp. 266–67.
17 Schroeder, op. cit., p. 200, pp. 202–03; Webster, *Castlereagh*, II, p. 472.
18 Metternich to Lebzeltern, 7 May 1822, quoted by Webster, *Ibid.*, II, p. 473.
19 Metternich to Castlereagh, 6 June 1822, *Ibid.*, II, pp. 541–44 (quotations from p. 542 and p. 543).
20 Castlereagh to Metternich, 29 July 1922, *Ibid.*, II, pp. 548–49.
21 *Ibid.*, pp. 486–88; Bartlett, *Castlereagh*, pp. 262–63; *Mémoires*, III, pp. 556–57; Quennell, *Lieven Letters*, pp. 198–205.
22 Dorothea Lieven to Metternich, 21 August 1822, *Ibid.*, p. 199.
23 Temperley, *Foreign Policy of Canning*, pp. 63–64; Rolo, *George Canning*, pp. 210–11; Srbik, I, p. 614; and see the article by Nichols on the Vienna Conference in JCEA for April 1961, XXI, p. 63.
24 Canning's speech at Liverpool, 30 August 1822, Rolo, op. cit., pp. 203–04.

25 Schroeder, op. cit., p. 281; cf. the article by Nichols, loc. cit., pp. 61–62; Sweet, *F. von Gentz*, p. 248.
26 Quoted by Srbik, I, p. 616.
27 Corti, *The Rise of the House of Rothschild*, pp. 245–97.
28 Private letter of Metternich, 9 October 1822, *Mémoires*, III, p. 538; cf. Quennell, op. cit., p. 207.
29 On Verona, see Schroeder, op. cit., pp. 211–36; Srbik, I, pp. 614–16; and Temperley (ed.), *Lieven Diary*, pp. 56–59.
30 Metternich to his wife, Eleonore, 12 November 1822, *Mémoires*, III, p. 560.
31 Crawley, *Question of Greek Independence*, p. 26.
32 Byron, 'The Age of Gold', Canto. XVI, *Poems*, I, p. 510.
33 Temperley, *Foreign Policy of Canning*, p. 67.
34 *Ibid.*, p. 68.
35 De Sauvigny, *Metternich and his Times*, pp. 285–86.
36 Private letters of Metternich, 22, 28, and 29 December 1822, *Mémoires*, III, pp. 563–65.

Chapter 14: The Shadow of Eclipse

1 Srbik, I, p. 622; Temperley, *Foreign Policy of Canning*, p. 145.
2 Metternich to Apponyi, 30 June 1823, *Mémoires*, IV, pp. 57–62. For his earlier comment over the question, see De Sauvigny, *Metternich and his Times*, p. 198.
3 See the classical account of the Italian patriots' tribulations in Silvio Pellico's *My Prisons*; cf. Srbik, I, pp. 488–89.
4 *Mémoires*, IV, pp. 27–34; and the private letter of Metternich, 2 February 1823, *Ibid.*, IV, pp. 3–4.
5 Metternich to his wife, Eleonore, 4 April 1823, *Ibid.*, IV, p. 6; cf. Corti, *Frauen*, II, p. 217.
6 Metternich to Lebzeltern, 22 May 1823, quoted by Grimsted, *Foreign Ministers of Alexander I*, p. 284.
7 *Ibid.*, pp. 282–84.
8 La Ferronays to Chateaubriand, 1 October 1823, *Ibid.*, p. 280.
9 For the journey eastwards and the illness at Lemberg, see *Mémoires*, IV, pp. 15–23.
10 Metternich to his wife, Eleonore, 27 October 1823, *Ibid.*, IV, p. 22.
11 Temperley, op. cit., p. 330.
12 *Ibid.*, p. 335.
13 *Mémoires*, IV, p. 12; Du Coudray, *Metternich*, pp. 221–22; Sweet, *F. von Gentz*, p. 256.
14 Metternich to Wellington, 10 June 1824, Wellington, *Supplementary Despatches*, II, p. 279.
15 Macartney, *Habsburg Empire*, pp. 190–93.
16 Sweet, op. cit., pp. 275–76.
17 Srbik, I, pp. 484–85; De Sauvigny, op. cit., p. 6 (quoting Andryane, *Memoirs of a State Prisoner*).
18 *Mémoires*, IV, pp. 116–28.

19 Private letter of Metternich, 23 September 1824, *Ibid.*, IV, p. 111; cf. De Sauvigny, op. cit., p. 287.

20 Metternich to Dorothea Lieven, 24 April 1819, Hanoteau, *Lettres*, p. 306.

21 Srbik, I, p. 623: Metternich to Esterhazy, 8 September 1825, printed in De Sauvigny, op. cit., p. 287. Esterhazy did, indeed, have a conversation with George IV at Windsor later in the month, but his despatch reporting it is concerned solely with foreign affairs (HHSA, Dipl. Korr., England, 1825, Karton 172, Fascicle 3) and there is no evidence the King ever received Metternich's gloomy message.

22 Private letter of Metternich, 12 January 1825, *Mémoires*, IV, p. 149; Corti, *Frauen*, II, pp. 256–62.

23 Metternich to Emperor Francis, 11 April 1825, *Mémoires*, IV, p. 172.

24 Corti, *Frauen*, II, p. 368; Temperley, op. cit., pp. 248–49; cf. Srbik, I, p. 628 and the letter to Emperor Francis cited immediately above; Dorothea Lieven to Metternich, 25 March 1825, Quennell, *Lieven Letters*, p. 348.

25 Dorothea Lieven to Metternich, 8 April 1825, *Ibid.*, p. 349.

26 Private letters of Metternich, 7 and 20 April 1825, *Mémoires*, IV, p. 156 and p. 160.

27 Metternich to Gentz, 3 July 1825, *Ibid.*, IV, pp. 180–81.

28 The same to the same, 7 July and 13 July 1825, *Ibid.*, IV, pp. 181–88.

29 Crawley, *Greek Independence*, p. 42.

30 Temperley, op. cit., p. 371.

31 Anderson, *Eastern Question*, p. 63; Schiemann, *Geschichte Russlands* ... *Nik. I*, I, pp. 608–10.

32 Dorothea Lieven to Metternich, 18 May 1825, Quennell, op. cit., p. 352.

33 Dorothea Lieven's account of her visit to St Petersburg and conversation with the Tsar has been printed by Temperley in the *Lieven Diary*, pp. 85–100.

34 Lebzeltern to Metternich, 30 July 1825, HHSA, Dipl. Korr., Russland, 1825, Karton 68, Fascicle 9.

35 Temperley (ed.), *Lieven Diary*, pp. 95–99.

36 Dorothea Lieven to Metternich, 2 September 1825, Quennell, op. cit., p. 353.

37 A despatch from Lebzeltern, sent on 13 September 1825, hints at 'new influences' hostile to Metternich. This is probably a discreet reference to Dorothea Lieven's activities (HHSA, Dipl. Korr., Russland, 1825, Karton 68, Fascicle 9).

38 Metternich to Dorothea Lieven, 1 October 1825, *Mémoires*, IV, p. 199.

39 The same to the same, 20 April 1825, Corti, *Frauen*, II, p. 269.

40 Metternich to Gentz, 28 September 1825, *Mémoires*, IV, pp. 198–99.

41 Private letter of Metternich, 17 August 1825, *Ibid.*, IV, p. 197.

42 Metternich to Dorothea Lieven, 1 October 1825, *Ibid.*, IV, p. 200.

43 Metternich to Szogenyi, 11 December 1825, *Ibid.*, IV, p. 243.

44 Barany, *Stephen Széchenyi and the Awakening of Hungarian Nationalism*, p. 124. Dr Barany's book gives a detailed account of the Diet and considerably modifies Srbik, I, pp. 466–67. See also, Bibl., *Metternich*, p. 197; and Macartney, op. cit., p. 223.

45 Barany, op. cit., pp. 125–30. For Metternich's version of events, see *Mémoires*, IV, pp. 246–57.
46 Wellesley to Canning, 25 December 1825, cited by Barany, op. cit., p. 123.
47 Private letter of Metternich, 22 December 1825, *Mémoires*, IV, p. 205; Metternich to Neumann, 1 January 1826, *Ibid.*, IV, p. 269.
48 Metternich to his son, Victor, 24 January 1826, *Ibid.*, IV, p. 271; for Metternich's comment, see Lebzeltern to Metternich, 15 December 1825 (received in Vienna, 6 January), HHSA, Dipl. Korr., Russland 1825, Karton 26, Fascicle 12.
49 Henry Wellesley to Wellington, 22 February 1826, Wellington, *Supplementary Despatches*, III, p. 141.
50 Temperley, *Foreign Policy of Canning*, p. 355 and pp. 390–91.
51 Metternich to Esterhazy, 2 December 1828, De Sauvigny, op. cit., p. 247.
52 Anderson, *Eastern Question*, p. 65.
53 Temperley, op. cit., pp. 357–58.
54 Metternich to Prince of Hesse-Hombourg, 13 November 1826, *Mémoires*, IV, p. 329.
55 Temperley, op. cit., p. 374.
56 Sweet, op. cit., p. 261.
57 Metternich to Dorothea Lieven, 28 April 1826, Corti, *Frauen*, II, p. 280.
58 Dorothea Lieven to Metternich, 16 May 1826, Quennell, op. cit., p. 369.
59 The same to the same, 22 November 1826, *Ibid.*, p. 376.
60 Corti, *Frauen*, II, p. 282.
61 *Ibid.*, p. 289; Srbik, I, p. 243.
62 Corti, *Frauen*, II, p. 284.
63 *Ibid.*, p. 292.

Chapter 15: Challenge Resisted

1 Anderson, *Eastern Question*, p. 67; Crawley, *Greek Independence*, pp. 85–86; Metternich to Apponyi, 13 November 1827, *Mémoires*, IV, p. 403.
2 Metternich to his son, Victor, 24 January 1828, *Ibid.*, p. 420.
3 Anderson, op. cit., p. 69; Guedalla, *The Duke*, p. 362.
4 Metternich to Esterhazy, 21 September 1829, *Mémoires*, IV, pp. 595–96; cf. Metternich to Emperor Francis, 9 October 1829, *Ibid.*, pp. 604–05.
5 Srbik, I, p. 622 and p. 629.
6 Metternich to Emperor Francis, 9 October 1829, *Mémoires*, IV, pp. 602–10.
7 Metternich to Countess Molly Zichy, 23 January 1829, *Ibid.*, IV, p. 540.
8 Corti, *Frauen*, II, pp. 303–04; cf. *Mémoires*, IV, pp. 562–63.
9 *Ibid.*, p. 594 and footnote; and see the article by Renesman on 'Metternich and Reform' in JMH, December 1970, Vol. 42, pp. 524–48.
10 Metternich to Esterhazy, 11 February 1830, De Sauvigny, *Metternich and his Times*, pp. 222–23.
11 Metternich to Apponyi, 5 June 1830, *Mémoires*, V, pp. 2–3.
12 *Ibid.*, V, p. 6.

13 For Gentz's personal affairs at this time, see Guest, *Fanny Elssler*, pp. 30–31.

14 Metternich to Emperor Francis, 31 July 1830, *Mémoires*, v, pp. 7–11.

15 Jäger's account of Metternich's dramatic reaction to the news from Paris is cited in Srbik, I, p. 781.

16 Metternich to Emperor Francis, 31 July 1830, *Mémoires*, v, pp. 7–11.

17 The same to the same, 4–5 August 1830, *Ibid.*, v, p. 15.

18 Metternich to Nesselrode, 1 September 1830, *Ibid.*, v, p. 23.

19 Metternich's summary of his conversation with General Belliard, 30 August 1830, *Ibid.*, v, p. 23.

20 Webster, *Palmerston, Metternich and the European System* (hereafter cited as *European System*), p. 20.

21 Ramm, *Germany*, pp. 162–63; Ridley, *Lord Palmerston*, p. 155.

22 Macartney, *Habsburg Empire*, pp. 232–33.

23 Barany, *Stephen Széchenyi*, p. 269.

24 Melanie's Journal, 16 October 1831, *Mémoires*, v, p. 112; Corti, *Frauen*, II, p. 313.

25 Srbik, I, pp. 244–45; Sainte-Aulaire, *Souvenirs*, pp. 26–28; Frances Trollope, *Vienna and the Austrians*, II, pp. 293–95; Pauline Metternich-Sandor, *Geschehenes, Gesehenes, Erlebtes*, p. 28.

26 Melanie's Journal, 1 February 1831, *Mémoires*, v, p. 89.

27 Srbik, I, p. 677. There is an interesting report, specially prepared for Emperor Francis by Werkheim, of events in Parma in February-March 1831, HHSA, Familienakten, Kaiser Franz, Karton 24.

28 Melanie's Journal, 12 February 1831, *Mémoires*, v, p. 90.

29 Macartney, op. cit., p. 237; Sweet, *F. von Gentz*, pp. 298–99.

30 Melanie's Journal, 18 April 1831, *Mémoires*, v, p. 95.

31 Metternich to Apponyi, 3 June 1831 (three letters), *Ibid.*, v, pp. 161–75.

32 Srbik, I, p. 676 (cf. Du Coudray, *Metternich*, pp. 254–56).

33 Grunwald, *Vie*, p. 255.

34 Metternich to Apponyi, 18 January 1831, *Ibid.*, p. 254; Metternich to Apponyi, 15 February 1831, *Mémoires*, v, p. 154.

35 The same to the same, 19 February 1831 (enclosing a letter from Joseph Bonaparte dated 9 October 1830), *Ibid.*, v, p. 158.

36 Melanie's Journal, 24 July 1832, *Ibid.*, v, p. 242.

37 Melanie's Journal, 17 February and 11 March 1831, *Ibid.*, v, p. 90 and p. 91.

38 Sweet, *F. von Gentz*, p. 300; Melanie's Journal, 23 July 1831 and 9 June 1832, *Mémoires*, v, p. 104 and p. 237.

39 Srbik, I, p. 245 and p. 730; Mazade, *Un Chancelier*, pp. 324–25; Grunwald, *Vie*, p. 265. Sainte-Aulaire's *Souvenirs* are silent over the crown incident, but it is mentioned in Melanie's Journal six times between 9 January and 5 March 1834, *Mémoires*, v, pp. 557, 558, 559, 562, 565 and 566.

40 Melanie's Journal, 19 December 1831, *Ibid.*, v, p. 115.

41 Corti, *Frauen*, II, p. 334 and p. 360.

42 Sainte-Aulaire, *Souvenirs*, pp. 39–43 and pp. 161–62; Srbik, I, p. 245.

43 Webster, *Palmerston*, I, pp. 207–36; Ridley, op. cit., pp. 138–41.

44 Metternich to Neumann, 31 October 1832, *Mémoires*, v, pp. 383–90; Melanie's Journal, 17 October 1832, *Ibid.*, v, p. 257.
45 Metternich to Neumann, 2 February 1833, De Sauvigny, op. cit., p. 224.
46 Neumann to Metternich, 8 January 1833, quoted in Webster, *European System*, pp. 10–11.
47 Anderson, op. cit., pp. 77–83.
48 Lamb to Palmerston, 14 April 1833, quoted in Webster, *Palmerston*, I, p. 294.
49 Webster, *European System*, pp. 12–14.
50 Macartney, op. cit., p. 234.
51 Webster, *Palmerston*, I, p. 298.
52 Webster, *European System*, p. 14.
53 See the letters of Metternich to Hügel, 16 August 1833, *Mémoires*, v, pp. 472–73.
54 Webster, *Palmerston*, I, p. 306 and pp. 309–10.
55 See Melanie's Journal, 7–17 August 1833, *Mémoires*, v, pp. 438–41.
56 Melanie's Journal, 4–20 September 1833, *Ibid.*, v, pp. 442–55.
57 Melanie's Journal, 10 September 1833, *Ibid.*, v, p. 446.
58 Schiemann, *Geschichte Russlands . . . Nik. I*, III, pp. 234–35.
59 Srbik, II, p. 472 (cf. *Ibid.*, I, pp. 686–87).
60 Schiemann, loc. cit.
61 See the article by Squire on Metternich and Benckendorff in *Slavonic and East European Review*, Vol. 45, p. 372.
62 Webster, *European System*, p. 15.
63 Webster, *Palmerston*, I, pp. 386–410.
64 Palmerston to William Temple, 21 April 1834, quoted in Ridley, op. cit., p. 172.
65 Metternich to Apponyi, 17 September 1834, *Mémoires*, v, p. 640.
66 Metternich to Hummelauer, 7 July 1834, Temperley, *The Crimea*, p. 81.
67 See the article by Bolsover, 'Palmerston and Metternich on the Eastern Question' in EHR for 1936, Vol. 51, pp. 237–50.
68 Hummelauer to Metternich, 1 October 1834, cited by Webster, *Palmerston*, I, p. 407.
69 Metternich to Hummelauer, 29 November 1834, *Mémoires*, v, p. 643; Webster, *Palmerston*, I, p. 410.

Chapter 16: Monarchy without a Monarch

1 Metternich to Dorothea Lieven, 20 December 1818, Hanoteau, *Lettres*, p. 71.
2 Kübeck, *Tagebücher*, 8 June 1831, I, ii, p. 438.
3 *Ibid.*, 28 November 1831, I, ii, p. 508.
4 See the article by Seton-Watson on 'Metternich and internal Austrian Policy,' in *Slavonic Year Book* (1939), XVIII, pp. 131–32.
5 Kübeck, *Tagebücher*, 11 January 1832, I, ii, p. 532.
6 *Ibid.*, 6 October 1834, I, ii, p. 662.
7 Melanie's Journal, 25–28 February 1835, *Mémoires*, v, pp. 645–48.
8 Corti, *Vom Kind zum Kaiser*, p. 100.

9   Melanie's Journal, 1 March 1835, *Mémoires*, v, p. 649.

10 Metternich to Marie Louise, 21 March 1835, quoted in Corti, *Frauen*, II, p. 371.

11 Metternich to Austrian representatives abroad, 12 March 1835, *Mémoires*, v, pp. 673–76 and vi, pp. 1–4.

12 Corti, *Frauen*, II, pp. 366–67; Macartney, *Habsburg Empire*, p. 255.

13 Kübeck, *Tagebücher*, 14 March 1835, I, ii, pp. 679–80.

14 *Mémoires*, VI, pp. 68–92; for Benckendorff's comment, see Squire's article, loc. cit., p. 370.

15 Srbik, II, p. 152.

16 Metternich to Apponyi, 12 October 1835, *Mémoires*, VI, pp. 89–92.

17 Webster, *Palmerston*, II, p. 559.

18 *Ibid.*, pp. 571–75; Webster, *European System*, p. 24.

19 Metternich to Apponyi, 30 September 1835, *Mémoires*, VI, p. 286.

20 Ramm, *Germany*, pp. 163–64.

21 For Metternich's memorandum on the *Zollverein*, written for Emperor Francis in June 1833, see *Mémoires*, v, pp. 517–36; cf. Seton-Watson article, loc. cit., p. 139.

22 Barany, *Stephen Széchenyi*, pp. 274–75; Melanie's Journal, 28 March 1835, *Mémoires*, VI, pp. 8–9.

23 Barany, op. cit., p. 250 and p. 319.

24 *Ibid.*, pp. 303–04.

25 *Ibid.*, pp. 328–29 (citing Erzebet Andics, *Á Habsburgok És Szövetsege Romanovok*, published in Budapest, 1961).

26 *Ibid.*, p. 310.

27 Srbik, II, pp. 8–9.

28 Taylor, *Habsburg Monarchy*, p. 48.

29 Srbik, II, pp. 9–12 and p. 572.

30 Melanie's Journal, 28 September 1836, *Mémoires*, VI, p. 125.

31 See the extract from Archduke John's journal, quoted by Srbik, II, pp. 14–15.

32 *Ibid.*, II, p. 16.

33 Palmerston to Ponsonby, 7 November 1836, Webster, *Palmerston*, II, p. 590; Srbik, II, p. 82.

34 See the analysis of the Chancellor's methods in Mayr, *Metternichs Geheimer Briefdienst*.

35 Metternich to his wife, Melanie, 19 July 1838, *Mémoires*, VI, p. 294.

36 On railway policy in general within the Habsburg Monarchy, see Macartney, op. cit., p. 259.

37 Melanie's Journal, 8 May 1838, *Mémoires*, VI, p. 242.

38 Melanie's Journal, 10 June 1840, *Ibid.*, VI, p. 400.

39 See, for examples, *Ibid.*, VI, pp. 305–07 and pp. 702–06.

40 Anderson, *Eastern Question*, pp. 95–100.

41 Metternich to Apponyi, 14 June 1839, *Mémoires*, VI, pp. 367–68; Webster, *European System*, p. 28.

42 Palmerston to Granville, 21 June 1839, *Ibid.;* and for Metternich's comments, *Ibid.*, p. 29 (cf. Webster, *Palmerston*, II, p. 631).

43   Palmerston to Lamb, 28 June 1839, quoted by Webster, *European System*, p. 28.
44   Metternich to Apponyi, 7 August 1839, *Mémoires*, VI, pp. 373-74; Webster, *Palmerston*, II, p. 642.
45   For Metternich's collapse and illness, see Melanie's Journal, beginning on 2 August 1839, *Mémoires*, VI, pp. 327-30. See also, Saint-Aulaire, *Souvenirs*, pp. 256-62 (a vivid account but chronologically confused).
46   Webster, *Palmerston*, II, pp. 660-65.
47   Metternich to Apponyi, 15 February 1839, *Mémoires*, VI, p. 359; cf. Bibl., *Metternich*, pp. 266-67.
48   Corti, *Frauen*, II, pp. 387-88.
49   Webster, *European System*, pp. 32-33.
50   Beauvale to Palmerston, 8 October 1840, quoted *Ibid.*, p. 33.
51   Nathan Rothschild to James Rothschild, 10 October 1840, subsequently forwarded to Metternich (HHSA, Dipl. Korr., Frankreich, Varia, Karton 101, Fascicle 130).
52   Webster, *European System*, p. 34.
53   *Ibid.*, p. 35.
54   *Ibid.*, p. 36 (citing F. S. Rodkey in *American Historical Review* for January 1921).

Chapter 17: *A Sense of Conflict*

1   Trollope, *Vienna and the Austrians*, II, p. 27.
2   Schuselka, *Deutsche Worte eines Oesterreichischers*, pp. 24-25; Macartney, *Habsburg Empire*, p. 306.
3   Namier, *1848, Revolution of the Intellectuals*, pp. 5-6.
4   Melanie's Journal, 13 March 1843, *Mémoires*, VI, p. 642.
5   See the article by Haas on Metternich and the Slavs in AHY for 1968-69, pp. 120-49.
6   Macartney, op. cit., pp. 315-16.
7   Metternich to Emperor Ferdinand, 9 March 1843, printed in Haas article, loc. cit., pp. 143-49.
8   Kübeck, *Tagebücher*, 27 December 1839, I, ii, pp. 846-47.
9   Melanie's Journal, 10 August 1843, *Mémoires*, VI, p. 659.
10   Franz, *Liberalismus*, pp. 29-33.
11   Srbik, II, p. 125.
12   Melanie's Journal, retrospective entry for August-September 1845, *Mémoires*, VII, p. 78; Metternich to Archduke Ludwig (with annexe), 20 August 1845, *Ibid.*, VII, pp. 127-37; Srbik, II, p. 95.
13   *Ibid.*, II, p. 95 and p. 582.
14   Corti, *Frauen*, II, pp. 412-17 and pp. 419-20.
15   Melanie's Journal, retrospective entry for December 1845, *Mémoires*, VII, p. 87.
16   Schiemann, *Geschichte Russlands . . . Nik. I*, IV, p. 377.
17   Melanie's Journal for November 1847, *Mémoires*, VII, p. 318; Corti, *Vom Kind zum Kaiser*, p. 231.
18   Melanie's Journal, 5 January 1840, *Mémoires*, VI, p. 387.

19 Grunwald, *Vie*, p. 302.
20 Namier, op. cit., pp. 15–17; Macartney, op. cit., pp. 307–09; Palmer, *Lands Between*, pp. 41–48.
21 Conference of State Agenda, Item 318 of 14 March and Item 347 of 18 March 1846, HHSA Staatskonferenzakten (1846), Karton 25.
22 Hartig, *Genesis der Revolution* in Coxe, *History of the House of Habsburg*, IV, pp. 61–62.
23 Srbik, II, pp. 149–66.
24 Ridley, *Lord Palmerston*, p. 316.
25 Conference of State Agenda, Items 522 of 8 February and 1370 of 30 November 1846, HHSA Staatskonferenzakten (1846), Karton 25.
26 Thomas's article 'L'Allemagne du Present' is printed in *Revue des Deux Mondes*, XIII (April 1846). The quotation is from p. 488. There is an English translation of the introductory open letter to Metternich in Mack Walker, *Metternich's Europe*, pp. 325–30.

Chapter 18: Challenge Triumphant

1 Srbik, II, p. 123; Langer, *Political and Social Upheaval*, p. 137.
2 Woodward, *Three Studies in European Conservatism*, pp. 281–82; Srbik, II, p. 130.
3 Metternich to Lützow, 19 August and 29 August 1847, *Mémoires*, VII, pp. 466–71; Srbik, II, p. 131; Ward, *1848, The Fall of Metternich*, p. 121.
4 Taylor, *The Italian Problem in European Diplomacy*, pp. 44–45.
5 Woodward, op. cit., pp. 178–200; *Mémoires*, VIII, pp. 388–404. For events in Switzerland, see Langer, op. cit., pp. 135–37.
6 Bibl., *Metternich*, p. 276; Ridley, *Lord Palmerston*, pp. 329–30.
7 Metternich to Apponyi, 29 December 1847, *Mémoires*, VII, pp. 356–57. This was a recurrent theme in Metternich's correspondence during the last weeks of the year. (Cf. *Ibid.* VII, p. 353, pp. 502–04 and p. 529).
8 Melanie's Journal, January 1848, *Ibid.*, VII, p. 532; Metternich to Lützow, 2 January 1848, *Ibid.*, VII, pp. 569–72.
9 Langer, op. cit., p. 255; Ward, op. cit., p. 118.
10 Taylor, op. cit., pp. 21–23, 56–58; Metternich to Hartig, 18 January 1848, *Mémoires*, VII, pp. 577–78; Hübner, *Une Année de Ma Vie*, p. 16.
11 Metternich to Apponyi, 29 January 1848, cited by Taylor, op. cit., p. 55.
12 Corti, *Vom Kind zum Kaiser*, pp. 247–48.
13 *Ibid.*, p. 245 and p. 251; Melanie's Journal for February 1848, *Mémoires*, VII, p. 534.
14 *Ibid.*, VII, p. 533; Macartney, *Habsburg Empire*, p. 325; Corti, *Vom Kind zum Kaiser*, pp. 249–53.
15 Macartney, op. cit., p. 322.
16 Hübner, op. cit., p. 12.
17 *Ibid.*, p. 16.
18 Corti, *Vom Kind zum Kaiser*, pp. 253–54; Robertson, *Revolutions of 1848*, pp. 206–07.
19 Macartney, op. cit., pp. 323–25.

20 *Ibid.*, p. 326; Melanie's Journal, mid-March 1848, *Mémoires*, VII, pp. 540–42; Ward, op. cit., pp. 136–38; Srbik, II, p. 258.
21 On Fuster and the students in general, see Robertson, op. cit., pp. 206–08; Hartig, *Genesis*, p. 99.
22 Srbik, II, p. 263.
23 Melanie's Journal, mid-March 1848, *Mémoires*, VII, pp. 541–42. As well as the references cited here, I have used for the events of 13 March 1848, Rath, *The Viennese Revolution* and Kiszling, *Die Revolution in Kaisertum Oesterreich*, Vol. I.
24 Srbik, II, pp. 276–77; Grunwald, *Vie*, pp. 315–16; Robertson, op. cit., pp. 209–11.
25 Corti, *Vom Kind zum Kaiser*, pp. 259–62; Srbik, II, p. 282.
26 Hügel article on 'The Escape of Prince Metternich', *National Review* for 1883, p. 596; Srbik, II, pp. 284–85.

Chapter 19 : Exile

1 Melanie's Journal, 14 March 1848, *Mémoires*, VII, p. 546.
2 Robertson, *Revolutions of 1848*, p. 217; Stiles, *Austria in 1848–49*, I, p. 108.
3 Quoted by his son, Baron C. von Hügel, in an article on 'The Escape of Prince Metternich' in *National Review* for 1883, No. 1, p. 596.
4 On these events, see the article of Hügel, cited above, and Melanie's Journal for April 1848, *Mémoires*, VIII, pp. 1–3. For Europe in general at this time, see Langer, *Political and Social Upheaval*, pp. 356–78.
5 Melanie's Journal, April 1848, *Mémoires*, VIII, pp. 5–6; Hügel article, loc. cit., p. 598.
6 Melanie's Journal, April 1848, *Mémoires*, VIII, p. 8.
7 Metternich to his daughter, Leontine, 20 April 1848, *Ibid.*, VIII, p. 154.
8 Letters of Metternich to his daughter, Leontine, 15 May, 18 May, 15 June 1848, *Ibid.*, VIII, p. 160, pp. 164–65 and pp. 170–71.
9 The same to the same, 12 July 1848, *Ibid.*, VIII, p. 178.
10 The same to the same, 7 September 1848, *Ibid.*, VIII, p. 186.
11 The same to the same, 26 June 1848, *Ibid.*, VIII, pp. 171–72.
12 Metternich to Archduke John, 10 July 1848, *Ibid.*, VIII, pp. 456–59; exchange of letters between Metternich and Radetzky, 18 August and 27 August 1848, *Ibid.*, VIII, pp. 32–33.
13 Guizot, *Mémoires*, IV, p.21.
14 Monypenny and Buckle, *Benjamin Disraeli*, III, pp. 181–83; Metternich to Wessenberg, 18 August 1848, *Mémoires*, VIII, pp. 477–78.
15 Extracts from the *Wiener Abendzeitung* of 23 June 1848, quoted by Srbik, II, pp. 332–33. For a full discussion of the issues involved, *Ibid.*, II, pp. 333–41.
16 Schwarzenberg on 14 November 1850, quoted by Srbik, II, p. 340.
17 Metternich to his daughter, Leontine, 15 June 1848, *Mémoires*, VIII, pp. 169–70.
18 Melanie's Journal, September 1848, *Ibid.*, VIII, p. 33.

19 Metternich to his daughter, Leontine, 17 September 1848, *Ibid.* VIII, p. 189.

20 Disraeli to his wife, 7 January 1849, Monypenny and Buckle, op. cit., III, p. 130.

21 Metternich to his daughter, Leontine, 20 and 22 December 1848, *Mémoires*, VIII, pp. 207–08; Melanie's Journal, December 1848, *Ibid.*, VIII, p. 42.

22 Temperley (ed.), *Lieven Diary*, pp. 183–206 (and see also, the biographies of Dorothea Lieven by Montgomery Hyde and Priscilla Zamoyska, already cited).

23 C. de Barante, *Souvenirs du Baron de Barante*, VII, p. 336; Melanie's Journal, November 1848, *Mémoires*, VIII, p. 36.

24 Melanie's Journal, late January 1849, *Ibid.*, VIII, pp. 45–46.

25 Dorothea Lieven to Barante, 19 January 1849, Barante, *Souvenirs*, VII, p. 421.

26 This incident was told by Aberdeen's son to Lord Rosebery and is recorded in Crewe's *Lord Rosebery*, p. 190. The anecdote is so much in character, for both Dorothea Lieven and Metternich, that it is probably true in substance.

27 Melanie's Journal, late April 1849, *Mémoires*, VIII, p. 51.

28 Metternich-Sandor, *Geschehenes, Gesehenes, Erlebtes*, p. 19.

29 Dorothea Lieven to Lady Holland, 2 July 1849, Smith (ed.), *Letters of Princess Lieven to Lady Holland*, p. 43.

30 Francis Joseph to Metternich, 26 July 1849, *Mémoires*, VIII, p. 62; Corti, *Mensch*, p. 40; Corti, *Frauen*, II, pp. 441–42.

31 Dorothea Lieven to Lady Holland, 4 September 1849, Smith, op. cit., p. 49.

32 Melanie's Journal, August 1849, *Mémoires*, VIII, pp. 65–66.

33 Melanie's Journal, October 1849, *Ibid.*, VIII, pp. 70–72; Monypenny and Buckle, op. cit., III, pp. 194–95.

34 Metternich to his daughter, Leontine, 3 November, *Mémoires*, VIII, p. 231. For other details of his residence in Brussels during this period, see *Ibid.*, VIII, pp. 71–102 and 229–69.

35 Kübeck, *Metternich und Kübeck, ein Briefwechsel*, p. 68 and p. 92; cf. Metternich to Kübeck, 31 December 1849, *Mémoires*, VIII, p. 301.

36 Leontine Sandor to Metternich, 8 November 1849, quoted from the family archives by Srbik, II, p. 360.

37 Metternich to his daughter, Leontine, 3 March 1850, *Mémoires*, VIII, p. 252.

38 Hübner, *Neuf Ans*, I, p. 18; Melanie's Journal, March 1851, *Mémoires*, VIII, p. 96; Metternich to Schwarzenberg, 29 March 1851, *Ibid.*, VIII, pp. 533–36; Schwarzenberg to Metternich, 6 April 1851, *Ibid.*, VIII, pp. 536–38.

39 Metternich to his daughter, Leontine, 14 September 1851, *Ibid.*, VIII, pp. 276–77; Hübner, op. cit., I, p. 24.

40 Melanie's Journal, August 1851, *Mémoires*, VIII, pp. 105–06; Srbik, II, pp. 414–15.

41 *Ibid.*, II, p. 416; Melanie's Journal, August 1851, *Mémoires*, VIII, p. 109.

42   Melanie's Journal, September 1851, *Ibid.*, VIII, pp. 110–15 (quotation from p. 114).

Chapter 20: Eldest Statesman

 1   Melanie's Journal, October 1851, *Mémoires*, VIII, p. 117; Corti, *Mensch*, p. 83.
 2   Walter, *Kübeck Nachlass*, p. 78.
 3   Melanie's Journal, September 1851, *Mémoires*, VIII, p. 115.
 4   Srbik, II, pp. 442–43.
 5   Melanie's Journal, January 1852, *Mémoires*, VIII, p. 123.
 6   Corti, *Mensch*, p. 87.
 7   Srbik, II, p. 444; Memorandum by Metternich, 2 January 1852, *Mémoires*, VIII, pp. 538–44.
 8   Corti, *Mensch*, pp. 91–92.
 9   Melanie's Journal, April 1852, *Mémoires*, VIII, p. 128.
10   Metternich to Buol, letters between 15 April and 15 December 1852, Burckhardt, *Buol*, pp. 1–49.
11   *Ibid.*, pp. 50–51; cf. note of 15 December 1852 in *Mémoires*, VIII, p. 346.
12   Note by Metternich, January 1853, *Ibid.*, VIII, p. 587.
13   *Ibid.*, VIII, pp. 589–90.
14   Melanie's Journal, February 1853, *Ibid.*, VIII, p. 140.
15   Hennings, *Fast Hundert Jahre Wien*, p. 54.
16   Melanie's Journal, May 1853, *Mémoires*, VIII, p. 145; Burckhardt, *Buol*, p. 79 and p. 85.
17   Metternich to Buol, 15 July 1853, Burckhardt, *Buol*, pp. 112–13.
18   Corti, *Mensch*, p. 118.
19   *Ibid.*
20   Metternich to Buol, 3 June 1854, Burckhardt, *Buol*, p. 159.
21   Walter, op. cit., p. 130; *Mémoires*, VIII, pp. 146–47; Metternich-Sandor, *Geschehenes, Gesehenes, Erlebtes*, p. 28 and p. 34.
22   Metternich to Buol, 12 May 1856, Burckhardt, *Buol*, p. 169.
23   Metternich-Sandor, op. cit., p. 31; Wassilko, *Fürstin Pauline Metternich*, pp. 26–27.
24   Metternich to Buol, 9 June 1856, Burckhardt, *Buol*, p. 170.
25   Quoted from the Prince's diary in the Windsor archives, by Magnus, *King Edward the Seventh*, p. 22; cf. Lee, *King Edward VII*, I, p. 64. On Thiers, and on Metternich's general interests in the autumn of 1857, see Hübner's account of his own visit to Johannisberg, *Neuf Ans*, II, p. 27.
26   Burckhardt, *Buol*, pp. 196–98.
27   Corti, *Mensch*, pp. 214–19.
28   Metternich-Sandor, op. cit., p. 35.
29   Corti, *Mensch*, pp. 224–25; Friedjung, *Struggle for Supremacy*, p. 13.
30   *Ibid.*, p. 227; Srbik, II, p. 513.
31   Hübner to Richard Metternich, 26 May 1883, *Mémoires*, VIII, pp. 646–47.
32   Metternich-Sandor, op. cit., p. 36.
33   *Ibid.*; Srbik, II, p. 514.
34   *Ibid.*, p. 515.

35 *Neue Öesterreischische Biographie*, III, pp. 43–52.
36 Recollections of Empress Zita, printed in Brook-Shepherd, *The Last Habsburg*, pp. 211–12.

N

SELECT BIBLIOGRAPHY

Archival Material

I *Staatskanzlei*: Haus-, Hof- und Staatsarchiv, Vienna:
   (i) Dip. Korrespondenzen:
     England: *Berichte* 172.
     Frankreich: *Berichte* 200, 205; *Varia* 58, 101.
     Russland: *Berichte* 67, 68.
   (ii) Interiora Korrespondenzen: 77, 78, 79.

II *Kabinettsarchiv*: Haus-, Hof- und Staatsarchiv, Vienna:
   (i) Familienakten, Kaiser Franz: 24.
   (ii) Staatskonferenzakten: 1837, 1846.

I would like to express my gratitude to the General Director and the staff of the Haus-, Hof- und Staatsarchiv, Vienna, for their assistance and advice during my visit to Vienna.

Books

ABRANTÉS, Laure, Duchesse d', *Mémoires de Madame la Duchesse d'Abrantés, ou Souvenirs Historiques*, Vol. VIII (Paris 1835).

ANDERSON, M. S., *The Eastern Question, 1774-1923* (London, 1966).

ANDREWS, Stuart, *Eighteenth Century Europe, the 1680s to 1815* (London, 1965).

ANON. *Correct Account of the Visit of H.R.H. the Prince Regent and his Illustrious Guests to the University and City of Oxford in June, 1814* (Oxford, 1814).

ASHLEY, E., *Life and Correspondence of the Hon. John Temple, Viscount Palmerston* (rev. ed., London, 1876).

BARANTE, Claude de, *Souvenirs du Baron de Barante*, Vol. 7 (Paris 1900).

BARANY, George, *Stephen Széchenyi and the Awakening of Hungarian Nationalism, 1791-1841* (Princeton, 1968).

BAREA, Ilsa, *Vienna* (London, 1966).

BARTLETT, C. J., *Castlereagh* (London, 1966).

BEER, Adolf, *Zehn Jahre Österreichischer Politik, 1801-1810* (Leipzig, 1877).

BELL, H. C. F., *Lord Palmerston* (London, 1936).

BERKELEY, G. F. H. and J., *Italy in the Making*, 1815-1846 (Cambridge, 1932).

BIBL, Victor, *Metternich, 1773-1859* (Paris, 1935).

BONNEFONS, André, *Un Allié de Napoléon, Frédéric Auguste, Premier Roi de Saxe, 1763-1827* (Paris, 1902).

BOTZENHART, Manfred, *Metternichs Pariser Botschafter zeit* (Münster, 1967).

BREYCHA-VAUTHIER, A., *Aus Diplomaten und Leben, Maximen des Fürsten Metternich* (Gräz, 1964).

BRION, M., *Daily Life in the Vienna of Mozart and Schubert* (London, 1961).

BROOK-SHEPHERD, Gordon, *The Last Habsburg* (London, 1968).

BRUFORD, W. H., *Germany in the Eighteenth Century* (rev. ed., Cambridge, 1965).

BRYANT, Sir Arthur, *The Years of Endurance* (London, 1942).

BUCKLAND, C. S. B., *Metternich and the British Government from 1809-1813* (London, 1932).

——, *Friedrich von Gentz' Relations with the British Government*, 1809-12 (London, 1933).

BURCKHARDT, Carl J., *Briefe des Staatskanzlers Fürsten Metternich-Winneburg an Grafen Buol-Schauenstein, 1852-59* (Munich and Berlin, 1934).

BYRON, George Gordon, Baron, *Poems*, Vol. 1 (Everyman ed., London, 1968).

CARTLAND, Barbara, *Metternich, the Passionate Diplomat* (London, 1964).

CAULAINCOURT, Armand de, *Memoirs of General de Caulaincourt, Duke of Vicenza*, 2 Vols (London, 1935).

CECIL, A., *Metternich* (London, 1933).

CHAMBONAS, Comte A. de la Garde, *Anecdotal Recollections of the Congress of Vienna* (London, 1902).

CHANDLER, D. G., *The Campaigns of Napoleon* (London, 1967).

CHANTENESSE, Robert, *The Secret Memoirs of the Duchesse d'Abrantés* (London, 1927).

COOPER, A. Duff, *Talleyrand* (London, 1932).

CORTI, E. C., *The Rise of the House of Rothschild* (London, 1928).

—— *Metternich und die Frauen*, 2 Vols (Vienna and Zurich, 1949).

—— *Vom Kind zum Kaiser* (Gräz, 1950).

—— *Mensch und Herrscher* (Gräz, 1952).

COUDRAY, H. du, *Metternich* (London, 1935).

COXE, Archdeacon, *History of the House of Austria*, Vol. IV (London, 1853). Contains a translation HARTIG, F., *Genesis der Revolution*.

CRAIG, Gordon A., *The Politics of the Prussian Army, 1640-1945* (New York, 1955).

CRANKSHAW, Edward, *The Fall of the House of Habsburg* (London, 1963).

CRAWLEY, C. W., *The Question of Greek Independence, 1821-1833* (Cambridge, 1930).

CREWE, Marquess of, *Lord Rosebery* (London, 1931).

DEUTSCH, Harold C., *The Genesis of Napoleonic Imperialism* (Cambridge, Mass., 1938).

EMERSON, Donald E., *Metternich and the Political Police, Security and Subversion in the Habsburg Monarchy, 1815-1830* (The Hague, 1968).

FAIN, P., *Manuscrit de Mille Huit Cent Treize* (Paris, 1827).

FORD, F. L., *Strasbourg in Transition, 1648-1789* (Cambridge, Mass., 1958).

FOURNIER, A., *Der Congress von Chatillon* (Vienna and Leipzig, 1900).

—— *Die Geheimpolizei auf dem Wiener Congress* (Vienna, 1913).

FRANZ, G., *Liberalismus* (Munich, 1955).

FRIEDJUNG, H., *The Struggle for Supremacy in Germany, 1859-66* (London, 1935).

GARROS, L., *Quel Roman que ma Vie - Itineraire de Napoléon Bonaparte* (Paris, 1947).

GORE, John (ed.), *The Creevey Papers* (rev. ed., London, 1963).

GRIMSTED, Patricia K., *The Foreign Ministers of Alexander I* (Berkeley, 1969).

GRUNWALD, C. de, *La Vie de Metternich* (Paris, 1938).

GUEDALLA, Phillip, *Palmerston* (London, 1926).

—— *The Duke* (London, 1931).

GUEST, Ivor, *Fanny Elssler* (London, 1970).

GUIZOT, François, *Mémoires pour servir a l'Histoire de mon Temps*, Vol. IV and Vol. VIII (Paris, 1859-61).

GULICK, Edward V., *Europe's Classical Balance of Power* (New York, 1955).

HAAS, Arthur G., *Metternich, Reorganization and Nationality, 1813-1818* (Wiesbaden, 1963).

HANOTEAU, Jean (ed.), *Lettres du Prince de Metternich à la Comtesse de Lieven, 1818-1819* (Paris, 1909).

HARTIG, F., *Genesis* (see COXE, Archdeacon).

HAUTERIVE, Ernest de, *La Police Secrete du Premier Empire*, Vol. 3 (Paris, 1922) and Vol. 4 (Paris, 1963).

HELLEINER, K. F., *The Imperial Loans* (Oxford, 1965).

HENNINGS, Fred, *Fast Hundert Jahre Wien, Rudolf von Alt, 1812-1905* (Vienna, 1967).

HERMAN, A., *Metternich* (London, 1932).

HEROLD, J. Christopher, *The Age of Napoleon* (London, 1964).

HOLBRAAD, Carsten, *The Concert of Europe* (London, 1970).

HÜBNER, J. A., *Une Année de ma Vie* (Paris, 1891).

—— *Neuf Ans de Souvenirs*, 2 Vols (Paris, 1904).

HYDE, H. Montgomery, *Princess Lieven* (London, 1938).

KISSINGER, H. A., *A World Restored* (London, 1957).

KISZLING, R., *Die Revolution in Kaisertum Oesterreich, 1848-9*, 2 Vols (Vienna, 1949).

KRAEHE, Enno E., *Metternich's German Policy, The Contest with Napoleon, 1799-1814* (Princeton, 1963).

KÜBECK, Karl von, *Tagebücher*, 2 Vols (Vienna, 1909-10).

KÜBECK, Max, *Metternich und Kübeck: ein Briefwechsel* (Vienna, 1910).

KÜHNEL, Harry, *Die Hofburg* (Vienna, 1971).

LANGER, William L. *Political and Social Upheaval, 1832-52* (New York, 1969).

LEE, Sir Sidney, *King Edward VII*, Vol. I (London, 1925).

LEFEBVRE, Georges, *Napoléon* (Paris, 1935).

—— *The French Revolution from its Origins to 1793* (London, 1962).

MACARINEY, C. A., *The Habsburg Empire, 1790-1918* (London, 1968).

MAGNUS, Philip, *King Edward the Seventh* (London, 1964).

MANN, Goldo, *Secretary of Europe* (rev. ed., New Haven, 1957).

MARKHAM, Felix, *Napoleon* (London, 1963).

MATHY, Helmut, *Franz Georg von Metternich* (Meisenheim, 1969).

MAY, Arthur J., *The Age of Metternich, 1814-1848* (rev. ed., New York, 1963).

MAYR, J.K., *Geschichte der Österreichischen Staatskanzlei im Zeitalter des Fürsten Metternich* (Vienna, 1935).

—— *Metternichs geheimer Briefdienst, Postlogen und Postkurse* (Vienna, 1935).

MAZADE, C. de, *Un Chancelier d'Ancien Régime* (Paris, 1889).

METTERNICH, Richard (ed.), *Mémoires, Documents et Écrits laissés par le Prince de Metternich*, 8 Vols (Paris, 1880-84).

METTERNICH-SANDOR, Pauline, *Geschehenes, Gesehenes, Erlebtes* (Vienna, 1921).

MISSOFFE, Michel, *Metternich, 1773-1859* (Paris, 1959).

MOLDEN, E., *Die Orientpolitik Metternichs, 1829-1833* (Vienna, 1913).

MONYPENNY, W. F. and BUCKLE, G. E., *The Life of Benjamin Disraeli, Earl of Beaconsfield*, Vol. 3 (London, 1914).

NAMIER, L. B., *1848: The Revolution of the Intellectuals* (London, 1945).

—— *Vanished Supremacies* (London, 1958).

NAPOLEON, *Correspondance de Napoléon I*, Vols XI-XXVII (Paris, 1863-68).

—— *Letters of Napoleon to Marie Louise* (London, 1935).

NESSELRODE, A. de, *Lettres et Papiers du Chancelier Comte de Nesselrode* (Paris, 1904-07).

NEUE OESTERREISCHISCHE BIOGRAPHIE (Vienna, 1923-35).

NICOLSON, Harold, *The Congress of Vienna* (London, 1946).

ONCKEN, Wilhelm, *Oesterreich und Preussen im Befreiungskriege, 1813*, 2 Vols (Berlin, 1876-79).

PALMER, Alan, *Napoleon in Russia* (London, 1967).

—— *The Lands Between* (London, 1970).

PELLICO, Silvio, *My Prisons* (English ed. of *Mie Prigioni*, translated and annotated by I. G. Capaldi, Oxford, 1936).

POLLARD, A. F., 'The Germanic Federation', Ch. XI of *Cambridge Modern History*, Vol. X (rev. ed., Cambridge, 1934).

QUENNELL, Peter (ed.), *The Private Letters of Princess Lieven to Prince Metternich* (London, 1937).

RAMM, Agatha, *Germany, 1789-1919* (London, 1967).

RATH, A. J., *The Viennese Revolution of 1848* (Austin, Texas, 1957).

REDLICH, Josef, *Emperor Francis Joseph* (London, 1929).

RIDLEY, Jasper, *Lord Palmerston* (London, 1970).

RIESBECK, Baron Caspar, *Travels through Germany* (London, 1787).

ROBERTSON, Priscilla, *Revolutions of 1848* (Princeton, 1952).

ROLO, P. J. V., *George Canning* (London, 1965).

SAINTE-AULAIRE, Beaupoil de, *Souvenirs, Vienne, 1832-41* (Paris, 1926).

SAUVIGNY, B. de, *Metternich and his Times* (London, 1962).

SCHENK, H. G., *The Aftermath of the Napoleonic Wars* (London, 1947).

SCHIEMANN, T., *Geschichte Russlands unter Kaiser Nikolaus I*, 4 Vols (Berlin, 1904-07).

SCHROEDER, P. W., *Metternich's Diplomacy at its Zenith, 1820-23* (Austin, Texas, 1962).

SCHUSELKA, Franz, *Deutsche Worte eines Oesterreichischers* (Hamburg, 1843).

SCHWARZ, Henry F. (ed.), *Metternich, the 'Coachman of Europe'* (Lexington, 1962).

SEALSFIELD, C., *Austria as it is* (London, 1828).

SMITH, E. A. (ed.), *Letters of Princess Lieven to Lady Holland, 1847-57* (Oxford, 1956).

SOREL, Albert, *Essais d'Histoire de Critique* (Paris, 1883).

—— *L'Europe et la Révolution Française*, Vols 7-8 (Paris, 1904).

SPIEL, Hilde, *Der Wiener Kongress in Augenzeugenberichten* (Düsseldorf, 1965).

SRBIK, Heinrich Ritter von, *Metternich, der Staatsmann und der Mensch*, Vols 1 and 2 (Munich, 1925) and Vol. 3 (Munich, 1954).

STACTON, David, *The Bonapartes* (New York, 1966).

STEARNS, Josephine B., *The Role of Metternich in Undermining Napoleon* (Urbana, Illinois, 1948).

STILES, W. H., *Austria in 1848-49*, Vol. 1 (New York, 1852).

STRACHEY, Lytton, *Portraits in Miniature* (London, 1931).

SWEET, Paul R., *Friedrich von Gentz, Defender of the Old Order* (Madison, Wisconsin, 1941).

SYDOW, Anna von (ed.), *Wilhelm und Caroline von Hümboldt in ihren Briefen*, Vol. 5 (Berlin, 1916).

TALLEYRAND-PERIGORD, C. M. de, *Correspondance Ihédite du Prince de Talleyrand, et du Roi Louis XVIII Pendant le Congrès de Vienne* (Paris, 1881).

TAYLOR, A. J. P., *The Italian Problem in European Diplomacy, 1847-49* (Manchester, 1934).

—— *The Habsburg Monarchy, 1809-1918* (rev. ed., London, 1948).

TEMPERLEY, H. W. V., *The Foreign Policy of Canning, 1822-27* (London, 1925).

—— *England and the Near East: The Crimea* (London, 1936).

—— (ed.), *The Unpublished Diary and Political Sketches of Princess Lieven* (London, 1925).

THOMPSON, J. M., *The French Revolution* (Oxford, 1943).

TREITSCHKE, Heinrich von, *Deutsche Geschichte in Neunzehnten Jahrhundert*, 2 Vols (Leipzig, 1880).

TROLLOPE, Frances, *Vienna and the Austrians*, 2 Vols (London, 1838).

TURNBULL, P. E., *Austria*, 2 Vols (Edinburgh, 1840).

ULLRICHOVA, Maria, *Clemens Metternich, Willhelmine von Sagan - Ein Briefwechsel, 1813-15* (Gräz and Cologne, 1966).

VALENTIN, Veit, *1848, Chapters of German History* (London, 1940).

VANDAL, Albert, *Napoléon et Alexandre I* (Paris, 1897).

VIERECK, Peter, *Conservatism Revisited, the Revolt against Reason* (New York and London, 1949).

WALKER, Mack (ed.), *Metternich's Europe, 1813-48* (New York, 1968).

WALTER, Friedrich, *Aus dem Nachlass des Frhr. Kübeck* (Gräz, 1960).

WARD, David, *1848, The Fall of Metternich* (London, 1970).

WASSILKO, Theophila, *Fürstin Pauline Metternich* (Vienna, 1959).

WEBSTER, C. K., *The Congress of Vienna, 1814-15* (London, 1919).

—— *British Diplomacy, 1813-15* (London, 1921).

—— *The Foreign Policy of Castlereagh*, Vol. 1 (London 1931) and Vol. 2 (London, 1925).

—— *Palmerston, Metternich and the European System, 1830-41* (London, 1934).

WEBSTER, Sir Charles, *The Foreign Policy of Palmerston*, 1830-41, 2 Vols (London, 1951).

WEIL, M. H. *Les Dessous de Congrès de Vienne*, 2 Vols (Paris, 1917).

WITTICHEN, F. C. and SALZER, E., *Briefe von und an Friedrich von Gentz*, 3 Vols (Munich, 1909-13).

WOODWARD, E. L., *Three Studies in European Conservatism* (London, 1929).

—— *War and Peace in Europe, 1815-70* (London, 1931).

YOUNG, Arthur, *Travels in France* (Cambridge, 1950).
ZAMOYSKA, P., *Arch Intriguer, a Biography of Dorothea de Lieven* (London, 1957).

Articles in Periodicals

BARANY, George, 'The Szechenyi Problem', *Journal of Central European Affairs* (Boulder, Colorado), Vol. 20, no. 3 (1960), pp. 249-69.

BOLSOVER, G. H., 'Palmerston and Metternich on the Eastern Question, 1834', *English Historical Review* (London), Vol. 51 (April 1936), pp. 237-56.

BUCKLAND, C. S. B. 'An English Estimate of Metternich in 1813', *English Historical Review* (London), Vol. 39 (April 1924), pp. 256-58.

FORCE, A. de C., Duc de la, 'Metternich Intime', *Revue des Deux Mondes* (Paris), (October 1936), pp. 650-66.

GRIMSTED, Patricia K., 'Capodistrias and a new Order for Restoration Europe', *Journal of Modern History* (Chicago), Vol. 40, no. 2 (1968), pp. 166-91.

GRUNWALD, C. de, 'Les débuts de Metternich', *Revue de Paris*, (August 1936), pp. 492-537.

—— 'La Fin d'une Ambassade', *Revue de Paris* (October 1937), p. 481-513 and pp. 819-46.

—— 'Le Mariage de Napoléon et de Marie Louise. Documents inédites', *Revue des Deux Mondes* (Paris), XXXVIII (1937), pp. 320-52.

HAAS, A. G. 'Metternich and the Slavs', *Austrian History Yearbook* (Rice University, Texas), Vols IV-V (1968-69), pp. 120-49.

HANOTEAU, J. (ed.), 'Une nouvelle relation de l'Entrevue de Napoléon et de Metternich à Dresden' (Caulaincourt), *Revue d'Histoire Diplomatique* (Paris), Vol. 47 (1933), pp. 421-40.

HÜGEL, Baron C. von, 'The Escape of Prince Metternich', *National Review* (London), Vol. 1 (1883), pp. 595-606.

KANN, Robert A., 'Metternich, a Reappraisal of his Impact on International Relations', *Journal of Modern History* (Chicago), Vol. 32, no. 4 (1960), pp. 333-39.

MARCHAND, Jean, 'Un Ambassadeur de Napoléon: Le Comte Alexandre de la Rochefoucauld', *Revue d'Histoire Diplomatique* (Paris), Vol. 48 (1934), pp. 217-30.

NICHOLS, Irby C., Jr, 'The Eastern Question and the Vienna Conference, September 1822', *Journal of Central European Affairs* (Boulder, Colorado), Vol. 21, no. 1 (1961), pp. 53-66.

RENESMAN, Alan, 'Metternich and Reform. The case of the Papal States, 1814-48', *Journal of Modern History* (Chicago), Vol. 42, no. 4 (1970), pp. 524-48.

RODKEY, F. S., 'The Views of Palmerston and Metternich on the Eastern Questions in 1834', *English Historical Review* (London), Vol. 45 (Oct. 1930), pp. 627-40.

ROTHENBERG, Gunther, 'The Austrian Army in Metternich's Day', *Journal of Modern History* (Chicago), Vol. 40, no. 2 (1968), pp. 155-65.

SCHROEDER, Paul W., 'Metternich Studies since 1925', *Journal of Modern History* (Chicago), Vol. 33, no. 3, (1961), pp. 237-60.

—— 'Austrian Policy at the Congresses of Troppau and Laibach', *Journal of Central European Affairs* (Boulder, Colorado), Vol. 22, no. 2 (1962), pp. 139-52.

SETON-WATSON, R. W., 'Metternich and Internal Austrian Policy', *The Slavonic Year Book* (London), Vol. 17 (1939), pp. 539-55; and Vol. 18 (1939), pp. 129-41.

SQUIRE, P. S., 'Metternich and Benckendorff, 1807-1834', *The Slavonic and East European Review* (London), Vol. 45, no. 104 (1967), pp. 135-63.

—— 'The Metternich-Benckendorff Letters, 1835-42', *The Slavonic and East European Review* (London), Vol. 45, no. 105 (1967) pp. 368-91.

THOMAS, A., 'L'Allemagne du Present', *Revue des Deux Mondes* (Paris), Vol. 13 (1846), pp. 488-93.

INDEX